Multithreading Programming Techniques

AF699058

The J. Ranade Workstation Series

BAMBARA AND ALLEN • *Powerbuilder: A Guide for Developing Client/Server Applications*

CERVONE • *AIX/6000 System Guide*

CHAPMAN • *OS/2 Power User's Reference: From OS/2 2.0 Through Warp*

CHAKRAVARTY • *Power RISC System/6000: Concepts, Facilities, and Architecture*

CHAKRAVARTY AND CANNON • *PowerPC: Concepts, Architecture, and Design*

DEROEST • *AIX for RS/6000: System and Administration Guide*

GOPAUL • *OS/2 Programmer's Desk Reference*

GRAHAM • *Solaris 2.X: Internals & Architecture*

HENRY AND GRAHAM • *Solaris 2.X System Administrator's Guide*

JOHNSTON • *OS/2 Connectivity & Networking: A Guide to Communication Manager/2*

JOHNSTON • *OS/2 Productivity Tool Kit*

KELLY • *AIX/6000 Internals & Architecture*

LAMB • *MicroFocus Workbench and Toolset Developer's Guide*

LEININGER • *AIX/6000 Developer's Tool Kit*

LEININGER • *HP-UX Developer's Tool Kit*

LEININGER • *Solaris Developer's Tool Kit*

LEININGER • *UNIX Developer's Tool Kit*

LOCKHART • *OSF DCE: Guide to Developing Distributed Applications*

MULLER • *The Webmaster's Guide to HTML: For Advanced Web Developers*

PETERSON • *DCE: A Guide to Developing Portable Applications*

RANADE AND ZAMIR • *C++ Primer for C Programmers*, 2/e

RIORDAN • *Windows NT Power User's Tool Kit*

ROBERTSON AND KOOP • *Integrating Windows & Netware*

ROBERTSON AND KOOP • *Windows 95 and Windows NT Networking*

SANCHEZ AND CANTON • *Graphics Programming Solutions*

SANCHEZ AND CANTON • *High Resolution Video Graphics*

SANCHEZ AND CANTON • *PC Programmer's Handbook*, 2/e

SANCHEZ AND CANTON • *Solutions Handbook for PC Programmers*, 2/e

WALKER AND SCHWALLER • *CPI-C Programming in C: An Application Developer's Guide to APPC*

WIGGINS • *The Internet for Everyone: A Guide for Users and Providers*

To order or receive additional information on these or any other McGraw-Hill titles, please call 1-800-822-8158 in the United States. In other countries, contact your local McGraw-Hill representative.

KEY = WM16XXA

Multithreading Programming Techniques

Shashi Prasad

McGraw-Hill

New York San Francisco Washington, D.C. Auckland Bogotá
Caracas Lisbon London Madrid Mexico City Milan
Montreal New Delhi San Juan Singapore
Sydney Tokyo Toronto

Library of Congress Cataloging-in-Publication Data

Prasad, Shashi.
Multithreading programming techniques / Shashi Prasad.
p. cm.—(J. Ranade workstation series)
Includes index.
ISBN 0-07-912250-7
1. Cross-platform software development. 2. Application software —Development. 3. C (Computer program language) I. Title. II. Series.
QA76.76.D47P72 1997
005.2—dc20 96-34490
CIP

McGraw-Hill
A Division of The ***McGraw·Hill*** *Companies*

Copyright © 1997 by The McGraw-Hill Companies, Inc. All rights reserved. Printed in the United States of America. Except as permitted under the United States Copyright Act of 1976, no part of this publication may be reproduced or distributed in any form or by any means, or stored in a data base or retrieval system, without the prior written permission of the publisher.

1 2 3 4 5 6 7 8 9 0 DOC/DOC 9 0 2 1 0 9 8 7

PN 0-07-050710-4
part of
ISBN 0-07-912250-7

The sponsoring editor for this book was John Wyzalek, the editing supervisor was Bernard Onken, and the production supervisor was Pamela Pelton. It was set in Century Schoolbook by Donald A. Feldman of McGraw-Hill's Professional Book Group composition unit.

Printed and bound by R. R. Donnelley & Sons Company.

McGraw-Hill books are available at special quantity discounts to use as premiums and sales promotions, or for use in corporate training programs. For more information, please write to the Director of Special Sales, McGraw-Hill, 11 West 19th Street, New York, NY 10011. Or contact your local bookstore.

Information contained in this work has been obtained by The McGraw-Hill Companies, Inc. ("McGraw-Hill") from sources believed to be reliable. However, neither McGraw-Hill nor its authors guarantee the accuracy or completeness of any information published herein and neither McGraw-Hill nor its authors shall be responsible for any errors, omissions, or damages arising out of use of this information. This work is published with the understanding that McGraw-Hill and its authors are supplying information but are not attempting to render engineering or other professional services. If such services are required, the assistance of an appropriate professional should be sought.

This book is printed on acid-free paper.

This book is dedicated in the memory of my mother,
Anima Prasad.

Contents

Preface

The performance of computer systems has constantly improved since the first computer was introduced. Today, processors have become cheap and powerful, and this has led to the popularity of technologies like multiprocessing and multithreading. Multithreading allows a developer to exploit the inherent parallelism of multiprocessor machines. One thing is for certain: applications will not run any faster on multiprocesser machines than on uniprocessor machines unless threads are used.

Multithreading is a new and exciting technology that holds a lot of promise if used correctly. One has to understand that not all applications can benefit from multithreading. It is important to first identify if your application can benefit from threads before you start using them. This book covers the application programming interface of the different thread implementations. The book is written for programmers, software engineers, and technical managers who are involved in developing multithreaded software. The purpose of the book is to cover the concepts and implementation of threads across multiple operating systems. The book does not focus on the design of threads or operating system design but rather focuses on the application programming interfaces.

The book covers five different thread implementations on operating systems such as UNIX (many flavors), Mach, Windows NT, and OS/2. The thread implementations can be broadly classified under two headings: POSIX style threads and WIN32/OS/2 style threads. The POSIX style thread implementation includes threads based on POSIX 1003.1c (Pthreads), UNIX International (UI Threads), and C Threads. All three of these thread implementations are similar; in fact, one can consider POSIX threads to be the improved and refined version of the other POSIX style thread implementations. Even though POSIX threads will soon become the de facto standard on UNIX platforms, I have covered UI and C Threads for completeness as this covers the three most popular implementations on UNIX style platforms.

WIN32 is the thread implementation of Microsoft and it runs on many platforms, like Windows NT and Windows 95. WIN32 and OS/2 style threads are quite similar; in fact, Microsoft implemented threads on OS/2 as well as

Windows NT. Since POSIX and WIN32 are two of the more popular thread implementations this book covers these implementations in more detail than the others.

The book does not assume any prior knowledge of multithreading, but it is helpful to have some experience in developing IPC style or client/server applications. The book assumes knowledge of C language on the platform of your choice. When I started writing the book I seriously contemplated writing all examples in C++, but after talking to many developers I decided that C was a better choice. The main reason for choosing C was that all operating systems covered in the book offer a C-based API for thread programming.

Plan of the Book

The book is divided into a different category for each thread implementation. The way the book is structured one does not have to read any one category before reading another. This means that one can start reading the chapters on UNIX International Threads without reading the POSIX chapters. The reader is advised that certain concepts and sections are repeated in multiple chapters; this has been done for completeness. The chapters break down as follows:

Chapter 1:	General Concepts of Multithreading
Chapters 2–6:	POSIX Threads
Chapters 7–9:	UNIX International Threads
Chapters 10–11:	C Threads
Chapters 12–16:	WIN32 Threads
Chapters 17–18:	OS/2 Threads
Chapter 19:	Portable Thread Implementation
Chapter 20:	Design Considerations

The examples in the book were developed in C language. The examples were chosen to be small and simple, and their purpose is to illustrate the various concepts of multithreading. Most of the example programs have been implemented across the different operating systems. The intention is to show how to develop modular and portable thread code across the different operating systems. Throughout the book I have snippets of code that are used to expand upon the subject matter. The code in Chapter 19 introduces Mthread, which is a portable thread interface for the various operating systems covered in the book. I had planned to implement a C++ implementation of Mthread but could not finish it on time for the different systems I have covered. I hope to finish it soon and announce the free software on the newsgroup comp.programming.threads.

Acknowledgments

I must admit that writing this book has been a memorable experience for me and my family. I am grateful to my wife Sweta, for being so understanding throughout the process. I would like to thank her for keeping up with me when I worked late nights and weekends on my book. I would like to thank Sweta for taking care of my son Curran, who missed so many great weekends because I worked on the book. Both of them have been greatly instrumental in my commitment to finish this project.

I would like to thank so many people who directly or indirectly helped me in writing this book. First of all I would like to thank Jerry Papke, my previous editor at McGraw-Hill, who convinced me to write the book in the first place. I would like to thank John Wyzalek, my current editor at McGraw-Hill, who was so supportive throughout. I would like to thank all the people who reviewed the book for technical accuracy and provided comments and technical expertise.

I would like to thank Sanjay Shrivastava of Momentum Software, who helped me a lot in developing the material for the OS/2 chapters. I would also like to thank the people on the Internet, who helped me very much. In spite of all the help I got from so many people, all shortcomings in this book are my responsibility.

Shashi Prasad

Chapter 1

Introduction

1.1 Multitasking

Operating systems have evolved considerably over the years. Back in the old days there was no operating system and programmers interfaced directly with the computer. After that came the era of simple batch processing, in which operating systems supported the execution of single tasks. In single-tasking systems, once a task was started, then it would run to completion before another task could be started. One of the most popular operating systems for personal computers, DOS, is a single-tasking operating system.

The normal evolution to simple batch processing was the ability to execute multiple tasks simultaneously. *Multitasking* is defined as the concurrent execution of two or more tasks on a central processing unit (CPU). Multiple tasks can be started to run on the CPU; the operating system is responsible for switching the tasks to execute on the CPU. The way the operating system handles the concurrent execution of multiple tasks is by assigning the CPU to a task for a time quantum. Multitasking operating systems provide the illusion of concurrent execution by timeslicing each task. In multitasking operating systems each task runs for a time quantum before it is preempted by the operating system. This process of preempting a task to run another task on the CPU is known as *context switching*.

Multitasking operating systems can either be preemptive or nonpreemptive. In the case of *preemptive* operating systems, the application is not aware of the periodic preemption by the operating system. This is different from *nonpreemptive* operating systems, in which the application is responsible for relinquishing the CPU. This form of multitasking is also referred to as *cooperative multitasking*. Operating systems such as Netware and Windows 3.X offer nonpreemptive multitasking, while MVS, VMS, UNIX, Mach, NT, and OS/2 are some examples of true preemptive multitasking operating systems.

Tasks and processes are fundamental concepts of any operating system. The operating system provides primitives for creating and destroying processes. A traditional program executes a sequence of instructions in a sequential manner. A *process* is a program in execution and constitutes the entities scheduled to execute on a CPU on most traditional operating systems. On most systems, a process is the basic unit of resource ownership.

1.1.1 Multiprocessing

Until recently, most machines were single-processor machines. A machine that has more than one processor (CPU) is called a *multiprocessor* (MP) *machine*. Multiprocessing technology has been around for a long time, but until recently it was considered to be an expensive solution. With the prices of chips falling and a need for better performance, multiprocessing machines are becoming increasingly popular. Theoretically, MP machines perform better than uniprocessor machines because they can run multiple programs concurrently.

Most MP machines fall under one of the following configurations:

- Symmetric MP
- Shared nothing MP
- Shared disk MP

1.1.2 Symmetric multiprocessing

In *symmetric multiprocessing* (SMP), multiple processors share a common memory space and have equal access to all peripheral devices. Since memory is shared, this kind of configuration is also known as *shared memory multiprocessors*. A bus connects all processors to the shared memory. Each CPU sees the memory coherently, and this allows a single copy of the operating system to be running on all processors. Most systems have additional memory known as *cache*. The hardware is responsible for maintaining the cache consistently across multiple CPUs.

One of the main advantages of SMP machines is that they offer the same programming model as a uniprocessor machine. This means that applications developed for uniprocessors run unchanged on SMP machines. This is important for developers who are migrating to MP machines. If the MP environment requires a change in their programming model, then it slows down the migration to MP technology.

Now let us look at the scaling of SMP machines. When one adds a new processor to the configuration, then one would expect that the performance would increase twofold. Similarly, when a third processor is added, one would expect the performance to increase threefold. In reality, this kind of linear scaling is hardly ever achieved on SMP machines.

As more processors are added to the configuration, the contention for the bus that connects all the processors increases. There is an overhead involved in keeping the memory and shared resources coherent across processors. The percentage increase in performance decreases as more processors are added until it reaches a point where performance does not increase with the addition of an additional CPU. In fact, performance tends to decrease once this critical point is reached.

An operating system has to be designed from ground up to support multiple processors. The SMP version of the operating system itself has to do more work than the uniprocessor version. It has to manage memory across multiple processors, and it has to ensure the integrity of the kernel data structures. It uses locks to serialize access to the shared kernel data structures. Depending on the locking scheme, the kernel spends considerable time in locking and unlocking these locks. The complexity, and thus the overhead, of the operating system also becomes one of the factors that prevents the linear scaling of SMP machines. The operating system must be well designed, and it must be tuned considerably to achieve scalability and efficiency on an SMP machine.

1.1.3 Shared nothing MP

In *shared nothing multiprocessing,* each CPU has its own memory and input-output (I/O) devices. Applications must be modified to run on these kinds of machines. Applications must be developed using some kind of message-passing interface (MPI). Shared nothing machines can scale better than SMP machines because there is no contention for the memory bus and the hardware does not have to keep the cache consistent across processors. The scalability advantage of SMP machines is somewhat reduced by the fact that they *require* a different programming model than uniprocessor machines.

1.1.4 Shared disk MP

In *shared disk multiprocessing,* each CPU has its own memory, but all share a common disk. In this kind of configuration, a centralized locking scheme is used to control access to the shared disk. These kinds of machines are better suited for clustered environments, where high data availability is required by applications. Applications must use the new programming application programming interfaces (APIs) to take advantage of the clusters. It is interesting to note that SMP machines can support clustering, and the combination of the two can be used to develop high-performance applications that are highly available.

SMP machines in general are the most popular kind of MP machines available today. In this book the discussion will be limited to SMP machines. SMP machines offer the benefit of increased throughput for applications. Since peripheral devices can be shared on SMP machines, they offer a better price performance. If applications can be split into smaller components, and if each of these components can run concurrently on different CPUs, then the performance of the application can increase. SMP machines offer the developer a true choice in exploiting the inherent parallelism of the hardware.

1.2 Multithreading

Traditional programs execute in a serial manner with a single thread of control. A sequential process has a single flow of control, a sequence of instructions executed by the process. A process with more than one thread of control is called a *multithreaded process*. A *thread* is a single sequential flow of control within a program; it is a sequence of instructions that are executed within a process.

Each thread has a single point of execution. Threads are often referred to as *threads of execution* because threads in a process are associated with a sequence of instructions. In a multithreaded program there can be multiple threads running concurrently within a single address space. Each thread can be considered to be a virtual processor having its own program counter, stack, and set of registers. Threads are the basic units of execution that utilize the CPU.

Each thread within a process runs independently of the other threads. All threads within a process share a common address space and have equal access to all process resources. Since threads share the same address space, the action of one thread can affect another thread within the same process. For example, when one thread closes a file, then that file is seen as closed by all threads within the process.

Threads and processes are similar in concept. A process can be considered as the unit of resource ownership (e.g., memory, open files, etc.), while threads are the dispatchable unit of work. Most multithreaded operating systems schedule threads to run on a CPU. Multiple threads do not necessarily run in parallel. On a uniprocessor machine the threads are timesliced by the operating system, while on SMP machines these threads can run in parallel on different processors.

Threads support the notion of concurrent programming and are often used to parallelize operations within an application. Traditionally, heavyweight processes were used to achieve parallelism in an application. Threads are cheaper to create than processes, and context switching is much faster for threads than for processes. Since the context maintained for threads is much lighter than that of processes, threads are also referred to as *lightweight processes*.

A very important thing to remember is that a single-threaded application will *not* run any faster on SMP machines until the application is split into multiple threads of execution. Each thread within the process is capable of running on any processor and thus has the potential to exploit the inherent parallelism of the SMP machine.

1.2.1 Kernel threads versus user threads

Threads can be supported either in kernel space or purely in user space. Operating systems that support kernel threads are known as *multithreading operating systems*. In the case of kernel threads, the kernel is aware of threads, while user threads are coroutine-based implementations. It is basically a cost versus performance issue when choosing between user and kernel threads.

User threads are faster to create than kernel threads, and also, the user-level thread context switching is must faster than kernel thread switching. One of the problems associated with pure user threads is that when one of the threads calls a blocking system call, then the whole process is suspended for the duration of the blocking call. For example, when one thread calls an I/O routine to read from a file, then the function does not return until the I/O operation completes. In coroutine-based implementations, the entire process blocks when a thread blocks on a system call, while in the case of kernel threads, only the calling thread is affected. Some coroutine-based implementations offer jacket routines for a subset of these blocking calls. Another disadvantage of user threads is that they cannot execute in parallel on multiple processors. User-based threads thus cannot take advantage of the performance benefits of SMP machines.

Traditionally, UNIX was a single-threaded operating system. Today, operating systems from IBM, DEC, SUN, Data General, and Novell are some of the examples of multithreaded UNIX kernels. On some UNIX systems such as HP/UX and earlier versions of AIX, threads are supported entirely in user space. Some non-UNIX operating systems such as Mach, Windows NT, and OS/2 were designed from the beginning to support multithreading.

1.2.2 Parallelism and threads

To take advantage of the parallelism offered by SMP machines, an application must be split into smaller components. The goal is to have each of these components run in parallel on different processors such that the multiple CPUs can be better utilized. The parallelism can be achieved in one of the following ways:

- *Coarse-grained parallelism.* In this kind of parallelism each component of the application is handled by a different process. The processes use some form of interprocess communication (IPC) (e.g., shared memory) to exchange information between themselves.
- *Medium-grained parallelism.* In this kind of parallelism each component of the application is handled by a different thread. In terms of performance, this model is much better than the process model because it avoids unnecessary IPC and context-switching overhead. The use of threads for concurrency or parallelizing the code is much more efficient than the process model.
- *Fine-grained parallelism.* This kind of parallelism is achieved by the use of parallelizing compilers. Today, such compilers exist for C, C++, and FORTRAN. The scope of such compilers is rather limited and is restricted to constructs such as loop parallelization.

One should spend time to identify portions of the problem that can be parallelized before jumping on to parallelize the application. In some cases, the complexity of the effort might not be worth it if the application does not run much faster than the nonparallelized version. According to *Amdahl's law,* a sufficient portion of the whole problem should be parallelized, or else the speedup might *not* be considerable.

Consider an application that reads 10,000 numbers from a file, sorts the numbers, and then writes the sorted numbers in a file. Assume that reading the numbers takes 1 second, sorting the numbers takes 2 seconds, and writing to the file takes another 1 second. Therefore, the total time spent is 4 seconds. Now, let us assume that we implement a parallel version of the sorting algorithm that sorts all the numbers in 1 second. Now the entire process takes 3 seconds instead of 4; therefore the speedup attained by parallelizing the sort algorithm is

$$\text{Speedup} = \frac{4}{3} = 1.33$$

This means that the overall performance gain is only 33 percent. Even if we are able to cut down the sorting time to almost 0 seconds, the application would still only run twice as fast as the nonparallel version. There is a limit to which the application's performance *can* increase because of the parallelization, and this is a important thing to keep in mind before really parallelizing the application.

This book focuses on medium-grained parallelism that can be achieved by using multiple threads. One should keep in mind that applications have the potential to run in parallel only on an SMP machine. On a uniprocessor machine threads run concurrently and will be timesliced by the operating system to run on a CPU.

1.2.3 When to use threads

Multithreading is a new and exciting technology, but knowing when to use threads is very important. One should have good reasons to use threads; otherwise, one is not going to see any of the benefits of threads. Do not use threads just because they are there and it is considered cool to use them. Threads can be helpful in the following situations:

- *Increased need for throughput.* Threads are ideal for "server" applications. The server application can be a file server, database server, or a Remote Procedure Call (RPC) server servicing client requests. The term *server* is used to describe the process that services client requests in a client-server environment. A multithreaded server has the potential to offer better throughput than a single-threaded server. A thread can be started for each client that connects to the server to handle the client's requests. Alternatively, a number of worker threads can be started to handle all client requests.
- *Need for performance.* Threads have the potential to increase performance on SMP machines. If a substantial portion of the application can be parallelized, then the application can run faster on an SMP machine. An application can be broken down into smaller components, and each compo-

nent can be executed by a separate thread potentially in parallel on an SMP machine.

- *I/O and CPU can be overlapped.* Threads are useful in applications where I/O and CPU can be overlapped. When a thread blocks on I/O, then the CPU is not utilized by the thread. If some other thread in the same process can still run, then the processor is better utilized. This is helpful not only on SMP machines but even on uniprocessor machines.
- *Processes are created frequently.* In client-server applications, concurrent servers often create a process for every client that connects to the server. As the number of clients increases, the overhead of multiple process and increased context switching can create a performance bottleneck. Consider the example of a TCP/IP server running on UNIX that creates a child process whenever a client connects to it. For such servers it is much more efficient to create a thread per user than "forking" a process. If you are developing *internet* applications using Common Gateway Interface (CGI), then you must be familiar with the overhead. The internet application on Web Server platforms (e.g., NSAPI, ISAPI) can be developed much more efficiently using threads.

1.2.4 Advantages of multithreading

Threads, if used properly, can offer many benefits, such as

- *Increased throughput and better performance.* Multithreaded programs can achieve performance in a multiprocessor environment. In an MP environment threads within a process can execute in parallel on multiple CPUs, thus offering a better throughput and better performance. Threads can exploit the inherent parallelism of SMP machines and thus reduce the time required to complete a given task.

Even on uniprocessor machines, threads offer better throughput because the CPU can handle multiple threads even when some threads are blocked on I/O operations. For example, consider a process with two threads executing on a single-processor machine. When one thread blocks on a blocking system call (e.g., file I/O), the other thread in the process can continue to run. This leads to a better CPU utilization.

- *Simplified algorithms.* Many programming tasks can be coded better by splitting the problem into smaller components and assigning threads to handle the execution of the individual components. Personally, I feel that this is one of the biggest advantages of multithreading, much more than the performance gains that can be achieved by using multiple threads. The coding of threaded programs can be much more complicated, but the code is much more modular. Threads improve the logical design of programs.

Before multithreading was widely supported, programs on multitasking operating systems such as VMS and UNIX simulated multiple threads of control by using interrupts or signals. These applications are generally difficult to code and debug, mainly because the application has to handle asynchronicity. The software architecture of threaded programs is much better, and it offers a much better environment for programming to asynchronous events.

- *More responsive programs.* Consider a single-threaded user-interface program that runs a lengthy calculation. While the calculation is in progress, the program cannot interface with the user. By using a separate thread to run the calculation, the main thread or the GUI thread can still be responsive to the user.
- *Cheaper concurrency model.* Threads offer a great advantage in today's client-server model of programming. Server programs can spawn off a thread to handle each client concurrently. It is less costly to create a thread than to create a heavyweight process. Since threads are lightweight, the context-switching overhead is greatly reduced. Threads provide a cheaper and better concurrency model than the traditional process.

1.2.5 Pitfalls of thread programming

Thread programming introduces new types of problems at the expense of solving old ones. Personally, I find that there is too much hype around the terms *multiprocessing* and *multithreading*. Today, it is common to see so many vendors touting the term *multithreading* in their advertisements without really having any reason to mention it in the first place. I find many users jumping on the bandwagon of multithreading without having valid reasons to use threads. These are some of the pitfalls of threads:

- *Added complexity.* It is possible that by using threads one might see no speedup in applications. In addition to not delivering the performance as one might have expected at the onset of developing the MT application, threads introduce another level of complexity to the development process. The complexity is added mainly in two areas: algorithm design and data synchronization.
- *Difficult to debug and test.* Multithreaded applications are always more difficult to debug than single-threaded applications. Since multithreading is a new technology, there is a lack of good debuggers and tools to help the developers in the development process. Sometimes, the biggest problem lies in recreating problems, since some of the problems do not happen frequently. An application can run fine on a single-processor machine, but bugs might show up when it is moved to a multiprocessor machine.
- *Data synchronization and race conditions.* Threads within the same process share the same address space and have access to all resources, including memory. Shared variables must be protected against simultaneous updates to ensure the data integrity. Consider two threads trying to insert an entry to the beginning of a list. It is possible that both the threads might change the global variable pointing to the beginning of the

list simultaneously. Since both threads can run in parallel on different processors, it is possible that one of the updates might be lost depending on the timing factors. The code that adds the entry to the beginning of the list is a critical section of code, and it must be protected against simultaneous execution by multiple threads. In multithreaded applications, mutual exclusion locks are used to prevent multiple threads from executing the critical section of code. Race conditions can be manifested in multithreaded applications without proper locking and data synchronization.

- *Potential for deadlocks.* Whenever multiple locks are used for data synchronization, a potential for deadlock exists. Deadlocks are not something introduced by thread programming; they can even happen when multiple processes are involved. A deadlock happens when a thread holding a lock is waiting for a lock that is held by another thread while the other thread is waiting for a lock held by the first thread. One should have strict locking rules when using multiple locks; otherwise, deadlock can happen.
- *Non-thread-safe environment.* Applications often use standard system libraries and third-party libraries. In a multithreaded application, a library that can be used safely in a threaded environment is called a *thread-safe library*. A function is called a *non-thread-safe* function if it cannot be called safely in a multithreaded application. A nonthreaded function can be made thread-safe by the use of global locks in the function such that access to the function is effectively serialized. A *reentrant* function is a function that can be called simultaneously by multiple threads safely without using any special locks to serialize the execution of these functions.

Generally, traditional libraries are nonreentrant because they use global and static data. For example, the standard C library was developed when no one was really concerned about multiple threads. Many C library functions use static data that do not work correctly in the presence of multiple threads. Many third-party libraries do not offer a reentrant version of their libraries, and this makes the use of threads with these libraries extremely difficult. For example, most of the UNIX database vendors do not provide a reentrant version of their library. The speed with which the vendors are providing support for reentrant libraries has been pretty slow, but this can be understandable considering the effort required to make libraries reentrant. The effort of conversion is just not limited to coding; much more time is spent in testing and debugging the library. Until threaded libraries become standard, the use of some of these libraries should be evaluated carefully in an MT application.

1.2.6 Designing multithreaded applications

Multithreaded programming is not difficult, but it does require a change in the way one thinks. The biggest challenge for the programmer lies in learning to think in terms of parallel activities rather than a sequential mode of execution. Multithreading requires careful design and planning in terms of algorithms, data synchronization, and interthread communication. Multithreading offers a lot of promise, but to achieve some of the benefits of threads, one has to design the application correctly. The design should reflect the reason for using threads in the first place.

The developer must first identify the areas of software that can be parallelized. Once you have identified such areas, then each of the areas must be broken down into smaller components that can be executed independently by separate threads. Once the algorithm design has been solved, then you should concentrate on data synchronization and interthread communication, since both of these are so crucial to effective multithreading.

Excessive data synchronization can cause performance bottlenecks, especially on SMP machines, and you might lose one of the most important benefits of threads, which is concurrent execution of threads. Since multiple threads can be used within an application, it is important to have an effective interthread communication method. The complexity of the code can increase greatly without the use of proper interthread communication. When splitting a problem into small components, one should not split the problem into such small components that the time required for interthread communication is longer than the time required to solve the actual problem. After reading the thread chapters of your favorite operating system, the reader is then advised to read Chap. 20 for more on design of multithreaded applications.

1.2.7 Models of thread programming

Threads are used in applications according to one of the software execution models:

- *Master/slave model.* In this model, one thread known as the *master thread* gets a request, and it creates one or more *slave threads* to handle the request. The code that will be executed by the slave threads is controlled by the master thread. This model is also known as the *boss/worker* thread model.
- *Worker model.* In this model, a number of worker threads are created to service the clients. Client requests are put on some queue that is used by the worker threads. Most server applications are either coded with the master/slave model or the worker model. Worker models are more complicated to implement than the master/slave model.
- *Pipelining model.* In this model, the task is broken down into smaller components, and each component feeds the input to the next component. Consider a single-threaded compiler that does the following steps in sequence: preprocess, compile, assemble, and optimize the code. If multiple threads were used in the compiler, then each step could be handled by a different thread. Each thread's output would become the input to the next thread in the pipeline.

1.2.8 Thread states

A thread within a process can be in one of many system-dependent states. For the sake of simplicity, threads can be assumed to be in one of these states:

- Running
- Ready
- Waiting

A thread that is actually in the running state is utilizing the processor (CPU). On uniprocessor machines, only one thread can be in the running state, while on an SMP machine, multiple threads can be in the running state (one per CPU). For example, on a four-way SMP machine, at most, four threads can be in the running state simultaneously.

A thread is classified in the *ready-to-run state* if the thread is waiting for a processor to run on. Only threads that are either in the running state or the ready-to-run state have the potential to utilize the CPU. If an application has multiple threads in the ready-to-run state, then the operating system will spend substantial time moving threads from the ready-to-run state to the running state. This process of moving threads from ready to running state is called *context switching* of threads. Context-switching overhead should be minimized in order to maximize performance gain of threads.

A thread is classified to be in the *waiting state* if it is waiting for some resource to be available. For example, a thread can be in the waiting state if it is waiting on I/O, mutex lock, or a page fault at the system level. The thread can move to the ready or running state only after the wait completes. Excessive synchronization may cause too many threads in the waiting state.

1.2.9 Thread implementations

Today, many operating systems such as Mach, NT, OS/2, and UNIX offer a multithreaded programming environment. From the developer's point of view, the operating system should provide some way to create and manage threads. The operating systems provide an application programming interface (API) for multithreaded programming. The question that everyone would then ask is, "Is there a standard API for threads for different systems?" Unfortunately, there is no universal standard for multithreaded programming to which all vendors conform.

On POSIX systems, after many years of effort, there is finally a thread programming standard that is better known as *POSIX.1c*. Even on UNIX systems, not every vendor implements POSIX.1c; in reality, most UNIX vendors seem to be leaning that way. Operating systems such as Mach, Windows NT, and OS/2 each have their own API for thread programming, and they do not conform to the POSIX.1c API. Welcome to the real world of open systems!

One should take comfort in the fact that even though the APIs are different, the concepts of thread programming are similar across these different operating systems. It is not difficult to develop applications that can be ported easily from one operating system to another. Before jumping on to the implementation, one should spend considerable time on the design of algorithms, interthread communication, and data synchronization issues. Knowing the differences and similarities between the operating systems helps in designing applications that can be ported easily from one system to the other.

Chapter

2

POSIX Thread Management

2.1 POSIX Standards

POSIX, the Portable Operating System Interface, is a standards document being produced by the Institute of Electrical and Electronics Engineers (IEEE). POSIX is a standard as well as an ongoing effort for future standards development. The goal of POSIX is to provide a standard interface for programming on different operating systems such that applications can be ported easily from one operating system to another by just a recompilation. It is important to understand that the POSIX programming interface is intended to provide source code portability and not binary compatibility across the different operating systems.

POSIX is not a single standard; rather, it is made up of different standards, each targeting different parts of an operating system. There are standards for the basic operating system interface, real-time extensions, transaction processing, system administration, and protocol-independent communication. Each of these standards has a dot extension to its name, such as POSIX.1 and POSIX.2.

IEEE has specified a standard for portable operating systems for open systems called *POSIX*. The POSIX 1 standard defines the basic set of system services provided by an operating system. The POSIX.1 standard includes mechanisms for process management (fork, exec, wait, exit), signals, I/O (read, write), and terminal handling. The POSIX.1 standard serves as the foundation for all the other POSIX standards.

List of POSIX Standards

POSIX.1	Basic OS Interfaces
POSIX.1b	Real-Time Extensions
POSIX.1c	Threads Extension
POSIX.2	Commands
POSIX.3	Test Methods
POSIX.5	Ada Bindings to POSIX.1
POSIX.6	Security Extensions
POSIX.7	System Administration
POSIX.8	Transparent File Access
POSIX.9	FORTRAN 77 Bindings to POSIX.1
POSIX.10	Supercomputing
POSIX.11	Transaction Processing
POSIX.12	Protocol-Independent Communications
POSIX.13	Real-Time Profiles
POSIX.14	Multiprocessor Profile
POSIX.15	Batch/Supercomputer Extensions
POSIX.16	Language-Independent POSIX.1
POSIX.17	Directory/Name Services
POSIX.18	Basic POSIX System Profile
POSIX.19	FORTRAN 90 Bindings to POSIX.1
POSIX.20	Ada Binding to POSIX.1b
POSIX.21	Distributed Real Time

Each of the standards groups is well represented by members of different groups such as operating system vendors, independent software vendors, universities, and members of other interest groups. This adds balance to the standards group, since no single vendor or group can enforce or influence any standard, but in reality, it becomes more of a compromise when members of the group have different views. The first step in any standard adoption process is the proposal for a standard. The proposal then goes through a series of balloting processes before it becomes a standard. IEEE uses the balloting processes as a standard way for standard adoption. Since POSIX standards are "designed by committee," it can take a long time to adopt any standard. Case in point, the threads standard proposal had been in the balloting process since 1990 before it was adopted as a standard in the summer of 1995.

2.1.1 POSIX and threads

POSIX.1b defines the real-time extensions to the base operating system standard POSIX.1. The thread extensions to the POSIX.1 and POSIX.1b (real-time extensions) standards are referred to as *POSIX.1c*. This standard defines the application programming interfaces (APIs) for developing multithreaded (MT) programs in a POSIX environment. The standard for threads is also commonly referred to as *Pthreads*. The Pthreads standard, which had been in draft form since 1990, was finally approved in the summer of 1995, and it is based on the draft 10 specification. Last year the POSIX.4 and POSIX.4a standards were renamed POSIX.1b and POSIX.1c, respectively.

The OSF DCE 1.1 threads interface is currently based on draft 4 of the Pthreads specification. OSF intends to support the adopted Pthreads standard (draft 10) in future versions of DCE. Remember, even though the focus of this discussion is Pthreads on UNIX systems, the theory and concepts explained in the chapters dealing with Pthreads can be applied easily to non-UNIX systems implementing the Pthreads API. In fact, many other non-UNIX operating systems such as LynxOS, MVS, and VMS either currently support or plan to support the Pthreads interface.

Most of the UNIX vendors are committed to providing the Pthreads interface as a part of their operating system, and it is expected that it will be the common standard for multithreaded programming on UNIX systems. The other UNIX thread standard that is popular is based on the UNIX International (UI) specification; operating systems such as SVR4/MP, Solaris, and Unixware support the UI threads interface. Now even these vendors are supporting or planning to support the Pthreads programming interface.

It seems that sooner or later Pthreads will be the de facto standard for thread programming on UNIX systems. Applications that are developed using the Pthreads API are intended to be portable across other POSIX.1c-compliant systems. Today, this is not always true, since OS vendors may support different draft standards of the Pthreads API. For example, IBM AIX 4.X supports draft 7 of the Pthreads standard, while Solaris 2.5 supports draft 10 (approved standard).

Operating systems can be POSIX.1-compliant and still not support the POSIX threads programming interface. There is no requirement that POSIX.1 systems have to support multiple threads; this means that Pthreads cannot become the common threads programming interface across the different operating systems. It is safe to assume that POSIX.1-compliant operating systems such as Windows NT will not provide the Pthreads API for multithreaded programming in the near future (if ever!).

2.1.2 Threads and the UNIX system

Traditional UNIX systems do not support the notion of threads. In earlier UNIX systems, a process consisted of a single thread of control within the process address space. Recently, with the increased popularity of symmetric multiprocessing (SMP) machines, many UNIX vendors have started offering multithreaded kernels with full multiprocessing support. Some of the operating systems that currently support a *multithreaded* UNIX kernel are AIX, Solaris, Digital UNIX (previously known as DEC OSF/1), SVR4/MP, DG/UX, and Unixware.

In a multithreaded UNIX system, the traditional process has been redefined to support multiple threads of execution within the same address space. Single-threaded programs do *not* require any changes when they are ported to a multithreaded UNIX system. Applications have only to be modified if they want to *exploit* the multithreading and multiprocessing features of the operating system.

Threads in the UNIX systems can be supported either in kernel mode or in user mode. Today, some UNIX systems offer a true multithreaded kernel, while many others implement threads entirely in user space without any support from the operating system. In the case of multithreaded kernels, there are two types of threads: *kernel* threads and *user* threads. Kernel threads are kernel entities that run in kernel space, while user threads run in user space. On multithreaded UNIX kernels, the unit of scheduling has changed from processes to threads.

In the case of nonthreaded UNIX systems, the kernel is *only* aware of the process, and all threads run entirely in user space. A run-time component that executes in user space is responsible for managing the threads within the process. The most noticeable example of a user thread package is OSF DCE threads. DCE threads have been implemented on certain single-threaded UNIX systems such as HP/UX and IBM AIX 3.2.5 and even on non-UNIX systems such as MVS. DCE does not require the support of a threaded kernel but maps DCE threads to native threads on operating systems that support kernel threads.

Threads that execute in kernel space are also known as *lightweight processes* (LWPs). This chapter uses the term *kernel thread* instead of LWP. Note that parallel execution of threads on multiple CPUs in an SMP environment can only be achieved on systems implementing kernel threads. True parallelism on SMP machines can *never* be achieved by just user-level threads. The use of threads on nonthreaded UNIX systems will not speed up your application on SMP machines.

2.2 Thread Execution Models

The threads library is the run-time component that provides various functions for creating and managing threads in a multithreaded process. The mapping between user and kernel threads in a multithreaded environment is handled by the threads library. On systems supporting POSIX threads, the mapping between user threads and kernel threads can be implemented in one or more of the following ways.

2.2.1 One-to-one mapping

In the 1:1 model, each user thread is mapped to a separate kernel thread. Each kernel thread runs in kernel space and uses kernel resources. In an SMP environment, each of these kernel threads can potentially execute in parallel on different CPUs. Each thread is scheduled *independently* of the others, and it continues to run even when some other thread blocks on a system call. In this model the number of threads that can be created successfully in a process is restricted because a kernel thread is created for each user thread. There is nothing wrong with this model except that it can be inefficient in terms of usage of kernel resources when the number of threads within a process is high. Although threads are much more lightweight than processes, it still does not make sense to create too *many* threads in a process. Always keep in mind that threads are cheap, but they are *not* free.

Today, most UNIX systems that implement the POSIX threads library offer this model; examples of such operating systems are IBM AIX 4.1, Digital UNIX 3.X, and Data General's DG/UX. If the application is designed correctly, then the limit on the maximum number of threads that can be created successfully in a process should *not* be a problem.

2.2.2 Many-to-one mapping

In the M:1 model, every user thread is mapped to the same kernel thread. The scheduling of threads is handled entirely by the threads library; the library is responsible for *multiplexing* user threads to the kernel thread. User threads can run entirely in user space, even without the support of a multithreaded kernel. This model is also supported by systems implementing kernel threads, where multiple user threads are mapped to the same kernel thread. On single-threaded systems, this is the *only* model that is supported by the threads library.

On certain operating systems that implement the M:1 model, the entire process is suspended when one of the threads blocks on a system call. Many vendors support the POSIX threads API as a part of OSF DCE, and in most cases, these are *coroutine*-based implementations. The coroutine-based implementations do not offer a true concurrent model of thread programming. For example, when a thread in AIX 3.2.5 (DCE) blocks on a call to *msgrcv,* then the entire process is *suspended,* and all other threads in the process cease to run until the blocking thread is resumed. It is very likely that most M:1 implementations on a single-threaded system have this limitation, although some vendors might provide jacket routines to a subset of these blocking calls. The topic of blocking calls and jacket routines is explained in Sec. 5.4.1.

2.2.3 Many-to-many mapping

In the M:N model, a group of user threads is mapped to a pool of kernel threads. The thread library is responsible for mapping one or more of these user threads to a given kernel thread. This model supports *mixed-scope* mapping, and the mapping can be a combination of the one-to-one model and the many-to-one model. This model cannot be implemented on a single-threaded operating system because it assumes multiple kernel threads. The M:N model is very flexible and is a good compromise between the 1:1 and M:1 models.

In the mixed-scope model, a user thread either can be bound to a specific kernel thread or multiple user threads can be mapped to the same kernel thread. A user thread is rescheduled either when it voluntarily gives up the CPU (e.g., block on I/O) or when it is preempted by a higher-priority running thread. This means that unless either of these things happens, the threads library cannot reschedule another thread, and this might delay execution of user threads bound to the same kernel thread. In these systems it is usually the programmer's responsibility to create the optimal number of kernel threads and ensure that all threads get a fair scheduling share. It is not easy to find out the optimal number of kernel threads in an M:N model. It *might* lead to "too few kernel threads" or "too many kernel threads" syndrome.

The Pthreads standard (post-draft 6) supports the mixed-scope thread model, but not all vendors actually support it as a part of their Pthreads library. It is obvious that any system that supports this model automatically supports the other two threading models. Although the M:N model adds much more responsibility on the programmer, it also allows for *cheaper* creation of user threads, thus using the system resources effectively. It is interesting to note that Digital has added support for the mixed-scope model in Digital Unix 4.0, and it is rumored that even IBM might support it in some future release of AIX.

2.2.4 Which threading model?

The question that is bound to arise is, "Which is the best threading model?" The discussion will be limited to the 1:1 and M:N models, since the M:1 model is really not of any great interest. The choice of the threading model depends on many factors, such as total number of CPUs, the number of threads, and the work performed by the threads in the application. Most applications do not have a large number of threads, and they would not have to worry too much about the threading model. If you are developing server applications such as a database server, RPC server, or tcp server to service a large number of clients, then the performance and scalability of the server will greatly depend on the threading model. Many server applications are developed to create a thread for every client that connects to the server, and this architecture is not a scalable one, especially in the 1:1 model. The use of worker threads to service a large number of clients should be considered seriously. This is a better alternative, in which case each of the worker threads can have a dedicated kernel thread.

If the number of threads in your application is low, then the M:N model does not give a lot of advantage over the 1:1 model. If the number of threads is high and the threads are active most of the time, then the overhead of too many kernel threads becomes an issue. This is where the 1:1 model can become inefficient. Keep in mind that user threads are much *more* lightweight and have less overhead than kernel threads. The context switch and creation time of user threads are much faster than those of kernel threads.

Some applications greatly benefit by using the M:N model. For example, one might create a bunch of low-priority user threads to watch certain low-frequency activities. All these user threads can be mapped to one kernel thread without the overhead of creating multiple kernel threads as would be in the case of 1:1 model. These kinds of threads are ideal for applications in which the threads are *idle* most of the time and the number of such threads is relatively high.

So what if my operating system does not support the M:N model? In the preceding example, rather than creating a separate thread to watch each of the low-frequency activities, a thread can be created for periodically monitoring (polling) all such activities. This is a design issue and is greatly influenced by the application requirements. Scalable systems can be designed without using the many-to-many threading model as long as the number of active threads is low.

There are definite advantages and disadvantages to each of these models. At first it seems that for most applications the M:N model is flexible and most efficient, but this is *not* necessarily true. One should remember that the operating system alone *cannot* be responsible for providing a scalable multithreaded application; applications must be designed correctly to achieve maximum scalabilty and performance. You should remember that a good design and a scalable architecture can be achieved with the 1:1 model just as they can be with the M:N model.

If *portability* of your application is a requirement to other POSIX systems, then use of the M:N model should be evaluated carefully, since many UNIX vendors do not yet support this model. Just imagine the ordeal of porting a multithreaded system with hundreds or even thousands of user threads (M:N) to an operating system that only supports the 1:1 model. If you are lucky, you might be able to create the same number of kernel threads, but you *should not* count on always being lucky in the real world. It might force a complete redesign and redevelopment of your application.

The situation can be much worse when your application has to be ported to another operating system that does not support the POSIX threads standard or the M:N threading model. Operating systems such as Windows NT, NeXTSTEP, or OS/2 currently only support the 1:1 threading model. If you are convinced that your system will only run on systems supporting the M:N model, then feel free to use it or else *think* twice. Personally, I feel that the key is to have a flexible design such that applications can work efficiently without any consideration of the underlying thread implementation. The key to an effective design is *not* to have too many active threads in the process; failure to do so usually will result in performance bottlenecks.

2.3 Processes and Threads

A traditional UNIX process consists of a single thread of execution and is defined to consist of an address space and a single thread executing within the address space. On systems that implement Pthreads, a process is redefined to consist of an address space with one or more threads of control. Threads share all process resources and have the same view of the address space. For example, if one thread frees a memory area, then a memory access violation occurs when some other thread tries to use the freed memory area. Similarly, when a file is closed by one thread, then it is seen as closed by all other threads in the process. All the threads within a process share many of the POSIX.1 system resources, such as

- The process ID, parent process ID, and parent group ID

- Session membership
- Real, effective, and saved-set user ID
- Real, effective, and saved-set group ID
- Supplementary group ID
- Current working directory, and root directory
- Signal state
- File mode creation mask
- File descriptor table

A thread is defined to be a sequential "flow of control" within a process. Each thread has

- Unique thread ID
- Scheduling priority and policy
- Per-thread signal mask
- The state of any timers
- Per-thread errno
- Unique stack and program counter

2.4 POSIX Threads API

The POSIX threads APIs are used to create and manage threads. The threads APIs can be broadly classified into areas such as thread management, thread synchronization, thread-specific data, and advanced thread topics. The advanced thread topics cover thread scheduling, priority, signals, and thread cancellation.

2.4.1 Checking POSIX options

Keep in mind that certain Pthreads functionality is optional and consequently might not be implemented on all systems supporting POSIX.1c threads. When functions that do not implement these optional features are called, they return ENOTSUP as the return value. For example, not every system implements the option to change the stack size attribute of the newly created thread. Supported options can be identified at *compile time* by checking if the options are defined in the header file *pthread.h*.

```
#ifndef_POSIX_THREAD_ATTR_STACKSIZE
#printf "Stacksize attribute is not supported"
#endif
```

Some UNIX systems provide a *sysconf* interface to query *run-time information* about the underlying thread implementation, although this might be limited to a subset only. The compile-time checking of POSIX options is a better way to find out support for optional features. If *portability* is of concern, then you should not rely on the optional features of Pthreads.

2.4.2 Naming conventions

The convention for naming functions and data types in the POSIX.1c standard is of the form pthread[_<object>]_<operation>, where *operation* describes the Pthread function, and *object* describes the type of the object to which the function is applied (e.g., pthread_mutex_init and pthread_mutex_lock). The object portion is omitted for functions that manipulate threads (e.g., pthread_create and pthread_exit). Data types have the _t suffix and are used to describe opaque data types (e.g., pthread_mutex_t). All macros are defined in uppercase though in pre-draft 7 versions they are defined in lowercase (e.g., PTHREAD_ONCE_INIT and pthread_once_init). All Pthread data types and macros are defined in the header file *<pthread.h>*.

2.4.3 Function return values and error number

The convention followed by most Pthreads functions in *pre-draft 7* versions is to return 0 on success and −1 on failure. On failure, these functions additionally set errno to the appropriate error code. In POSIX.1 the error variable errno is a per-process global variable, while on a POSIX.1c system the variable errno is nonglobal and is maintained on a per-thread basis. On most systems, errno is usually redefined to be a function returning a pointer to an integer. Note that starting from draft 7 the Pthread functions return 0 on success and return the error number instead of setting the variable errno on failure.

> Applications that are currently using pre-draft 7 APIs and are planning to use the newer versions of Pthreads should make the necessary changes in error handling.

The following code segment illustrates such a change in the code.

2.4.3.1 Pre-draft 7 and DCE 1.1

```
int       ret;

ret = pthread_create (......);
if (ret = = -1 && errno = = ENOMEM)
{
     fprintf (stderr, "Insufficient memory to create threads \n");
     exit (1);
}
```

2.4.3.2 Draft 7 or higher

```
int     ret;
ret = pthread_create (.......);
if (ret ! = 0 && ret = = ENOMEM)
{
     fprintf (stderr, "Insufficient memory to create threads \n");
     exit (1);
}
```

2.4.4 Portability of Pthreads

As with any standard process, the POSIX threads standard proposal had been in draft form for quite some time, and it was recently finalized as the draft 10 version. In 1991, some vendors started supporting the POSIX threads API based on the draft 4 version. Since then, there have been *numerous* changes to the APIs, return codes, functional interface, and functionality of Pthreads. Many functions supported in the approved standard (draft 10) are *not* supported in lower versions, and vice versa. If you are porting your code from a lower draft version (e.g., draft 4) to a higher version (e.g., draft 10), then you should check all APIs in use for any *changes* in terms of parameters, return codes, and functionality. If you fail to do so, then chances are very good that your application will *not* work correctly.

As an example of the change, consider the function pthread_mutex_trylock. The function returns 1 if the calling thread acquires the lock (draft 4), while the function returns 0 in later versions (draft 7 and higher). I will try to point out the changes in API in the discussion, but it is beyond the scope of this book to refer to all such changes. See Sec. 5.5.6 for a complete list of Pthread functions and data types. The version and threading model of Pthreads as supported by some of the vendors is shown below.

AIX 3.2.5	Draft 4	M:1
AIX 4.X	Draft 7	1:1
DG/UX 5.4	Draft 6	1:1
Digital Unix 3.2	Draft 4	1:1
Digital Unix 4.0	Draft 10	M:N
HP/UX 10.X	Draft 4	M:1
Solaris 2.5	Draft 10	M:N
VMS 6.X	Draft 4	M:1
VMS 7.X	Draft 10	M:N

2.5 Thread Attributes

POSIX thread attributes define the characteristics of a thread. When you change the attributes of a thread, you change the properties of a thread. Threads can be created with different attributes; e.g., a thread can be created to be either bound or unbound. *Bound* threads have a dedicated kernel thread, while *unbound* threads do not have a dedicated kernel thread. Thread attributes specify the attributes of the thread when they are *created.* The *default* thread attributes with which a thread is created are implementation-specific.

The attributes of a thread as defined in the attribute object are only used at thread creation. If an attribute object is subsequently changed and is used to create another thread, then the change does *not* affect the properties of the previous thread that was created using the original thread attribute values. For example, an attribute object can be created and initialized to specify a stack size of 16,384 bytes. When a thread is created using this thread object attribute, then the stack size of the newly created thread is 16,384. After creating the first thread, the stack value in the attribute object can be changed to 32,768 bytes. Now all other threads created using the modified attribute object have a stack size of 32,768 bytes. The first thread is *not* affected by the changes made to the stack attribute and still has a stack size of 16,384 bytes.

Pthreads uses an attribute object defined by the data type *pthread_attr_t*. Before attribute objects can be used to change the characteristics of a thread, these attribute objects have to be created. If *portability* is of concern, then one should use attributes prudently. It is a good idea to keep your application flexible in terms of thread attributes and not dependent on any thread attribute. One vendor might allow you to set the stack address attribute of a thread, while others might not. Rather than specifying your stack address for the thread, you should leave such details to the underlying thread implementation. If you are curious to know which thread attributes are supported by your vendor, then check the header file *pthread.h,* and search for the thread attribute defines.

2.5.1 Creating attributes object

```
Pre-draft 7 and DCE 1.1
int pthread_attr_create (pthread_attr_t *attr)

Draft 7 or higher
int pthread_attr_init (pthread_attr_t *attr)
```

The function pthread_attr_create or pthread_attr_init creates a thread attributes object specified by the *attr* argument and initializes it with the default values. The same attributes object can be applied to *multiple* threads. The attributes object should be destroyed before it can be reinitialized again.

2.5.2 Deleting attributes object

```
Pre-draft 7 and DCE 1.1
int pthread_attr_delete (pthread_attr_t *attr)

Draft 7 or higher
int pthread_attr_destroy (pthread_attr_t *attr)
```

The function pthread_attr_delete or pthread_attr_destroy is used to delete the thread attributes object specified by the argument *attr*. It allows storage for the attributes object to be reused. The deletion of the attributes object has *no* effect on threads that were created using these attributes objects. The attributes objects should not be used once they are deleted, until they are reinitialized.

> Applications that are currently using the pre-draft 7 version should make the API changes when moving to systems implementing draft 7 version or higher.

Threads have many characteristics that can be defined at *creation* time. Other than the scheduling attributes, most of the thread attributes are *static* in nature. Changing a static attribute does *not* change the characteristic of the thread that was created using the attributes object. If static attributes of a thread have to be modified, then they should be changed *before* the thread creation function is called. The attributes of a thread that can be modified are

- Contention scope
- Detach state
- Stack size
- Stack address
- Scheduling parameters, policy, and inheritance

2.5.3 Thread contention scope

The contention scope attribute defines the scheduling scope of the thread, and it can be either process- or system-wide. The possible values for contention scope are

PTHREAD_SCOPE_PROCESS	Process contention scope means that the thread is scheduled locally within a process. This is similar to the M:1 or the M:N thread model, which was discussed earlier in Sec. 2.4.
PTHREAD_SCOPE_SYSTEM	System contention scope means that all threads within a process are scheduled globally in the system. This is similar to the 1:1 thread model, which was discussed earlier in Sec. 2.4.

Operating systems that implement a 1:1 mapping between a user and a kernel thread support the PTHREAD_SCOPE_SYSTEM contention scope. Similarly, certain nonthreaded operating systems only support the PTHREAD_SCOPE_PROCESS contention scope, as in the case of DCE threads on HP/UX. Systems such as Solaris 2.5 that support the M:N threading model support both contention scope attributes. The default value for the contention scope is *implementation-dependent*. For example, the default contention scope on Solaris 2.5 is PTHREAD_SCOPE_PROCESS, while on AIX 4.1 it is PTHREAD_SCOPE_SYSTEM. The choice of using the appropriate contention scope depends on the application, and this was discussed earlier in Sec. 2.4.4.

2.5.3.1 Get/set contention scope attribute value

```
int pthread_attr_getscope (pthread_attr_t *attr, int *scope)

int pthread_attr_setscope (pthread_attr_t *attr, int scope)
```

The function pthread_attr_setscope sets the thread contention scope attribute value in *attr* as specified by *scope*. The function pthread_attr_getscope returns the value of the contention scope of the thread attribute object *attr* in *scope*. The valid values for scope are PTHREAD_SCOPE_SYSTEM and PTHREAD_SCOPE_PROCESS.

The following code segment checks if the process contention scope is supported by the underlying implementation.

```
CheckProcessContentionScope ()
{
  pthread_attr_t threadAttr;
  int            ret;

#ifdef PTHREAD_SCOPE_PROCESS
    pthread_attr_init (&threadAttr); /* initialize the attributes to default
                                        values */

    ret = pthread_attr_setscope (&threadAttr, PTHREAD_SCOPE_PROCESS);

    if (ret = = ENOTSUP)
         fprintf (stderr, "Process Contention Scope is not supported by the
         implementation \n");
    else
         fprintf (stderr, "Process Contention Scope is supported by the
         implementation \n");

    pthread_attr_destroy (&threadAttr); /* destroy them after use */
#else
   fprintf (stderr, "Process Contention Scope is not supported by the
   implementation \n");
#endif
}
```

2.5.4 Thread detach state

The thread detach attribute defines if the thread is created either in a detached or nondetached state. Nondetached threads *can* be joined (waited on) by other threads. Even when the thread terminates, the storage for the nondetached thread is saved until the thread is joined. The storage, among other things, includes the exit value of the thread. When a thread is created in a detached state, then the storage for the thread is immediately reclaimed after thread termination.

On most draft 4 implementations, threads were created in a nondetached state, which meant that the application was responsible for implicitly detaching the thread on termination. On systems supporting the draft 7 version and higher, threads are often created in the detached state (e.g., AIX 4.X). Since detached threads *cannot* be joined, these applications when ported to the draft 7 version or higher *fail* when the target thread is joined. The default value for the detach attribute is implementation-specific; e.g., Solaris 2.5 creates a thread in a nondetached state. This means that applications *should* change the detached state explicitly to the desired value and not rely on any particular implementation.

Threads should be created in a nondetached state *only* if they have to be joined later in the application. If threads are created in a nondetached state and never joined, then the storage for the thread is never released. This might cause your application to fail when trying to create additional threads.

2.5.4.1 Get/set detached state attribute value

```
int pthread_attr_getdetachedstate (pthread_attr_t *attr, int *detachedstate)

int pthread_attr_setdetachedstate (pthread_attr_t *attr, int detachedstate)
```

The function pthread_attr_setdetachedstate sets the thread detached state attribute value in *attr* as specified by *detachedstate*. The function pthread_attr_getdetachedstate returns the value of the detached state attribute of the thread attribute object *attr* in *detachedstate*. The possible values for the detachedstate attribute are PTHREAD_CREATE_DETACHED and PTHREAD_CREATE_UNDETACHED (draft 7) or PTHREAD_CREATE_JOINABLE (draft 10).

2.5.5 Thread scheduling policy

The scheduling policy attribute defines the scheduling policy of the thread. The possible defines for the scheduling policy are

`SCHED_FIFO`	Preemptive, priority-based scheduling.
`SCHED_RR`	Preemptive, priority-based scheduling with timeslicing.
`SCHED_OTHER`	None of the above, and it is usually an implementation-defined policy.

The topic of thread scheduling will be discussed in detail later in Sec. 5.2

2.5.6 Thread stack size

The stack size attribute is used to specify the stack size in bytes of the newly created thread. Keep in mind that for most applications the default stack size is sufficient. If an application is heavily threaded and you want to conserve the address space, then you should change the default stack size. Since the stack of a thread grows dynamically, reserving a bigger stack size than needed is not a problem, but having a smaller stack can cause many problems.

When a thread exceeds its stack limit, then the signal SIGSEGV is raised in the faulting thread. These are generally nasty bugs to track down because they do not happen with any frequency. Your application might work fine for a long time and then suddenly start to crash once you insert a call to a new function. The stack size value is implementation-dependent.

2.5.6.1 Get/set stack size attribute value

```
Pre-draft 7
unsigned long pthread_attr_getstacksize (pthread_attr_t *attr)
int pthread_attr_setstacksize (pthread_attr_t *attr, long stacksize)

Draft 7 and higher
int pthread_attr_getstacksize (pthread_attr_t *attr, size_t *stacksize)
int pthread_attr_setstacksize (pthread_attr_t *attr, size_t stacksize)
```

The function pthread_attr_setstacksize sets the stack size attribute value in *attr* as specified by *stacksize*. The value of stacksize should be at least PTHREAD_STACK_MIN bytes. The function pthread_attr_getstacksize returns the value of the stack size attribute of the thread attribute object *attr* in *stacksize*.

> Applications that are currently using the pre-draft 7 version should make the API changes when moving to systems implementing draft 7 version or higher.

In the following code segment, thread attributes are used to change the default stack size attribute of a newly created thread.

```
ChangeThreadStackSize ()
{
  pthread_attr_t  threadAttr;
  size_t          oldStackSize;

  pthread_attr_init (&threadAttr);

  pthread_attr_getstacksize (&threadAttr, &oldStackSize);

  if (oldStackSize > 65536)
      pthread_attr_setstacksize (&threadAttr, 65536);

  pthread_create (....);

  pthread_attr_destroy (&threadAttr);
}
```

2.5.7 Thread stack address

The stack address attribute can be used to specify the starting address of the thread's stack. This is usually done by the system, and it is very rare that applications would ever need to specify a specific stack address. One should be careful *not* to specify the same starting stack address for multiple threads. If you create threads frequently with large stack requirements, then it might be a good idea to cache the stacks for these threads (for performance reasons) and specify a stack address at creation time. It is the application's responsibility to reuse/deallocate the stack, since user-supplied stacks are not destroyed when the thread terminates.

2.5.7.1 Get/set stack address attribute value

```
int pthread_attr_getstackaddr (pthread_attr_t *attr, void **stackaddr)

int pthread_attr_setstackaddr (pthread_attr_t *attr, void *stackaddr)
```

The function pthread_attr_setstackaddr sets the stack address attribute value in *attr* as specified by *stackaddr*. The function pthread_attr_getstackaddr returns the value of the stack address attribute of the thread attribute object *attr* in *stackaddr*.

2.6 Thread Management Functions

`pthread_create`	Create a thread
`pthread_join`	Wait for a thread termination
`pthread_exit`	Terminate a thread
`pthread_detach`	Detach a thread
`pthread_self`	Find thread ID
`pthread_yield`	Yield processor to other threads
`pthread_once`	Initialization of package

2.6.1 Create a thread

When a process begins execution, it has a single thread of control. The process is automatically created with one thread, which is commonly referred to as the *main thread*. The creation of the main thread maintains binary compatibility with single-threaded programs. If a process needs additional threads of control, then they have to be created by calling the thread creation API.

When threads are created, they begin executing a start routine. Creating a thread is somewhere in between calling a function and creating a process. The start routine specifies the entry point at which the newly created thread starts execution. Multiple threads can execute the same start routine, or each thread can have a separate start routine. If multiple threads call the same thread routine and they modify shared data within the routine, then the routine must be written to be thread-safe. Unlike the parent-child relationship, when a new process is created via the *fork* call in POSIX, there is no relationship between the threads. In Pthreads all threads are considered equal. The thread does not maintain a list of created threads or have any knowledge of other threads in the process.

```
Pre-draft 7
int pthread_create (pthread_t *thread, pthread_attr_t attr,
                void * (*start_routine) (void *arg), void *arg)

Draft 7 and higher
int pthread_create (pthread_t *thread, pthread_attr_t *attr,
                void * (*start_routine) (void *arg), void *arg)
```

The function pthread_create is used to create a new thread of control in the process. The first argument is a pointer to an opaque object of type *pthread_t*. Pthreads uses this data type to identify threads. On success, the function pthread_create places the identifier of the newly created thread in *thread*. Each thread within a process is identified by a thread identifier (TID). The TID of the newly created thread is only known to be usable and *unique* within the context of the process creating the thread.

The second argument *attr* defines the attribute of the newly created thread. Depending on the draft version, the default thread attributes are specified by using the constant pthread_attr_default or NULL. The third argument is a pointer to a function that is executed as the thread's *start_routine*. The start routine should be defined to return a void *. The fourth argument *arg* is a pointer to an optional argument passed to the thread's *start_routine,* and it can be NULL in the case when no arguments are passed to the thread routine. Passing integer values and casting it to void * is a bad programming practice and should be avoided.

The function pthread_create does *not* start executing the newly created thread right away; rather, it creates a thread that is a schedulable entity. Do not *depend* on the order in which the new thread starts executing. The new thread can start running even before the function pthread_create returns in the calling thread. It is possible that the new thread can terminate and its TID be reused by the time the function pthread_create returns to the caller.

Some operating systems allow the thread to be created in a suspended state that can be resumed later by the creator. This is helpful when the creator has to create some context information for the new thread before the new thread can begin execution. Even though in POSIX it is not possible to create a thread in suspended state, it is possible for the creator of the thread to synchronize with the new thread using condition variables or some other synchronization primitive.

> In draft 7 of Pthreads the second argument to pthread_create was changed.

The following code segment illustrates the creation of a new thread. The newly created thread is created to start executing the routine LoopThread (). The routine LoopThread executes a loop; the number of iterations to loop is specified as an argument to the thread routine. If you do not wait for the thread to finish, and exit in the main thread, then the entire process will exit.

This includes the newly created thread. The reason for the wait will be explained later in the chapter.

```
main (int argc, char **argv)
{
      pthread_t  threadId;
      void       *LoopThread ();
      int        numRows;
      int        *pThrArg;

      numRows = 1000;
      pThrArg = &numRows;

      /* create a thread using default attributes */
      pthread_create (&threadId, NULL, LoopThread, (void *) pThrArg);

      /*
      */

      /* Wait for the thread to complete */

      exit (0);
  }

  void *
  LoopThread (void * pThrArg)
  {
      int j;
      int numRows;

      numRows = *((int*)pThrArg);
      for (j = 0; j < numRows; ++j)
           printf ("loop iteration j: [%d]\n", j);

  /* Exit Thread */
  }
```

2.6.1.1 Passing multiple arguments to a thread routine. How do we pass multiple arguments to a thread routine? To pass multiple arguments to the thread routine, you should place the arguments in a structure, and pass the address of the structure as an argument to the thread's start routine. The only argument that can be passed to the thread routine is a void *, and it can be the address of a string or the address of a structure.

```
typedef struct _THRARG
{
   int rows;
   int cols;
} THRARG;

main (int argc, char **argv)
{
      pthread_t  threadId;
      void       *LoopThread();
      THRARG     thrArg;

      thrArg.rows = 10;
      thrArg.cols = 20;

      /* create a thread using default attributes */
      pthread_create (&threadId, NULL, LoopThread, (void *) &thrArg);
```

```
        /* Wait for the thread to complete */

        exit (0);
}

void *
LoopThread (THRARG *pThrArg)
{
  int j;
  int k;

  for (j = 0; j < pThrArg->rows; ++j)
       for (k = 0; k < pThrArg->cols;++k)
           printf ("loop iteration j: [%d]\t k: [%d]\n", j, k);

  /* Exit Thread */
}
```

2.6.1.2 Passing different parameters to a thread routine. In multithreaded applications, it is common to create multiple threads to execute the same routine but with different parameters. How do we pass different parameters to a thread routine such that each thread has its own context? Dynamically allocated memory can be used to maintain context for each thread. This guarantees that each thread will have the information it needs in a unique memory area. An incorrect version of the code will be implemented first for illustration purposes, and later the correct version will be implemented.

```
main (int argc, char **argv) /* Incorrect Version - might!! work correctly */
{
        pthread_t   threadId1;
        pthread_t   threadId2;
        void        *LoopThread ();
        THRARG      thrArg;

        thrArg.rows = 10;
        thrArg.cols = 20;

        /* Create Thread #1 using default attributes */
        pthread_create (&threadId1, NULL, LoopThread, (void *) &thrArg);

        /* Change the information for thread #2 */
        thrArg.rows = 30;
        thrArg.cols = 40;

        /* Create Thread #2 using default attributes */
        pthread_create (&threadId2, NULL, LoopThread, (void *) &thrArg);

        /* Wait for both the threads to complete */
        exit (0);
}

void *
LoopThread (THRARG *pthrArg)
{
  int j;
  int k;
  int numRows;
  int numCols;

  numRows = pthrArg->rows; /* assume T1 is preempted before executing this
                              statement */
  numCols = pthrArg->cols;
```

```
    for (j = 0; j < numRows; ++j)
        for (k = 0; k < numCols; ++k)
            printf ("loop iteration j: [%d]\t k: [%d]\n", j, k);

    /* Exit Thread */
}
```

You would expect that when the first thread runs it would print the values 10 and 20, while the second thread would print 30 and 40. The question that then arises is, "How can such a simple code not work correctly all the time?" This might work correctly depending on some other factors such as thread scheduling or the number of processors. If threads were sequential entities, then the code would have worked correctly every time the preceding program ran. Remember that threads are *concurrent* entities and can even run in parallel on an SMP machine. Examine the following sequence of events under which the preceding code will work incorrectly.

- The main thread creates thread T1 and is scheduled to run on the first processor P1. T1 is preempted by a higher-priority thread on P1 *before* it starts executing the assignment statements in the function LoopThread (see code above).
- The main thread now changes the values in the global structure and creates the second thread T2. The thread T2 starts running immediately on a different processor P2. When T2 executes the routine ThreadRoutine, it prints the values 30 and 40.
- T1 is rescheduled to run on P1 and resumes executing the routine ThreadRoutine. It will print the values 30 and 40.

You can see that under such a situation the data for thread T1 are lost. The preceding program will work correctly if T1 executes the routine LoopThread before the main thread updates the structure with both new values for T2. This can happen if the main thread is rescheduled right after it creates the first thread, in which case the value of numRows and numCols inside LoopThread will be 10 and 20 when T1 executes both the assignment statements.

It is possible that the main thread is rescheduled after it updates one of the values, in which case when T1 runs, it will print the values 30 and 20. By now you must have observed that many things can go wrong and are very much dependent on timing and scheduling of the threads. Welcome to the real world of thread programming, where all kinds of things can go *wrong* depending on thread scheduling, number of processors, and other factors (including your own programming bug). Most of these problems can be solved by coding the application correctly.

```
main (int argc, char **argv) /* Correct version */
{
  pthread_t  threadId1;
  pthread_t  threadId2;
  void       *LoopThread ();
```

```
    THRARG      *pthrArg1;
    THRARG      *pthrArg2;

    pthrArg1 = (THRARG *) malloc (sizeof (THRARG));
    pthrArg1->rows = 10;
    pthrArg1->cols = 20;

    /* Create Thread #1 using default attributes */
    pthread_create (&threadId1, NULL, LoopThread, (void *) pthrArg1);

    /* Change the information for thread #2 */
    pthrArg2 = (THRARG *) malloc (sizeof (THRARG));
    pthrArg2->rows = 30;
    pthrArg2->cols = 40;

    /* Create Thread #2 using default attributes */
    pthread_create (&threadId2, NULL, LoopThread, (void *) pthrArg2);

    /* Wait for both the threads to complete */
    free ( (void *) pthrArg1);
    free ( (void *) pthrArg2);

    exit (0);
}
```

Now you can observe that by using different variables for each of the threads, the *race* condition associated with the use of a single variable is eliminated. When you pass dynamically allocated variables as arguments to a thread routine, you *should* deallocate the memory when the thread terminates, or else you will have a memory leak in your application. It makes more sense to deallocate such variables in the thread routine unless the thread returns some result in the thread argument to the caller.

2.6.1.3 Scope of start routine argument. The variable that is passed to the thread start routine is usually a dynamically allocated variable or a global variable. When stack variables are used, one should make sure that the scope of the variable is *valid* throughout the execution of the thread using the variable. The scope of stack variables is limited to the routine in which the variable is declared, and these variables cease to exist after the caller returns from the routine in which the thread was declared.

The following code segment shows a programming bug that can be caused by using stack variables to pass arguments to a thread routine. The main thread calls the function DoFunc, which creates a new thread to execute the routine LoopThread. When the routine DoFunc returns, the variable thrArg is automatically *destroyed,* and this can potentially cause problems in the thread when it begins executing the routine LoopThread. The same code might work depending on the scheduling of the threads. As a general rule, one should avoid using stack variables for passing arguments to another thread.

```
main (int argc, char **argv)
{

    DoFunc ();
```

```
  /* do some other stuff */
}

DoFunc ()
{

  pthread_t  threadId;
  void       *LoopThread ();
             THRARG thrArg;

  thrArg.rows = 10;
  thrArg.cols = 20;

    /* create a thread using default attributes */
  pthread_create (&threadId, NULL, LoopThread, (void *) &thrArg);

  return; /* the variable thrArg ceases to exist after the return - bug! */
}
```

To avoid this nasty bug, either declare the variable thrArg to be global or define thrArg to be a pointer and dynamically allocate the memory for the variable. I would recommend that you use the latter method, since this will ensure that the routine DoLoop can be used safely by multiple threads.

2.6.1.4 Maximum threads allowed. Threads are much more lightweight than a process. Even though threads are cheap, they are *not* free. Threads use system resources like kernel stack and also involve scheduling overhead. The maximum number of threads that can be created successfully in a process in UNIX is limited by system resources, and it is usually vendor- and operating system–specific. For example, in IBM's AIX 4.1, the maximum number of threads that can be created successfully in a single process is 512 (hard-coded limit). Some operating systems might allow you to change the maximum value by rebuilding the kernel. Check your vendor's documentation to find out the maximum threads that can be created in a process.

There is no portable way to find out the maximum number of threads that can be created successfully in a process. The function pthread_create returns EAGAIN (draft 7 and higher) when the maximum allowable limit is reached. Some operating systems allow you to retrieve this value through the *sysconf* interface. The following code segment returns the maximum number of threads that can be created in a process on AIX 4.1.

```
GetSysThreadsMax ()
{
  int maxThreads;

  maxThreads = sysconf (_SC_THREAD_THREADS_MAX);
  fprintf (stderr, "Maximum number of threads allowed per process is [%d]\n",
           maxThreads);
}
```

2.6.1.5 Create bound thread. Depending on the value of the contention attribute, the newly created thread is mapped either to a new kernel thread or to an existing kernel thread. The following segment of code creates a bound thread on Solaris 2.5, thus overriding the default of unbound threads.

```
CreateBoundThread ()
{
  pthread_attr_t  threadAttr;
  pthread_t       threadId;
  void            *ThreadRoutine ();

  pthread_attr_init (&threadAttr);
  pthread_setscope (&threadAttr, PTHREAD_SCOPE_SYSTEM);
  pthread_create (&threadId, &threadAttr, ThreadRoutine, NULL);
}
```

2.6.1.6 Create undetached thread. Depending on the detach state attribute, the newly created thread is created in either a detached or a nondetached state. On some operating systems the default is to create threads in a detached state, in which case the calling thread cannot join (wait for) the created thread. The following segment of code creates an undetached thread on AIX 4.1 (overriding the default of detached threads).

```
CreateUndetachedThread ()
{
  int             detachState;
  pthread_attr_t  threadAttr;
  pthread_t       threadId;
  void            *ThreadRoutine ();

  pthread_attr_init (&threadAttr);

  pthread_getdetachstate (&threadAttr, &detachState);
  if (detachState = = PTHREAD_ATTR_UNDETACHED) /* assumes draft 7*/
    pthread_attr_setdetachstate (&threadAttr, PTHREAD_ATTR_DETACHED);

  pthread_create (&threadId, &threadAttr, ThreadRoutine, NULL);
}
```

2.6.2 Thread termination

Everything that is created must come to an end, and so must the life of a thread. A thread terminates when

- It exits the start_routine.
- It calls pthread_exit.
- It is terminated by some other thread.

```
void pthread_exit (void *status)
```

The function pthread_exit terminates the calling thread and stores the exit status in the variable *status,* which is later made available to any thread waiting for this thread to terminate. The function pthread_exit is called implicitly when a thread returns from the start routine that was used to create the thread. In such a case, the function return value serves as the exit status. The routine pthread_exit does *not* return to the calling thread. The variable status *must* be valid even after the thread exits; therefore, do not use an automatic variable when calling the function pthread_exit. Remember, the stack of a terminating thread is destroyed, except when the stack is user-supplied.

When an initial thread returns from the main routine, then *exit* routine is called, thus terminating *all* the threads in the process. It is a good practice to call pthread_exit to terminate all threads. When the initial thread calls pthread_exit, it does *not* terminate the entire process. The process terminates when the last thread in the process terminates.

A POSIX.1 process can terminate itself by calling the *exit* system call. In a multithreaded process, the routine *exit* terminates the entire process, and this includes all threads in the process. This preserves the semantics of a single-threaded process in POSIX.1. A thread should *never* call *exit* unless the entire process needs to be terminated. For example, on a fatal error when the integrity of the entire process is questionable, then it is better to exit the entire process than just the calling thread in which the error was detected.

2.6.3 Waiting for thread termination

In the worker thread model it is common for a thread to suspend execution until some other thread terminates. For example, consider a program in which a boss thread creates multiple worker threads to perform parallel queries on different databases. The boss thread has to wait for all the worker threads to terminate before it can continue processing with the result of the queries.

The function *pthread_join* is used to wait for the termination of nondetached threads. This is similar in concept to the POSIX *wait* system call used to wait for a child process. The result of calling pthread_join on a detached thread is *undefined.*

```
int pthread_join (pthread_t thread, void **status)
```

The function pthread_join suspends the calling thread and then waits for termination of the thread specified by *thread.* On return from a successful join, the variable *status* contains the exit status of the terminating thread. If thread has already terminated, then pthread_join sets status and returns immediately without blocking.

When multiple threads call pthread_join to join a nonterminated thread, only one of them will be successful, while the rest will fail with an error code of ESRCH. Prior to the draft 10 version of Pthreads, multiple threads could join the same *nondetached* thread. The target thread is *immediately* detached after the notification. If the target thread has already terminated and multiple threads call pthread_join, then only the *first* thread calling pthread_join will succeed. All subsequent calls to pthread_join will fail because the thread is detached as a result of the first thread's pthread_join. Do not use the TID of a thread once it has been detached.

> In draft 10 of Pthreads, pthread_join has been changed, and it returns an error to all but one thread when multiple threads call pthread_join on the same thread.

There is a limit to the number of threads that can be created in a process. Upon thread termination, the resources of the terminating thread must be released. Resources such as thread ID, thread termination status, and internal thread storage for the threads are stored until the thread is detached. The thread resources are automatically released for detached threads. If the thread is created as an undetached thread, then pthread_join *must* be called to ensure that resources are freed. Depending on the implementation, a deadlock may be detected if a thread wants to join itself; similarly, when two threads try to join each other, then they might deadlock.

The routine pthread_join along with pthread_exit also can be used to *return* information to the waiting thread. It is important that the returned variable be valid even after the thread has terminated. Returning a pointer to a stack variable is a programming *bug* because the routine pthread_exit frees the stack of the thread when it exits.

In the following code segment the main thread creates a thread to execute a query. The thread returns the results of the query in a dynamically allocated buffer. On return, the main thread prints the results and then frees the buffer.

```
main (int argc, char **argv)
{
  pthread_t  threadId;
  char       *query;
  void       *QueryThread ();
  char       *queryResults;

  pthread_create (&threadId, NULL, (void *) QueryThread, (void *)query);

  pthread_join (threadId, (void **)&queryResults);
  if (queryResults ! = NULL)
  {
      /*print results returned by the thread */
      free (void*) queryResults); /* assumes only one thread will do a join
      */
  }

  exit (0);
}

void *
QueryThread (void *pquery)
{
  int j;
  void *pqueryResults;

  /* pqueryResults on return is either NULL or points to the result set */
  DoQuery (pquery, &pqueryResults); /* malloc is done inside this routine */

  pthread_exit (pqueryResults);
}
```

2.6.4 Detaching a thread

The Pthreads library maintains some information internally, such as thread ID, termination status, thread-specific data, thread stack, and internal thread storage for each created thread until the thread is detached. This information is saved so that other threads can perform a successful pthread_join operation. The function pthread_detach is used to suggest to the Pthreads library that all information maintained for the thread can be deleted after the thread terminates.

In draft 10 of Pthreads when a thread is joined, then it is *automatically* detached. In earlier versions, the function pthread_detach had to be called to detach a thread that was joined, since pthread_join did not automatically detach the thread. This function is helpful in detaching a running thread and is also used when a thread waiting on a pthread_join is canceled. The canceled thread can call pthread_detach on itself in its thread cleanup handler.

```
Pre-draft 7
int pthread_detach (pthread_t *thread)

Draft 7 and higher
int pthread_detach (pthread_t thread)
```

The routine pthread_detach marks the thread specified by *thread* for deletion. A thread may no longer be joined by another thread *after* it has been detached. If the thread has not terminated, then pthread_detach does not cause the thread to terminate but will cause the thread data structure to be released after the thread terminates.

2.6.5 Thread identifier

Each thread within a process is uniquely identified by a thread identifier. The thread identifier (TID) is only guaranteed to be unique within the context of the calling process. The TID of a new thread is returned in the call to pthread_create. A TID is an opaque object referenced by *pthread_t*. It is important that TID should always be considered an opaque data type. The definition of the data type pthread_t for some operating systems is shown below.

AIX 4.1

```
typedef void *pthread_t;
```

Solaris 2.5

```
typedef unsigned int pthread_t;
```

DEC-Unix 3.2 (DCE 1.1 also)

```
typedef struct
{
  int field1;
  int field2;
  int field3;
} pthread_t;
```

```
pthread_t pthread_self ()
```

The function pthread_self returns the TID of the calling thread.

2.6.5.1 Compare thread identifiers

```
int pthread_equal (pthread_t t1, pthread_t t2)
```

The function pthread_equal returns a nonzero value if the two identifiers are the same; otherwise, 0 is returned. It is important to consider pthread_t as an *opaque* data type and always use pthread_equal to compare two thread identifiers. It does not make sense to use the = = operator for comparing thread identifiers.

In multithreaded programs, ownership information is often associated with resources. In such cases, the TID can be used for identifying the owner of a shared resource. For example, consider the function IsResourceOwner, which returns 1 if the calling thread is the owner of the resource and 0 otherwise. Each thread, upon acquiring the resource in the routine ResourceLock, will store the TID of the calling thread. This can be used to build a recursive lock or to avoid deadlocks when locks are acquired recursively.

```
typedef struct_resource
{
  pthread_t owner;
  /* additional resource specific information */
} RESOURCE;

int
ResourceLock (RESOURCE *pResource)
{

  if (IsResourceOwner (pResource))
    return (-1); /* already owner of resource */

  /*
  Lock resource
  */

  pResource->owner = pthread_self (); /* store thread identifier */
}
```

```
int
IsResourceOwner (RESOURCE * pResource)
{
  pthread_t mySelf;

  mySelf = pthread_self (); /* find out my thread identifier */

  if (pthread_equal (pResource ->owner , mySelf))
      return (1); /* same thread */
  return (0); /* different */
}
```

2.6.6 Yielding processor

```
Pre-draft 10 version
void pthread_yield ()

Draft 10 version (POSIX.1b function)
int sched_yield ()
```

The function pthread_yield or sched_yield *can* be used by the calling thread to release its processor. It allows the scheduler to determine if another thread of higher priority can be run instead of the calling thread. If no suitable thread exists, then the calling thread continues to run. The function sched_yield is part of the POSIX.1b standard and is not a part of POSIX.1c.

In the case of CPU-intensive threads, it is a good idea to yield the processor periodically. This function also can be very useful on operating systems where there is no support for kernel threads or on systems that support the M:N threading model. On such systems, if one thread is in a busy loop without releasing the processor, then the other threads might never get a chance to run.

On systems that implement the PTHREAD_SCOPE_SYSTEM, this function will cause the underlying kernel thread to yield the processor. In the case of threads with PTHREAD_SCOPE_PROCESS contention scope, the threads library will schedule another user thread. On systems that implement PTHREAD_SCOPE_PROCESS contention scope, a thread that does not block or give up CPU might prevent other threads bound to the same kernel thread from running. The yield function provides the ideal solution to such problems.

If you are developing Pthread programs to be portable across operating systems, it might be a good idea to use pthread_yield or sched_yield. Note, *misuse* of this call may hurt rather than help, since it may cause lots of unnecessary context switches. For example, it does not make sense to call this function while holding a lock to a shared data structure, since the other threads might not be able to continue processing unless the shared lock is released.

> In Draft 10 of Pthreads, the function pthread_yield was dropped in favor of sched_yield.

2.6.7 Dynamic package initialization

While developing a multithreaded library or application, it might be necessary to execute some initialization routine before any thread starts execution. Furthermore, this initialization should be *only* done by the first thread calling the routine. In the case of multithreaded servers, this is usually done by the initial thread, and there is no need for any special functionality, since all the initialization work is done even before any additional threads are started.

These routines are used primarily when developing a multithreaded library to perform once-only library initialization. In a traditional single-threaded system, the use of a static variable is adequate to perform such initialization. For example, consider the following segment of the code:

```
static int LibInitialized;
void LibInitOnce ();

void
LibInitOnce ()
{
   if (!LibInitialized)
   {
       LibInit (); /* code to initialize library */
       LibInitialized = 1; /* mark it initialized */
   }
}
```

This code will work incorrectly in the presence of multiple threads. For example, consider the following sequence of events in a multithreaded environment:

- Thread T1 enters the routine LibInitOnce and checks the variable LibInitialzed. It finds that the value of LibInitialized is 0; therefore, it proceeds to execute the function LibInit ().
- Thread T1 is preempted before setting the variable LibInitialized to 1.
- Thread T2 enters the routine LibInit and checks the variable LibInitialized. It finds that the value is 0, so it proceeds to execute the function LibInitOnce (). After executing the function, it sets the value of the variable LibInitialized to 1.
- Thread T1 is rescheduled, and it sets the variable LibInitialized to 1.

It is apparent that in such a situation the library will be initialized *twice*. It can be debated that the preceding problem can be solved by the use of a mutual exclusion (mutex) to guard the variable LibInitialized. Mutexes must be created before they can be used. If two threads proceed to create the mutex concurrently, then each thread has a different view of the mutex. The creation of a mutex itself should be done exactly once, which requires a recursive solution to the problem of once-only initialization. The preceding explanation regarding mutexes is true for pre-draft 7 versions of Pthreads. Note that in draft 7 and beyond, mutexes can be initialized statically and hence can be used to implement a once-only function.

On systems that support the atomic test and set instruction, it is possible to enforce once-only semantics (using some assembly language code). They tend to be nonportable in nature. The Pthreads interface solves the problem by providing a function that safely performs once-only initialization in a portable manner.

2.6.8 Once-only initialization

```
void pthread_once (pthread_once_t *once_block, void (*once_routine) ())
```

The function pthread_once calls *once_routine* with no arguments after checking that once_routine has not been called by a previous thread. On return from the function pthread_once, it is guaranteed that once_routine has returned. Since there is no way to find out if the once routine executed successfully, you *should* use some kind of global error variable within the once routine and check the status of the global variable on return from the pthread_once function.

If multiple threads call pthread_once before once_routine has completed, then they will block until the thread currently executing the once_routine returns. The *once_block* variable is used to determine if the once_routine is called. The once_block variable should be a global variable and should be initialized to pthread_once_init or PTHREAD_ONCE_INIT. A separate once_block variable should be specified for each initialization routine.

The implementation of LibInitOnce using pthread_once could be as follows:

```
static pthread_once_t LibInitialized = PTHREAD_ONCE_INIT;
void LibInit ();

void
LibInitOnce ()
{

   pthread_once (&LibInitialized, LibInit);
}
```

It is a common practice to create all per-process global resources like per-process data structures, keys, mutexes, etc., in the initialization routine. Since these resources require a global scope and have the lifetime of the process, once_routine serves as a natural place to create such resources.

> In draft 7 of Pthreads, the macro pthread_once_init has been replaced by PTHREAD_ONCE_INIT. Applications that are currently using pre-draft 7 versions and are planning to use the newer versions of Pthreads should make the necessary changes.

Chapter

3

POSIX Thread Synchronization

3.1 Thread Synchronization

In a multithreaded process, all threads execute in a single address space and hence share most of the process resources. Process resources such as open files descriptors, IPC identifiers, static variables, and dynamically allocated memory variables are shared by all the threads. For example, if one thread closes a file, then that file is considered closed for all other threads within the process. Similarly, if one thread frees a dynamically allocated buffer using the C library *free* routine, then no other thread can safely reference the same buffer without causing an access violation.

Consider two threads running on different processors trying to update a shared variable simultaneously (e.g., ++SharedVariable). If the value of the variable before the update is 3, then the correct value after the update should be 5. If both threads update the variable concurrently, then one of the updates can be lost, and the value of the variable will be 4. Even though the statement ++SharedVariable looks atomic, keep in mind that the assembly code generated for the statement might not be atomic. This lack of atomicity can cause one of the updates to be lost.

One of the main advantages of threads is easy data sharing, but along with this comes the added responsibility to guard such data against corruption. Threads need to synchronize data that are shared and can be modified by multiple threads. If shared data are modified without any synchronization by multiple threads, then the data can become inconsistent. All access to shared resources must be protected by some mutual exclusion lock. The use of locks to synchronize access to shared data is called *data synchronization*.

In a boss/worker thread model it is common to divide work between multiple threads. In such a case, one thread might wait for another thread to reach a particular state before proceeding, or one thread might wait for a particular condition to be true before proceeding. In these cases, threads are not necessarily synchronizing on data but more on conditions or events. Data synchronization is usually for shorter duration, while event synchronization can be for much longer duration.

Let us consider an example of a producer and a consumer thread writing and reading from a shared buffer. When the threads are reading or writing from the buffer, they have exclusive access to the buffer. The producer cannot write to the buffer until the consumer has finished reading from the buffer, and the consumer cannot read from the buffer until the producer has finished writing to the buffer. Each thread waits for notification from the other thread that the buffer is available. When the producer thread is finished writing to the buffer, it notifies the consumer, and vice versa. This form of synchronization is often called *event synchronization*.

3.1.1 Why mutual exclusion?

To get a better understanding of mutual exclusion, consider a function that adds a new item to the beginning of a list. This list is global and is shared by multiple threads within the process.

```
typedef struct_List
{
   struct_List   *next;
   void          *data;
} SHARED_LIST;
static SHARED_LIST *gpListHead; /* global variable pointing to the beginning
                                   of list */

AddToList (SHARED_LIST *pnewEntry)
{
   pnewEntry->next = gpListHead;
   gpListHead = pnewEntry;
}
```

Assume further that the list is empty when two threads T1 and T2 start executing the routine AddToList. Consider the following sequence of events:

- After the thread T1 executes the first statement, it is preempted by the operating system.
- T2 is scheduled, and it executes both the statements. The global variable gpListHead now points to the new element added by T2.
- T1 is rescheduled, and then it executes the second statement. The global variable gpListHead now points to the element added by T1.

3.1.2 Race condition

It is obvious that in the scenario just described the item added by thread T2 will be *lost*. This is a programming bug that is caused by a race condition. A *race condition* is described as a condition in which two or more threads perform an operation, and the result of the operation depends on thread scheduling (timing). The results of the operation depend on which thread wins the race to execute the statements. Race conditions are often caused by lack of proper synchronization.

In the preceding example, the item added for thread T2 will be preserved if thread T1 executes the routine AddToList before thread T2 enters the routine. These kinds of timing bugs are very *difficult* to find because they do not occur with any defined frequency. Since on SMP machines threads can run in parallel, these kinds of bugs can occur with more frequency on multiprocessor machines than on uniprocessor machines.

Race conditions can happen even when proper locking strategies are used, and depending on the scheduling of the threads, the results can be different. Consider an example of two threads T1 and T2 sharing a global variable Total. Thread T1 executes the routine Add, while thread T2 executes the routine Multiply. If the value of Total is 10 before either thread starts execution, then, depending on the scheduling of the threads, the final value of Total could be either 75 (T1 runs first) or 55 (T2 runs first). The final results depend on the scheduling of threads.

```
Add ()
{
  Acquire mutual exclusion lock;
  Total = Total + 5;
  Release mutual exclusion lock;
}
```

```
Multiply ()
{
  Acquire mutual exclusion lock;
  Total = Total * 5;
  Release mutual exclusion lock;
}
```

3.1.3 Critical section

It is obvious that the function AddToList shown above is a critical section of the code. A *critical section* (CS) is defined as a segment of the code in which a thread accesses shared, modifiable data and where these state changes happen over several instructions. If you have to maintain the data integrity, then it is important that only *one* thread should be inside the critical section code. When one thread is executing the critical section code, then all other threads must *wait* to enter the critical section until the thread inside *leaves* the critical section.

If you do not want more than one thread in the critical section, then access to the critical section should be serialized by some form of locking mechanism. The use of a lock to guard the critical section will guarantee that only one thread will execute the critical section. Failure to use such locks will result in *corruption* of the data. For performance reasons, it is important to keep the critical section code as small as possible. Avoid calling blocking functions inside the CS code, since this might cause preemption of the thread holding the lock to the critical section, which in turn would further delay other threads trying to enter the CS code.

Now implementation of the routine AddToList using some critical section lock will be considered. After entering the routine, each thread will acquire a lock, add the new entry, and then release the lock when it leaves the function. This will guarantee that only one thread will update the global variable gpListHead.

```
AddToList (LIST *pnewEntry)
{
  Acquire critical section lock;
  pnewEntry->next = gpListHead;
  gpListHead = pnewEntry;
  Release critical section lock;
}
```

Let us see how the routine AddToList serializes access to the critical section of code using some critical section (CS) lock under the scenario that we discussed earlier.

- The thread T1 acquires the CS lock on entry to the routine AddToList.
- T1 executes the first statement and is preempted by the operating system.
- T2 enters the routine AddToList and tries to acquire the CS lock. It will *block* until the lock is released by T1.
- T1 is rescheduled, and then it executes the second statement. The global variable gpListHead points to the element added by T1.
- T1 releases the CS lock, which unblocks T2.
- T2 acquires the CS lock and executes the rest of the code.

Consider the example we discussed in the beginning of this chapter where two threads execute the statement ++SharedVariable. The pseudocode for the generated assembly statements could look like

```
LOAD SharedVariable, X      /* load the value of SharedVariable into the reg-
                            ister X */
ADD X                       /* add one to it */
STORE X, SharedVariable     /* store the results into the variable
                            SharedVariable */
```

Now apply the scheduling scenario discussed in Sec. 3.1.1 to these statements, and you can see how one of the updates can be lost. Now that we have discussed some of the concepts of thread synchronization, I will present an overview of the Pthreads synchronization primitives that can be used for data and event synchronization.

3.2 Mutex Functions and Macros

pthread_mutex_init	Initializes a mutex and sets default attributes
pthread_mutex_destroy	Deletes a mutex
pthread_mutex_lock	Locks a mutex
pthread_mutex_trylock	Conditionally locks a mutex
pthread_mutex_unlock	Unlocks a mutex
PTHREAD_MUTEX_INITIALIZER	Initializes a static mutex with default attributes

3.2.1 Mutual exclusion locks

Mutex locks are generally used to synchronize access to and ensure atomic updates of shared data. A *mutex* (mutual exclusion) lock is a data structure in memory that processes or threads use to *serialize* access to shared data. Mutex locks are meaningful only for data that can be *modified* by multiple threads or processes. This means that you do *not* need to serialize access to shared read-only data items.

The state of the mutex can be either *locked* or *unlocked*. The basic assumption behind mutexes are that threads must lock the mutex before accessing shared, modifiable data and unlock the mutex after the thread has completed accessing the shared data. If one thread has acquired the mutex, then all other threads requesting to lock the mutex will *wait* until the mutex is released by the thread owning the mutex. It is important to remember that for data synchronization, all threads must strictly *enforce* the mutex locking protocol. Note that if threads do not check the locks before entering the critical section, then mutex locks cannot be of any help. One possible solution to enforce mutual exclusion is to provide well-defined interfaces (functions) to allow access to shared resources and then implement the mutex locking and unlocking within these interfaces. In this way, the details of locking and unlocking are hidden from the user of these interfaces.

Acquiring a mutex is itself a critical section because it might require multiple steps such as read, test, and set the mutex. On both uniprocessor and multiprocessor machines, the hardware must provide a mechanism for atomic test and set kinds of operations. An *atomic* instruction is an instruction or a sequence of instructions that is uninterruptable. This atomic test and set instruction guarantees that the read, test, and set happen as one atomic instruction. When multiple CPUs try to get/set the same lock, only one of them will succeed. All SMP machines use this atomic operation as the basis for providing mutex locks. The following code segment is a high-level implementation of the function TestAndSet (the code below is for illustration purposes and is not atomic).

```
TestAndSet (int lock)
{
   if (lock = = 0)
   {
      lock = 1;
      return (1);
   }
   return (0);
}
```

3.2.2 Creating a mutex

Mutexes have to be created before they can be utilized for mutual exclusion. Normally, mutexes are created in some initialization code of the process.

Pre-draft 7
```
int pthread_mutex_init (pthread_mutex_t *mutex, pthread_mutexattr_t attr)
```

Draft 7 and higher
```
int pthread_mutex_init (pthread_mutex_t *mutex, pthread_mutexattr_t *attr)
```

The function pthread_mutex_init is used to create a new mutex object with the attributes specified by *attr*. When the function succeeds, the identifier of the newly created mutex is returned in *mutex*. Depending on the draft version, either the constant *pthread_mutexattr_default* or *NULL* should be used for default attributes. Keep in mind that many Pthreads implementations do *not* support any mutex attributes. Mutex attributes are discussed in Sec. 3.5 in much more detail.

By default, mutexes are created as nonrecursive, and the initial state of the mutex is *unlocked*. It is a programming error to initialize the same mutex lock more than once. Mutexes should be created in a once-only function, or the creation of the mutex should be serialized using some other mutex.

> In draft 7 of Pthreads, the arguments to pthread_mutex_init have changed. The value for the default mutex attribute value also was changed from pthread_mutexattr_default to NULL. A new macro was added to initialize static mutexes.

3.2.3 Initializing static mutex variables

In draft 7 of Pthreads, a new macro was introduced to initialize a static mutex with default attributes. Static initialization of mutex guarantees that the mutex will be initialized even before any thread starts execution. With static initialization, mutexes are guaranteed to be initialized once, and this is different from pthread_mutex_init, where it is the programmer's responsibility to ensure that the mutex is initialized only once. Static mutex initialization is equivalent to calling the function pthread_mutex_init and initializing the mutex to default attributes.

```
InitializeMutex ()
{
   static pthread_mutex_t mutex;

   mutex = PTHREAD_MUTEX_INITIALIZER;
}

The above code is equivalent to:
InitializeMutex ()
{
   static pthread_mutex_t mutex;
   pthread_mutex_init (&mutex, NULL);
}
```

3.2.4 Destroying a mutex

When mutexes are no longer needed, they should be destroyed. The Pthreads library does not delete information for the mutex until the mutex is destroyed. Mutexes are *not* deleted when the thread that created the mutex terminates, since mutexes are considered to be shared resources of a process. Mutexes are deleted automatically when the process exits, assuming the scope of the mutex is PTHREAD_SCOPE_PRIVATE. Once a mutex is destroyed, it can be reinitialized by calling the function pthread_mutex_init.

```
int pthread_mutex_destroy (pthread_mutex_t *mutex)
```

The function pthread_mutex_destroy is used to delete a previously created mutex identified by *mutex*. This routine should be called only when the mutex is *no* longer referenced. Deleting a mutex allows all the resources associated with the mutex to be reclaimed. Since this function does not free the memory associated with the dynamically allocated mutex, you should deallocate the memory (e.g., call the *free* routine). The result of deleting a *locked* mutex is implementation-specific. Some Pthreads implementations set *errno* to EBUSY or return EBUSY when trying to delete a locked mutex. The results are undefined if the operation is performed on a nonexisting mutex.

3.2.5 Acquiring the mutex lock

Before executing a critical section (CS) code, a thread must *acquire* the mutex lock guarding the CS. After executing the CS, the thread that locked the mutex must *release* the mutex. The locking of the mutex in Pthreads can be either blocking or nonblocking in nature.

```
int pthread_mutex_lock (pthread_mutex_t *mutex)
```

The function pthread_mutex_lock is used to acquire a lock of a valid unlocked mutex identified by *mutex*. If the mutex is currently locked by some other thread, then the calling thread is *blocked* until the mutex lock is released. When the function returns successfully, then the state of the mutex becomes *locked,* and the calling thread becomes the *owner* of the mutex. The calling thread remains the owner of the mutex lock until it unlocks the mutex later. If the mutex is never unlocked, then some other thread will block *indefinitely* on the mutex lock when it tries to acquire the locked mutex.

Any attempt by the calling thread to lock a mutex that is already locked by the calling thread might result in *deadlock* or in an unspecified behavior. Some Pthreads implementations either set errno to EDEADLK or return EDEADLK on deadlock. It is your responsibility to ensure that you do *not* call this function while owning the mutex lock. Sometimes there is a *need* for recursive mutexes, and recursive mutexes can be built easily using the Pthreads primitives without much overhead. Any attempt to lock a mutex that has been deleted also might result in unspecified behavior.

When *multiple* threads call pthread_mutex_lock at the same time, they are suspended and are placed on a queue of threads waiting for the mutex to be released. Certain factors such as thread priority and scheduling determine which thread will be woken up first, and it does *not* necessarily have to be first in, first out (FIFO) policy. As a general rule, mutex locks should only be held for *short* durations to avoid performance problems.

3.2.6 Nonblocking mutex lock

The function pthread_mutex_trylock is similar to pthread_mutex_lock except that the function returns immediately if the mutex identified by *mutex* is currently locked by any thread, and this includes the calling thread.

```
int pthread_mutex_trylock (pthread_mutex_t *mutex)
```

Nonblocking mutex locks can be used to implement *spinlocks*. When the overhead of suspending and resuming a thread is higher than the time a thread would spend spinning (busy wait) on the mutex, then the use of nonblocking mutexes should be considered. Spinlocks can be helpful for short sections of the code, but they also can burn expensive CPU cycles and should only be considered on SMP machines. Spinlocks can even cause deadlocks on uniprocessor machines. Consider the following code segment that implements a version of a simple spinlock.

```
SpinLockAcquire(pthread_mutex_t *psharedMutex)
{
   while(pthread_mutex_trylock(psharedMutex) = = EBUSY)
         ; /* busy wait */
}
```

In draft 7 of Pthreads, the return value of pthread_mutex_trylock has changed.

3.2.7 Unlocking a mutex

The mutex lock should be released after the thread executes the critical section of the code, or else no other thread can enter the critical section guarded by the mutex.

```
int pthread_mutex_unlock (pthread_mutex_t *mutex)
```

The function pthread_mutex_unlock is used to unlock a mutex lock identified by *mutex*. On success, the mutex lock is released, and the state of the mutex is marked as *unlocked*. If no other thread is waiting for the mutex to be released, then the mutex is marked as having no owner. If one or more threads are waiting for the mutex to be released, then one of them is woken up. Thread priority and scheduling determine which thread is woken up. You should *not* rely on the order in which threads are woken up.

The results are unspecified if the mutex is *unlocked* or the calling thread is not the *owner* of the mutex. Some Pthreads implementations either set errno to EPERM or return EPERM if the mutex is not locked by the calling thread.

Let us implement the routine AddToList that we discussed earlier using mutexes to guard the critical section code.

```
typedef struct List
{
   struct List  *next;
   void         *data;
}SHARED_LIST;

static SHARED_LIST *gpListHead; /* pointer to beginning of list */

pthread_mutex_t ListMutex;

InitListMutex()
{
   pthread_mutex_init(&ListMutex, NULL);
}

AddToList (SHARED_LIST *pnewEntry)
{
   /* Assume the function InitListMutex is called before */

   pthread_mutex_lock (&ListMutex);

   /* Critical Section of Code */
   pnewEntry->Next = gpListHead;
   gpListHead = pnewEntry;

   pthread_mutex_unlock (&ListMutex);
}
```

3.2.8 DCE mutex types

A mutex attributes object specifies nondefault values for mutexes when the routine pthread_mutex_init is called to create a mutex. Most draft 4 implementations do *not* support attributes for mutexes. The DCE thread implementation supports the notion of mutex attributes object. In DCE threads there are three types of mutexes:

- Fast mutex
- Recursive mutex
- Nonrecursive mutex

Fast mutexes can be locked only once; deadlock happens when an attempt is made to lock the mutex again. This is the default mutex and is the fastest to lock and unlock. *Recursive mutexes* have a lock count, and they can be locked multiple times. In the case of the recursive mutex, the only requirement is that the mutex should be unlocked the same number of times it was locked. *Nonrecursive mutexes* are just like fast mutexes except that they return an error rather than deadlock when an attempt is made to lock an already locked mutex.

The following code can be used to create a recursive mutex in *DCE* threads using mutex attributes. Mutex attributes are explained in detail in Sec. 3.5.

```
CreateRecursiveMutex ()
{
   pthread_mutexattr_t   mutexAttr;
   pthread_mutex_t       recursiveMutex;
```

```
    pthread_mutexattr_create (&mutexAttr);
    pthread_mutexattr_setkind_np (&mutexAttr, MUTEX_RECURSIVE); /* non-
    portable */
    pthread_mutex_init (&recursiveMutex, &mutexAttr);
}
```

If *portability* is of concern, then the use of nonportable thread functions should be avoided. These functions, like any other nonportable Pthreads functions, are not guaranteed to be on all systems supporting Pthreads. All nonportable Pthreads functions end with an *_np* suffix.

3.2.9 Recursive mutexes

Recursive mutexes are used in situations where a thread that owns a mutex calls another function that needs to lock the same mutex. For example, consider two functions Func1 and Func2 that can be called independently; in addition, Func2 also can be called by the function Func1. One option for the thread executing Func1 could be to release the mutex before calling Func2, but it might *not* be possible because shared data structures might not have been fully updated in Func1. This is where recursive mutexes are a big help. Let us see the implementation of the functions Func1 and Func2.

```
int                                 int
Func1 ()                            Func2 ()
{                                   {
   Lock Mutex (M);                     Lock Mutex (M);

   Begin updating shared data;         Update shared data;
   if (SomeCondition)                  Unlock Mutex (M);
       Func2 ();
                                    }
   Finish updating shared data;

   Unlock Mutex (M);
}
```

In standard Pthreads, deadlock happens when the owner of the mutex tries to acquire the locked mutex. The following section of the code shows one possible implementation of *recursive* mutexes without using the nonportable extensions of DCE threads. The routine RMutexInit should be called only once. Warning: This code makes certain assumptions about memory sharing, and might not work on certain SMP processors (see file `mthrmutx.c` on disk).

```
typedef struct _recurmutex
{
   int               lockCnt;
   int               maxRecursion;
   pthread_t         owner;
   pthread_mutex_t   mutex;
} RECURSIVE_MUTEX;

int
RMutexInit (RECURSIVE_MUTEX *prmutex, int maxRecursion)
{
```

```
    prmutex->lockCnt = 0;
    /* you should set it to a reasonably high number */
    prmutex->maxRecursion = maxRecursion;
    pthread_mutex_init (&prmutex->mutex, NULL); /* assumes draft 7 or higher */
}

int
RMutexLock (RECURSIVE_MUTEX *prmutex)
{
    pthread_t myself;

    myself = pthread_self ();

    if (prmutex->lockCnt && pthread_equal_np (prmutex->owner, myself))
    {
          if (prmutex->lockCnt == prmutex->maxRecursion)
          {
                fprintf(stderr, "Failure to lock mutex: max recursion count
                reached\n");
                return(-1);
          }

          ++prmutex->lockCnt; /* increment lock count */
          return (prmutex->lockCnt); /* return the count */
    }
    /*Warning: Will not work on certain SMP processors */
    pthread_mutex_lock (&prmutex->mutex); /* wait for lock */
    prmutex->owner = myself;
    prmutex->lockCnt = 1;

    return (prmutex->lockCnt);
}

int
RMutexUnlock (RECURSIVE_MUTEX *prmutex)
{
    pthread_t myself;

    myself = pthread_self ();

    if (!pthread_equal (prmutex->owner,myself))
        return(-1);

    -prmutex->lockCnt; /* decrement lock count */
    /* Should set the owner field to 0 */
    if (!prmutex->lockCnt)
        pthread_mutex_unlock (&prmutex->mutex);

    return (prmutex->lockCnt);
}
```

3.3 Priority Inversion

Priority inversion can happen for threads that are not in the SCHED_OTHER scheduling policy class (see Sec. 5.2.2). *Priority inversion* happens when a lower-priority thread holding the mutex blocks a higher-priority thread trying to lock the same mutex lock, thus delaying the execution of the higher-priority thread. When a higher-priority thread tries to acquire a lock held by the lower-priority thread, the higher-priority thread has to wait until the lock is released by the lower-priority thread. The wait time is determined by the time the lock is held by the lower-priority thread, and sometimes priority inversion can cause a higher-priority thread to block indefinitely.

Consider a process with three threads, namely, T1, T2, and T3, with descending priorities. The priority of thread T1 is highest, while the priority of thread T3 is lowest. Two threads T1 and T3 use a mutex to execute a critical section of the code.

```
CriticalSectionAcquire ()
{
   pthread_mutex_lock (&CriticalSectionMutex);

   /* logic inside the critical section of code */

   pthread_mutex_unlock (&CriticalSectionMutex);
}
```

Let us now consider the possible sequence of events: Thread T3 is scheduled and is preempted after acquiring the mutex lock. Now, when thread T1 executes the routine CriticalSectionAcquire, it blocks, because T3 owns the mutex lock. This will cause T1 to be preempted and some other thread in the process to be executed. Since T3 is a low-priority thread, it might not be rescheduled for some time; chances are that thread T2 might be scheduled before T3. If thread T2 is scheduled, then threads T1 and T3 cannot run until thread T2 ceases to run.

Priority inversion can be a problem for certain applications (real-time class) that require more deterministic scheduling of threads. This kind of scheduling delay should not be a problem for most applications when the wait time is short. The problem happens only with threads of fixed priorities. If *default* thread attributes are used for thread creation, then all threads are created with the same priority. Note that the priorities of threads that fall under the SCHED_FIFO or SCHED_RR scheduling class are never changed by the system.

The Pthreads library provides two mutex protocols to *avoid* priority inversion, namely:

- Priority protection protocol
- Priority inheritance protocol

The priority of the thread holding the mutex is *boosted* in both protocols. Each of these protocols can be applied individually to a mutex.

3.3.1 Priority inheritance protocol

In this protocol, the thread holding the mutex receives the priority of the highest-priority thread trying to acquire the mutex. When a thread blocks on a mutex, the owner of the mutex gets the priority of the blocking thread only if the priority is higher than the priority of the thread holding the mutex. The owner's original priority is restored after it unlocks the mutex.

3.3.2 Priority protection protocol

In this protocol, each mutex has a *priority ceiling,* which is the minimum priority level at which the code guarded by the mutex is executed. If a thread acquires a mutex, and if the ceiling is higher than its own priority, then it receives the mutex priority ceiling. The owner's original priority is restored after it unlocks the mutex. Usually, the priority ceiling is assigned the highest priority value of all threads that might acquire the mutex lock. This means that the priority of all the threads that can use the mutex should be known in advance. In this respect the priority inheritance protocol is better.

3.4 Deadlocks

Deadlock occurs when two threads stop execution and then wait for events that might *never* happen. For example, consider two threads T1 and T2 using two mutexes Mutex1 and Mutex2. Thread T1 acquires Mutex1, while thread T2 acquires Mutex2. Now, thread T1 tries to acquire Mutex2 and thread T2 tries to acquire Mutex1. Deadlock will happen!

A deadlock happens when a thread holding a resource is waiting for a resource that is held by another thread while the other thread is waiting for a resource held by the first thread. There can be multiple threads involved in a deadlock. Deadlocks can happen even when a single thread is involved. If the owner of a mutex tries to acquire the mutex, it may deadlock. These kinds of deadlocks are called *recursive* deadlocks.

Deadlocks also can happen when the thread owning the mutex *terminates* in the middle of the critical section of code without releasing the mutex lock. Any other thread trying to acquire the mutex will wait *indefinitely* because there is no way the mutex can be released. These kinds of deadlocks are detected once the deadlock happens. The problem is worsened by the fact that even when you detect that the thread holding the mutex has terminated, there is still *no* way to release the lock. The guiding principle behind mutex locks is that *only* the owner of the lock can release the lock.

Assume that the lock could have been released by some other thread. This cannot guarantee that the state of the shared data is *consistent.* The terminating thread could have crashed in the middle of updating a linked list so that even if the mutex could have been released, it cannot guarantee the integrity of the data. One of the best things to do in this case is to *exit* the program and then try to find the bug that abnormally terminated the thread in the critical section.

Personally, I would have preferred that the function pthread_mutex_lock return some form of error code when it detected that the thread owning the mutex had terminated abnormally. This would have made the deadlock-detection part easier, but unfortunately, nothing like this exists. It is entirely for the application developer to program some means to detect the death of a thread owning the mutex. Some other operating systems such as Windows NT and OS/2 *notify* the threads trying to lock the mutex when the owner of the mutex terminates abnormally without releasing the mutex.

3.4.1 Deadlock avoidance techniques

There are a couple of ways to avoid deadlocks with synchronization objects. If you are interested in learning more about the topic of deadlock avoidance and detection, then you should read any decent operating system book. Let us consider one of the ways to avoid deadlocks with mutexes.

The protocol states that all mutexes should be assigned a sequence number and that one should always lock mutexes in sequence and should never try to lock a mutex with a sequence number that is lower than the one of the mutex the thread holds. If a thread has to acquire a lock with a lower sequence number, it should first release all mutexes of higher sequence numbers.

The protocol is simple to understand, but in reality, this is *not* a practical solution. The unlocking of mutexes with higher sequence numbers to acquire a mutex of lower sequence number can lead to performance problems. This solution for deadlock avoidance comes at the expense of performance. To detect recursive deadlocks, you can build your own recursive mutex, such as the one that was discussed earlier.

3.5 Mutex Attributes Functions

Just like thread attributes objects, in Pthreads, mutex attributes objects define the characteristics of the mutex when it is created. Keep in mind that currently some vendors do not support any mutex attributes objects.

3.5.1 Initializing/destroying mutex attributes objects

Pre-draft 7
```
int pthread_mutexattr_create (pthread_mutexattr_t *attr)

int pthread_mutexattr_delete (pthread_mutexattr_t *attr)
```
Draft 7 or higher
```
int pthread_mutexattr_init (pthread_mutexattr_t *attr)

int pthread_mutexattr_destroy (pthread_mutexattr_t *attr)
```

The function pthread_mutexattr_init is used to initialize a mutex attributes object identified by *attr* to its default values. The same attribute object can be used to create multiple mutexes. It is a programming error to initialize the mutex attribute more than once.

The function pthread_mutexattr_destroy is used to delete mutex attributes objects. Deleting the attributes object does not affect the mutexes created using this attributes object. The attributes object can be reused if it is again initialized.

> In draft 7, the functions pthread_mutexattr_create and pthread_mutexattr_delete were renamed to pthread_mutexattr_init and pthread_mutexattr_destroy.

3.5.2 Process shared mutex attribute

The *process shared attribute* defines if the mutex can be shared with other processes in the system. If the attributes object is defined to be PTHREAD_SCOPE_PROCESS, then the mutex can be used with other processes in the system. If the attribute is PTHREAD_SCOPE_PRIVATE, then the mutex is *only* accessible to the threads in the process. The process scope mutexes are not interesting when we are dealing with threads but definitely can be useful when mutexes are to be used across processes.

If *portability* of your system is a requirement to other POSIX systems, then use of the process scope attribute should be evaluated carefully because many vendors implementing Pthreads do not support this feature.

Draft 7 or higher

```
int pthread_mutexattr_getpshared (pthread_mutexattr_t *attr, int *pshared)

int pthread_mutexattr_setpshared (pthread_mutexattr_t *attr, int pshared)
```

The function pthread_mutexattr_setpshared sets the mutex process shared attribute *attr* as specified by *pshared*. The function pthread_mutexattr_getpshared returns the value of the mutex process shared attribute of the mutex attributes object *attr* in *pshared*. The valid values for pshared are PTHREAD_SCOPE_SYSTEM and PTHREAD_SCOPE_PRIVATE.

3.5.3 Mutex protocol attribute

Section 3.3 briefly discussed the two different protocols that can be used to prevent priority inversion. If the attributes object is defined to be PTHREAD_PRIO_INHERIT, then the priority inheritance protocol is used, whereas the priority protection protocol is used when the value is PTHREAD_PRIO_PROTECT. No priority inversion protocol is used if the value is PTHREAD_PRIO_NONE. When a mutex is created, neither of the priority inversion protocols is enabled for the mutex.

Draft 7 or higher

```
int pthread_mutexattr_getprotocol (pthread_mutexattr_t *attr, int *protocol)

int pthread_mutexattr_setprotocol (pthread_mutexattr_t *attr, int protocol)
```

The function pthread_mutexattr_setprotocol sets the mutex protocol attribute *attr* as specified by *protocol*. The function pthread_mutexattr_getpshared returns the value of the mutex protocol attribute of the mutex attribute object *attr* in *protocol*. The valid values for protocol are PTHREAD_PRIO_INHERIT and PTHREAD_PRIO_PROTECT.

3.6 Guidelines for Using Mutex

- Always use global or dynamic variables for storing mutex identifiers. Do not try to use stack variables for mutexes, because the stack of a thread is destroyed when the thread terminates. Other threads in the process can still be referencing the mutex, and the address of the mutex identifier is invalid after the stack is destroyed.
- Initialize the mutex before using it, and initialize it only once so that all threads have the same view of the mutex. Statically initialize mutexes whenever possible.
- Delete mutexes after they are no longer used.
- Avoid locking the mutex in a recursive fashion unless you have implemented your own recursive mutex.
- Avoid using any nonportable extensions (e.g., pthread_setkind_np).
- Do not rely on any special mutex attribute in your code. Mutex attributes are not implemented on all systems (e.g., PTHREAD_SCOPE_SYSTEM).
- While locking multiple mutexes simultaneously, be sure that all threads acquire the locks in the same order to avoid deadlocks.
- Lock mutexes for a short time. Keep the critical section of code small, and avoid any blocking operation (I/O, another synchronization lock) inside the critical sections.
- Do not use mutex locks excessively. Excessive synchronization will cause performance problems, and you will tend to lose one of the foremost benefits of multithreading, which is concurrent execution of threads. If all threads reference the shared data in *read-only mode,* then there is no need to serialize access to this piece of shared data.
- If your application runs slower on a multiprocessor machine than on a uniprocessor machine, it is very likely that your application is suffering because of excessive locking.

3.7 Event Synchronization

Consider a boss/worker thread model in which the boss thread puts new work items on a work queue and worker threads dequeue new work items from the queue. It is assumed that the threads use a mutex to guard the work queue while the actual enqueue/dequeue operation happens. The question that arises then is, "How can the worker threads know when a new work item has been placed on the queue?" The worker thread can

- Continuously check the work queue for arrival of new work items.
- Poll the work queue at specified intervals for arrival of new work items.
- Wait on the work queue for new items until the boss thread notifies the worker thread that a new work item has been placed on the work queue.

The first two methods are extremely inefficient when it comes to CPU utilization, whereas the last option provides the *best* solution. In this case the worker thread is suspended when there are no work items on the queue and is only woken up when a new work item is placed on the queue. This form of event synchronization is the most efficient and highly desirable in a multithreaded environment. In the POSIX threads library, *condition variables* are used for event notification and synchronization. It is important that one should never use global flags or shared variables to enforce event synchronization.

3.8 Condition Variable Functions and Macros

`pthread_cond_init`	Create a condition variable
`pthread_cond_destroy`	Destroy a condition variable
`pthread_cond_wait`	Wait for a condition (blocking)
`pthread_cond_timedwait`	Wait for a condition (time-out)
`pthread_cond_signal`	Signal a condition
`pthread_cond_broadcast`	Broadcast a condition
`PTHREAD_COND_INITIALIZER`	Initialize a static condition variable

3.8.1 Condition variables

Condition variables (CVs) are yet another kind of Pthreads synchronization objects that are used for event synchronization. CVs allow threads to block until a particular condition is satisfied and are most useful when multiple threads coordinate together to solve a task. A state change of a variable (condition) can be signalled to one or more threads at the same time.

The question that can be asked is, "Why can't mutexes be used to wait until a particular condition is true?" The answer is simple: It is inefficient in terms of CPU utilization. On some systems, mutexes can be implemented using the hardware test and set instruction and waiting for a condition to be true; using mutexes can easily create a spinloop. Condition variables are used whenever the thread has to wait for *longer* periods on a specified condition. Mutexes, on the other hand, are used for implementing critical sections of code where locks are generally held for a *short* time. Condition variables should be never used for serializing access to some shared data.

Condition variable are used along with a mutex and a boolean variable (condition predicate). The three objects used together for event notification are

- A *condition expression* to indicate whether the condition is met (e.g., $X < 15$ && $Y > 12$)
- A *condition variable* (CV) to wait for the condition
- A *mutex variable* that is used to synchronize access to the condition expression

Condition variables should be always used in conjunction with mutexes. The thread *locks* the mutex and then checks if the condition expression is in the desired state. The state is defined by a boolean variable called a *predicate*. If the condition expression is not in the desired state, then the thread *waits* on the CV associated with the predicate. The mutex is atomically released when a thread waits on a CV. The atomicity of the release and wait operation ensures that no other thread can change the predicate between the operations. It is important to release the mutex because some other thread will lock the mutex before setting the condition expression to the desired state.

When the other thread sets the predicate to the desired state, it then signals the CV. The thread *relocks* the mutex after coming out of the wait, since a return from the wait does not guarantee that the predicate is true or false. The thread that is woken up reexamines the predicate, since more than one thread can be woken up when the condition is broadcasted and the predicate can still be false when it resumes execution after the wait.

3.8.2 Creating condition variables

Condition variables have to be created before they can be used for event notification. Normally CVs are created in some initialization code of the process.

Pre-draft 7

```
int pthread_cond_init (pthread_cond_t *condition, pthread_condattr_t attr)
```

Draft 7 and higher

```
int pthread_cond_init (pthread_cond_t *condition, pthread_condattr_t *attr)
```

The function pthread_cond_init is used to create a new condition variable object with the attributes specified by *attr*. When the function succeeds, the identifier of the newly created condition variable is returned in *condition*. Depending on the draft version of Pthreads, the constant pthread_condattr_default or NULL is used for default attributes. It is a programming error to initialize a CV multiple times without destroying the CV object. Condition variable attributes are discussed in detail later in Sec. 3.10.

In draft 7 of Pthreads, the arguments to pthread_cond_init have changed; the value for the default condition attribute also was changed from pthread_condattr_default to NULL. A new macro was added to initialize static condition variables.

3.8.3 Initializing static condition variables

In draft 7 of Pthreads, a new macro was introduced to initialize a static condition variable with default attributes. Static initialization of a CV guarantees that the CV will be initialized even before any thread starts execution. With static initialization, CVs are guaranteed to be initialized once, and this is different from pthread_cond_init, where it is the programmer's responsibility to ensure that the CV is initialized only once. Static CV initialization is equivalent to calling the function pthread_cond_init and initializing to default attributes.

```
InitializeCondition ()
{
     static pthread_cond_t someCondition; /* should be a static CV */

     someCondition = PTHREAD_COND_INITIALIZER;
}
```

The preceding code is equivalent to

```
InitializeCondition ()
{
     static pthread_cond_t someCondition;

     pthread_cond_init (&someCondition, NULL);
}
```

3.8.4 Destroying condition variables

The function pthread_cond_destroy is used to destroy the state of an initialized condition variable. When condition variables are no longer referenced, they should be destroyed, since the Pthreads library does not delete information for the CV until it is destroyed. Condition variables are not deleted when the thread that created them terminates, since CVs are considered to be shared resources of a process. CVs are deleted automatically when the process exits, assuming the scope of the CV is PTHREAD_SCOPE_PRIVATE.

```
int pthread_cond_destroy (pthread_cond_t cond)
```

The function pthread_cond_destroy is used to destroy the state of the condition variable identified by *cond*. This routine should be called only when *cond* is no longer referenced. Deleting a CV allows all the resources associated with that CV to be reclaimed. The result of deleting a CV on which a thread is currently waiting is implementation-specific. Some Pthreads implementations set errno to EBUSY or return EBUSY when trying to delete a CV on which a thread is currently waiting.

3.8.5 Wait for a condition variable

```
int pthread_cond_wait (pthread_cond_t *cond, pthread_mutex_t *mutex)
```

The function pthread_cond_wait causes the thread to be suspended until the CV *cond* is signalled. The mutex should be *locked* by the calling thread before waiting on the CV. The mutex lock of *mutex* is released atomically, and the thread waits on the CV to be signalled. When the wait on the condition variable is satisfied, then the lock on the mutex variable is reacquired automatically. When multiple threads are woken up as a result of some thread calling pthread_cond_broadcast, then these threads contend for the mutex lock.

Note that if the CV is never signalled, then the thread will block *indefinitely* on the condition variable unless the wait is canceled after a specified time. The function pthread_cond_wait is a cancellation point; cancellation points are discussed in detail later in Sec. 4.4. The following code segment shows a typical use of waiting on condition variables.

```
pthread_mutex_t conditionMutex;
pthread_cond_t conditionVariable;
int            conditionExpression;

WaitForCondition ()
{
    pthread_mutex_lock (&conditionMutex);
    while (conditionExpression = = FALSE)
          pthread_cond_wait (&conditionVariable, &conditionMutex);

    /* do something */

    pthread_mutex_unlock (&conditionMutex);
}
```

3.8.6 Timed wait for a condition variable

```
int pthread_cond_timedwait (pthread_cond_t *cond, pthread_mutex_t *mutex,
struct timespec *abstime)
```

The function pthread_cond_timedwait is similar to pthread_cond_wait except that the wait on the condition variable *cond* is canceled after the time period specified by *abstime*. The time-out parameter abstime is specified as an *absolute* date. The function acquires the mutex even when it returns in case of a time-out. The function pthread_cond_timedwait is also a cancellation point.

The following code segment shows a typical condition timed wait logic.

```
pthread_mutex_t conditionMutex;
pthread_cond_t  conditionVariable;
int             conditionExpression;

TimedWaitForCondition ()
{
   struct timespec  timeOut;
   int              ret;

   timeOut.tv_sec = time(NULL) + 2; /* timeout after 2 seconds */
   timeOut.tv_nsec = 0;
```

```
    pthread_mutex_lock (&conditionMutex);
    while (conditionExpression = = FALSE)
       ret = pthread_cond_timedwait (&conditionVariable, &conditionMutex,
       &timeOut);
    /* do something */

    pthread_mutex_unlock (&conditionMutex);
    if (ret = = ETIMEDOUT)
         return(-1);

    return(0);
}
```

It is *important* to check the condition expression even after a successful return from pthread_cond_wait or pthread_cond_timedwait because a successful return from either of these functions does *not* guarantee that the predicate is either true or false. In the case of a time-out, there is a race condition between the expiration of the time-out and the predicate change, and it is possible that the predicate will be true even though the wait time expired. It is recommended that a while loop (as shown above) *always* should be executed for checking the predicate and waiting on the condition variable. The mutex *always* should be unlocked, even when the function pthread_cond_timedwait is canceled due to a time-out.

3.8.7 Signal a condition variable

```
int pthread_cond_signal (pthread_cond_t cond)
```

The function pthread_cond_signal is used to wake up a thread that is currently waiting on the condition variable *cond*. When multiple threads are waiting on a condition variable, only one of them is woken up, and the rest continue to wait on the condition variable. The scheduling policy and the priority of the thread determine which thread is woken up. After the CV is signalled, the ownership of the mutex lock is granted to the thread that is woken up. If no thread is waiting on the condition variable, then the threads library does *not* save the condition signalling. This means that the next thread calling pthread_cond_wait will block.

On some SMP systems it is possible that the function pthread_cond_signal under some circumstances might wake up more than one thread. This is self-correcting as long as the waiting thread executes a while loop as shown before. It is safe to assume that more than one thread can be woken up by pthread_cond_signal. The following code shows a typical condition signal logic.

```
pthread_mutex_t   conditionMutex;
pthread_cond_t    conditionVariable;
int               conditionExpression;
```

```
SignalCondition () /* version 1 */
{
   pthread_mutex_lock (&conditionMutex);

   conditionExpression = = TRUE;

   pthread_cond_signal (conditionVariable); /* interchangeable with the above
   statement */

   pthread_mutex_unlock (&conditionMutex);
}
```

The condition predicate *always* should be checked and modified under the mutex lock. It is possible to signal the condition variable *after* releasing the mutex. The code below is another version of the function SignalCondition; in fact, it can even be *more* efficient. Whenever data are modified in some critical section of code and some other thread has to be informed of the change, then it is better to unlock the lock first and then notify the thread.

Unlocking the mutex before signalling can *avoid* the double wakeup problem and sometimes can be a better locking alternative. When a condition variable is signalled *without* holding the mutex, chances are that the thread will be successful in acquiring the mutex when it returns from pthread_cond_wait without blocking. Remember, the thread coming out of the function pthread_cond_wait *must* acquire the mutex lock before it can return control to the thread.

```
SignalCondition () /* version 2 */
{
   pthread_mutex_lock (&conditionMutex);

   conditionExpression = = TRUE;

   pthread_mutex_unlock (&conditionMutex);

   pthread_cond_signal (conditionVariable);
}
```

3.8.8 Broadcast a condition variable

```
int pthread_cond_broadcast (pthread_cond_t cond)
```

The function pthread_cond_broadcast is similar to pthread_cond_signal except that it can notify multiple threads instead of a single thread as in the case of pthread_cond_signal.

```
pthread_mutex_t   conditionMutex;
pthread_cond_t    conditionVariable;
int               conditionExpression;

BroadcastCondition ()
{
   pthread_mutex_lock (&conditionMutex);
```

```
    conditionExpression = = TRUE;

    pthread_cond_broadcast (conditionVariable);

    pthread_mutex_unlock (&conditionMutex);
}
```

Let us turn the discussion to the boss/worker queue model that we discussed earlier and see the appropriate use of the signalling functions. When the boss thread adds a new item, it has two choices: It can either wake up *one* worker thread, or it can wake up *all* the workers. Even when multiple workers are woken up, only one of them will be able to dequeue a work item, since only one work item was added by the server. In this case it makes sense to use pthread_cond_signal; the boss thread, after adding a new work item, will wake up one of the worker threads waiting on the queue to dequeue a work item. Generally, when a condition is set and a *single* thread has to be notified of the state change, then pthread_cond_signal should be called. Now assume that the queuing model supports broadcast facility, in which case all worker threads should be notified via pthread_cond_broadcast when a new work item is enqueued.

3.9 Race Condition

Signalling a condition variable *without* being the owner of the mutex lock can cause *race conditions,* thus leading to program errors. For example, consider the modified implementation of the routines SignalCondition and WaitForCondition executed by threads T1 and T2, respectively.

The function SignalCondition has been changed to release the mutex before it signals the condition, and the function WaitForCondition has been changed to destroy the condition variable after acquiring the mutex. The CV is destroyed when the last thread using the CV has terminated. This has been done to illustrate the potential race condition.

```
pthread_mutex_t  conditionMutex;
pthread_cond_t   conditionVariable;
int              numActiveThreads;

SignalCondition ()
{
   pthread_mutex_lock (&conditionMutex);

   —numActiveThreads;

   pthread_mutex_unlock (&conditionMutex);

   pthread_cond_signal (conditionVariable);
}

WaitForCondition ()
{
   pthread_mutex_lock (&conditionMutex);

   while (numActiveThreads 7 0)
      pthread_cond_wait (&conditionVariable, &conditionMutex);
```

```
    pthread_mutex_unlock (&conditionMutex);

    if (!numActiveThreads) /* means no other thread is referencing the CV */
       pthread_cond_destroy (conditionVariable);
}
```

Let us now consider the following scheduling scenario and see how the program can fail.

- Thread T1 starts executing the function SignalCondition, decrements numActiveThreads, and then unlocks the mutex. It is preempted by the operating system before it can execute the pthread_cond_signal function. Also, assume that the value of numActiveThreads becomes 0 after it is decremented.
- When thread T2 begins executing the function WaitForCondition, it finds the value of numActiveThreads to be 0 and hence does not block on the pthread_cond_wait statement. It then proceeds to destroy the condition variable ConditionVariable with the assumption that no thread is referencing the CV.
- Thread T1 is rescheduled, and it executes the statement pthread_cond_signal. The signalling of the CV will fail because the condition variable was destroyed by T2.

It is obvious that this is a race condition that could have been avoided if thread T1 had finished execution of the function SignalCondition before thread T2 started execution of WaitForCondition. These kinds of problems can be eliminated by signalling the condition with the mutex *locked*. The correct version of the function SignalCondition is shown in an earlier section. The lock on the mutex will prevent thread T2 from deleting the condition variable because in the scenario described above, thread T2 will be blocked on the pthread_mutex_lock function.

3.9.1 Deadlocks

When the function pthread_cond_signal is called and there are no threads waiting on the condition variable, then the function does not wake up any threads. The threads library does not *remember* that the condition variable was signalled. This can cause any thread doing a condition wait to *deadlock*.

Consider the modified implementation of the functions SignalCondition and WaitForCondition executed by threads T1 and T2, respectively. The function SignalCondition has been changed so as not to acquire the mutex before it signals the condition. This has been done to illustrate the deadlock condition.

```
pthread_mutex_t  conditionMutex;
pthread_cond_t   conditionVariable;
int              conditionExpression;

SignalCondition ()
```

```
{
   /* mutex is not used to illustrate the problem */

   conditionExpression = TRUE;

   pthread_cond_signal (conditionVariable);
}

WaitForCondition ()
{
   pthread_mutex_lock (&conditionMutex);

   while (conditionExpression == FALSE)
      pthread_cond_wait (&conditionVariable, &conditionMutex);

   pthread_mutex_unlock (&conditionMutex);

   pthread_cond_destroy (conditionVariable);
}
```

Consider the following scheduling scenario that will cause a deadlock.

- Thread T2 begins executing the function WaitForCondition. It checks the condition predicate ConditionExpression and finds it to be FALSE. Soon after this it is preempted by the operating system before it calls pthread_cond_wait.
- Thread T1 is scheduled, which sets ConditionExpression to TRUE and then executes the statement pthread_cond_signal. This will *not* wake up T2 because it is not waiting on the condition yet.
- Thread T2 is rescheduled, executes pthread_cond_wait, and can potentially block indefinitely. The signalling of the condition was *lost* by the threads library.

These kinds of race conditions can be prevented easily by locking the mutex before modifying the condition predicate. It is important that the condition predicate should be tested and modified while holding the mutex lock.

3.10 Condition Attributes

Just like thread and mutex attributes objects in Pthreads, condition attributes objects define the characteristics of the condition variable when it is created.

3.10.1 Initializing/destroying condition attributes objects

Draft 4 and DCE 1.1

```
int pthread_condattr_create (pthread_condattr_t attr)
int pthread_condattr_delete (pthread_condattr_t attr)
```

Draft 7 and higher

```
int pthread_condattr_init (pthread_condattr_t *attr)
int pthread_condattr_destroy (pthread_condattr_t *attr)
```

The function pthread_condattr_init can be used to create condition variable attributes objects and then initialize them to default attributes. The same attributes object can be used to create multiple condition variables. The function pthread_condattr_destroy is used to delete condition attributes objects. Deleting the attributes object does not affect the condition variables created using this attributes object. Once an object is deleted, it can then be reinitialized.

> In draft 7, the functions pthread_condattr_create and pthread_condattr_delete were renamed to pthread_condattr_init and pthread_condattr_destroy.

3.10.2 Process shared condition attribute

The process shared attribute defines if the CV can be shared with other processes in the system. If the attributes object is defined to be PTHREAD_SCOPE_PROCESS, then the CV can be used with other processes in the system. If the attribute is PTHREAD_SCOPE_PRIVATE, then the CV is only accessible to the threads in the process.

If *portability* of your system is a requirement to other POSIX systems, then use of the process scope attribute should be evaluated carefully because many vendors implementing Pthreads do not support attributes of a CV.

3.10.3 Set/get condition process shared attribute

Draft 7 or higher

```
int pthread_condattr_getpshared (pthread_condattr_t *attr, int *pshared)

int pthread_condattr_setpshared (pthread_condattr_t *attr, int pshared)
```

The function pthread_condattr_setpshared sets the condition variable process shared attribute *attr* as specified by *pshared.* The function pthread_condattr_getpshared returns the value of the condition variable process shared attribute of the condition attribute object *attr* in *pshared.* The valid values for pshared are PTHREAD_SCOPE_SYSTEM and PTHREAD_SCOPE_PRIVATE.

3.11 Guidelines for Using Condition Variables

- Always use global or static variables for CVs. Do not try to use stack variables for CVs because the stack of a thread is destroyed when the thread terminates. Other threads in the process can still be referencing the CV even though the address of the CV is invalid after stack destruction.

- Initialize the CV before using it, and initialize it only once such that all threads have the same view of the CV.
- Delete the CV after it is no longer used.
- Do not rely on any special CV attribute in your code. CV attributes are not implemented on all systems.
- Associate a condition predicate with your CV.
- Use CVs in a while loop, as shown in Sec. 3.8.5.
- When the wait function (pthread_cond_wait or pthread_condtimed_wait) returns, then the mutex is locked. It is important to unlock the mutex after you are done with the CV.

3.12 POSIX.1b Semaphores

POSIX.4, which is a standard for real-time extensions, was renamed recently to POSIX.1b. The POSIX.1b standard provides real-time extensions to the base POSIX.1 standard, and it deals with such things as scheduling, timers, I/O, and interprocess communication (IPC). As a synchronization mechanism, POSIX.1b provides counting semaphores. Even though this is not part of the POSIX.1c (Pthreads) standard, it deserves mention in this chapter along with the other synchronization mechanisms presented in this chapter.

Semaphores are used to enforce mutual exclusion and for coordinating events. Counting semaphores were invented by a Dutch professor named Edsger Dijsktra. These semaphores have a count associated with them, and the count can be incremented to any high value but can only be decremented to zero. The value of the counting semaphore can never be less than zero. The *post* (*verhogen* in Dutch) operation increments the semaphore count, while the *wait* (*proberen* in Dutch) decrements the semaphore count.

POSIX.1b implements counting semaphores, and each semaphore has an integer count associated with it. When a process *waits* on a semaphore and the count is greater than zero, the process acquires the semaphore. The integer count is decremented as a result of acquiring the semaphore. When the count associated with the semaphore becomes zero, the process blocks on the wait operation until the integer count is incremented as a result of the *post* operation by some other process. The count associated with a semaphore can never be less than zero. When a process posts a semaphore, the semaphore count is incremented, and any thread waiting to acquire the semaphore is notified.

Counting semaphores are *useful* in restricting access to a shared resource but not necessarily in a mutually exclusive manner. You can think of a semaphore as a gate through which a variable number of threads can pass simultaneously. The maximum number of threads entering the gate can be limited, and the gate remains open as long as resources are available. When the number of resources reaches the maximum limit, then the gate is closed, and it is reopened *only* when resources are freed.

In POSIX.1b there are two kinds of semaphores:

- Named semaphores
- Unnamed semaphores

Named semaphores have a name associated with them, while *unnamed semaphores* do not have names associated with them. Named semaphores are useful when the semaphores are used by different processes. Unnamed semaphores can be used by the threads or child processes of a process. This discussion will be restricted to unnamed semaphores because our interest is in the use of semaphores in a multithreaded environment. Currently, not all UNIX systems implement the POSIX.1b semaphores. If the macro _POSIX_SEMAPHORES is defined in <unistd.h>, then POSIX.1b semaphores are supported by the system. Some systems might define _POSIX_SEMAPHORE, but when you call the semaphore functions, they fail and set *errno* to ENOSYS, which means that POSIX.1b semaphores are not implemented.

A POSIX.1b semaphore is defined by the data type *sem_t*. All semaphore functions return −1 on failure and additionally set the global error variable *errno* to the error code.

3.12.1 Creating an unnamed semaphore

Just like any synchronization object, semaphores have to be created before they can be used by the threads in a process. Unnamed semaphores are memory-based; thus, if multiple processes need to share the unnamed semaphores, then the semaphores should be created in shared memory. In the case of threads, the semaphores can be created in the address space of the process.

```
int sem_init (sem_t *sem_loc, int pshared, unsigned int init_val)
```

The function sem_init creates an unnamed semaphore at address *sem_loc* and initializes it to *init_val*. The semaphore count should be a positive number and should be initialized to the number of initially available resources. When the semaphore count is 0, this means that none of the resources is available initially. This can be used to restrict the use of the resource during some initialization phase. After initialization is done, it can be made available by releasing all instances of the resource by calling the function sem_post. If the value of *pshared* is 1, then the semaphore can be shared across processes, or else it can be shared only by threads within the process.

3.12.2 Destroying a semaphore

When a semaphore is not needed, it can be destroyed to free up all resources used by the system. No process or thread should be blocked on the semaphore when it is destroyed. POSIX.1b does not guarantee that a blocked process or thread will be notified when the semaphore is destroyed. Unnamed semaphores are destroyed automatically when the process exits.

```
int sem_destroy (sem_t *sem_loc)
```

The function sem_destroy destroys the semaphore pointed to by the address *sem_loc*.

3.12.3 Wait on a semaphore

If the semaphore count associated with the semaphore *sem_loc* is greater than zero, then the wait is successful and the semaphore count is decremented. If the count is zero, then the wait operation *blocks* until some other thread or process increments the semaphore count. A nonblocking version of the function is implemented as sem_trywait.

```
int sem_wait (sem_t *sem_loc)

int sem_trywait (sem_t *sem_loc)
```

3.12.4 Post a semaphore

When a semaphore is posted, the semaphore count is incremented, and one of the blocked threads or processes is woken up.

```
int sem_post (sem_t *sem_loc)
```

The following code segment illustrates the use of semaphores for the shared buffers example discussed earlier in the chapter. Two semaphores bufEmpty and bufFull are used by the producer and consumer threads to control access to the shared buffer. Assume that the routine InitSemaphores is called before either thread begins executing.

```
#define  THREAD_SCOPE 0
sem_t    bufEmpty;
sem_t    bufFull;

InitSemaphores()
{
   sem_init(&bufEmpty, THREAD_SCOPE, 1);
   sem_init(&bufFull, THREAD_SCOPE, 0); /* none available */
}

Producers()
{
```

```
    sem_wait(&bufEmpty);
    Produce();
    sem_post(&bufFull);
}

Consumers()
{
    sem_wait(&bufFull);
    Consume();
    sem_post(&bufEmpty);
}
```

3.13 Choosing Synchronization Primitives

Mutexes should be used only to control access to shared, modifiable data. For event synchronization, one has a choice between CVs and semaphores. Semaphores are *simpler* to use than CVs for waiting on events. If you want to have simple event wait semantics and you want to wait for some event no matter when it happens, then a semaphore is a better choice than a CV. However, if you want to wait until some condition is true, then the use of CVs is better. There are more chances of error with CVs than with semaphores because with CVs you have more states to manage. Semaphores are a better choice than CVs when access to shared resources has to be controlled.

In the case of semaphores, any thread or process can release the semaphore, even if some other thread or process had acquired it. This is different from mutexes, where only the owner of the mutex can unlock the mutex. In the case of semaphores, there is no concept of ownership. If your system implements POSIX.1b, then you should definitely consider using semaphores in multithreaded applications.

Often applications require complex synchronization primitives such as barriers, monitors, queues, reader/writer locks, and priority locks and much more. POSIX provides the basic building blocks for all your synchronization needs. You should refer to the examples in Chap. 6 for the implementation of some of these complex synchronization schemes.

Chapter

4

POSIX Thread-Specific Data

4.1 Threads and Variables

Threads in a process run in the same address space and have access to all process resources, including variables in memory. These variables can be of the type

- Static variables
- Dynamic variables
- Stack variables

Static variables have a global scope and are allocated by the compiler (e.g., static variables in the C language). Threads have access to all static variables, and they exist for the entire duration of the process. *Dynamic variables* can be created by calling the allocation routine (e.g., malloc routine of the C library). Any thread that knows the address of the dynamic variable can access it safely. Dynamic variables are destroyed when the deallocation routine is called (e.g., the free routine of the C library). *Stack variables* or *automatic variables* are accessible in the routine where the variable is declared, and they cease to exist when the thread returns from the routine in which the variable is declared.

4.1.1 Thread-specific data

In a multithreaded application it is often necessary to create variables whose scope is nonglobal. There are two ways that threads can create data items whose scope is limited to a single thread. Threads can use either stack or local variables. The scope of such variables is limited to the routine in which the variable is declared. The usefulness of local variables is sometimes *limited* when these variables have to be made accessible across function calls. In a single-threaded process, the C language keyword *extern* is used to make global variables accessible across function calls. If a multithreaded application wants the same data to be maintained on a per-thread basis across function calls, then global variables *cannot* be used. What is really needed is a per-thread global variable that is accessible across function calls.

There are a couple of ways this can be achieved in a multithreaded environment. The compilers can be changed to generate a per-thread global variable (e.g., MS Visual C++). Even though these kinds of variables might require support from the operating system, it can be argued that from an application point of view it becomes real *easy* to support per-thread variables. Just a new compiler directive, and you are set! To the best of my knowledge, none of the UNIX compilers supports this directive.

Yet another method could involve a convention among threads that would require each thread to store/retrieve variables at a well-known location reserved for each thread. While the compiler option is not portable across operating systems, the second option is feasible as long as the application maintains the thread-data association. Lastly, the threads library can maintain the thread-data association for the application. The last option is most desirable and is supported by Pthreads. One important thing to remember about TSD: Even though other threads cannot access another thread's TSD it is possible for a thread to corrupt another thread's TSD. This is due to the fact that TSD for all threads share the same address space.

4.1.2 Why is TSD required?

In a multithreaded environment, library functions can be called reentrantly on a per-user or a per-thread basis. Since these functions have to be thread-safe, either all variables within the function must be stack variables or the function must use some mutual exclusion lock to serialize access to the global variables. When these functions are executed by multiple threads, then these functions sometimes maintain context information on a per-thread basis. The data or context to be maintained on a per-thread basis is referred to as *thread-specific data* (TSD). On some operating systems, the concept of thread-specific data is also known as *thread local storage* (TLS on Windows NT).

Let us consider an example of a multithreaded library that requires each thread to call an initialization function ThreadLibraryInit before the thread can call any other function in the library. If the thread calls any other library function before calling the function ThreadLibraryInit, then the library flags it as an error. The function ThreadLibraryInit creates a thread context structure, and this information is used by the library functions to maintain thread global variables across function calls. Basically, the thread context information can be accessed by each library function in one of the two ways:

- Each library function can take an extra argument that is the pointer to the thread context structure created by ThreadLibraryInit. This becomes a bit awkward when the thread context has to be passed to each of the subsequent functions that the library function calls. Adding an additional argument also requires changing the existing functional interface of the library functions.

- Set up a TSD variable that can be accessed globally across functions with a thread scope.

Another good example of the need for thread-specific data is the *errno* variable. In a single-threaded system, *errno* is defined to be a static variable. In a multithreaded application, consider the following situation:

- Thread T1 calls the system call *msgget* with an invalid argument. The function fails and sets errno to EINVAL.
- Thread T2 calls the system call *semget* to create a semaphore when the maximum semaphore limit has been reached. The function fails and sets errno to ENOSPC.

Later, when thread T1 checks the value of errno, it might have the wrong errno value (ENOSPC). The value of errno for thread T1 is *lost* because both threads share the same global errno. This can be avoided by maintaining a per-thread errno variable. On most systems supporting Pthreads, the variable errno is maintained on a per-thread basis and has been redefined to be a function returning a pointer to a per-thread errno variable.

4.2 POSIX TSD Mechanism

Pthreads provides a simple yet powerful mechanism for storing TSD. This scheme uses a key for storing and retrieving per-thread data. To store data on a per-thread basis, the application must first create a key and then use the set/get routines to store or retrieve TSD. Threads in the process use the same key, but they set and get different TSD values.

4.2.1 TSD functions

`pthread_keycreate`	Creates a TSD key
`pthread_key_create`	Creates a TSD key
`pthread_key_delete`	Deletes a TSD key
`pthread_setspecific`	Sets TSD associated with the specific key
`pthread_getspecific`	Gets TSD associated with the specific key

4.2.2 Creating a key

Thread-specific keys must be created before threads can use them to bind TSD. The key is used to maintain association between thread and data. The same key can be used by multiple threads, and a thread can bind values to multiple keys. Each thread binds a unique value to the key such as an address of a dynamically allocated variable.

Draft 4
```
int pthread_keycreate (pthread_key_t *key, void * (*destructor_routine)
(void *));
```

Draft 7 or higher
```
int pthread_key_create (pthread_key_t *key, void * (*destructor_routine)
(void *));
```

The function pthread_key_create is used to create a new *key* accessible to all threads within a process. When the key has to be shared by more than one thread within the process, it is *important* to store the key identifier in a global or static variable. When a new key is created, the TSD are set to a value of NULL for *all* existing threads in the process. Whenever a thread is created afterwards, the TSD value for the thread is set to NULL for *all* keys in the process. The TSD value associated with a key remains NULL unless the thread binds a new value to the key.

When multiple threads use a key to maintain per-thread context, then it is important to create the key only once. The key can be created once, either by creating the key before any thread starts using it or by creating the key in the one-time initialization routine (using pthread_once). It is a programming error to create the same key multiple times.

Destructor routines optionally can be associated with thread-specific keys and are called when the thread terminates normally. If a TSD value is a dynamically allocated variable, then these routines can be used to deallocate the TSD when the thread terminates. Destructor routines are called *only* when a non-NULL value is bound to the key. When the destructor routine is called, then the current TSD value associated with the key is passed to it. Multiple keys either can have the same destructor routine or each key can have its own destructor routine. On some systems it is possible for the destructor routine to be called several times. When multiple keys with their own destructor routines exist in an application, then the order in which these destructor routines are called at thread termination is unspecified.

On some systems, the number of TSD keys per process is limited to some number that can be retrieved by the PTHREAD_KEYS_MAX constant or by calling *sysconf* and passing the macro _SC_THREADS_KEYS_MAX.

The function pthread_keycreate was renamed to pthread_key_create in draft 7.

4.2.3 Deleting a key

```
int pthread_key_delete (pthread_key_t key)
```

In draft 7, thread-specific keys can only be destroyed when *no* TSD are currently bound to them. The key is considered to have data bound to it when one of the threads has a non-NULL TSD value associated with the key. The function pthread_key_delete is used to free the storage associated with the key. After the key has been destroyed, it can be reused. The function does not call the destructor function for each thread TSD, which means that threads are not *notified* when a key is destroyed.

4.2.4 Get value from a key

Draft 4 or DCE 1.1
```
int pthread_getspecific (pthread_key_t key, void **value)
```
Draft 7 or higher
```
void * pthread_getspecific (pthread_key_t key)
```

The function pthread_getspecific is used to get a TSD *value* associated with a valid *key*. If no value was bound previously to the key, then a value of NULL is returned. The return value of NULL *usually* means that the calling thread never set a TSD value. This function only returns the TSD value of the calling thread and cannot be used to get the TSD value of some other thread.

```
pthread_key_t threadKey;
GetThreadData () /* Draft 7 and higher */
{
        void *pthrData;

        pthrData = pthread_getspecific (threadKey);
        if (pthrData == NULL)
                printf ("Null value set \n");
}

GetThreadData () /* Draft 4 or DCE 1.1 */
{
        void *pthrData;

        pthread_getspecific (threadKey, &pthrData);
        if (pthrData == NULL)
                printf ("Null value set \n");
}
```

The routine pthread_getspecific returns a NULL either when no value is set or when the key is invalid. It is the programmer's responsibility to differentiate between a NULL thread-specific data value and an invalid key. The following segment of the code checks to see if the key is valid after the function pthread_getspecfic returns NULL.

```
pthread_key_t threadKey ;

CheckThreadKey ()
{
```

```
    char   *pthrData;
    int    ret;

    pthrData = pthread_getspecific (threadKey);
    if (pthrData = = NULL)
    {
      ret = pthread_setspecific (threadKey, NULL);
      if (ret = = EINVAL)
          printf ("Thread key is invalid \n");
    }
}
```

The function pthread_getspecific was changed in draft 7. Applications that are currently using draft 4 of Pthreads and are planning to use the newer versions of Pthreads should make the necessary changes.

4.2.5 Set value to a key

```
int pthread_setspecific (pthread_key_t key, void *value)
```

The function pthread_setspecific is used to set a TSD *value* associated with a *key*. The value bound to the key is maintained by the threads library, assuming that the thread does not bind a new value to the key. Since the TSD value is a void pointer, any kind of data can be stored (e.g., pointer to a structure or pointer to a string). It is a bad programming practice to cast int values to void pointers. Note that if a thread binds the value NULL or 0 to a key, then the destructor function will not be called when the thread terminates. Usually, the TSD value is an address of a dynamically allocated variable, as shown below.

```
pthread_key_t threadKey;
SetThreadData ()
{
      char *pthrData;

      pthrData = malloc (....);

      pthread_setspecific (threadKey, pthrData);
}
```

4.2.6 Potential problems with keys

A thread cannot bind multiple values to the same key. When a thread binds a new value to a key, the old value is lost. The man pages on some systems (draft 4) suggest that the destructor routine is called even when a new value is bound to it. I tried it on couple of platforms but could never verify this behavior. In draft 7 and higher, whenever a new value is bound to a key, it overwrites the old value *without* calling the destructor routine. If the TSD value associated with a key is some dynamic variable, then it is the application's responsibility to *deallocate* the storage for the old TSD before assigning the new value. Failure to deallocate storage will result in a memory leak in your application.

The following code sample illustrates the problem of *lost* values. Since this is for illustration purposes, two consecutive calls to set data in the routine SetThreadData are shown; in reality, these calls could have been done in separate routines.

```
pthread_key_t  threadKey;
void           *DestructorRoutine();

CreateKey ()
{
       pthread_key_create (&threadKey, DestructorRoutine);
}

void *
DestructorRoutine (void *pthrData)
{
   If (pthrData)
   {
         free (pthrData);
         pthrData = NULL;
   }
}

SetThreadData () /* memory leak */
{
   void *poldThrData;
   void *pnewThrData;

   poldThrData = malloc (....);
   pthread_setspecific (threadKey, poldThrData);

   /* do something */

   pnewThrData = malloc (....);
   pthread_setspecific (threadKey, pnewThrData);
}
```

Since the memory is freed in the destructor routine, one can see that the storage for the variable poldThrData is *never* deallocated, thus causing the memory leak. In the code segment below, the memory leak is prevented by calling the function pthread_getspecific *before* doing the second pthread_setspecific.

```
SetThreadData ()
{
   void *poldThrData;
   void *pnewThrData;
   void *pcurrThrData;

   poldThrData = malloc (....);
   pthread_setspecific (threadKey, poldThrData);

   /* check if an old TSD value is bound to the key */
   if (pcurrThrData = pthread_getspecific (threadKey )
        DestructorRoutine (pcurrThrData);
```

```
    pnewThrData = malloc (....);
    pthread_setspecific (threadKey, pnewThrData);
}
```

In certain applications, a generic cleanup handler is called when an error happens in a thread. It is important that if the TSD value was dynamically allocated, then it should be deallocated only *once,* either in the error handler routine or in the destructor function associated with the key. Consider the following example in which the ThreadCleanup routine frees up the TSD value. Assume that the routine CreateKey shown above has been called to create the key. When the thread terminates, the destructor routine associated with the key will be called with a pointer that has already been freed.

```
ThreadCleanup () /* potential problem */
{
   char *pthrData;

   /* logic for other thread cleanup - application specific

   */
   pthrData = pthread_getspecific (threadKey);

   If (pthrData)
         free (pthrData);

   pthread_exit (NULL);
}
```

This can be *avoided* by setting the TSD value to NULL after the TSD has been freed. When the thread terminates and the TSD value bound to the key is NULL, the destructor routine will not be called. Remember, the destructor routine is only called if the value bound to the key is a non-NULL value.

```
ThreadCleanup () /* correct version */
{
   char *pThrData;
   /* logic for other thread cleanup - application specific

   */
   pThrData = pthread_getspecific (threadKey);

   If (pThrData)
   {
        free (pThrData);
        pthread_setspecific (threadKey, NULL);
   }
   pthread_exit (NULL);
}
```

If the application uses a dynamically allocated variable for the TSD value, then it is a good practice to set the TSD value to NULL when it is deallocated. The destructor routine should always check for non-NULL values before using them. This will guarantee that there will be no error even if the TSD value was deallocated in some other routine or the destructor routine was called multiple times.

4.2.7 TSD and thread-safe functions

Certain functions use static data or return a pointer to static data and therefore are considered non-thread-safe. These functions can be made thread-safe by using TSD. I would *not* recommend this technique for making functions thread-safe, but sometimes you might not have much choice, especially when the functional interface and use of the function cannot be changed. The techniques for writing reentrant code are explained in detail in Chap. 20.

The following example shows how to use TSD for making a function thread-safe. In the following example, the function DbOpen opens a file and allocates a buffer for reading records. For illustration purposes, assume that the implementation allows only one database to be open at a time. The non-thread-safe version of the function uses a global variable pointed to by CurrDb to store the information.

```
#define MAXREC 512
typedef struct _dbrec
{
   int     fd;
   char    *buffer;
} DBREC;

static DBREC *gpCurrDb; /* global variable */

int DbOpen (char *DbName) /* non-thread safe */
{
   /* assume mutex locks are used to serialize this function */
   if (gpCurrDb == NULL)
   {
        gpCurrDb = (DBREC *) malloc (sizeof (DBREC));
        gpCurrDb->fd = open (DbName.....);
        gpCurrDb->buffer = malloc (sizeof (MAXREC));
   }
   else
   {
        printf ("Error: cannot open more than one database at a time \n");
        return (-1);
   }
   return (0);
}
```

Assume the following sequence of events in a process with two threads T1 and T2:

- Thread T1 calls the function DbOpen to open database D1. The global variable gpCurrDb is used to store the information for the database.
- Thread T2 calls the function DbOpen to open database D2. Since the function DbOpen uses a global variable to store the information, the function assumes that a database was already opened by the thread and therefore returns an error to the calling thread.

Let us examine one of the ways to make the function DbOpen thread-safe so that it can be called by multiple threads. For illustration purposes, assume that the functional interface cannot be changed; therefore, the only choice is to eliminate the use of the global variable and store the information in a per-thread variable.

```
pthread_key_t            dbKey;
static pthread_once_t    keyCreated = PTHREAD_ONCE_INIT;

CreateDbKey ()
{
       pthread_key_create (&dbKey, DbClose);
}

DbOpen (char *pdbName) /* thread safe */
{
   DBREC *pthrDbRec;

   /* create the key once */
   pthread_once (&keyCreated, CreateDbKey);

   /* check if the key/value binding is already done */

   pthrDbRec = pthread_getspecific (dbKey);

   if (pthrDbRec == NULL) /* first time called */
   {
        pthrDbRec = (DBREC *) malloc (sizeof (DBREC));
        pthrDbRec->fd = open (DbName.....);
        pthrDbRec->buffer = malloc (sizeof (MAXREC));
        pthread_setspecific (dbKey, pthrDbRec);
   }
   else
   {
        printf ("Error: cannot open more than one database at a time \n");
        return (-1);
   }
   return (0);
}

DbClose (void *pthrData)
{
   DBREC *pthrDbRec;

   pthrDbRec = (DBREC *) pthrData;
   If (pthrDbRec)
   {
        close (pthrDbRec->fd);
        free (pthrDbRec->buffer);
        free (pthrDbRec);
   }
}
```

4.2.8 Guidelines for using thread-specific data

- Always use global or static variables for thread-specific keys. Do not try to use stack variables for keys because the stack of a thread is destroyed when the thread terminates. Other threads in the process can still be referencing the key, which is invalid after stack destruction.
- Create a key only once, either in a process initialization routine or use pthread_once.

- Use a destructor function to deallocate storage for TSD (dynamic variables only).
- If a new value is set to a key, then the old TSD value should be deallocated (dynamic variables only).
- The routine pthread_getspecific returns NULL either when the key is invalid or when no value is bound to the key. It is your responsibility to check that the key is valid when a NULL is returned.
- When freeing any dynamically allocated TSD, set the value to NULL. Also, if the TSD value is freed in some routine other than the destructor routine, then the application should call pthread_setspecific with a NULL value.

4.3 Thread Cancellation

Sometimes in a threaded application one thread might want to terminate another thread. This is required when a thread is no longer responding or is blocked on some operation that will never happen (e.g., blocked on a condition variable). For example, consider an application where a master thread creates several slave threads to run a search query in parallel on multiple databases. The master thread waits for the result to come back from any one of the slave threads. When the first thread comes back with the results, the master thread cancels all other query requests in progress. This would essentially mean terminating all these threads in some orderly manner. In POSIX.1c the term *cancellation* is used for thread termination. Before you read further, let me warn you that cancellation should only be used as a last resort for terminating threads. There are *many* pitfalls associated with thread cancellation.

Pthreads provides a mechanism for one thread to terminate the execution of another thread in the same process. In POSIX jargon this is also called a *cancellation request*. The termination is controlled, and the thread that is being cancelled can hold the cancellation request pending for later delivery. This allows for easier coding, since thread cancellation can only happen at well-defined points. These well-defined points are known as *cancellation points*.

Threads can control cancellation requests similarly to the way a process can control the delivery of signals. Signals, just by their asynchronous behavior, add complexity to applications. In a single-threaded process, signals generally are programmed to be delivered at well-defined points. The results of a signal being delivered while the process is executing some critical section of code can be disastrous. To avoid asynchronous signal notification, the process usually blocks the delivery of a signal while the process executes some critical section of code. When the process unblocks the signal upon exiting the critical section, all pending signals are delivered to the process.

Similarly, in a multithreaded process, a thread can block and unblock its own cancellation requests. This guarantees that the thread cannot be terminated while it is in the middle of some critical section of code. Just as a process can ignore the signal, threads also can disable cancellation, in which case the thread can never be terminated by some other thread. The terminating thread can perform application-specific *cleanup* when the cancellation request is actually handled.

4.3.1 Cancelability state and type

The *cancelability state* specifies *if* the thread can be cancelled. Each thread can set its own cancelability state and also can disable cancellation. The *cancelability type* specifies *how* the thread can be cancelled. The cancellation request for a thread either can be handled on a *deferred* basis or can be acted on *immediately*. There are three possible cancellation situations:

- *Cancellation state is disabled.* If a thread tries to terminate a thread that has disabled termination, then the target thread cannot be terminated. All cancellation requests are held pending until the cancellation state is enabled. By default, the cancellation state is *enabled,* which means that threads can be terminated.
- *Cancellation state is enabled and the cancellation type is immediate.* In this case the cancellation request is handled, and the thread is terminated immediately. This can be *dangerous* because the thread that is terminated could be in the middle of some critical processing, and the cancellation can leave the process in an inconsistent state. I would recommend *not* enabling the immediate cancellation type in applications unless you are sure that there will be no side effects. The better alternative is to use the deferred cancellation type, which allows the thread to be cancelled only at well-defined points.
- *Cancellation state is enabled and the cancellation type is deferred.* In this case the cancellation request is held *pending* until the thread reaches a cancellation point. Since the thread can be cancelled only at a well-defined point, the target thread can perform a cleanup operation (e.g., unlock a held mutex) in its cleanup handlers. This is the *preferred* mechanism for the cancellation type.

4.3.1.1 Pre-draft 7 and DCE 1.1 thread cancellation states. The terms *cancellation state* and *type* were introduced in the draft 7 version of Pthreads. In earlier versions, a thread had two kinds of cancelability states: *general cancelability* and *asynchronous cancelability*. General cancelability is the same as cancellation state, and asynchronous cancelability is the same as cancellation type. Each of the cancelability states also can be disabled or enabled programmatically in draft 4. The functionality for thread cancellation has not changed, even though the functional interface changed in draft 7.

4.3.2 Cancellation points

Cancellation points (CPs) are well-defined points in a program where a cancellation request is acted on if the cancellation state is *enabled* and the cancellation type is *deferred*. CPs allow a program to protect critical sections of code, and they allow cleanup handlers to be executed when a thread is terminated. *Explicit* CPs can be created by calling the pthread_testcancel routine. The pthread_testcancel routine creates a CP and then acts on any pending cancellation requests. The thread is terminated on handling of the cancellation. If no cancellation requests are pending, then the routine pthread_testcancel returns without doing anything.

The following functions in Pthreads are cancellation points:

- pthread_cond_wait
- pthread_cond_timedwait
- pthread_join
- pthread_setcancel and pthread_testcancel

The functions pthread_mutex_lock and pthread_mutex_trylock do *not* provide a cancellation point. Mutex locks are not supposed to be held for a long time, and it is very unlikely that a thread needs to be cancelled when it is blocked waiting for a mutex lock. If a thread that is an owner of the mutex is cancelled and the mutex is not released as a part of cleanup, then all other threads will wait *indefinitely* on the mutex lock.

4.3.2.1 List of POSIX.1 cancellation points. POSIX requires that certain functions support cancellation points, while others are optional. In general, POSIX.1 functions that possibly return EINTR can be considered to be cancellation points. For a complete list, please check your vendor's documentation, but do not rely on support for cancellation points in optional POSIX functions.

4.3.3 Async-cancel-safe functions

A function is called *async-cancel-safe* if a thread that has the immediate cancelability type enabled is terminated while the thread is blocked on the function and the cancellation does *not* cause any side effect. The function should not hold any resources after it has been terminated. Most C library functions *cannot* be considered to be async-cancel-safe. This makes the use of the immediate async cancellation type almost *impossible*.

Asynchronous cancellation should be *enabled* only if you know that the thread does not hold any resource (e.g., mutex), does not require any cleanup, or is currently blocked on an async-cancel function. This is very difficult to design in your application; the simplest solution is to disable immediate asynchronous cancellation. Unless a function is documented to be async-cancel-safe, it is safe to assume that most functions are non-async-cancel-safe. The following Pthreads functions are async-cancel-safe:

- pthread_cancel
- pthread_setcancelstate

- pthread_setcanceltype
- pthread_setcancel (pre-draft 7 only)

4.3.4 Request cancellation of a thread

```
int pthread_cancel (pthread_t thread)
```

The function pthread_cancel *starts* the termination of the thread identified by *thread*. The cancellation request for the target thread is

- Pending if the cancelability state is disabled. The target thread is not terminated until the target thread enables cancelability state.
- Pending if the cancelability state is enabled and the cancellation type is deferred. In this case the target thread is terminated when the thread reaches the next cancellation point.
- Acted on immediately if the cancellation state is enabled and the cancellation type is immediate. The target thread is terminated immediately.

Once the target thread is terminated, all threads that are waiting for the thread to terminate via pthread_join are notified immediately. The exit status of the thread is marked as (void *) −1, and it is made available to any other thread performing a pthread_join. All registered cleanup routines are executed on behalf of the target thread.

4.3.5 Setting cancelability state

Draft 7 and higher

```
int pthread_setcancelstate (int state, int *oldstate)
```

The function pthread_setcancelstate sets the calling thread's cancellation state to *state*. The cancelability state specifies if a thread can be cancelled. The possible values for state are

PTHREAD_CANCEL_DISABLE	All cancellation requests for the thread are held pending until the thread enables cancellation.
PTHREAD_CANCEL_ENABLE	All cancellation requests for the thread are acted on depending on the cancellation type: immediate or deferred. This is the default value for thread cancellation state.

The function returns the old cancellation state in the variable *oldstate*. This information can be very helpful for library functions that might want to disable cancellation in their critical section of code and would later restore it to the old cancellation state when exiting the critical section of code. The following segment of code disables the cancellation state and then restores it back to the original state. One should never enable cancellation in a library routine since the calling thread might not want it enabled.

```
CriticalSectionCancellationDisable ()
{
   int  oldState;
   pthread_setcancelstate (PTHREAD_CANCEL_DISABLE, &oldState);

   /*

   Do Critical section code
   */
   /* restores the old cancellation state */
   pthread_setcancelstate (oldState, NULL);
}
```

4.3.6 Setting cancelability type

> Draft 7 and higher
> `int pthread_setcanceltype (int type, int *oldtype)`

The function pthread_setcanceltype sets the calling thread's cancellation type to *type* and returns the old value of cancellation type in *oldtype*. The cancelability type specifies how a thread can be cancelled, and it is meaningful when the cancellation state is enabled. The possible values for type are

PTHREAD_CANCEL_DEFERRED	This disables the thread cancellation until the thread reaches a cancellation point (this is the default).
PTHREAD_CANCEL_ASYNCHRONUS	The cancellation request is acted on immediately.

4.3.7 Setting general cancelability state

> Pre-draft 7
> `int pthread_setcancel (int state)`

The function pthread_setcancel sets the calling thread's cancellation state to *state*. The cancelability state specifies if a thread can be cancelled. The possible values for state are

PTHREAD_CANCEL_ON	All cancellation requests for the thread are pending until the thread enables cancellation.
PTHREAD_CANCEL_OFF	All cancellation requests for the thread are acted on depending on the cancellation type: immediate or deferred. This is the default value.

4.3.8 Setting asynchronous cancelability state

```
Pre-draft 7
int pthread_setasyncancel (state)
```

The function pthread_setasyncancel sets the calling thread's async cancellation state to *state*. The cancelability state specifies if a thread can be cancelled. The possible values for *newstate* are

PTHREAD_CANCEL_OFF	This disables the thread cancellation until the thread reaches a cancellation point (this is the default).
PTHREAD_CANCEL_ON	The cancellation request is acted on immediately.

> The Pthreads cancellation APIs were changed in draft 7. Applications that are using pre-draft 7 versions of Pthreads and are planning to migrate to the approved standard should make the necessary changes.

4.3.9 Creating cancellation points

```
void    pthread_testcancel ()
```

The function pthread_testcancel *creates* a cancellation point in the calling thread. If the thread has enabled cancellation and a cancellation request is pending, then the thread is terminated. If there are no pending cancellation requests, then the function simply returns. The following section of the code illustrates the use of cancellation points. Assume that a master thread creates a thread to execute the routine LongLoop. For illustration purposes, the master thread cancels the thread if the work does not complete in a second.

```
int  workDone; /* assume that access is protected by some mutex variable */
main ()
{
     pthread_t   workerThread;
    void        *LongLoop ();

    /* Create Worker Thread using default attributes */
    pthread_create (&workerThread, NULL, LoopThread, NULL);

    pthread_mutex_lock(...);

    while (!workDone)
            pthread_cond_timedwait(....); /* wait for one second */

    if (!workDone)
            pthread_cancel (workerThread);

    pthread_mutex_unlock(....);
}
```

```
LongLoop (void *)
{
    int   j;
    for (j = 0; j < 1000000; ++j)
    {
             /* do something with the variable j */
    if (j % 1000) /* periodically check if I have been cancelled */
        pthread_testcancel ();
    }

    pthread_mutex_lock(....);

    workDone = 1;

    pthread_cond_signal(...);

    pthread_mutex_unlock(...);
}
```

4.4 Thread Cleanup Handlers

Cleanup handlers provide a mechanism for a cancelled thread to release all acquired resources and restore all invariants when they are terminated. For example, a thread can have the lock of a shared mutex when it is cancelled by another thread. If the cancelled thread does not release the mutex, then all other threads waiting for the mutex lock to be released will wait indefinitely. This can be avoided if the cancelled thread unlocks the mutex in some cleanup handler before it terminates.

Cleanup handlers are user-specified routines and are maintained on a thread-specific stack. Cleanup handlers are pushed on the stack and are popped off the stack when the thread is cancelled. Multiple cleanup handlers can be pushed, in which case they are popped off in LIFO order.

Cleanup handlers are maintained on a *per-thread basis* and are called when

- The thread exits (either returns from the start routine or calls pthread_exit).
- The thread cancellation request is handled.
- The thread calls pthread_cleanup_pop with a nonzero argument.

4.4.1 Pushing cleanup handlers

```
void pthread_cleanup_push (void (*routine) (void *), void *arg)
```

The function pthread_cleanup_push pushes the function *routine* on the calling thread's LIFO stack. When the thread exits or is cancelled, the cleanup routine is called with *arg* as its argument.

4.4.2 Popping cleanup handlers

```
void pthread_cleanup_pop (int execute)
```

The function pthread_cleanup_pop pops the topmost function from the calling thread's LIFO stack, and then it executes the function if *execute* is nonzero.

These functions may be implemented as *macros* and therefore must be used in pairs within the same lexical scope. The macro pthread_cleanup_push might open a block of statements; similarly, the macro pthread_cleanup_pop might close a statement. Each call to pthread_cleanup_push *must* be matched by a call to pthread_cleanup_pop.

The following segment of code illustrates the use of cleanup handlers.

```
void MutexCleanupHandler (void *);

typedef struct _Sema
{
   pthread_mutex_t  mutex;
   pthread_cond_t   cond;
   int              semaCnt;
} SEMA;

void MutexCleanupHandler (void *pmutex)
{
   pthread_mutex_unlock ( (pthread_mutex_t) *pmutex);
}

AcquireSemaphore (SEMA *psema)
{
   pthread_mutex_lock (&psema->mutex);

   /* push cleanup handler */

   pthread_cleanup_push (MutexCleanupHandler, &psema->mutex);

   while (psema->semaCnt = = 0) /* if cancelled, cleanup handlers will be
   called */
   pthread_cond_wait (&psema->cond, &psema->mutex);

   --psema->semaCnt;

   /* pop cleanup handler and execute it*/
   pthread_cleanup_pop (1);
}

ReleaseSemaphore (SEMA *psema)
{
   pthread_mutex_lock (&psema->mutex);

   /* push cleanup handler */
   pthread_cleanup_push (MutexCleanupHandler, &psema->mutex);

   ++psema->semaCnt;

   pthread_cond_signal (&psema->cond);

   /* pop cleanup handler and execute it*/
   pthread_cleanup_pop (1);
```

```
}

InitSemaphore (SEMA *psema, int count)
{
   pthread_mutex_init (&psema->mutex, NULL);
   pthread_cond_init (&psema->cond, NULL);
   psema->semaCnt = count;
}
```

4.5 Guidelines for Thread Cancellation

- Do not enable asynchronous cancellation unless you are sure that the thread does not hold a shared resource, it does not need to run a cleanup handler, and it is not blocked on any non-async-cancel-safe function.
- Allow cancellations only at some well-defined points in your code.
- Test explicitly for cancellation in routines where no cancellation point exists.
- Register cleanup cancellation handlers and always use the Pthreads cleanup functions (macros) pthread_cleanup_push and pthread_cleanup_pop in pairs.
- Threads that are cancelled should clean up all resources, including thread-specific data.
- Do not assume that functions are cancellation-safe unless documented otherwise.

4.6 Signals in a POSIX System

Signals in a POSIX environment are used for notification purposes and can be either synchronous or asynchronous. When a process receives a signal, it means that some event has happened that the process needs to handle. Historically, signals in UNIX have been overloaded to do many things.

- Signals are generated when a hardware trap or an operating system exception occurs. For example, when a floating-point exception occurs, the signal SIGFPE is raised in the faulting process. Similarly, when a process accesses an invalid memory area, the signal SIGBUS is generated. These kinds of signals are synchronous in nature (e.g., SIGFPE, SIGBUS, SIGPIPE).
- Signals are also used to signal a process termination. For example, when the signal SIGTERM is delivered to a process, it is a request for the process to terminate. When someone types CTRL-C while a process is running, the signal SIGQUIT is generated. These kinds of signals are asynchronous in nature (e.g., SIGTERM, SIGQUIT, SIGHUP).
- A process with the right permission can send a signal to some other process and interrupt the processing of the target process. Signals are also used by some applications as an interprocess communication (IPC)

method. Personally, I feel that this is a very weak form of IPC, but some programmers use it anyway. These kinds of signals are asynchronous in nature (e.g., SIGUSR1, SIGUSR2).

- On UNIX systems, I/O can be done asynchronously, in which case the signal SIGIO is delivered to the process when a pending I/O completes. Signals are also used to install alarms and timers in the process, in which case the signal SIGALRM is generated. These kinds of signals are also asynchronous in nature (e.g., SIGIO, SIGALRM).
- Signals are also used for job control. For example, a user might type CTRL-Z to suspend the process, in which case the signal SIGSTOP is delivered to the process. These kinds of signals are also asynchronous in nature (e.g., SIGSTOP, SIGCONT).

One of the main *advantages* of signals is that the process is notified immediately when an event happens. Signals also can be used to simulate *multiple* flows of control within a process by using asynchronous I/O and timers (SIGIO and SIGALRM). There are some advantages and many more disadvantages to using signals in a single-threaded system. The main disadvantage is that it adds *complexity* to the program code. The process must be coded to handle signals at any given point, thus making the code complex, error-prone, and difficult to understand. A process can arrange to block and unblock signals such that signals are delivered only at well-defined points, but this does not decrease the program complexity. Signals in UNIX cannot be queued and hence are considered unreliable. Note that in POSIX.1b signals can be queued, but it does not make the use of signals less complicated.

I am not going to discuss the merits and demerits of using signals in an application but rather discuss how to use signals in a multithreaded process. Programmers who rely on signals too much for IPC purposes might have a difficult time trying to use them in multithreaded applications. Signals, just by virtue of their being totally asynchronous, are difficult to use in any application; the problems are just *magnified* in a multithreaded application. It is better to handle asynchronous events in a separate thread rather than use signals. Remember, one of the main motivations for using threads is to simplify the handling of asynchronous events. I strongly feel that signals should not have been supported in POSIX.1c multithreaded environment.

4.6.1 Signal handlers and process signal masks

A process has to notify the operating system about how it wants to handle the arrival of signals. Failure to do so might terminate the process when the signal arrives. A process can handle signals in one of the three ways:

- The process can notify the system that it wants to *ignore* the signal, in which case the signal is never delivered to the process.

- The process can notify the system that it wants to *block* the signal temporarily. The signal is held pending, and it is delivered when the signal is unblocked later.
- A process can *catch* a signal by installing a signal handler for the signal. The signal handler is a user-supplied function that is called when the signal arrives. The signal handler can be unique for signals, or multiple signals can have the same signal handler.

In a POSIX.1 system, the function *sigaction* is used to specify how a process wants to handle a signal.

```
int sigaction (int signal, struct sigaction *new, struct sigaction *old)
```

The following code installs a signal handler for the signal SIGUSR1.

```
InstallSignalHandler ()
{
            void SigUsr1Handler ();
   struct   sigaction   oldSig, newSig;

   newSig.sa_flags = 0;
   newSig.sa_handler = SigUsr1Handler;

   /* install new signal handler and save old handler */
   sigaction (SIGUSR1, &newSig, &oldSig);

   /*
        do something
   */

   /* restore old signal handler */
   sigaction (SIGUSR1, &oldSig, NULL);
}
```

It is important for the processes to control when a signal can be delivered to the process. When a process is in some critical section of code, then it might want all signals to be held until it exits the critical section. The function sigprocmask can be used to install signal *masks* in a process, and it also can be used to block and unblock signals.

```
int sigprocmask (int how, sigset_t *newset, sigset_t *oldset)
```

The first argument *how* can have the values SIG_BLOCK, SIG_UNBLOCK, and SIG_SETMASK. Generally, SIG_BLOCK is used to block signals, SIG_UNBLOCK is used to unblock signals, and SIG_SETMASK is used to restore the mask returned by the sigprocmask in *oldset*. There are various functions such as *sigemptyset, sigfillset, sigaddset, sigdelset,* and *sigismember* that operate on signal sets. The reader is advised to consult the vendor's documentation for more explanation on these functions. The following code blocks the signal SIGUSR1 from delivery in its critical section.

```
CriticalSectionRoutine ()
{
    sigset_t  newSet;
    sigset_t  oldSet;

    sigemptyset (&newSet);
    sigaddset (SIGUSR1, &newSet);

    /* block SIGUSR1 while in critical section */
    sigprocmask (SIG_BLOCK, &newSet, &oldSet);

    /* do critical section processing */

    /* restore original signal mask */
    sigprocmask (SIG_UNBLOCK, &oldSet, NULL);
}
```

4.6.2 Threads and signals

Now that we have seen how signals work in a POSIX.1 process, let us turn our attention to signals in a multithreaded process. I feel that by trying to preserve the signal semantics of the POSIX.1 process, the Pthreads implementation has become unnecessarily complicated. Some of the Pthreads implementations have to go to great lengths to simulate POSIX signals in a multithreaded process.

The use of signals in a multithreaded process can make the program unnecessarily complicated and still not work as it would in a single-threaded application. Furthermore, one of the main reasons for using threads in a program is to avoid using signals for handling asynchronous events. A word of advice: If possible, *do not* use signals in multithreaded applications. If you agree with my previous comment, then you should skip reading the rest of this chapter.

Signals are a process resource and are installed on a *per-process* basis. In a single-threaded process, signals often are used to send notification between processes. In a multithreaded process, there might be multiple threads sending or receiving signals, and this means that a signal handler that is installed for one thread is installed for *all* threads in the process.

When a process installs a signal handler and a signal arrives, then, on delivery of the signal, the signal handler starts executing. On return from the signal handler, the process resumes execution at the location where it was interrupted. In a threaded environment, the issue of signals becomes more complex, especially when it is not clear *which* thread is interrupted when a signal is received. This depends on the *type* of signal that is received.

In a multithreaded process, the signal-handling mechanism is different for synchronous and asynchronous signals. Synchronous signals (SIGFPE, SIGBUS) are delivered to the faulting thread, and multiple threads can handle the signal at the same time. The mechanism for asynchronous signals is different and involves much more detail.

Pthreads provides a function *sigwait* that a thread must use to wait for asynchronous signals. When a thread calls *sigwait,* it blocks until a signal is delivered to the process. Keep in mind that not all signals can be used in a threaded process. For example, on certain DCE systems the signals SIGIO, SIGURG, and SIGVTALRM are used by the thread library for internal thread scheduling and I/O. In DCE threads, when a signal handler is not established for a synchronous signal, then the signal is converted to an exception, and an exception is raised in the thread.

Signal handlers are installed on a *per-process* basis, which means that there is only one handler routine for a given signal. The handler is executed when the synchronous signal is received in *any* thread. If more than one thread is interested in receiving the signal, then only one of the threads will receive the signal. Which one? The thread that will receive the signal in such a case is *unspecified.* If two threads install different signal handlers for the same signal, then the signal handler registered by the last thread is used. The application should use the function sigaction to install signal handlers for synchronous signals in a threaded process. *None* of the Pthreads functions should be called from the signal handlers that are installed using sigaction.

4.6.3 Thread signal mask

Draft 7

```
int sigthreadmask(int how, sigset_t *newset, sigset_t *oldset)
```

Draft 10

```
int pthread_sigmask(int how, sigset_t *newset, sigset_t *oldset)
```

Signal handlers are maintained on a per-process basis, whereas signal masks are maintained on a *per-thread* basis. The function pthread_sigmask or sigthreadmask is used to install a per-thread signal mask. The function sigprocmask should *never* be used in a multithreaded application for masking signals. The function pthread_sigmask is identical in use to the sigprocmask, except that it registers signal masks on a per-thread basis. The function sigthreadmask can be used to install signal masks in a thread and can be used to block and unblock signals.

> A new function sigthreadmask was introduced in draft 7. Users of DCE threads should change the code to use sigthreadmask instead of sigprocmask. The function sigthreadmask was changed to pthread_sigmask in draft 10.

4.6.3.1 Sending a signal to a thread. In UNIX it is possible to send a signal to another process by calling the *kill* system call. Similarly, it is possible for one thread to send a signal to another thread within the same process, although one could seriously question such a use in a threaded application.

```
int pthread_kill (pthread_t thread, int sig)
```

The function pthread_kill sends the signal *sig* to the *thread* within the same process. If the target thread has blocked the signal from delivery, then the signal is set pending in the *thread* until the target thread unblocks the signal from delivery. The signal should be a valid signal number; if the signal number specified by sig is 0, then no signal is actually sent but just error checking is performed. This behavior is similar to the POSIX.1 *kill* system call.

When the target thread is blocked on some system call and the signal *sig* is delivered to it, then it interrupts the system call, and EINTR is returned in the target thread. When the thread receives the signal, then the signal handler (if any) is invoked in the context of the target thread. All blocking Pthreads functions return EINTR when they are interrupted by a signal; therefore, applications must be designed to handle this error condition if signals are used in the application. None of the Pthreads functions are *thread-safe,* and thus they should not be called from the signal handlers. A function is said to be async-safe if it can be called from signal handlers.

4.6.4 Waiting for signals synchronously

In a threaded process, asynchronous signals should be handled synchronously. In Pthreads, asynchronous signals can be handled synchronously by waiting for the signals at well-defined points. The well-defined point where threads must wait for signals to be delivered is at the function *sigwait.* Threads should *not* use the function sigaction to install signal handlers for asynchronous signals when they intend to wait for signals synchronously using sigwait.

Threads should *never* wait for synchronous signals such as SIGILL, SIGTRAP, SIGIOT, SIGEMT, SIGFPE, SIGBUS, SIGSEGV, SIGSYS, and SIGPIPE. Signals such as SIGKILL and SIGSTOP cannot be caught by sigwait.

Pre-draft 7

```
int sigwait (sigset_t *set)
```

Draft 7 and later

```
int sigwait (sigset_t *set, int *sig)
```

The function sigwait can be used by a thread to wait for asynchronous signals. The first argument *set* specifies the signal mask, and it is used by the thread to specify all signals that the thread is interested in waiting for. The signals that are masked in set *must* be blocked before the thread calls the function *sigwait*. The function *blocks* until one of the signals currently masked in the set arrives. When a signal arrives, then the function sigwait unblocks, and the signal number is returned either as the function return value or in *sig* (depending on the Pthreads version).

If multiple threads call sigwait simultaneously, then only *one* thread will be woken up when the signal arrives. This order of waking threads is *undefined* and is usually implementation-dependent. It is a good idea to have one dedicated thread calling sigwait on behalf of all threads. Cancellation of a thread *can* happen when a thread is blocked on sigwait because the function is a cancellation point.

Before a thread calls sigwait, it blocks all signals that it wants to receive. The question that arises then is, "How are the signals delivered when the signals are blocked?" It is confusing, but all the details of catching signals are handled internally by the function sigwait. For example, in the DCE threads implementation, the function sigwait installs a internal signal handler that unblocks all signals that are specified in the signal mask to sigwait. The threads then block on a special condition variable, and it is woken up by the thread run-time library when a signal arrives. The signal is reblocked in the calling thread on return from the function sigwait. In general, the thread run-time library acts as the traffic cop between the application and the operating system to handle asynchronous signals.

> The function sigwait was changed in draft 7. Applications should make the necessary changes when moving from a pre-draft 7 version of POSIX threads.

The following code illustrates how a dedicated thread can wait for signals to arrive. The term *sigwaiter thread* is used commonly for the dedicated thread handling signals. In our example, the thread is only interested in receiving signals SIGUSR1 and SIGUSR2.

```
SigWaiterThread ()
{
   sigset_t  newSet;
   sigset_t  oldSet;
   int       sigReceived;

   sigemptyset (&newSet);

   sigaddset (SIGUSR1, &newSet);
   sigaddset (SIGUSR2, &newSet);

   pthread_sigmask (SIG_BLOCK, &newSet, NULL);

   sigwait (&newSet, &sigReceived);

   switch (sigReceived)
   {
       case SIGUSR1:
                    /* handle SIGUSR1*/
            break;
```

```
        case SIGUSR2:
                        /* handle SIGUSR2*/
                break;
        default:
                printf ("not expecting any signals \n");
                pthread_exit (NULL);
        }
}
```

The functions that can be called within the sigwaiter thread do *not* have to be async-safe. A function is considered to be async-safe if the function is interrupted by a signal and the same function can be invoked safely in the signal handler. For example, if the routine printf acquires a global lock and then is interrupted by a signal, then the function printf would deadlock if it were called again from the signal handler. Most functions can be considered *non-async-safe,* but this problem is eliminated when using the sigwait mechanism in a dedicated thread. Although the sigwaiter thread catches signals, it should not be considered a signal handler. The use of sigwait converts asynchronous signals to synchronous signals and therefore places *no* restriction on the functions that can be called from within the sigwaiter thread routine.

It is possible to implement a mechanism such that multiple threads can be notified when a signal arrives. Threads that are interested in receiving signals should register with the sigwaiter thread, and then the threads should wait on a condition variable. The sigwaiter thread can wait for the arrival of any of the registered signals using sigwait. When the signal arrives, the sigwaiter thread can notify all waiting threads by broadcasting the condition variable.

4.6.4.1 Potential problems with sigwait. Even though a dedicated thread can be used to handle asynchronous signals, the user should be aware of some potential problems with threads. If multiple threads do not block a signal, then these threads can be interrupted when a signal arrives. For example, in AIX 4.1, when a signal arrives, the run-time library directs the signal to the thread blocked on a sigwait or to any other thread that has not masked the signal. This can potentially *interrupt* another thread blocked on a system call. The system call will fail, and it will set the errno variable to EINTR. The interrupted thread should either handle the interrupted system call or arrange that signals are not delivered to it. The latter is preferred; otherwise, you have to handle EINTR being returned by system calls throughout the code.

On arrival of a signal, a process can exit if signals are *not* masked in nonsigwaiter threads. Consider the following example, in which the dedicated thread handles the signal SIGUSR1.

```
SignalHandlerThread ()
{
   sigset_t   newSet;
   int        sigReceived;

   sigemptyset (&newSet);
   sigaddset (SIGUSR1, &newSet);
   pthread_sigmask (SIG_BLOCK, &newSet, NULL);
```

```
    for (;;)
    {
         sigwait (&newSet, &sigReceived);
         if (sigReceived = = SIGUSR1)
                 HandleSigUsr1 ();
}
```

Now consider the case where the thread unblocks from sigwait and enters the function HandleSigUsr1. If another signal arrives while the thread is executing the routine HandleSigUsr1, the kernel can deliver the signal to *any* other thread (at random) that has the signal unmasked. When a signal is delivered to some other thread other than the one doing sigwait, then the default action for the signal is taken, since the process never installed a signal handler for SIGUSR1. In the case of SIGUSR1, the default action is to terminate the process.

Both these problems can be solved by *masking* unwanted signals in all threads except the sigwaiter thread. Any thread that is not interested in receiving signals should block all such signals using the pthread_sigmask/ sigthreadmask function. This can be done in one of the two ways:

- At thread creation time the thread creator can mask signals it does not want the new thread to receive. Since signal masks are inherited from the creator, the signals are blocked in the new thread. If signals are masked in the main thread, then each thread in the process will inherit the signal mask.
- Each created thread upon entering the routine that it starts executing on creation should mask the signals it is not interested in receiving.

The following example shows how threads can mask out the signal SIGUSR1.

Method 1 (thread creator masks signals before creating new threads)

```
main ()
{
   pthread_t    threadId;
   void         *ThreadRoutine ();
   void         *SigWaiterThread ();
   sigset_t     newSet;
   int          j;

   /* create signal handler thread to handle SIGUSR1 */
   pthread_create (&threadId, NULL, SigWaiterThread, NULL);

   /* create a signal mask */
   sigemptyset (&newSet);
   sigaddset (SIGUSR1, &newSet);
   pthread_sigmask(SIG_BLOCK, &newSet, NULL);

   /* all new threads inherit signal mask of creator */
   for (j = 0; j <10; ++j)
        pthread_create (&threadId, NULL, ThreadRoutine, NULL);
```

```
   /* wait for threads to complete: assume threads are nondetached */
}

void *
ThreadRoutine (void *pdata)
{
   /* do something */
}

void *
SigWaiterThread (void *pdata)
{
   sigset_t   newSet;
   int        sigReceived;

   sigemptyset (&newSet);
   sigaddset (SIGUSR1, &newSet);
   pthread_sigmask(SIG_BLOCK, &newSet, NULL);

   for (; ;)
   {
        sigReceived = sigwait (newSet);
        switch (sigReceived)
        {
                case SIGUSR1:
                /* handle SIGUSR1 */
                break;
        }
   }
}
```

Method 2 (each thread blocks signals in the start routine)

```
main ()
{
   pthread_t   threadId;
   void        *ThreadRoutine ();
   void        *SigWaiterThread();
   int         j;

   /* first create signal handler thread to handle SIGUSR1 */
   pthread_create (&threadId, NULL, SigWaiterThread, NULL);
   for (j = 0; j <10; ++j)
        pthread_create (&threadId, NULL, ThreadRoutine, NULL);

   /* wait for threads to complete: assume threads are nondetached */
}

ThreadRoutine (void *Arg)
{
   sigset_t   newSet;

   sigemptyset (&newSet);
   sigaddset (SIGUSR1, &newSet);

   /* a potential for a signal arriving before the next statement exists */
   pthread_sigmask (SIG_BLOCK, &newSet, NULL);

   /* do something */
}
```

4.6.5 Guidelines for using signals in a multithreaded process

- Remember, signals are a per-process resource (e.g., SIGALRM).
- Always use sigwait in a dedicated thread to handle asynchronous signals. Never block synchronous signals when calling sigwait.
- Before calling sigwait, the thread should block all asynchronous signals it wants to receive.
- Do not use sigaction to install a signal handler, and also wait for the same signal synchronously using sigwait.
- Never use sigprocmask in a multithreaded process.
- Never use alarms or timers in multiple threads.
- Always block unwanted signals in threads that are not interested in receiving them.
- The signal handler routine should be reentrant if multiple threads can call the handler routine concurrently. Also, do not call non-async-safe functions from the signal handler.
- None of the Pthreads functions are async-safe, and thus they should not be called from signal handlers.

4.6.6 Thread, sleep, and timers

On most systems when a thread calls the *sleep* function call, only the calling thread is suspended. Having said this, let me mention that this might *not* be true on some Pthreads implementations. On systems that do not have support for native threads, "sleep" can suspend the *entire* process, and this includes all other threads in the process.

Timers are maintained on a per-process basis, and the signal SIGALRM is delivered to the process when the alarm expires. The thread that receives the signal SIGALRM is undefined; in fact, it might not be the thread that started the alarm. If possible, *avoid* using alarms in a multithreaded process. According to the POSIX specifications, alarms are a *per-process* resource, and keeping this in mind, applications should design their applications accordingly. Signals and alarms are *not* suitable for a multithreaded programming environment and should be avoided at all costs.

Chapter

5

POSIX Thread Scheduling

5.1 Scheduling of Threads

On most multithreaded operating systems the unit of scheduling is threads. Systems that support system contention scope may have either a one- or two-level scheduling algorithm. Kernel threads are scheduled by the scheduler, and the thread library schedules user threads to run on these kernel threads (on systems supporting the M:N model). In coroutine-based implementations the kernel is only aware of processes, and the thread run-time library schedules user threads. The scheduling of threads is handled differently on uniprocessor and multiprocessor machines. On a uniprocessor machine the operating system timeslices threads to run on a single processor, while on an SMP machine multiple threads can execute in parallel on different processors.

Most programmers will never have to deal with the scheduling details of threads. POSIX thread scheduling is an extension of POSIX.1b process scheduling. The POSIX scheduling interface provides application developers with finer control on how the threads interact with the system scheduler. Scheduling will only be covered as it relates to threads because it is beyond the scope of this book to cover process scheduling in a POSIX.1b environment.

5.1.1 Thread states

A thread within a process can be in one of many system-dependent states. For the sake of simplicity, threads can be assumed to be in one of these states:

- Running
- Ready
- Waiting

A thread that is actually in the running state is utilizing the processor (CPU). On uniprocessor machines, only one thread can be in the running state, while on an SMP machine, multiple threads can be in the running state (one per CPU). For example, on a four-way SMP machine, at most four threads can be in the running state simultaneously.

A thread is classified in the ready-to-run state if the thread is waiting for an idle processor to run on. Only threads that are either in the running state or the ready-to-run state have the potential to utilize the CPU. If an application has multiple threads in the ready-to-run state, then the operating system will spend substantial time moving threads from the ready-to-run state to the running state. This process of moving threads from ready to running state is called *context switching* of threads. Context-switching overhead should be minimized in order to maximize the performance gain of threads.

A thread is classified to be in the waiting state if it is waiting for some resource to be available. For example, a thread can be in the waiting state if it is waiting on I/O, mutex lock, condition variable, or even a page fault at the system level. The thread can move to the ready or running state only after the wait completes. Excessive synchronization may cause too many threads in the waiting state.

5.2 POSIX Thread Scheduling

Most operating systems maintain a priority-based queue for each of the different thread states. The term *thread scheduling* means selecting a thread from the ready-to-run queue to execute on a processor. The scheduling of threads can be controlled in a couple of ways: It can be altered dynamically or statically defined via thread attributes at creation time. There are three factors that influence the scheduling of Pthreads in a multithreaded process.

- Scheduling scope
- Scheduling policy
- Scheduling priority

5.2.1 Thread scheduling scope

As you might recall from the discussion in Sec. 2.7.3, contention scope for threads can be either global or process-wide. If contention scope is global, then the thread is scheduled with respect to other threads in the system. Process contention scope threads are scheduled by the threads library, and the threads library maps these threads to run on a pool of kernel threads. Threads that are bound to the same kernel thread can never run concurrently.

When the scheduling attributes of a global contention scope thread are changed, this affects the scheduling of the underlying kernel thread. On the other hand, changing the scheduling attributes of a process contention scope thread does not affect the scheduling attributes of the kernel thread.

5.2.2 Scheduling policy

The scheduling *policy* attribute defines which thread is chosen to run next on the CPU. The POSIX.1b standard defines three scheduling policies:

- SCHED_FIFO
- SCHED_RR
- SCHED_OTHER

5.2.2.1 First in, first out (FIFO) scheduling. SCHED_FIFO is a priority-based preemptive scheduling scheme. Each thread is assigned a fixed priority, and the operating system scheduler always picks up the highest-priority thread to run from the run queue. When multiple threads are on the same priority level, they are chosen to run in FIFO order.

The thread continues to run until it voluntarily gives up the CPU or is preempted by a higher-priority thread. The scheduler or the threads library selects another thread to run when the currently executing thread blocks (e.g., I/O, mutex, or a condition variable). When a thread voluntarily gives up the CPU by calling the routine sched_yield, then the scheduler picks up the next-highest-priority thread from the run queue and runs it. In a given priority level, the first thread in at a priority level will be the first thread to run, and this is why the scheduling is called FIFO.

5.2.2.2 Round robin (RR) scheduling. The round robin (RR) scheduling scheme is similar to the SCHED_FIFO scheme except that threads have a time quantum assigned to them. In RR scheduling, each thread has a fixed priority, and threads run for a time quantum in round robin fashion. The scheduler preempts running threads at fixed intervals (implementation-dependent), thus allowing every thread to execute. When multiple threads have the same priority level, they run for a fixed time slice in FIFO order. An application can retrieve the time quantum by calling the function sched_rr_get_interval.

5.2.2.3 SCHED_OTHER scheduling. This is implementation-dependent and usually is the default scheduling behavior on most operating systems. The scheduling algorithm tries to give each thread some execution time independent of the thread priority. On most systems the priority of the thread is constantly adjusted according to the workload, and threads are timesliced on a round robin basis.

5.2.2.4 Which scheduling policy? Most applications would hardly ever need to change the scheduling characteristics of a thread. FIFO scheduling has the property that a thread continues to run until it blocks or gives up the CPU voluntarily, and is useful when threads run for a short duration before blocking. This means that if a high-priority thread spends a lot of time in a non-blocking routine, then all other threads in the system would starve for CPU time. The RR scheduling scheme is preferable over FIFO scheduling because it avoids indefinite starvation. Applications that need to be portable should not depend on SCHED_OTHER scheduling because it is implementation-dependent. Most vendors do *not* support all these scheduling policies.

5.2.3 Thread scheduling attributes

The default scheduling attributes of a thread can be modified by changing the scheduling attributes of a thread attributes object at its creation time.

5.2.3.1 Get/set scheduling policy attribute

Pre-draft 7 and DCE 1.1

```
int pthread_attr_getsched (pthread_attr_t attr)
int pthread_attr_setsched (pthread_attr_t *attr, int scheduler)
```

Draft 7 and later

```
int pthread_attr_getschedpolicy (pthread_attr_t *attr, int *schedpolicy)
int pthread_attr_setschedpolicy (pthread_attr_t *attr, int schedpolicy)
```

The function pthread_attr_setschedpolicy sets the thread scheduling value in attribute *attr* as specified by *schedpolicy*. The function pthread_attr_getschedpolicy returns the value of the scheduling policy of the thread attributes object *attr* in *schedpolicy*. The valid values for schedpolicy are SCHED_FIFO, SCHED_RR, and SCHED_OTHER. On some UNIX systems it might require *superuser* privileges to set the scheduling policy to SCHED_FIFO or SCHED_RR.

The following code segment shows how to change the schedpolicy attribute of a thread such that the newly created thread runs under the FIFO scheduling.

```
main(int argc, char **argv)
{
    pthread_attr_t   threadAttr;
    pthread_t        threadId;
    int              schedPolicy;
    /* initialize attributes objects */
    pthread_attr_init (&threadAttr);

    pthread_attr_getschedpolicy(&threadAttr, &schedPolicy);

    if (schedPolicy ! = SCHED_FIFO)
        pthread_attr_setschedpolicy(&threadAttr, SCHED_FIFO);

    /* create thread using the threadAttr attribute structure */
    pthread_create (&threadId, &threadAttr, ThreadRoutine, NULL);
    .
    ./* do something */
    .
}
```

> Applications that are using the draft 4 version should make the API changes when moving to systems implementing draft 7 or higher.

5.2.3.2 Thread inheritsched attribute. The inheritsched attribute specifies that threads either *inherit* the scheduling attributes of the creator or use the scheduling attributes specified in the thread attributes object when they are created. The possible values are

PTHREAD_INHERIT_SCHED. This specifies that the thread will *implicitly* inherit the scheduling attributes from its creator. This means that if the creator has FIFO scheduling, then all threads it creates also will have the FIFO scheduling behavior. In earlier versions of Pthreads this constant was defined as INHERIT_SCHED.

PTHREAD_EXPLICIT_SCHED. This specifies that the thread will *explicitly* get its scheduling attributes from the thread attribute at creation. The scheduling attribute can be specified in the thread attributes object when the function pthread_create is called. In earlier versions of Pthreads this constant was defined as DEFAULT_SCHED.

5.2.3.3 Getting/setting inheritsched attribute

Pre-draft 7 and DCE 1.1

```
int pthread_attr_getinheritsched (pthread_attr_t attr)
```

Draft 7 or higher

```
int pthread_attr_getinheritsched (pthread_attr_t *attr, int *inheritsched)
int pthread_attr_setinheritsched (pthread_attr_t *attr, int inheritsched)
```

The function pthread_attr_getinheritsched returns the inherit scheduling attribute of the thread attributes object *attr* in *inheritsched*. The function pthread_attr_inheritsched sets the inherit scheduling attribute in the *attr* object as specified by *inheritsched*. The possible values for the inheritsched attributes are PTHREAD_INHERIT_SCHED and PTHREAD_EXPLICIT_SCHED.

The default value for inheritsched is implementation-dependent. For example, on AIX and DCE threads the default value is PTHREAD_INHERIT_SCHED, while on Solaris 2.5 the default value is PTHREAD_EXPLICIT_SCHED. To avoid dependence on any implementation, *always* use the explicit inheritsched scheme.

> Applications that are currently using the draft 4 version should make the API changes when moving to systems implementing draft 7 or higher.

5.2.4 Scheduling priority

The scheduling priority is an integer value that defines the execution priority of a thread. Priority defines the importance of a thread's work relative to other threads in the process. Priority values are similar to *nice* values of a process.

Priorities of threads are modified through the *sched_param* structure. The structure sched_param is defined in the header file *<sched.h>*, and it is used to set and retrieve the priority of a thread. The structure currently has one member, but vendors are free to add additional members to implement their own scheduling priority scheme. The functions pthread_attr_setschedparam and pthread_attr_getschedparam are used to set and get thread priority.

5.2.4.1 Setting/getting priority attribute

Draft 4 or DCE 1.1 threads

```
int pthread_attr_getprio (pthread_attr_t attr)
int pthread_attr_setprio (pthread_attr_t *attr, int priority)
```

Draft 7 or higher

```
int pthread_attr_getschedparam (pthread_attr_t *attr, struct sched_param
*param)
int pthread_attr_setschedparam (pthread_attr_t *attr, struct sched_param
*param)
```

The function pthread_attr_getschedparam returns the scheduling priority attribute of the thread attributes object *attr* in struct *param*. The function pthread_attr_setschedparam sets the priority attribute in the *attr* object as specified by *param*. The only value that can be specified in the param structure is the priority value.

Users of DCE threads should use the pre-draft 7 version of these functions. The minimum and maximum priority values of DCE threads depend on the scheduling class. These constants are defined in the header file <pthread.h>.

Scheduling class	Minimum value	Maximum value
SCHED_FIFO	PRI_FIFO_MIN	PRI_FIFO_MAX
SCHED_RR	PRI_RR_MIN	PRI_RR_MAX
SCHED_OTHER	PRI_OTHER_MIN	PRI_OTHER_MAX

Applications that are currently using the draft 4 version should make the API changes when moving to systems implementing draft 7 or higher.

The following code segment illustrates the use of the scheduling function to change the scheduling priority of a thread.

```
#include <sched.h>
#include <pthread.h>

main(int argc, char **argv)
{
   pthread_attr_t       threadAttr;
   pthread_t            threadId;
   struct sched_param   schedParam;

   /* set the priority of the newly created thread */
   schedParam.sched_priority = 49;

   /* initialize attributes objects */
   pthread_attr_init (&threadAttr);

   /* change the schedinheritsched attribute */
   pthread_attr_setinheritsched (&threadAttr, PTHREAD_EXPLICIT_SCHED);

   /* change the scheduling priority attribute of the thread */
   pthread_attr_setschedparam (&threadAttr, &schedParam);

   /* create thread using the threadAttr attribute structure */
   pthread_create (&threadId, &threadAttr, ThreadRoutine, NULL);

   /* destroy the attributes object */
   pthread_attr_destroy (&threadAttr);

   /*
      Do something
   */
}
```

5.2.5 Dynamically changing scheduling attributes

The scheduling attributes can be defined statically in the thread attributes. The scheduling behavior of an existing thread in the process can be altered dynamically. The changes to the scheduling attributes of the target thread might *not* be immediate. If the thread is not currently running, then these changes take effect the next time the thread is scheduled to run.

The functions for dynamically changing the scheduling parameters of a thread are similar to the scheduling policy and scheduling priority attributes functions discussed earlier. These functions take the thread identifier of the thread whose scheduling attributes have to be altered.

5.2.5.1 Dynamically changing priority and scheduling policy

Draft 4 or DCE 1.1 threads

```
int pthread_setprio (pthread_thread_t *thread , int priority)
int pthread_setscheduler (pthread_t *thread, int scheduler, int priority)
```

Draft 7 or higher

```
int pthread_getschedparam (pthread_thread_t , int *policy, struct sched_param
*param)
int pthread_setschedparam (pthread_thread_t thread , int policy, struct
sched_param *param)
```

The function pthread_setprio changes the priority of the target *thread* to *priority*. The function pthread_setscheduler changes the scheduling policy of the *thread* to *scheduler* and the scheduling priority to *priority*. This routine should be called only when both policy and priority of the thread have to be changed at the same time. The function pthread_setprio can be called to modify only the priority.

The function pthread_setschedparam sets the scheduling policy and priority of the target *thread*. The scheduling policy is changed to the value specified in *policy*. The scheduling priority can be changed by setting the priority field of the *param* structure. The function pthread_getschedparam gets the scheduling policy and priority of the target *thread*. The scheduling policy is retrieved in *policy,* while the scheduling priority is returned in the priority field of the *param* structure.

Some of these functions might not be implemented on your system. For example, Solaris 2.5 only allows policy to be SCHED_OTHER. If *portability* is of concern, do not rely on these functions to be available on all operating systems supporting Pthreads.

5.2.6 Mutex scheduling protocols

In Sec. 3.3 we discussed the problem of priority inversion in a multithreaded application. To avoid priority inversion for threads that have the scheduling policy SCHED_FIFO or SCHED_RR, Pthreads defines three scheduling classes for mutexes. The classes are

- *PTHREAD_PRIO_NONE.* Thread priorities are ignored if a mutex is created using this scheduling class.
- *PTHREAD_PRIO_INHERIT.* This is an implementation of priority inheritance in which the priority of the thread holding the mutex (mutex owner) is changed to the priority of the highest-priority thread waiting for the mutex. The boost in priority is temporary and is reversed after priority inversion is corrected.
- *PTHREAD_PRIO_PROTECT.* In this class the mutex is assigned a fixed priority. If a thread that acquires the mutex has a priority lower than the mutex priority, then the thread temporarily receives the priority of the mutex. In the case of multiple mutexes with different priority values, the thread will get the maximum priority value assigned to the mutex in the list. Refer to the functions pthread_mutexattr_setprotocol and pthread_mutexattr_getprotocol for more information.

5.2.7 Yielding the scheduler

```
void sched_yield (void)
```

The function *sched_yield* can be used by the calling thread to yield its processor. It allows the scheduler to determine if another thread can be run instead of the calling thread. If no suitable thread exists, then the calling thread continues to run. The function *pthread_yield* was dropped in the final Pthreads standard, and applications should use the function sched_yield instead.

> Applications that are currently using the earlier versions should make the API changes when moving to systems implementing draft 10.

5.3 DCE Threads

As part of DCE a thread package is provided, and it currently supports *draft 4* of Pthreads. It is expected that future versions of DCE will comply with the adopted Pthreads standard. The current provider of DCE threads is Digital Equipment Corporation, and it is based on Digital's proprietary Concert Multithread Architecture (CMA) interface. The DCE threads interface has several extensions to the draft 4 version of Pthreads; these extensions are considered nonportable and end with an *_np* suffix (e.g., pthread_delay_np). One should be careful while using these nonportable extensions because they might *not* be supported on many systems.

One major difference between DCE threads and the standard POSIX.1c threads is in the area of exception management. DCE threads support exception management, which aids in the development of more robust applications. I feel that POSIX should have addressed the issue of exception management, but I am not surprised to see it excluded (just like I am not surprised by some of its complexity).

DCE threads do not rely on the native threads of an operating system. On systems that support native threads, DCE threads are mapped to the native threads. On operating systems that do not implement kernel threads, DCE threads are implemented as *coroutines,* and they run in the address space of the process. Programmers using DCE threads are not aware of the fact that the underlying operating systems supports native threads. By providing a coroutine-based implementation, the support for Pthreads is available on many nonthreaded operating systems.

Ideally, a programmer should not be concerned if the Pthreads library is a coroutine-based implementation. In reality, it *does* matter, because applications do *not* behave the same way when they are developed using coroutine-based thread packages. Timing bugs are hard to detect in such implementations, and debugging the application is much more challenging. Even though the APIs are the same, there are other implications of using threads on a nonthreaded operating system. The support for reentrant library functions and the semantics of blocking system calls are some of the main problem areas. As part of DCE threads, jacket routines are provided to address both these issues.

5.3.1 DCE jacket routines

Multithreading is gaining popularity in the POSIX world, but today the number of nonthreaded operating systems far outweighs the true multithreaded kernels. Many system calls are non-thread-safe, and to avoid reentrancy problems, DCE provides jacket routines that act as wrappers for regular system calls.

The header file <cma_ux.h> *redefines* the list of functions for which a jacket routine exists. It seems that the jacket routines were provided mainly to help in the development of multithreaded DCE RPC servers. The programmer does not have to call these jacket routines directly; instead, the header file cma_ux.h redefines lots of these system calls.

Jacket routines primarily address the issue of reentrant libraries and blocking system calls. The jacket routine internally calls a function, which locks a global mutex before calling the system service. This ensures that even when non-thread-safe functions are called by multiple threads, they are single-threaded and effectively serialized by the use of global lock. Even though the routines are single-threaded, jacket routines have helped in the acceptance of threads in the UNIX world. They made it possible to introduce Pthreads even on single-threaded operating systems.

Jacket routines ensure that if one thread blocks on a system call, then only the calling thread and not the entire process is suspended. For example, if one thread is blocked on a read from a slow device, the wrapper for the read system call ensures that only the calling thread is suspended, thus allowing other threads in the process to execute.

Does this mean that jacket routines are provided for all system calls and library functions? The answer is *no,* and do not be surprised to find out that your DCE vendor only provides nonblocking calls for a subset of these functions. On most DCE systems on which I have worked, I have found that the SYSV IPC routines do not have jacket routines. This means that if one thread blocks on the system call *msgrcv,* then no other thread will get a chance to run until the thread returns from the call to *msgrcv.* On some systems, the jacket routines for certain systems calls (e.g., semop) *can* be grossly inefficient. With coroutine-based implementations, one should be careful while calling blocking system calls.

5.3.1.1 How to stop using jacket routines. If the application does not want to use these jacket routines, then one can add the following line before including the header file <pthread.h>:

```
#define _CMA_NOWRAPPERS
#include <pthread.h>
```

The definition of _CMA_NOWRAPPERS prevents the jacket version of the routine from being included in the application code. Another method is to #undef the routine name you do not want to be substituted after including the header file <pthread.h>. For example, if you do not want to use the jacket version of the routine *read,* then you should add these lines to your code.

```
#include <pthread.h>
#undef read
```

5.3.2 Differences between DCE threads and draft 10 of Pthreads

As discussed earlier, DCE threads are based on draft 4 of Pthreads. There are many differences between the draft 4 version of Pthreads and the approved standard. This section will highlight the major differences and can be used by application developers who migrate their applications using DCE threads or draft 4 of Pthreads to the approved Pthreads standard. This can be helpful if you are migrating your application to the newer version and also can be used to develop threaded DCE applications keeping draft 10 portability in mind.

There are many issues to consider when porting an application from draft 4 to draft 10 of Pthreads. These issues generally involve such things as

- Data types (mainly DCE threads)
- Error handling
- Pthreads APIs (added/modified/deleted)
- Exception handling
- Nonportable code using DCE extensions

5.3.2.1 Data types. DCE threads define data types that are not part of the POSIX.1c standard. The following table shows a mapping of DCE and POSIX.1c data types:

DCE data types	POSIX.1c data types
pthread_addr_t	void *
pthread_start_routine	void * (*) (void *arg)
pthread_cleanup_t	void * (*) (void *arg)
pthread_destructor_t	void * (*) (void *arg)

Personally, I never used the DCE data types because applications that were developed using draft 4 of Pthreads compiled cleanly on systems supporting DCE threads. Substituting these data types is a fairly simple exercise, and you can even typedefs the DCE data types to the POSIX.1c equivalent in some application header files.

5.3.2.2 Error handling. Error handling has changed in draft 7 of Pthreads. In draft 4 of Pthreads, most functions returned 0 on success and −1 on failure. On failure, these functions would additionally set the per-thread errno variable. Beginning with draft 7, all Pthreads functions return the error condition on failure and 0 on success. The variable errno is *not* set on error conditions.

5.3.2.3 Exception handling. Exception management in DCE threads is supported as an extension to the Pthreads. DCE threads support exception management and handling on a per-thread basis using the TRY/CATCH/FINALLY clause. Since exception management is not part of the official POSIX.1c standard, the exercise of porting exception management code might not be that easy. All exception management features of DCE have to be removed when moving to POSIX.1c.

5.3.2.4 Thread APIs. Many new functions have been added to Pthreads since the early draft 4 version. Many draft 4 Pthreads functions were either modified or deleted from the draft 10 Pthreads interface. The modifications were in terms of syntax, return values, and arguments. Some of the more obvious changes made since draft 4 will be covered here, even though they may have been covered in earlier chapters. The reader is advised to consult the vendor's manual for a complete description of these changes.

5.3.2.5 Changes in thread default attributes. When an application calls the function pthread_create, the default thread attributes are no longer specified by pthread_attr_default. Now the applications must either initialize a thread attributes object and pass the thread attributes object to pthread_create or a NULL value can be passed for the thread attributes structure while calling pthread_create.

The following example illustrates such a change in the code.

Pre-draft 7 and DCE 1.1

```
int         ret;
pthread_t   threadId;
void        *ThreadRoutine (void *);

ret = pthread_create (&threadId, pthread_attr_default, ThreadRoutine, NULL);
```

Draft 7 or higher

```
int ret;
pthread_t        threadId;
pthread_attr_t   threadAttr;
void             *ThreadRoutine (void *);

pthread_attr_init (&threadAttr);

/* for default attributes one can pass NULL instead of ThreadAttr */
ret = pthread_create (&threadId, &threadAttr, ThreadRoutine, NULL);
```

5.3.2.6 Changes in thread detach state. Many DCE thread implementations create undetached threads and therefore can be joined by some other thread in the process. On some systems this has been changed, and now the default behavior is to create detached threads (e.g., AIX 4.1). This means that if a thread has to be joined, then the detach state attribute of a thread must be set to PTHREAD_CREATE_JOINABLE when the thread is created. This change has an impact on applications that call pthread_join; these applications *might* fail when pthread_join is called because detached threads cannot be joined.

5.3.2.7 Nonportable DCE functions. In DCE thread implementation there are many extensions to the draft 4 version of Pthreads. Since these functions are nonportable, all functions that are nonportable end with an *_np* suffix. The following are some of the nonportable DCE functions.

```
pthread_global_lock_np pthread_global_unlock_np   pthread_signal_to_cancel_np
pthread_delay_np       pthread_cond_signal_int_np pthread_get_unique_np
```

5.3.2.8 Other changes

- The one-time initialization macro has changed from pthread_once_init to PTHREAD_ONCE_INIT.
- The function pthread_join has changed.
- The default attribute specification for mutex creation has changed.
- The POSIX.1c standard only implements nonrecursive mutexes, while DCE threads support fast, nonrecursive, and recursive mutexes.
- Mutex attribute functions have changed.
- The default attribute specification for condition variable has changed.
- Condition variable attribute functions have changed.
- The return value for pthread_cond_timedwait has changed.
- The function pthread_getspecific has changed.
- Thread cancellation APIs are different.
- The signal-handling API has changed.
- The pthread_atfork function has changed.
- Thread attribute (creation/destroy) functions have changed.
- The scheduling and priority functions have changed.
- The function pthread_yield is superseded by sched_yield.
- All nonportable DCE extensions are not part of the POSIX.1c standard.

5.3.3 DCE RPC and threads

Threads are becoming popular in remote procedure call (RPC) applications. Threads are used by both the client and server components of an RPC application. RPC is synchronous by nature, which means that when a process initiates an RPC request, control is not returned to the caller until the request completes. On the client side, threads can be used to provide support for asynchronous RPC. The client thread that initiates the RPC request can block while other threads in the process can continue to run, thus increasing responsiveness of the clients. On the server side, RPC stub routines use threads to concurrently service multiple client requests.

In a DCE RPC environment, the maximum number of worker threads on the server side can be specified in the function *rpc-server-listen*. Whenever a client makes an RPC call to the server, then the request is passed on to a thread when the number of threads is less than what was configured; otherwise, the request is placed on a queue that is picked up later by one of the worker threads. It is inefficient to create too many unnecessary worker threads. Threads are automatically created and managed by DCE, but the programmer is still responsible for most of the data synchronization and interthread communication.

5.3.4 Pitfalls of DCE threads

There are certain limitations of DCE threads on *coroutine-based* implementations. All POSIX I/O functions have a nonblocking call interface, but there are many other functions that block the entire process (e.g., msgrcv). On systems that do not implement native threads, the use of DCE threads should be limited to applications that are not time *critical*. When DCE threads are used heavily on nonthreaded systems, there can be a *performance bottleneck*. Application developers should understand that *coroutine-based* DCE threads cannot exploit the power of multiple CPUs. Know the limitations in terms of jacket routines, blocking calls, etc., when designing applications using DCE threads. Keep in mind that applications *might* even run slower.

5.3.5 Threads and exception handling

When the functions in DCE threads fail, then they can either return an error value or raise an exception. Exceptions are events that you do not expect to happen in your application. For example, when a thread does a divide by zero, an exception can be raised; the thread can handle the exception and continue processing.

The exception returning interface of Pthreads functions is not automatically invoked; rather, the application *must* include the header file <pthread_exc.h> instead of the file <pthread.h>. When the application includes this header file, all exception returning interfaces of Pthreads functions are invoked. All exceptions are handled in the file <exc_handling.h>. Exception handling defines macros such as TRY, CATCH, FINALLY, and RERAISE. Since exception handling is not part of the official POSIX.1c standards, I am not going to discuss it further. Refer to the DCE threads documentation for more information.

5.4 Threads, POSIX.1, and C-Library Functions

The name of the threads standard was changed from POSIX.4 (previous name) to POSIX.1c, and this shows how closely the threads standard is integrated with the base POSIX standard. The intention of POSIX is to ensure that all POSIX.1 functions work identically for single-threaded and multithreaded applications. Many POSIX.1 functions and the C-library functions were developed at a time when nobody really cared for supporting multiple threads and hence cannot be used safely in a threaded environment.

Most vendors offer a thread-safe version of these functions, and in some cases, only the internal implementation of these functions differs. A reentrant version is provided for functions that *cannot* be made reentrant without changing the existing functional interface. These functions have the same name as the nonreentrant version, except the reentrant version of these functions ends with an *_r* suffix. Most of the functions that offer a reentrant interface use static data internally, thus making their use unsafe in a multithreaded application. If two threads call such a function at the same time, then the results of the invocations cannot be predicted. To solve this problem, these functions additionally take extra arguments instead of using the static storage.

Consider the POSIX.1 function ctime; the nonreentrant version of the function takes one argument that is the time in seconds. The function returns a pointer to a static storage. The reentrant version of the code takes an extra argument, and the function returns the time string in this buffer.

```
char *ctime (const time_t *clock); /* nonreentrant version */
char *ctime_r (const time_t *clock, char *buf); /* reentrant version */
```

Multithreaded applications should always use the reentrant version of the POSIX.1 and C-library functions. On some systems the reentrant functions are defined in the library libc_r.a and should be used with applications that use Pthreads. Note that the compiler *cannot* detect if an application uses the nonreentrant version of these functions. It is the programmer's responsibility to use the right interface in the application.

Most blocking POSIX.1 functions are considered cancellation points. In reality, any POSIX.1 function that returns EINTR on error potentially can be a thread cancellation point. I would recommend that you consult your vendor's documentation to find out the list of POSIX.1 functions that *can* be canceled safely. Note that most of these functions are non-async-cancel safe.

5.4.1 List of functions with a reentrant version

Many functions on systems supporting the POSIX threads environment support reentrant versions. For example, the functions ctime_r, getlogin_r, rand_r, and readdir_r provide a new interface and are reentrant. For a complete listing of all reentrant functions supported by your vendor, please check your vendor's manual (e.g., ls -R *_r.* in the man3 directory will list all functions that have a reentrant interface).

5.4.2 Fork in a multithreaded environment

In a traditional POSIX.1 environment, fork is called to

- Create a new thread of control
- Create a new thread of control to run a different program

Multithreaded applications should *not* call *fork* system call to create a new thread of control. In a POSIX.1 environment, *fork* copies the entire address space from the parent to the child process, and this can be inefficient if child processes are created frequently. In a multithreaded process, threads can be used to create a new thread of control. Programs can continue to call *fork* if is followed by an *exec*. *Avoid* calling fork in a multithreaded process unless it is going to be followed by an exec.

The developers of Pthreads felt that there was no need to copy all the threads of the calling process in the newly created process when *fork* is called. The fork system call *only* copies the calling thread's state, and this includes all data and mutex states. If your application needs to copy *all* threads, then it should call the function *forkall*. Unixware and Solaris implement *forkl,* which is identical to the *forkall* of POSIX in a multithreaded application.

Deadlock can happen if fork is used in a multithreaded application. For example, consider two threads T1 and T2 sharing a mutex M. Let us assume that before the thread T2 calls fork it acquires the mutex lock for the mutex M. After the fork, the child process *will* deadlock when it tries to acquire the mutex M because the state of the mutex was copied from the thread that created it. To avoid such recursive deadlocks, POSIX.1c defines a function pthread_atfork that *should* be used in conjunction with fork. The function pthread_atfork protects many states, including the state of the mutex.

```
int pthread_atfork(void (*prepare)(void), void (*parent)(void), void *(child)
(void))
```

The function pthread_atfork takes pointers to three functions. The function pointed to by *prepare* is called in the context of the parent process before fork is called, the function *parent* is called in the parent after returning from fork, and the function *child* is called in the child after returning from fork.

The following code segment illustrates the use of fork in a multithreaded process. Let us assume that the parent process wants to lock a mutex M and then wants to create a child process by calling the routine fork.

```
void prepare_routine()
{
   pthread_mutex_lock(&M);
}

void parent_routine()
{
   pthread_mutex_unlock(&M);
}
```

```
void child_routine()
{
   pthread_mutex_unlock(&M);
}

main()
{
   /* assume that mutex is locked before fork is called */

   pthread_atfork(prepare_routine, parent_routine, child_routine);

   switch fork())
        {
   case 0: /* child process */
           do_child();
           exit(0);
      default: /* parent process */
           do_parent(); /*mutex can be locked within */
   }
```

5.4.3 Threads and file I/O

Open file descriptors are shared resources of a process. In a multithreaded application when multiple threads share an open file descriptor (e.g., file, socket, etc.), then the issue of concurrent access to these file descriptors *must* be addressed. Consider two threads T1 and T2 that share an open file descriptor, and both threads attempt to write to the end of the file at the same time by calling the function AppendToFile.

```
AppendToFile (int fd, char *buf, int bufLen)
{
   lseek (fd, 0, 0); /* seek to the end of file */
   write (fd, buf, bufLen);
}
```

Now, consider the following sequence of events:

- T1 seeks to the end of the file (executes call to lseek).
- T1 is preempted by thread T2.
- T2 seeks to the end of the file (executes call to lseek) and writes to the file.
- T1 resumes execution, and now it writes to the file.

Under the scenario described above, the *write* of thread T1 will *not* be at the location as a result of the original *lseek*. The file pointer offset is changed by the *write* of thread T2. Open file descriptors are shared resources, and they should be protected by mutual exclusion locks. Things could have been much worse if the threads were doing a read as in the following example.

The function FindRecord returns the starting offset of a record based on some key value passed to it. Let us assume that threads T1 and T2 call the routine ReadRecord with different key values and that all records are fixed-size records.

```
ReadRecord (int fd, char *key, char *precBuf, int recBufSize)
{
   int recOffset;
   recOffset = FindRecord (fd, key);
   lseek (fd, recOffset, 0); /* seek to recOffset bytes from the beginning */
   read (fd, precBuf, recBufSize);
}
```

In the preceding code segment if T1 is preempted after the call to lseek and T2 runs to completion, then thread T1 will read the wrong record. This *can* be avoided easily by using some mutual exclusion lock to guard the lseek/read combination. Some UNIX vendors provide the functions *pread* and *pwrite* that combine the lseek/read or lseek/write as one *atomic* operation. Rather than depending on some system-dependent function, you can easily write your own thread-safe implementation of the function ReadRecord. Note that a *more efficient* implementation of the function ReadRecord is shown later in this chapter using POSIX.1b asynchronous I/O.

```
ReadRecord (int fd, char *key, char *precBuf, int recBufSize)
{
   int recOffset;

   recOffset = FindRecord (fd, key);
   pthread_mutex_lock(....);
   lseek (fd, recOffset, 0); /* seek to recOffset bytes from the beginning */
   read (fd, precBuf, recBufSize);

   pthread_mutex_unlock(....);
}
```

5.4.4 Threads and asynchronous I/O (POSIX.1b option)

The POSIX.1 I/O model is *synchronous* in nature. When a process initiates an I/O operation, the entire process is suspended until the I/O completes. For example, when a process calls the *read* system call, the process blocks until the data are read into the user buffer. Similarly, when the process calls the *write* system call, the process waits until the operating system saves the data in the buffer cache. The saved buffer cache is later flushed to the disk.

Over the years, processors have become very fast, but I/O has *not* been able to keep up with the performance of these processors. Most applications are limited by an I/O bottleneck, and one should *not* expect threads alone to improve an application's responsiveness. The use of threads helps alleviate some of the problems of synchronous I/O, since only the calling thread blocks on the I/O operation while allowing others threads in the process to continue.

Even though asynchronous I/O is a part of POSIX.1b and not part of POSIX.1c, it is worth mentioning because asynchronous I/O and threads *can* be a very powerful combination for developing scalable and efficient multithreaded applications. Applications that have high I/O requirements are generally written with the asynchronous I/O model. This allows the application to perform other tasks while the I/O happens asynchronously in parallel. Asynchronous I/O allows processing and I/O to be overlapped and in many cases *can* be considered to be an alternative to threads. On threaded kernels, asynchronous I/O can execute in parallel on a separate processor while the thread/process that initiated the I/O can run on a different processor. If you are developing the worker thread model for an I/O-intensive application, then asynchronous I/O is a big win. High-performance applications on other operating systems such as VMS and Windows NT use asynchronous I/O heavily.

5.4.4.1 POSIX.1b asynchronous I/O. If the macro _POSIX_ASYNCHRONOUS_IO is defined, then POSIX.1b asynchronous I/O is supported on your POSIX operating system. Asynchronous I/O is different from synchronous I/O in the sense that when you call the read or write system call, the operating system simply queues the request and returns to the caller. The application is free to do any other thing while the I/O request is handled. The application can check the completion of I/O in one of the following ways:

- Poll for I/O completion by calling the function *aio_error*.
- Wait synchronously for I/O completion by calling the function *aio_suspend*.
- Be notified asynchronously by a signal.

Polling for completion of I/O can be a waste of CPU cycles, and the use of signals in a multithreaded application can be difficult to manage. In a threaded environment, the best way to wait for I/O completion is to call aio_suspend. Additionally, the thread that initiated the I/O can synchronously wait for notification via a signal using *sigwait,* but there is not much of an advantage. It might not be possible to use signals for notification when multiple threads initiate asynchronous I/O simultaneously.

5.4.4.2 AIO control block. All asynchronous functions use a structure called an *asynchronous control block* (ACB); the ACB structure *aiocb* is defined in the header file *<aio.h>*. Note that the definition of the structure aiocb on your system *can* be different, and it depends on the version of POSIX.1b supported. The definition of the structure aiocb is as follows (on a Digital UNIX 3.X system).

```
struct aiocb
{
   int              aio_fildes; /* file descriptor used for I/O */
   offset_t         aio_offset; /* offset where I/O should happen */
   void             *aio_buf; /* buffer to read to or write from */
   size_t           aio_nbytes; /* number of bytes of I/O operation */
   struct sigevent  aio_sigevent; /* signal delivery operation */
   int              aio_lio_opccde; /* opcode - list of async i/o to be
                    performed */
   int              aio_reqprio; /* AIO priority */
};
```

5.4.4.3 AIO functions. It is beyond the scope of this book to cover the asynchronous I/O functions in detail. The APIs will be explained briefly in the examples in this chapter. The following is a list of AIO functions as defined in POSIX.1b.

```
int  aio_read (struct aiocb *acb);
int  aio_write (struct aiocb *acb);
int  lio_listaio (int waittype, struct aiocb *lacb[], int num_acb,
     structsigevent*notification);
int  aio_cancel (int fd, struct aiocb *acb);
int  aio_suspend (struct aiocb *lacb[], int num_acb, struct timespec
     *timeout);
int  aio_fsync (int type, struct aiocb *acb);
int  aio_return (struct aiocb *acb);
int  aio_error (struct aiocb *acb);
```

5.4.4.4 AIO in a threaded process. The following example shows the use of AIO functions in a threaded process. In the example, the thread initiates an I/O and then does other things before checking the completion of the I/O request.

```
ReadRecord (int fd, char *key, char *precBuf, int recBufSize)
{
   int          recOffset;
   struct aiocb aioCb;
   struct aiocb *pAiocb[1];

   recOffset = FindRecord (key);

   /* fill up the AIO structure */
   aioCb.aio_fildes = fd;
   aioCb.aio_offset = recOffset;
   aioCb.aio_buf = precBuf;
   aioCb.aio_nbytes = recBufSize;
   aioCb.aio_reqprio = 0;
   aioCb.aio_sigevent.sigev_signo = 0; /* no signal needed when I/O
   completes */

   /* fire the asynchronous I/O */
   aio_read (&aioCb);

   /* do some other stuff while I/O is in progress */
   DoStuff ();

   /* check I/O completion synchronously */
   pAioCb[1] = &aioCb;
   aio_suspend (pAioCb, 1, NULL); /* wait for I/O to complete */
}
```

In the preceding example, the thread fills up the AIO block and then initiates an asynchronous I/O. Generally, applications do some other processing while the I/O operation is in progress before they check for I/O completion. It does *not* make sense to check the completion of I/O right away, since in that case it becomes more of a synchronous I/O (so why use async I/O!). Finally, the thread waits for the completion of the I/O by calling the function aio_suspend.

Readers should note that in the version of ReadRecord using AIO, mutex locks were *not* used. When an application uses AIO functions, they do *not* have the concurrency problems we discussed in Sec. 5.5.3. The *aio_offset* element in the structure aiocb is used by the API to do an lseek each time a read/write is performed. This alone can be a compelling reason to use the AIO routines for FILE I/O rather than using locking with the POSIX.1 read or write interfaces. In fact, the UNIX functions *pread* and *pwrites* can be implemented easily using the POSIX.1b aio routines.

5.4.5 Performing multiple I/O requests

Multiple I/O requests (combination of read and write) can be performed in one system call. The functions *lio_listaio* can be very useful when multiple I/O requests have to be performed on a file. The function WriteBuffersToFile writes several buffers at once to the file. For the sake of simplicity, it has been assumed that all buffers are of fixed length and that the buffers are to be written from the beginning of the file.

```
WriteBuffersToFile (int fd, int numBuffers, char **ppbuffers, int bufLen)
{
   struct aiocb *aioCbList[AIO_LISTAIO_MAX];
   int  aioIndex;
   int  aioOffset;
   int  aioCompleted;

   aioOffset = 0; /* start from beginning of file */
   /* set up multiple AIO blocks , assume NumBuffers is <= AIO_LISTAIO_MAX */
   for (aioIndex = 0; aioIndex < numBuffers; ++aioIndex)
   {
        aioCbList[aioIndex].aio_fildes = fd;
        aioCbList[aioIndex].aio_offset = aioOffset;
        aioCbList[aioIndex].aio_buf = ppbuffers[aioIndex];
        aioCbList[aioIndex].aio_nbytes = bufLen;
        aioCbList[aioIndex].aio_reqprio = 0;
        aioCbList[aioIndex].aio_sigevent.sigev_signo = 0; /* do not deliver
        signal */
      aioCbList[aioIndex].aio_lio_opcode = LIO_WRITE; /* perform a
      synchronous write */
      aioOffset += bufLen; /* increment offset by size of each buffer */
   }

   /* Fire off multiple asynchronous I/O */
   lio_listio (LIO_NOWAIT, acbList, numBuffers, NULL);

   /* do some other stuff while I/O is in progress */
   DoStuff ();

   /* check I/O completion synchronously */
   for (aioCompleted = 0; aioCompleted < numBuffers; ++ aioCompleted)
   {
      aio_suspend (aioCbList, numBuffers, NULL); /* wait for ever */
     /* call aio_error and aio_return on each acb */
   {
}
```

The function aio_suspend returns 0 when *any* one of the asynchronous operations completes. It is your responsibility to find out which I/O operation has completed by calling the function aio_error and aio_return on *each* of the ACBs.

5.4.5.1 Which I/O to use: synchronous or asynchronous I/O? In the UNIX world, the functions *select* and *poll* can be used (on some devices) for non-blocking read and write system calls. The functions select and poll simply tell you that there are data to read or room to write. These functions are helpful in avoiding a long delay on a read/write call, but the process probably will have to block for the read or write function to complete even after the select/poll notification. Additionally, these functions are inefficient when the list is big, and they involve a context-switching overhead.

Most applications would never need to use asynchronous I/O, but if your application has high-performance I/O requirements, then async I/O is the better way. The performance gains on an SMP machine can be multifold, since it is possible that multiple asynchronous I/Os can happen in parallel. When you are developing a multithreaded server to service a large number of clients, then every bit of performance gain counts, and it can be helpful to combine I/O and computation.

Let us consider the design of a tcp/ip server servicing a large number of clients. One can create a separate thread for each client that connects to the server, but studies show that this can be inefficient for a large number of clients. The other approach could be to create fewer worker threads to service all clients. Each of the worker threads could either do a *select* to read new requests or it could use asynchronous I/O for the read operations. With asynchronous I/O one can avoid the overhead of the *select* system call. The POSIX.1b functions *would* have been more powerful if some function notified which pending I/O operation completed. The reader is advised to read the samples on the disk that use asynchronous I/O.

5.4.6 Listing of POSIX.1c functions

5.4.6.1 Thread attributes functions. (TAO stands for thread attributes object.)

`pthread_attr_destroy`	Deletes a TAO.
`pthread_attr_getdetachstate`	Gets detachstate attribute value of a TAO.
`pthread_attr_getinheritsched`	Gets inheritsched attribute value of a TAO.
`pthread_attr_getschedparam`	Gets schedparam attribute value of a TAO.
`pthread_attr_getschedpolicy`	Gets schedpolicy attribute of a TAO.
`pthread_attr_getscope`	Gets contention-scope attribute value of a TAO.
`pthread_attr_getstackaddr`	Gets stackaddr attribute value of a TAO.
`pthread_attr_getstacksize`	Gets stacksize attribute value of a TAO.
`pthread_attr_init`	Creates and initializes a TAO with default values.
`pthread_attr_setdetachstate`	Sets detachstate attribute value of a TAO.
`pthread_attr_setinheritsched`	Sets inheritsched attribute value of a TAO.
`pthread_attr_setschedparam`	Sets schedparam attribute value of a TAO.
`pthread_attr_setschedpolicy`	Sets schedpolicy attribute of a TAO.
`pthread_attr_setscope`	Sets contention-scope attribute value of a TAO.
`pthread_attr_setstackaddr`	Sets stackaddr attribute value of a TAO.
`pthread_attr_setstacksize`	Sets stacksize attribute value of a TAO.

5.4.6.2 Thread management functions

`pthread_create`	Creates a new thread of control.
`pthread_equal`	Compares two thread IDs.

`pthread_exit`	Terminates the calling thread.
`pthread_getschedparam`	Gets SchedPolicy and SchedParam attribute of a thread.
`pthread_join`	Waits for a thread to terminate.
`pthread_kill`	Sends a signal to the specified thread.
`pthread_once`	Executes a routine exactly once in a process.
`PTHREAD_ONCE_INIT`	Initializes a once synchronization control structure.
`pthread_self`	Returns the calling thread's ID.
`pthread_setschedparam`	Sets the schedpolicy and schedparam attributes.
`pthread_yield`	Yields the CPU voluntarily.

5.4.6.3 Thread mutex functions. (MAO stands for mutex attributes object.)

`pthread_mutex_destroy`	Deletes a mutex.
`pthread_mutex_getprioceiling`	Gets value of the prioceiling attribute of a mutex.
`pthread_mutex_init`	Initializes a mutex and sets its attributes.
`PTHREAD_MUTEX_INITIALIZER`	Initializes a static mutex with default attributes.
`pthread_mutex_lock`	Locks a mutex (wait).
`pthread_mutex_setprioceiling`	Sets value of the prioceiling attribute of a mutex.
`pthread_mutex_trylock`	Locks a mutex (nowait).
`pthread_mutex_unlock`	Unlocks a mutex.
`pthread_mutexattr_destroy`	Deletes a MAO.
`pthread_mutexattr_getprioceiling`	Gets prioceiling attribute value of MAO.
`pthread_mutexattr_getprotocol`	Gets value of the protocol attribute of a MAO.
`pthread_mutexattr_getpshared`	Gets value of the process-shared attribute of a MAO.
`pthread_mutexattr_init`	Creates MAO and initializes it with default attributes.
`pthread_mutexattr_setprioceiling`	Sets the value of the prioceiling attribute of a MAO.
`pthread_mutexattr_setprotocol`	Sets the value of the protocol attribute of a MAO.
`pthread_mutexattr_setpshared`	Sets the value of the process-shared attribute of a MAO.

5.4.6.4 Condition variables. (CAO stands for condition attributes object.)

`pthread_cond_broadcast`	Broadcasts condition to multiple waiting threads.
`pthread_cond_destroy`	Deletes a condition variable.
`pthread_cond_init`	Initializes a condition variable with default attributes.
`pthread_cond_signal`	Signals a condition to a waiting thread.
`pthread_cond_timedwait`	Waits for a condition variable with time-out.
`pthread_cond_wait`	Waits for a condition indefinitely.
`pthread_condattr_destroy`	Deletes a CAO.
`pthread_condattr_getpshared`	Gets pshared attribute of a CAO.
`pthread_condattr_init`	Creates and initializes a CAO.
`pthread_condattr_setpshared`	Sets pshared attribute of a CAO.
`pthread_cond_initializer`	Initializes a static condition variable with default values.

5.4.6.5 Thread-specific data. (TSD stands for thread-specific data.)

`pthread_getspecific`	Gets TSD associated with a key.
`pthread_key_create`	Creates a TSD key.
`pthread_key_delete`	Deletes a TSD key.
`pthread_setspecific`	Sets TSD associated with a key.

5.4.6.6 Thread cancellation and cleanup

pthread_cancel	Cancels a thread.
pthread_cleanup_pop	Pops cleanup handlers in LIFO order.
pthread_cleanup_push	Pushes cleanup handlers.
pthread_getcancelstate	Gets the calling thread's cancelability state.
pthread_getcanceltype	Gets the calling thread's cancelability type.
pthread_setcancelstate	Sets the calling thread's cancelability state.
pthread_setcanceltype	Sets the calling thread's cancelability type.
pthread_testcancel	Creates a cancellation point in the calling thread.

5.4.6.7 Miscellaneous functions

pthread_sigmask	Sets thread signal mask
pthread_atfork	Registers atfork handlers

5.4.6.8 List of POSIX.1c data types

pthread_t	Thread data type
pthread_attr_t	Thread attributes data type
pthread_cond_t	Condition variable data type
pthread_condattr_t	Condition variable attributes data type
pthread_key_t	Thread-specific key data type
pthread_mutex_t	Mutex data type
pthread_mutexattr_t	Mutex attributes data type
pthread_once_t	One-time initialization data type

Chapter

6

POSIX Programming Examples

6.1 Compiling and Linking Programs

Every program that uses the threads library should include the header file *pthread.h*. The compiler and linker options depend upon the operating system. The compiler and linker options for some of the platforms are listed below.

Solaris 2.5

```
cc -D_POSIX_C_SOURCE-199506L foc.c -o foo -lpthread
```

AIX 4.1

Depending on the compiler, the programs can be compiled and linked using:

```
cc_r foo.c -o foo (draft 7 threads)
xlc_r foo.c -o foo (draft 7 threads)
```

For draft 4 compatibility you should use:

```
cc_r4 foo.c -o foo
xlc_r4 foo.c -o foo
```

Digital Unix 3.X

```
cc foo.c -o foo -threads
cc foo.c -o foo -lpthreads -lmach -lc_r
```

Digital Unix 4.0

```
cc foo.c -o foo -lpthread (draft 10 - POSIX)
cc foo.c -o foo -lthread (draft 4 - POSIX)
```

6.2 Queue Implementation

Queues are a simple yet powerful interthread communication paradigm. Queues can be used effectively in applications that use worker threads to service clients. Threads, instead of waiting on semaphores or condition variables, can wait on queues for work items to be added. It should be noted that threads that use queues for servicing requests are much easier to program and test. POSIX.1c does not provide a standard queue mechanism, but it can be easily implemented using condition variables and mutexes. Queues can also be implemented by using the POSIX.1b semaphores and mutexes. The reader is advised to see Section 16.2 for a queue implementation using POSIX.1b counting semaphores.

```
#include <pthread.h>
#include <stdio.h>

typedef struct _qmsg QMSG;
struct _qmsg
{
   void  *msg;
   int   msgLen;
   QMSG  *next;
};

typedef struct _queue
{
   int       qMsgs;   /* current number of msgs on queue */
   int       qMax;    /* max depth of queue */
   pthread_mutex_t   qMutex; /* mutex guarding the queue */
   pthread_cond_t    qEmptyEvent; /* queue empty event */
   pthread_cond_t    qFullEvent; /* queue full event */
   QMSG              *qHeadMsg; /* pointer to first msg */
   QMSG              *qTailMsg; /* pointer to last msg */
} QUEUE;

QUEUE gQueue; /* global queue shared by all threads */

main(int argc, char **argv)
{
   int              numThr;
   pthread_t        threadId[NUMTHREADS];
   pthread_attr_t   threadAttr;
   void             *Readers();
   void             *Writers();
   int              i;
   int              *status;

   numThr = NUM_WRITERS + NUM_READERS;

   if (numThr > NUMTHREADS)
        exit(0);

   QueCreate(&qQueue, 10);

   pthread_attr_init(&threadAttr);
   pthread_attr_setdetachstate(&threadAttr, PTHREAD_CREATE_JOINABLE);

   for (i = 0; i < NUM_WRITERS; ++i)
       pthread_create(&threadId[i], &threadAttr, Writers, NULL);

   for (i = NUM_WRITERS ; i < numThr; ++i)
       pthread_create(&threadId[i], &threadAttr, Readers, NULL);
```

```
    for (i = 0; i < numThr; ++i)
        pthread_join(threadId[i],(void**) &status);

    exit(0);
}

void *
Writers(void *pThrArg)
{
    pthread_t  threadId;
    int        i;
    char       msg[256];

    threadId = pthread_self();

    for (i = 0; i < NUMMSGS; ++i)
    {
        sprintf(msg,"msg %d from thread %d", i, threadId);
        QuePut(msg, sizeof(msg), &qQueue);
    }
    fprintf(stderr,"writer put [%d] msgs\n", i);
    return(NULL);
}

void *
Readers(void *pThrArg)
{
    int        i;
    int        nMsgs;
    int        retCode;
    char       msg[256];
    pthread_t  threadId;

    threadId = pthread_self();

    nMsgs = (NUMMSGS * NUM_WRITERS) / NUM_READERS;

    for (i = 0; i < nMsgs; ++i)
         retCode = QueGet(msg, sizeof(msg), &gQueue);

    fprintf(stderr,"reader got [%d] msgs\n", i);
    return(NULL);
}

int
QueGet(void *pmsg, int msglen, QUEUE *pQueue)
{
        int retCode;

        pthread_mutex_lock(&pQueue->qMutex);

        while (pQueue->qMsgs == 0)
           pthread_cond_wait(&pQueue->qEmptyEvent, &pQueue->qMutex);

        if (pQueue->qMsgs == pQueue->qMax)
           pthread_cond_broadcast(&pQueue->qFullEvent);

        retCode = DeleteQueueMsg(pmsg, msglen, pQueue);
        --pQueue->qMsgs;

        pthread_mutex_unlock(&pQueue->qMutex);
        return(retCode);
}

int
QuePut(void *pmsg, int msglen, QUEUE *pQueue)
{
```

```
    pthread_mutex_lock(&pQueue->qMutex);

    while (pQueue->qMsgs == pQueue->qMax)
       pthread_cond_wait(&pQueue->qFullEvent, &pQueue->qMutex);

    InsertQueueMsg(pmsg, msglen, pQueue);

    ++pQueue->qMsgs;
    pthread_cond_signal(&pQueue->qEmptyEvent);
    pthread_mutex_unlock(&pQueue->qMutex);
}

QueCreate(QUEUE *pQueue, int Maxmsgs)
{
   pthread_mutex_init(&pQueue->qMutex , NULL);
   pthread_cond_init(&pQueue->qFullEvent , NULL);
   pthread_cond_init(&pQueue->qEmptyEvent , NULL);

   pQueue->qMax = Maxmsgs;
   pQueue->qMsgs = 0;
   pQueue->qHeadMsg = NULL;
   pQueue->qTailMsg = NULL;
}

InsertQueueMsg(void *pMsg, int msgLen, QUEUE *pQueue)
{
   QMSG *newMsg;

   newMsg = (QMSG *) calloc(1,sizeof(QMSG));
   newMsg->msgLen = msgLen;
   newMsg->msg = (void *) malloc(msgLen);

   memcpy(newMsg->msg, pMsg, msgLen);

   if (pQueue->qHeadMsg == NULL)
   {
       pQueue->qHeadMsg = newMsg;
       pQueue->qTailMsg = newMsg;
   }
   else
   {
       pQueue->qTailMsg->next = newMsg;
       pQueue->qTailMsg = newMsg;
   }
   return(0);
}

DeleteQueueMsg(void*Msg, int msgLen, QUEUE *pQueue)
{
   QMSG   *currMsg;
   int    len;

   currMsg = pQueue->qHeadMsg;
   len = currMsg->msgLen;

   memcpy(Msg,currMsg->msg, currMsg->msgLen);

   if (pQueue->qHeadMsg == pQueue->qTailMsg)
       pQueue->qTailMsg = NULL;

   pQueue->qHeadMsg = pQueue->qHeadMsg->next;
   free(currMsg->msg);
   free(currMsg);

   return(len); /* length of message */
}
```

6.3 Barrier Synchronization

Barrier is a synchronization point in the program where threads wait to synchronize with each other. It is used to ensure that cooperating threads have reached a point before they can proceed to the next step. All threads wait at a synchronization point until the last thread reaches the point at which all of them can proceed.

```
#include <pthread.h>
#include <stdio.h>

typedef struct _barrier
{
   int               bCount;
   int               bResetCount;
   int               bReset;
   int               bWaiters;
   pthread_mutex_t   bMutex;
   pthread_cond_t    bCond;
} BARRIER;

BARRIER   Tbarrier; /* global barrier variable */

main(int argc, char **argv)
{
   int              numThr;
   int              *pThrArg;
   pthread_t        threadId[NUMTHREADS];
   pthread_attr_t   threadAttr;
   void             *ThrRoutine(void *);
   int              i;
   int              *status;

   numThr = NUMTHREADS;
   pThrArg = &numThr;

   BarrierInit(&TBarrier, NUMTHREADS);

   pthread_attr_init(&threadAttr);
   pthread_attr_setdetachstate(&threadAttr, PTHREAD_CREATE_JOINABLE);

   for (i = 0; i <numThr; ++i)
       pthread_create(&threadId[i], &threadAttr, ThrRoutine, NULL);

   for (i = 0; i <numThr; ++i)
       pthread_join(threadId[i], (void**) &status);

   exit(0);
}

void *
ThrRoutine(void *pThrArg)
{
   int i;

   for (i = 0; i < 5; ++i)
        BarrierSync(&TBarrier); /* all threads call BarrierSync to
        synchronize */
   return(NULL);
}

BarrierInit(BARRIER *pBarrier, int bCount)
{
```

```
    pBarrier->bResetCount = bCount;
    pBarrier->bCount = bCount;
    pBarrier->bReset = TRUE;

    pthread_mutex_init(&pBarrier->bMutex, NULL);
    pthread_cond_init(&pBarrier->bCond, NULL);
}

BarrierSync(BARRIER *pBarrier)
{
    int wakingThread = 0;

    /* this is executed by threads that have finished executing */
    /* BarrierSync, and started executing again before all threads */
    /* have exited the routine BarrierSync - referred to as fast threads */

    while (pBarrier->bReset == FALSE && !pBarrier->bCount)
        sched_yield(); /* fast threads yield processor */

    pthread_mutex_lock(&pBarrier->bMutex);

    --pBarrier->bCount;

    if (!pBarrier->bCount) /* last thread entering the barrier */
    {
        wakingThread = 1;
        pBarrier->bReset = FALSE;
    }

    while (pBarrier->bCount != 0) /* all, but the last thread */
    {
        ++pBarrier->bWaiters;
        fprintf(stderr,"thread [%d] waiting\n", pthread_self());
        pthread_cond_wait(&pBarrier->bCond, &pBarrier->bMutex);
        --pBarrier->bWaiters;
    }

    if (wakingThread) /* wake up all waiters */
    {
        pBarrier->bCount = 0;
        fprintf(stderr,"thread [%d] waking ......\n\n\n", pthread_self());
        pthread_cond_broadcast(&pBarrier->bCond);
        pthread_mutex_unlock(&pBarrier->bMutex);
        return (0);
    }

    if (!pBarrier->bWaiters) /* last waiter leaving the routine BarrierSync */
    {
        fprintf(stderr,"barrier [%d] reset ......\n\n\n", pthread_self());
        pBarrier->bCount = pBarrier->bResetCount; /* reset barrier count */
        pBarrier->bReset = TRUE;
    }

    pthread_mutex_unlock(&pBarrier->bMutex);

    return(0);
}
```

6.4 Semaphore Synchronization

Semaphores are used to enforce mutual exclusion and for coordinating events. Each semaphore has a count associated with it; the count can be incremented to any high value but can be only decremented to zero. The value of the counting semaphore can never be less than zero. Counting semaphores are useful in restricting access to a shared resource, but not necessarily in a mutually exclusive manner. In the following example, two semaphores are used by the reader and writer threads to control access to a shared buffer.

```
#include <pthread.h>
#include <stdio.h>
#include <fcntl.h>
#include <sys/types.h>
#include <sys/stat.h>

typedef struct _SEMA
{
   int               semCnt;
   int               sWaiters;
   pthread_mutex_t   mutex;
   pthread_cond_t    cond;
} SEMA;

typedef struct _linebuf
{
   char  line[MAXLINE];
   int   lineLen;
   SEMA  lineEmpty;
   SEMA  lineFull;
} LINEBUF;

LINEBUF lineBuf[MAX_BUFFERS];

void main(int argc, char **argv)
{
   int              i;
   char             *oldfile;
   char             *newfile;
   void             *Consumer();
   void             *Producer();
   int              *status;
   pthread_t        threadId[NUMTHREADS];
   pthread_attr_t   threadAttr;
   if (argc < 3)
   {
      printf("USAGE: %s input-file output-file\n", argv[0]);
      exit(0);
   }
   oldfile = argv[1];
   newfile = argv[2];

   for (i = 0; i < MAX_BUFFERS; ++i)
   {
      CreateSemaphore(&lineBuf[i].lineEmpty, 1);
      CreateSemaphore(&lineBuf[i].lineFull,0);
   }

   pthread_attr_init(&threadAttr);
   pthread_attr_setdetachstate(&threadAttr, PTHREAD_CREATE_JOINABLE);

   pthread_create(&threadId[0], &threadAttr, Consumer, (void *)oldfile);
   pthread_create(&threadId[1], &threadAttr, Producer, (void *)newfile);

   for (i = 0; i < NUMTHREADS; ++i)
        pthread_join(threadId[i],(void**) &status);
   return;
}
```

```
void *
Consumer(char * file)
{
   int  nRead;
   int  i = 0;
   int  inFd;

   inFd = open(file, O_RDONLY, 0666);
   if (inFd == -1)
   {
        printf("main:error opening file %s\n", file);
        pthread_exit(NULL);
   }

   i = 0;

   while(1)
   {
      AcquireSemaphore(&lineBuf[i].lineEmpty);

      nRead = read(inFd, lineBuf[i].line, MAXLINE);
      lineBuf[i].lineLen = nRead;

      ReleaseSemaphore(&lineBuf[i].lineFull);

      if (nRead <= 0)
          break;

      if (i++ == MAX_BUFFERS -1)
          i = 0;
   }

   close(inFd);
   return(0);
}

void *
Producer(char * file)
{
   int  ret;
   int  outFd;
   int  i;

   outFd = open(file, O_CREAT|O_WRONLY, 0666);
   if (outFd == -1)
   {
       printf("error opening file %s\n", file);
       pthread_exit(NULL);
   }
   i = 0;
   for (;;)
   {
       int j;

       AcquireSemaphore(&lineBuf[i].lineFull);

       if (lineBuf[i].lineLen <= 0)
            break;

       j = 0;
       for (j = 0; j < lineBuf[i].lineLen; ++j)
            lineBuf[i].line[j] = toupper(lineBuf[i].line[j]);

       ret = write(outFd, lineBuf[i].line, lineBuf[i].lineLen);
       if (ret == -1 )
       {
       printf("error writing to file %s\n", file);
```

```
            pthread_exit(NULL);
        }

        ReleaseSemaphore(&lineBuf[i].lineEmpty);
        if (i++ = = MAX_BUFFERS -1)
            i = 0;
    }
    close(outFd);
    return(NULL);
}

CreateSemaphore(SEMA *pSema, int semCnt)
{
    pSema->semCnt = semCnt;
    pSema->sWaiters = 0;
    pthread_mutex_init(&pSema->mutex, NULL);
    pthread_cond_init(&pSema->cond, NULL);
}

AcquireSemaphore(SEMA *pSema)
{
    pthread_mutex_lock(&pSema->mutex);

    while(pSema->semCnt = = 0)
    {
        ttpSema->sWaiters;
        pthread_cond_wait(&pSema->cond, &pSema->mutex);
        --pSema->sWaiters;
    }

    --pSema->semCnt;

    pthread_mutex_unlock(&pSema->mutex);
}

ReleaseSemaphore(SEMA *pSema)
{
    pthread_mutex_lock(&pSema->mutex);

    ++pSema->semCnt;

    If (pSema->sWaiters)
        pthread_cond_signal(&pSema->cond);

    pthread_mutex_unlock(&pSema->mutex);
}
```

6.5 Reader/Writer Locks

In certain applications data are much more frequently read than they are modified. Reader/writer (RW) locks allow multiple threads to read data simultaneously but serialize writers when data have to be updated. One of the main advantages of reader/writer locks over mutex locks is that they allow multiple threads to share data in read mode without the overhead of locking. The payoff of RW locks over mutexes is not evident when the code guarded by the RW lock is short. RW locks are better when the frequency of read operations is higher than write operations, and the read operations are somewhat lengthy. The following implementation favors readers over writers and can cause starvation for writers. (See example on disk that favors writers.)

```
#include <pthread.h>
#include <stdio.h>

typedef struct _rwlock
{
   pthread_mutex_t  mutex;
   pthread_cond_t   cond;
   int              count;
} RWLOCK;

RWLOCK rwLock;

main(int argc, char **argv)
{
   int              numThr;
   pthread_t        threadId[NUMTHREADS];
   pthread_attr_t   threadAttr;
   void             *Readers();
   void             *Writers();
   int              i;
   int              *status;

   numThr = NUM_WRITERS + NUM_READERS;

   InitReadWriteLock(&rwLock);

   pthread_attr_init(&threadAttr);
   pthread_attr_setdetachstate(&threadAttr, PTHREAD_CREATE_JOINABLE);

   for (i = 0; i < NUM_WRITERS; ++i)
        pthread_create(&threadId[i], &threadAttr, Writers, NULL);

   for (i = NUM_WRITERS ; i < numThr; ++i)
        pthread_create(&threadId[i], &threadAttr, Readers, NULL);

   for (i = 0; i <numThr; ++i)
        pthread_join(threadId[i],(void**) &status);

}

void *
Writers(void *pThrArg)
{
   int i;

   for (i = 0; i < NUMMSGS; ++i)
   {
        AcquireWriteLock(&rwLock);
        /* do some update to shared data */
        ReleaseWriteLock(&rwLock);

        /* sleep for some time before updating data again to simulate
          infrequent writes*/
   }
   fprintf(stderr,"writer:wrote [%d] msgs\n", i);
   return(NULL);
}

void *
Readers(void *pThrArg)
{
   int  i;
   int  nMsgs;
```

```
    nMsgs = NUMMSGS / NUM_WRITERS ;
    for (i = 0; i < nMsgs; ++i)
    {
         AcquireReadLock(&rwLock);
         /* read shared data */
         ReleaseReadLock(&rwLock);
    }
    fprintf(stderr,"reader: read [%d] msgs\n", i);
    return(NULL);
}

AcquireReadLock(RWLOCK *pRwLock)
{
    pthread_mutex_lock(&pRwLock->mutex);

    while(pRwLock->count < 0)
        pthread_cond_wait(&pRwLock->cond, &pRwLock->mutex);

    ++pRwLock->count;

    pthread_mutex_unlock(&pRwLock->mutex);
}

ReleaseReadLock(RWLOCK *pRwLock)
{
    pthread_mutex_lock(&pRwLock->mutex);

    --pRwLock->count;

    if (!pRwLock->count)
         pthread_cond_broadcast(&pRwLock->cond);

    pthread_mutex_unlock(&pRwLock->mutex);
}

AcquireWriteLock(RWLOCK *pRwLock)
{
    pthread_mutex_lock(&pRwLock->mutex);

    while(pRwLock->count != 0)
        pthread_cond_wait(&pRwLock->cond, &pRwLock->mutex);

    pRwLock->count = -1;

    pthread_mutex_unlock(&pRwLock->mutex);
}

ReleaseWriteLock(RWLOCK *pRwLock)
{
    pthread_mutex_lock(&pRwLock->mutex);
    pRwLock->count = 0;
    pthread_cond_broadcast(&pRwLock->cond);
    pthread_mutex_unlock(&pRwLock->mutex);
}

InitReadWriteLock(RWLOCK *pRwLock)
{
    pthread_mutex_init(&pRwLock->mutex, NULL);
    pthread_cond_init(&pRwLock->cond, NULL);
    pRwLock->count = 0;
}
```

Chapter

7

UNIX International Thread Management

7.1 Introduction

UNIX International (UI) has defined an application programming interface (API) for developing multithreaded applications. This interface is also known as *UI threads,* and it is very similar to the POSIX.1c threads interface. The reader is advised to read the chapters on POSIX threads for more detailed information on Pthreads. Operating systems such as Solaris 2.X, Unixware 2.0, and SVR4/MP support the UI threads interface for developing multithreaded applications. If portability is of concern to other UNIX systems, then one *should* use the POSIX threads interface even though the UI threads interface offers sufficient functionality to develop multithreaded applications. Some operating systems such as Solaris 2.5 support both POSIX.1c and UI threads interfaces, while others such as Unixware 2.0 only support UI threads. On systems that support only the UI threads interface one should develop applications that can be easily ported to the POSIX.1c threads interface.

Discussion of some of the concepts of thread programming has been avoided because this was done already in the earlier chapters on Pthreads. The reader also might find that some of the text has been repeated from earlier chapters, and this has been done for the sake of completeness. If you are reading this chapter after reading the POSIX threads chapters, then you should not have any problem understanding these concepts and APIs. Readers who have not yet read the chapters on Pthreads are advised to read relevant sections from the POSIX threads chapters. The differences between POSIX.1c and UI threads will be pointed out throughout the chapters and can be used as guidelines for developing applications using UI threads but keeping Pthreads *portability* in mind.

This discussion is limited to the Solaris and UNIX SVR4/MP implementations of UI threads. Since Solaris threads are a subset of the UI threads interface, some of the APIs mentioned in these chapters are not implemented on Solaris. The reader is advised to refer to the vendor's documentation for a detailed description of the APIs and the error code returned by each of the APIs.

7.1.1 Threads and the UNIX system

Traditional UNIX systems did not support the notion of threads. In earlier UNIX systems, a process consisted of an address space and a single thread of control. Recently, with the increased popularity of symmetric multiprocessing (SMP) machines, many UNIX vendors have started offering multithreaded kernels with full multiprocessing support.

In a multithreaded UNIX system, a process has been redefined to support multiple threads of execution within the same address space. Single-threaded programs do *not* require any changes when they are ported to a multithreaded UNIX system. Applications have only to be modified when they want to *exploit* the multithreading and multiprocessing features of the operating system. In the case of multithreaded kernels, there are two types of threads: *kernel* threads and *user* threads. Kernel threads are kernel entities that execute in kernel space, while user threads run entirely in user space. The kernel handles the scheduling of kernel threads, while the threads library is responsible for the scheduling of user threads.

UI threads are pure user-level entities and are mapped by the threads library to kernel threads via a structure called a *lightweight process* (LWP). An LWP is a kernel entity and is scheduled by the kernel to execute on the CPU. Each LWP maps to a kernel thread, and it is independent of the other LWPs in the system. By default, LWPs are not bound to any particular processor and can be scheduled to run on any processor. A user thread cannot execute unless it is mapped to an LWP, since the LWP acts as the execution resource for the user thread.

7.1.2 Thread execution models

The mapping between user threads and LWPs is handled by the threads library. The threads library is the *run-time* component that provides various functions for creating and managing threads in a multithreaded process. On a system supporting UI threads, the mapping between user threads and kernel threads can be implemented in one or more of the following ways:

- One-to-one mapping
- Many-to-one mapping
- Many-to-many mapping

The reader is advised to read Sec. 2.4 for a more detailed description on the thread execution models.

7.1.3 Process, LWP, and threads

Traditional UNIX processes consist of a single thread of execution, and they are defined to consist of an address space and a single thread executing within the address space. On systems that implement UI threads, a process is redefined to consist of an address space with one or more LWPs and threads. Each LWP is scheduled independently by the kernel, and they can even run in parallel on SMP machines. The reader is advised to read Sec. 2.3 for a more detailed description of the attributes shared between processes and threads.

UI threads support a two-tiered threads library model; at the top layer are the user threads, and at the bottom layer are lightweight processes (LWPs). The kernel is only aware of LWPs, knows nothing about user threads, and is responsible for the scheduling of kernel threads. User threads are managed by the threads library, and the library supports 1:1, M:N, or M:1 mapping between the user threads and the LWPs. The multiplexing of user threads to a pool of LWPs and the scheduling of user threads are handled entirely by the threads library. Although the two-tiered threads model adds some extra responsibility on the user, it allows for the cheaper creation of user threads without using a lot of system resources.

In UI threads there are two kinds of threads: *bound* and *unbound*. A bound thread has a 1:1 mapping between a user thread and the LWP, while an unbound thread does not have a dedicated LWP. Unbound threads are also known as *multiplexed threads*. In the case of bound threads, the mapping between the thread and the LWP is maintained for the entire life of the thread. When an unbound thread runs, it is temporarily bound to an LWP in the pool of available LWPs. When one of the threads blocks, then the library schedules another runnable thread to run on the LWP. The threads library is responsible only for the scheduling of unbound threads, while the kernel is responsible for the scheduling of LWPs. Applications that require global scheduling with respect to other LWPs in the system would be better suited to the use of bound threads. Refer to Sec. 7.2.1.1 for more on bound threads.

7.1.4 UI threads APIs

The UI threads APIs are used to create and manage threads. The threads APIs can be broadly classified into areas such as threads management, threads synchronization, thread-specific data, and advanced threads topics. The advanced threads topics deal with such things as scheduling, priority, and signals. Most thread functions return 0 on success and the error code on failure. Unlike other UNIX functions, the threads APIs do *not* set the error variable errno on failure.

The discussion of UI threads will be limited to the threads interface and not the low-level LWP interface. The LWP interface (e.g., _lwp_create) is not portable, and it can be changed by the vendor. The LWP interface is used by the threads library, and it should *never* be used by application programs.

7.2 Thread Management Functions

thr_create	Creates a thread
thr_join	Waits for a thread termination
thr_exit	Terminates a thread
thr_self	Finds thread ID
thr_setconcurrency	Sets concurrency level
thr_getconcurrency	Gets concurrency level
thr_suspend	Suspends a thread
thr_resume	Resumes a thread
thr_setscheduler	Sets scheduling policy and priority
thr_getscheduler	Gets scheduling policy and priority
thr_getprio	Gets priority of a thread
thr_setprio	Sets priority of a thread
thr_yield	Yields processor to other threads

7.2.1 Create a thread

When a process begins execution, it has a single thread of control. The process is automatically created with one thread that is commonly referred to as the *main thread*. The creation of the main thread maintains binary compatibility with single-threaded programs. If a process needs additional threads of control, then they have to be created by calling the thread creation API.

When threads are created, they begin executing a start routine. Creating a thread is somewhere between calling a function and creating a process. The start routine specifies the entry point at which the newly created thread starts execution. Multiple threads can execute the same start routine, or each thread can have a separate start routine. If multiple threads call the same thread routine and they modify shared data within the routine, then the routine must be written to be thread-safe. Unlike the parent/child relationship, when a new process is created via the fork call in POSIX, there is no relationship between the threads. The thread does not maintain a list of created threads does not have any knowledge of other threads in the process.

```
int thr_create(void *stack_address, size_t stack_size, void *(*start_
routine)(void *), void *arg, long flags, thread_t *new_thread)
```

The function thr_create is used to create a new thread of control in the current process. The first argument *stack_address* can be used to specify the starting address of the new thread's stack. When a NULL value is passed, the system assigns the default stack address. It is very rare that applications would need to specify a user-supplied stack. If you supply your own user stack, then you should reclaim the stack when the thread terminates. A word of caution: One should *never* use the same stack address for multiple threads.

The second argument *stack_size* is used to specify the stack size in bytes of the newly created thread. If the stack requirements of the thread will be greater than the default size, then the default stack size of the thread should be changed. If the value 0 is specified, then the default stack size is used. The size of the stack must be at least THR_MIN_STACK or *thr_min_stack()* bytes in size. When a user-supplied stack address is used, then a nonzero value should be used, and it should be equal to the size of the user-supplied stack. The stack size can be changed even when the default stack address is used.

Since the stack of a thread grows dynamically, reserving a bigger stack size than needed is not a problem, but having a smaller stack can cause some nasty bugs. When a thread exceeds its stack limit, the signal SIGSEGV is raised in the faulting thread. The default stack size is *implementation-dependent,* and I would recommend that you check your vendor's documentation for details.

The third argument is a pointer to a function that is executed as the thread's *start routine.* The start routine should be defined to return a void *. The fourth argument *arg* is a pointer to an optional argument passed to the thread's start_routine, and it can be NULL in the case when no arguments are passed to the thread routine. Passing integer values and casting them to void * constitute a bad programming practice and should be avoided.

The last argument is a pointer to an opaque object of type *thread_t.* UI threads uses thread_t as the data type to identify threads, and it is defined to be an unsigned integer. Each thread within a process is identified by a thread identifier (TID). The TID of the newly created thread is *only* known to be usable and unique within the context of the process creating the thread. If new_thread is non-NULL, then the function thr_create stores the identifier of the newly created thread in *new_thread.* Pass a NULL value if you are not interested in the TID of the new thread.

The argument *flags* can be used to define the attributes of the newly created thread and are very similar to the threads attributes of Pthreads. The argument flags can have the following values:

- THR_SUSPENDED
- THR_BOUND
- THR_DETACHED
- THR_DAEMON
- THR_INC_CONC or THR_NEW_LWP

When a thread is created, by default it enters the *runnable* state. Threads can be created in a *suspended* state by passing the value THR_SUSPENDED to flags. The newly created thread will not start executing the start_routine until it is resumed by the creating thread or some other thread in the process. For example, one might want to create a thread in suspended state, alter the thread priority, and then resume the thread. Another time you might want to create a thread in suspended state is when some state of the thread has to be initialized before it can run (e.g., create a mutex for the new thread).

If you are new to thread programming, then I recommend that you *should* read Secs. 2.6.1.1 through 2.6.1.3, where topics like passing different arguments to a thread routine and the scope of the thread argument are covered in detail.

The following example illustrates the creation of a new thread. The newly created thread is created to start executing the routine LoopThread (). The routine LoopThread executes a loop, and the number of iterations to loop is specified as arguments to the thread routine.

```
typedef struct _THRARG
{
   int rows;
   int cols;
} THRARG;

main (int argc, char **argv)
{
   thread_t  threadId;
   void      *LoopThread();
   THRARG    thrArg;

   thrArg.rows = 10;
   thrArg.cols = 20;

   thr_create (NULL, 0, LoopThread, (void *) &thrArg, 0, &threadId);

   /* Wait for the thread to complete */

   exit (0);
}

void *
LoopThread (THRARG *pThrArg)
{
   int j;
   int k;

   for (j = 0; j < pThrArg->rows; ++j)
        for (k = 0; k < pThrArg->cols;++k)
            printf ("loop iteration j: [%d]\t k: [%d]\n", j, k);

   /* Exit Thread */
}
```

7.2.1.1 Bound and unbound threads. A thread, by default, is created as an unbound thread, which means that no LWP is dedicated to the thread. An unbound thread does not run until an LWP is assigned to it, and the system takes care of binding LWPs to threads. A thread can be created as a bound thread using the THR_BOUND *flag* in the call to thr_create function. This creates a new LWP that is permanently bound to the thread and does not terminate until the thread terminates.

Since bound threads are more resource expensive than unbound threads, it is generally inefficient to create too many bound threads. If your application *needs* true concurrency, then you should create bound threads. Note, two unbound threads mapped to the same LWP cannot run concurrently on different processors. Bound threads are created when performance is of utmost importance and applications cannot tolerate the LWP allocation delay. Scheduling of bound threads is handled strictly by the kernel, while unbound threads depend on the threads library for scheduling. Additionally, if the thread *needs* an alternate signal stack, a unique alarm, or timers, then you should create bound threads. The following code segment creates a bound thread.

```
CreateBoundThread ()
{
   thread_t   threadId;
   void       *ThreadRoutine ();

   thr_create (NULL, 0, ThreadRoutine, NULL, THR_BOUND, &threadId);
}
```

> Bound threads are similar to POSIX.1c threads that are created with a contention scope of PTHREAD_SCOPE_SYSTEM, while unbound threads are similar to threads that are created with a contention scope of PTHREAD_SCOPE_PROCESS.

7.2.1.2 Detached and nondetached threads. The thread detach attribute defines if the thread is created either in a detached or nondetached state. Nondetached threads *can* be joined (waited on) by other threads, and the storage for the thread is saved until the thread is joined. The storage, among other things, includes the exit value and TID of the thread. When a thread is created in detached state, the storage for the thread is immediately reclaimed after thread termination.

By default, threads are created as nondetached, which means they *have* to be joined explicitly by calling the thr_join function. When nondetached threads are not joined, the memory and internal resources of the thread are never released by the threads library. This might cause an application to fail when trying to create threads. If one knows at thread creation time that the new thread will *never* be joined, then the thread should be created as detached by using the THR_DETACHED flag in the call to the thr_create function. The following code segment creates a detached thread.

```
CreateDetachedThread ()
{
   thread_t  threadId;
   void     *ThreadRoutine ();
   thr_create (NULL, 0, ThreadRoutine, NULL, THR_DETACHED, &threadId);
}
```

> Detached threads are similar to POSIX.1c threads that are created with a detach state attribute of PTHREAD_CREATE_DETACHED, while nondetached threads are similar to threads that are created with a detach state attribute of PTHREAD_CREATE_JOINABLE.

7.2.1.3 Daemon threads. A daemon thread usually performs background tasks for multiple threads. *Daemon* threads are service threads, and they are designed to support other threads in the application. These other threads are known as *nondaemon* threads. When there are no more nondaemon threads, then the daemon thread automatically terminates. To create a daemon thread, use the THR_DAEMON flag in the call to thr_create.

> If *portability* is of concern to Pthreads, then keep in mind that there is no equivalence of a daemon thread in POSIX.1c.

7.2.1.4 Controlling the number of LWPs. Since LWPs are kernel resources, one should not create "too many" LWPs in a process, but at the same time one should be concerned about creating "too few" LWPs in a process. When unbound threads are used, the threads library is responsible for managing the number of LWPs in the pool dynamically. In addition to this default behavior, the threads library allows the programmer to control the number of LWPs in a process.

When a thread is created using the THR_NEW_LWP or THR_INC_CONC flag, then a new LWP is created, and it is added to the pool of available LWPs. When both flags THR_BOUND and THR_NEW_LWP are passed to the function thr_create, then two LWPs are created, one for the bound thread and one for the pool of LWPs. Additionally, the number of LWPs in the pool can be controlled by thr_setconcurrency function. The function thr_setconcurrency is a better way to control the concurrency of LWPs in a process rather than using the flags in the function thr_create.

> If *portability* is of concern to Pthreads, then keep in mind that currently in POSIX.1c one cannot control the number of LWPs required to multiplex the unbound threads.

7.2.1.5 Maximum threads allowed. Threads are much more lightweight when compared with a process. Even though threads are cheap, they are *not free*. Threads use system resources such as kernel stack and memory and also involve scheduling overhead. The maximum number of threads that can be created successfully in a process in UNIX is limited by system resources, and it is vendor and operating system–specific. The function *thr_create* returns *EAGAIN* when the maximum allowable limit is reached. There is *no* portable way to determine the maximum number of threads that can be created in a process.

7.2.2 Thread termination

Everything that is created must come to an end, and so must the life of a thread. A thread terminates when:

- It exits the start_routine.
- It calls thr_exit.

```
void thr_exit (void *status)
```

The function thr_exit terminates the calling thread and stores the exit status in the variable *status,* which is later made available to any thread waiting for this thread to terminate. The function thr_exit is called implicitly when a thread returns from the start routine that was used to create the thread. In such a case, the function return value serves as the exit status. The routine thr_exit does *not* return to the calling thread. The variable status *must* be valid even after the thread exits; therefore, do not use an automatic variable when calling the function thr_exit. Remember, the stack of a terminating thread is destroyed except when the stack is user-supplied.

When an initial thread returns from the main routine, the *exit* routine is called, thus terminating *all* the threads in the process. It is a good practice to call thr_exit to terminate all threads. When the initial thread calls thr_exit, it does *not* terminate the entire process but only terminates the main thread. The process terminates when the last nondaemon thread in the process terminates.

A process can terminate itself by calling the *exit* system call. In a multithreaded process, the routine *exit* terminates the entire process, and this includes all threads in the process. This preserves the semantics of a single-threaded process in UNIX. A thread should *never* call *exit* unless the entire process needs to be terminated.

7.2.3 Waiting for thread termination

In the worker thread model it is common for a thread to suspend execution until some other thread terminates. For example, consider a program in which a master thread creates multiple worker threads to perform parallel queries on different databases. The master thread has to wait for all the worker threads to terminate before it can continue processing with the result of the queries.

The function thr_join is used to wait for the termination of nondetached threads. Resources such as thread ID and thread termination status for the thread are saved until the thread is detached. The thread resources are released *automatically* if the thread is a detached thread. If the thread is created as an undetached thread, then the function thr_join *must* be called to ensure that resources are released by the threads library. It is a programming error to wait for detached threads.

```
int thr_join (thread_t wait_for, thread_t *departed, void **status)
```

The function thr_join suspends the calling thread and waits for termination of the thread specified by the thread *wait_for.* On return from a successful join, the variable *status* contains the exit status of the terminating thread. If the target thread has already terminated, then thr_join returns immediately without blocking.

If the value passed to wait_for is NULL, then the function waits for the next nondetached thread to terminate. This can be used to wait for the termination of *any* thread in the process. When multiple threads call thr_join to join a thread, then only one thread succeeds, while the rest fail with an error code of ESRCH. The following code segment waits for the termination of all threads in a process.

```
WaitForAllThreads()
{
    /* wait for all nondaemon and nondetached threads */
    while (thr_join(NULL, NULL, NULL) == 0)
        ;
}
```

The routine thr_join along with thr_exit also can be used to *return* some information to the calling thread. It is important that the returned variable should be valid even after the thread has terminated. In the following code segment the main thread creates a thread to execute a query. The thread returns the results of the query in a dynamically allocated buffer. On return, the main thread prints the results and then frees the buffer.

```
main (int argc, char **argv)
{
    thread_t  threadId;
    char      *query;
    void      *QueryThread ();
    char      *queryResults;

    thr_create ( NULL, 0, (void *) QueryThread, (void *)query, 0, &threadId);

    thr_join (threadId, NULL, (void **)&queryResults);

    if (queryResults != NULL)
    {
        /*print results returned by the thread */
        free (void*) queryResults);
    }

    exit (0);
}

void *
QueryThread (void *pquery)
{
    int j;
    void *pqueryResults;

    /* pqueryResults on return is either NULL or points to the result set */
    DoQuery (pquery, &pqueryResults); /* malloc is done inside this routine */

    thr_exit (pqueryResults);
}
```

If *portability* is of concern to Pthreads, then keep in mind that the function pthread_join can only be used to wait for the termination of a thread whose identifier is known. In UI threads one can wait for the termination of *any* thread in the process even when the TID of the thread is unknown.

7.2.4 Thread identifier

Each thread within a process is uniquely identified by a thread identifier. The thread identifier (TID) is only guaranteed to be unique within the context of the calling process. Once a thread terminates and it is detached, then the TID can be reused by the threads library.

```
thread_t thr_self (void)
```

The function thr_self returns the TID of the calling thread. In UI threads, the function *thr_main* can be used to determine if the calling thread is the main or primary thread in the process.

If *portability* is of concern to Pthreads, then the use of thr_main should be avoided. Additionally, one should keep in mind that the data type pthread_t is an opaque data type that does not necessarily map to an unsigned integer as in UI threads.

7.2.5 Thread concurrency control

The number of threads that can execute concurrently on any processor is determined by the number of LWPs in a process. The number of LWPs in a process is a sum of the number of bound threads plus the number of LWPs in the pool used for multiplexing the unbound threads. *Concurrency level* is defined as the number of LWPs in the pool that service the unbound threads. The threads library provides functions to determine and change the concurrency level, since the default concurrency algorithm used by the threads library might *not* be suitable for all applications.

```
int thr_getconcurrency (void)
int thr_setconcurrency (int new_level)
```

The function thr_getconcurrency returns the current concurrency level, while the function thr_setconcurrency is used to increase the number of LWPs to *new_level* in a process. If new_level is 0, then the default concurrency level is used. When a nonzero value is passed to new_level, it does not mean that the concurrency level will be set to that value but is used *only* as a hint by the threads library. The following code segment increases the concurrency level for every fourth thread created in the process.

```
#define NUM_CPU          4 /* number of CPU */
static int NumThreads;   /* counter for number of threads in the process */

main (int argc, char **argv)
{
   thread_t  threadId;
   int       currentConcurrency;
   char      *query;
   void      *QueryThread ();

   thr_create ( NULL, 0, (void *) QueryThread, (void *)query, 0, &threadId);
   ++NumThreads; /* assumes thr_create is successful */
   if (NumThreads && NumThreads % 4)
   {
      currentConcurrency = thr_getconcurrency();
      if (currentConcurrency < NUM_CPU * 4)
         thr_setconcurrency(currentConcurrency + 1); /* increase the number
         of LWPs */
   }

   /*wait for threads to terminate */
}
```

If *portability* is of concern to Pthreads, then keep in mind that currently in POSIX.1c one cannot control the number of LWPs required to multiplex the unbound threads.

7.2.6 Suspending and resuming threads

A thread can be created in a suspended state by calling the function thr_create and using the flag THR_SUSPEND. A suspended thread will not run unless some other thread resumes the thread by calling the thr_continue function. It is possible to suspend a thread even after it has been created by calling the function thr_suspend.

In some cases it might be useful to create a thread in suspended state, alter the thread priority, and then resume the thread. Another situation in which you might want to create a thread in suspended state occurs when the state of the thread has to be initialized before it can run. These functions should *never* be used for mutual-exclusion purposes. Using thread scheduling for synchronization purposes is likely to cause you problems later.

```
int thr_suspend (thread_t target_thread)
int thr_continue (thread_t target_thread)
```

The function thr_suspend is used to suspend a thread specified by *target_thread*. The control is not returned to the caller until the target thread is suspended. When an unbound thread is suspended, the LWP assigned to the target thread is mapped to some other thread in the process. The function thr_continue is used to resume a previously suspended thread identified by the TID *target_thread*.

> If *portability* is of concern to Pthreads, then keep in mind that in POSIX.1c there is no equivalent function to suspend or resume threads.

When a thread is suspended while holding a mutex lock and some other thread tries to acquire the same lock, then a deadlock can happen. Note that when you are using external libraries it might *not* be possible to predict when a thread is holding a lock. For example, consider the following code segment of a function that is in some external library. If thread T1 is suspended while it is in the middle of the function DoFunc and thread T2 calls the same function, then thread T2 will block trying to lock the mutex until thread T1 is resumed by some other thread. If thread T1 can only be resumed by T2, then a deadlock *will* happen. Before using the function thr_suspend, be aware of the potential problems.

```
ExternalFunc()
{
   ...
   ...
   LockMutex();
     DoFunc();
   UnlockMutex();
}
```

7.3 Threads and Scheduling

UI threads architecture employs a two-tiered scheduling policy in which the kernel is responsible for scheduling LWPs on processors and the threads library is responsible for scheduling threads on LWPs. LWPs are scheduled by the kernel according to their scheduling class and priority. A process is created with an initial LWP that inherits the scheduling class and priority of the parent process. Bound threads inherit the scheduling class and priority of the underlying LWP, while unbound threads that are created by other unbound threads inherit the scheduling class of the creator.

The kernel employs a preemptive priority-based scheduling system and always executes the highest-priority LWP on the CPU. The threads library schedules user threads using priority levels on a pool of LWPs. Threads do not yield the LWP until they block on a synchronization object, call thr_yield, or are preempted by a higher-priority thread. The priority of an unbound thread is *never* altered by the threads library, while the priority of an LWP can be adjusted by the operating system.

The threads library usually creates a sufficient number of LWPs to ensure that the process can proceed without an indefinite wait. When *all* LWPs in a process block, then the kernel sends the signal SIGWAITING to the process, which is handled by the threads library. The signal SIGWAITING is a new signal that was added on systems that support UI threads. Upon receiving the signal, a new LWP is only created if there are more runnable threads in the process. Once the LWP is created, the new LWP is assigned to the runnable thread.

LWPs are *aged,* which means that if an LWP is idle for some time, then it is deleted by the kernel. The time period on most systems is 5 minutes. When an unbound thread terminates, the LWP becomes idle, and it is automatically deleted if the library does not map another user thread to the LWP. If an application creates threads frequently and lots of idle LWPs hang around, then it is possible that the thread creation function will fail due to lack of resources.

7.3.1 Scheduling policy and priority

The scheduling *policy* defines which thread is chosen to run next on the CPU. The UI threads standard defines three scheduling policies:

- SCHED_FIFO
- SCHED_RR
- SCHED_TS or SCHED_OTHER

Since the scheduling policies are similar to the POSIX scheduling policies, the reader is advised to read Sec. 5.2 for more information on scheduling policies. Unbound or multiplexed threads *must* run under the time-sharing policy, while bound threads can run under any scheduling policy. Some operating systems such as Solaris only implement the SCHED_TS scheduling policy. The functions thr_setscheduler and thr_getscheduler can be used to change the scheduling policy and priority of the thread. Since multiplexed threads generally use the SCHED_TS policy, these functions can be used to alter the priority of a thread. The functions to change the scheduling policy might *not* be implemented on all systems.

```
int thr_setscheduler(thread_t thread, sched_param_t *param)
int thr_getscheduler(thread_t thread, sched_param_t *param)
int thr_getprio(thread_t thread, int *priority)
int thr_setprio(thread_t thread, int priority)
```

The scheduling priority is an integer value that defines the execution priority of a thread. This defines the importance of a thread's work relative to other threads in the process. The function thr_setprio sets the priority of the thread identified by *thread* to *priority,* while the function thr_getprio returns the *priority* of the thread identified by *thread*. The function thr_setprio is an easier interface than thr_setscheduler to change the priority of a thread. These functions are more useful for unbound threads because they compete for access to an LWP. Bound threads *should* use the function *priocntl* to modify the scheduling class and priority.

The following code segment creates a thread in a suspended state and then alters the priority of the thread before resuming the thread.

```
main (int argc, char **argv)
{
   thread_t  threadId;
   void      *ThrRoutine();
   int       priority;

   thr_create ( NULL, 0, (void *) ThrRoutine, NULL, THR_SUSPENDED,
   &threadId);

   thr_getprio(threadId, &priority);

   /* increase the priority of the thread by 2 */
   thread_setprio(threadId, priority + 2);

   thr_continue(threadId);
   /* wait for thread to complete */
}
```

7.3.2 Yielding processor

```
int thr_yield ()
```

The function thr_yield can be used by the calling thread to yield its processor. It allows the scheduler to determine if another thread of higher priority can run instead of the calling thread. When no suitable thread exists, then the calling thread continues to run on the CPU.

This function *should* be used with CPU-intensive threads because it allows other threads a chance to run. Remember that a user thread that does not block or give up the CPU might prevent other threads bound to the same LWP from running. The thr_yield function provides the ideal solution to such problems. If the calling thread is a bound thread, then the LWP yields the processor. In the case of unbound threads, the threads library maps another thread to run on the LWP.

Note that misuse of this call may hurt rather than help because it may cause lots of unnecessary context switches. For example, it does not make sense to call this function while holding a lock to a shared data structure, since the other threads might not be able to continue processing unless the shared lock is released.

> If *portability* is of concern to Pthreads, then keep in mind that the POSIX.1b function sched_yield can be used to yield the processor.

7.4 Thread Synchronization

In a multithreaded process, all threads execute in a single address space and hence share most of the process resources. Process resources such as open file descriptors, IPC identifiers, static variables, and dynamically allocated memory variables are shared by all the threads. For example, if one thread closes a file, then that file is considered closed for all other threads within the process. Similarly, if one thread frees a dynamically allocated buffer using the C-library *free* routine, then no other thread can safely reference the same buffer without causing an access violation.

One of the main advantages of threads is easy data sharing, but along with this comes the added responsibility to guard such data against corruption. Threads need to synchronize data that are shared and can be modified by multiple threads. If shared data are modified without any synchronization by multiple threads, then the data can become inconsistent. All access to shared resources must be protected by some mutual exclusion lock. The use of locks to synchronize access to shared data is called *data synchronization*.

In a boss/worker thread model it is common to divide work between multiple threads. In such a case, one thread might wait for another thread to reach a particular state before proceeding, or one thread might wait for a particular condition to be true before proceeding. In these cases, threads are not necessarily synchronizing on data but more on conditions or events. Data synchronization is usually for shorter duration, while event synchronization can be for much longer duration.

Let us consider an example of a producer and a consumer thread writing and reading from a shared buffer. When the threads are reading or writing from the buffer, they have exclusive access to the buffer. The producer cannot write to the buffer until the consumer has finished reading from the buffer, and the consumer cannot read from the buffer until the producer has finished writing to the buffer. Each thread waits for notification from the other thread that the buffer is available. When the producer thread is finished writing to the buffer, it notifies the consumer, and vice versa. This form of synchronization is often called *event synchronization*.

If you have read Chap. 3, then most of these APIs should be very simple; otherwise, I would recommend that you should *read* Secs. 3.1.1 through 3.1.3 to better understand some of the basic concepts of mutual exclusion and event synchronization.

The UI threads interface provides many synchronization primitives, not all of which might be implemented on systems supporting UI threads. For example, barriers, spinlocks, and recursive mutexes are implemented on Unixware 2.0 but are *not* implemented on Solaris 2.5.

- Mutexes
- Condition variables
- Semaphores
- Reader/writer locks
- Barriers
- Spinlocks
- Recursive mutexes

The functions for mutex locks and condition variables in UI threads are *identical* to the POSIX.1c counterparts. POSIX.1c *only* implements mutex and condition variables for synchronization, but it is possible to implement most of the other synchronization primitives on top of the basic POSIX.1c synchronization primitives.

7.4.1 Mutex functions and macros

`mutex_init`	Initializes a mutex
`mutex_destroy`	Deletes a mutex
`mutex_lock`	Locks a mutex
`mutex_trylock`	Conditionally locks a mutex
`mutex_unlock`	Unlocks a mutex

7.4.2 Mutual exclusion locks

Mutex locks generally are used to synchronize access to and ensure atomic updates of shared data. A *mutex* (mutual exclusion) lock is a data structure in memory that processes or threads use to *serialize* access to shared data. Mutex locks are meaningful only for data that can be *modified* by multiple threads or processes. This means that you do *not* need to serialize access to shared read-only data items.

The state of the mutex can be either *locked* or *unlocked*. The basic assumption behind mutexes is that threads must lock the mutex before accessing shared modifiable data and unlock the mutex after the thread has completed accessing the shared data. If one thread has acquired the mutex, then all other threads requesting to lock the mutex will *wait* until the mutex is released by the thread owning the mutex. It is important to remember that for data synchronization all threads must *enforce* the mutex locking protocol strictly. Note that if threads do not check the locks before entering the critical section, then mutex locks cannot be of any help. One possible solution to enforce mutual exclusion is to provide well-defined interfaces (functions) to allow access to shared resources and then implement the mutex locking and unlocking within these interfaces. In this way the details of locking and unlocking are hidden from the user of these interfaces.

7.4.3 Initializing a mutex

UI threads use the data type *mutex_t* to identify nonrecursive mutexes. Mutexes have to be initialized before they can be utilized for mutual exclusion. Mutexes, by default, are created as nonrecursive, and the initial state of the mutex is unlocked. A mutex variable should only be initialized *once*.

```
int mutex_init (mutex_t *mutex, int type, void *arg)
```

The function mutex_init initializes the mutex pointed by *mutex*. The *type* of the mutex can be either USYNC_THREAD or USYNC_PROCESS. Mutexes of type USYNC_THREAD can only be used by threads within a process, while mutexes of type USYNC_PROCESS can be used for interprocess mutex synchronization. If a mutex has to be shared between processes, then the mutex should be created in shared memory. The third argument *arg* is reserved for future use and should always be passed as NULL.

A mutex can be initialized statically by zero filling the mutex, in which case the mutex_init function does *not* have to be called. Static initialization of the mutex guarantees that the mutex will be initialized even before *any* thread starts execution. Further, with static initialization, mutexes are guaranteed to be initialized once, and this is different from mutex_init, where it is the programmer's responsibility to ensure that the mutex is initialized only once. Static mutexes *can* be used to implement a function similar to the pthread_once function of Pthreads (see examples on disk).

```
InitializeMutex ()
{
   mutex_t mutex;

   mutex = DEFAULTMUTEX; /* on Solaris */
      or
   mutex = calloc(1, sizeof(mutex_t)); /* do a free after mutex-destroy */
      or
   mutex_init (&mutex, USYNC_THREAD, NULL);
}
```

> The USYNC_THREAD type of mutex is similar to the PTHREAD_SCOPE_PRIVATE mutex, while the USYNC_PROCESS type is similar to the PTHREAD_SCOPE_PROCESS. Static initialization is similar to the PTHREAD_MUTEX_INITIALIZER macro.

7.4.4 Destroying a mutex

When mutexes are not needed, they should be destroyed. Mutexes are *not* deleted when the thread that created the mutex terminates, since mutexes are considered to be shared resources of a process. Mutexes are deleted automatically when the process exits, assuming the scope of the mutex is USYNC_THREAD.

```
int mutex_destroy (mutex_t *mutex)
```

The function mutex_destroy is used to delete the state of a previously initialized mutex identified by *mutex*. This routine should be called only when a mutex is *no* longer referenced. Deleting a mutex allows all the resources associated with the mutex to be reclaimed. It is a programming error to delete a locked mutex or when some other thread is blocked trying to lock a mutex.

7.4.5 Acquiring mutex lock

Before executing a critical section of code, the thread must *acquire* the mutex lock. After executing the critical section, the thread that locked the mutex must then *release* the mutex. The locking of the mutex can either be blocking or nonblocking in nature.

```
int mutex_lock (mutex_t *mutex)
```

The function mutex_lock is used to acquire a lock of a valid unlocked mutex identified by *mutex*. If the mutex is currently locked by some other thread, then the calling thread blocks until the mutex lock is released. When the function returns successfully, then the state of the mutex becomes locked, and the calling thread becomes the owner of the mutex. The calling thread remains the owner of the mutex lock until it unlocks the mutex later. If the mutex is never unlocked, then some other thread will block *indefinitely* on the mutex lock when it tries to acquire the locked mutex.

Any attempt by the calling thread to lock a mutex that is already locked by the calling thread will result in *deadlock*. It is your responsibility to ensure that you do not call this function while owning the mutex lock. When multiple threads call mutex_lock at the same time, they are suspended and are placed on a queue of threads waiting for the mutex to be released. Certain factors such as thread priority and scheduling determine which thread will be woken first, and it does *not* necessarily have to be FIFO policy. It is safe to assume that there is *no* defined order in which blocked threads are unblocked. Bound threads are given preference over unbound threads when they are woken up. As a general rule, mutexes should only be held for short duration to avoid performance problems.

7.4.6 Nonblocking mutex lock

The function mutex_trylock is similar to mutex_lock except that the function returns immediately if the mutex identified by *mutex* is currently locked by any thread. This function returns an error even when the calling thread owns the mutex lock and therefore can be used to detect recursive deadlocks.

```
int mutex_trylock mutex_t *mutex)
```

Nonblocking mutex locks can be used to implement *spinlocks*. The UI threads interface also provides its own spinlock routines (see Sec. 7.5), but they are *not* implemented on all systems (e.g., Solaris). Consider the following code segment, which implements a simple spinlock routine.

```
SpinLockAcquire(mutex_t *SharedMutex)
{
   while(mutex_trylock(SharedMutex) = = EBUSY)
          ; /* busy wait */
}
```

7.4.7 Unlocking a mutex

The mutex lock should be released after the thread executes the critical section of the code; otherwise, no other thread can enter the same critical section.

```
int mutex_unlock (mutex_t *mutex)
```

The function mutex_unlock is used to unlock a mutex lock identified by *mutex*. On success, the mutex lock is released, and the state of the mutex is marked as *unlocked*. If no other thread is waiting for the mutex to be released, then the state of the mutex is not changed, and the mutex is marked as having no owner. If one or more threads are waiting for the mutex to be released, then one of them is woken up. One should *not* rely on the order in which threads are woken up.

On some systems the function mutex_unlock does *not* enforce that the owner of the mutex should unlock the mutex. When I tried it on Unixware 2.0, I found that the threads library *allows* any thread to unlock the mutex, even though the thread might not have locked the mutex. This *can* cause nasty bugs in your code. I would advise that you implement your own version of mutex locking and unlocking functions that detects this error (see Sec. 7.4.8).

Let us consider a function that adds a new item to the beginning of a list. This list is shared by multiple threads within the process. For a detailed description on critical sections and race conditions, please refer to Sec. 3.1.

```
typedef struct List
{
   struct List  *next;
   void         *data;
}SHARED_LIST;

static SHARED_LIST *gpListHead; /* pointer to beginning of list */

mutex_t          ListMutex;

InitListMutex()
{
   mutex_init(&ListMutex, USYNC_THREAD, NULL);
              or
   ListMutex = DEFAULTMUTEX;
}

AddToList (SHARED_LIST *pnewEntry)
{
   /* Assume the function InitListMutex is called before */

   mutex_lock (&ListMutex);

   /* Critical Section of Code */
   pnewEntry->next = gpListHead;
   gpListHead = pnewEntry;

   mutex_unlock (&ListMutex);
}
```

7.4.8 Recursive mutexes

Recursive mutexes are used in situations where a thread that owns a mutex calls another function that needs to lock the same mutex. The reader is advised to read Sec. 3.2.9 for a detailed description of recursive mutexes. Sometimes there is a *need* for recursive mutexes, and recursive mutexes can be built easily using the primitives without much overhead. Operating systems such as Unixware 2.0 have implemented recursive mutexes, but they are not available on all systems implementing UI threads. Even POSIX.1c does *not* support recursive mutexes.

In the standard threads implementations, deadlock can happen if the owner of the mutex tries to acquire the same locked mutex. The following section of the code shows one possible implementation of *recursive* mutexes without using the UI recursive mutexes. The routine RMutexInit should be called only once. When the maximum recursion count passed to RMutexInit is 1, then it does not act as a recursive mutex. Note that this routine can be called to prevent or detect mutex deadlocks. Warning: This code makes certain assumptions about memory sharing, and might not work on certain SMP processors (see file `mthrmutx.c` on disk).

```
typedef struct _recurmutex
{
   int        lockCnt;
   int        maxRecursion;
   thread_t   mutexOwner;
   mutex_t    mutex;
} RECURSIVE_MUTEX;

int
RMutexInit (RECURSIVE_MUTEX *prmutex, int maxRecursion)
{
   prmutex->Lockcnt = 0;

   /* you should set it to a reasonably high number */
   prmutex->MaxRecusion = maxRecursion;

   mutex_init (&prmutex->mutex, USYNC_THREAD, NULL);
}

int
RMutexLock (RECURSIVE_MUTEX *prmutex)
{
   thread_t myself;

   myself = thr_self ();

   if (prmutex->lockCnt && prmutex->mutexOwner == = myself)
   {
        if (prmutex->lockCnt = = prmutex->maxRecursion)
        {
            fprintf(stderr, "Failure to lock mutex: max recursion count
            reached \n");
            return(-1);
        }
        /* will not work on certain SMP processors */
        ++prmutex->lockCnt; /* increment lock count */
        return (prmutex->lockCnt); /* return the count */
   }
```

```
    mutex_lock (&prmutex->mutex); /* wait for lock */

    prmutex->lockCnt = 1;
    prmutex->mutexOwner = myself;

    return (prmutex->lockCnt);
}

int
RMutexUnlock (RECURSIVE_MUTEX *prmutex)
{
    thread_t myself;

    myself = thr_self ();

    if (prmutex->mutexOwner != myself) /* not owner of mutex */
        return(-1);

    --prmutex->lockCnt; /* decrement lock count */
    /* should reset the owner field to 0 /*
    if (!prmutex->lockCnt)
        mutex_unlock (&prmutex->mutex);

    return (prmutex->lockCnt);
}
```

7.4.9 UI recursive mutexes

UI threads provide recursive mutexes that can be used for interprocess or interthread mutex synchronization needs. The UI threads library uses the data type *rmutex_t* to identify recursive mutexes. The functions are similar in use and syntax to the nonrecursive counterparts. The only *difference* is that these functions operate on the rmutex_t data type instead of mutex_t. Since these functions might not be implemented on all platforms, one should use them with caution (e.g., Solaris 2.5 does not implement these functions). Note also that POSIX.1c does *not* implement recursive mutexes.

rmutex_init	Initializes a recursive mutex
rmutex_destroy	Deletes a recursive mutex
rmutex_lock	Locks a recursive mutex
rmutex_trylock	Conditionally locks a recursive mutex
rmutex_unlock	Unlocks a recursive mutex

7.4.10 Mutexes, deadlocks, and priority inversion

In a multithreaded application when you are dealing with multiple mutexes, deadlock can happen. Similarly, some applications might be affected by priority inversion. The topics of deadlock and priority inversion are explained in detail in Secs. 3.3 and 3.4. Since UI threads do not address the issue of priority inversion directly, you would have to build your own priority locks. For example, if one would like to implement the POSIX priority-inheritance protocol, then one could use thr_setpriority to alter priorities of threads.

7.4.11 Guidelines for using mutex

- Always use global or dynamic variables for storing mutex identifiers. Do not try to use stack variables for mutexes because the stack of a thread is destroyed when the thread terminates. Other threads in the process can still be referencing the mutex, and the address of the mutex identifier is invalid after the stack is destroyed.
- Initialize the mutex before using it, and initialize it only once so that all threads have the same view of the mutex. Statically initialize mutexes whenever possible.
- Delete mutexes after they are no longer used.
- Avoid locking the mutex in a recursive fashion unless you have implemented your own recursive mutex.
- While locking multiple mutexes simultaneously, be sure that all threads acquire the locks in the same order to avoid deadlocks.
- Lock mutexes for a short time. Keep the critical section of code small, and avoid any blocking operation (I/O, another synchronization lock) inside the critical section.
- Do not use mutex locks excessively. Excessive synchronization will cause performance problems, and you will tend to lose one of the foremost benefits of multithreading, which is concurrent execution of threads. If all threads reference the shared data in *read-only* mode, then there is no need to serialize access to this piece of shared data.
- If your application runs slower on a multiprocessor machine than on a uniprocessor machine, it is very likely that your application is suffering because of excessive locking.

7.5 Spinlocks

Spinlocks can be employed wherever mutexes are used, but unlike mutexes, threads *spin* in a loop busy waiting when the lock is acquired by some other thread. There are some cases where the use of spinlocks can be justified. When the overhead of suspending and resuming a thread is higher than the time a thread would spend spinning (busy wait) on the mutex, then the use of spinlocks should be considered. It is not a good idea to use spinlocks on uniprocessor machines, and the use of spinlocks on uniprocessor machines might even cause a deadlock. Remember, spinlocks can be helpful for short sections of the code, but they also can burn expensive CPU cycles.

Spinlocks in UI threads are represented by the data type *spin_t*. Spinlocks are nonrecursive and can only be used by threads within a process. The spinlock must first be initialized using the _spin_init function before it can be used. Spinlocks can be acquired either by calling the _spin_lock or _spin_trylock function. In the case of _spin_trylock, the function returns immediately if the lock is held by some other thread. Spinlocks must be unlocked by calling the _spin_unlock function.

`_spin_init`	Initializes a spinlock
`_spin_destroy`	Deletes a spinlock
`_spin_lock`	Locks a spinlock
`_spin_trylock`	Conditionally locks a spinlock
`_spin_unlock`	Unlocks a spinlock

Chapter

8

UNIX International Thread Synchronization

8.1 Event Synchronization

Consider a boss/worker thread model in which the boss thread puts new work items on a work queue and worker threads dequeue new work items from the queue. It is assumed that the threads use a mutex to guard the work queue while the actual enqueue/dequeue operation happens. The question that arises then is: "How can the worker threads know when a new work item has been placed on the queue?" The worker threads can:

- Continuously check the work queue for arrival of new work items.
- Poll the work queue at specified intervals for arrival of new work items.
- Wait on the work queue for new items until the boss thread notifies the worker thread that a new work item has been placed on the work queue.

The first two methods are extremely inefficient when it comes to CPU utilization, while the last option provides the *best* solution. In this case, the worker thread is suspended when there are no work items on the queue and is only woken up when a new work item is placed on the queue. This form of event synchronization is the most efficient and highly desirable in a multithreaded environment. In the UI threads library, *condition variables* are used for event notification and synchronization. It is inefficient to use global flags or shared variables to enforce event synchronization.

8.1.1 Condition variable functions

`cond_init`	Creates a condition variable
`cond_destroy`	Destroys a condition variable
`cond_wait`	Waits for a condition (blocking)
`cond_timedwait`	Waits for a condition (timeout)
`cond_signal`	Signals a condition
`cond_broadcast`	Broadcasts a condition

8.1.2 Condition variables

Condition variables (CVs) are yet another kind of synchronization object used for event synchronization. CVs allow threads to block until a particular condition is satisfied and are most useful when multiple threads coordinate together to solve a task. State change of a variable (condition) can be signaled to one or more threads at the same time.

The question that can be asked is: "Why can't mutexes be used to wait until a particular condition is true?" The answer is simple: It is inefficient in terms of CPU utilization. Condition variables are used whenever the thread has to wait for *longer* periods on a specified condition. Mutexes, on the other hand, are used for implementing critical sections of code where locks are generally held for a *short* time. Condition variables should never be used for serializing access to some shared data.

Condition variables are used along with a mutex and a boolean variable (condition predicate). The three objects used together for event notification are:

- A *condition expression* to indicate whether the condition is met (e.g., X < 15 && Y > 12).
- A *condition variable* (CV) to wait for the condition.
- A *mutex variable* to synchronize the access to the condition expression.

Condition variables always should be used in conjunction with mutexes. The thread *locks* the mutex and then checks if the condition expression is in the desired state. The state is defined by a boolean variable called a *predicate.* If the condition expression is not in the desired state, then the thread *waits* on the CV associated with the predicate. The mutex is released automatically when a thread waits on a CV. The automaticity of the release and wait operation ensures that no other thread can change the predicate between the operations. It is important to release the mutex because some other thread will lock the mutex before setting the condition expression to the desired state.

When the other thread sets the predicate to the desired state, it then signals the CV. The thread *relocks* the mutex after coming of out the wait, since a return from the wait does not guarantee that the predicate is true or false. The thread that is woken up reexamines the predicate, since more than one thread can be woken up when the condition is broadcasted and the predicate can still be false when it resumes execution after the wait.

8.1.3 Creating condition variables

UI threads use the data type *cond_t* to identify condition variables (CVs). A condition variable has to be initialized before it can be used for event notification.

```
int cond_init (cond_t *condition, int type, void *arg)
```

The function cond_init initializes the CV pointed to by *cond*. The *type* of the CV can be either USYNC_THREAD or USYNC_PROCESS. CVs of type USYNC_THREAD can only be shared by threads within a process, while USYNC_PROCESS CVs can be used for interprocess event synchronization. The third argument *arg* is reserved for future use and always should be passed as NULL. Do *not* initialize a CV more than once or when some other thread is using it.

A CV can be initialized statically by zero filling the CV, in which case the cond_init function does not have to be called. Static initialization guarantees that the CV will be initialized *once* even before any thread starts execution.

```
InitializeCondition ()
{
   cond_t cond;

   cond = DEFAULTCV; /* on Solaris */

         or

   cond = calloc(1, sizeof(cond_t)); /* call free after cond_destroy */

         or

   cond_init(&Cond, NULL, NULL);

}
```

8.1.4 Destroying condition variables

```
int cond_destroy (cond_t cond)
```

The function cond_destroy is used to invalidate a previously initialized condition variable identified by *cond*. This routine should be called when *cond* is no longer referenced. Deleting a CV allows all the resources associated with that CV to be reclaimed. When a thread is waiting on a CV and the CV is deleted, then the function cond_destroy returns EBUSY. It is a programming error to delete a CV while some other thread is still referencing it.

8.1.5 Wait for a condition variable

```
int cond_wait (cond_t *cond, mutex_t *mutex)
```

The function *cond_wait* causes the thread to be suspended until the condition variable *cond* is signaled. This function must be called only when the mutex is *locked* by the calling thread. The *mutex* is released automatically, and the thread blocks on the condition variable. When the wait on the condition variable is satisfied, then the lock on the mutex variable *mutex* is reacquired automatically. When multiple threads are woken up as a result of some thread calling cond_broadcast, then these threads contend for the mutex lock.

Note that if the condition is never signaled, then the thread will block *indefinitely* on the condition variable. The following code segment shows a typical use of waiting on condition variables.

```
mutex_t conditionMutex = DEFAULTMUTEX;
cond_t  conditionVariable = DEFAULTCV;
int     conditionExpression;
WaitForcondition ()
{
    mutex_lock (&conditionMutex);

    while (conditionExpression = = FALSE)
           cond_wait (&conditionVariable, &conditionMutex);

    /* do something */

    mutex_unlock (&conditionMutex);
}
```

8.1.5.1 Timed wait for a condition variable

```
int cond_timedwait (cond_t *cond, mutex_t *mutex, struct timespec *abstime)
```

The function cond_timedwait is similar to cond_wait except that the wait on the condition variable *cond* is canceled after the time period specified by *abstime*. The function acquires the mutex even when it returns the timeout error ETIME.

It is *important* to check the condition expression again even on a successful return from cond_wait or cond_timedwait. A successful return from either of these functions does *not* guarantee that the predicate is either true or false. In case of timeout, there is a race condition between the expiration of the timeout and predicate change, and it is possible that the predicate will be true even though the function timed out. It is recommended that a while loop (as shown above) always should be executed for checking the predicate and waiting on the condition variable.

```
TimedWaitForCondition (time_t seconds)
{
   struct abstime timeout;
   int            ret;

   timeout.tv_sec = time(NULL) + seconds; /* timeout in seconds */
   timeout.tv_nsec = 0;

   mutex_lock (&conditionMutex);

   while (conditionExpression = = FALSE)
   {
         ret = cond_wait (&conditionVariable, &conditionMutex, &timeout);
         if (ret = = ETIME)
         {
             fprintf(stderr, "condition wait timed out...\n);
             mutex_unlock(&conditionMutex);
             return(-1);
         }
   }

   /* do something */

   mutex_unlock (&conditionMutex);
}
```

8.1.6 Signal a condition variable

```
int cond_signal (cond_t *cond)
```

The function cond_signal is used to wake up a thread that is currently waiting on the condition variable *cond*. When multiple threads are waiting on a condition variable, then only one of them is woken up, and the rest continue to wait on the condition variable. The scheduling policy and the priority of the threads determine which thread is woken up. It is safe to assume that there is no *defined* order in which blocked threads are unblocked. Ownership of the mutex lock is granted to the thread that is woken up. If no thread is waiting on the condition variable, then the threads library does not *save* the condition signaling. This means that the next thread calling cond_wait will block.

The following code segment shows a typical condition signal logic.

```
mutex_t  conditionMutex = DEFAULTMUTEX;
cond_t   conditionVariable = DEFAULTCV;
int      conditionExpression;

SignalCondition ()
{
    mutex_lock (&conditionMutex);

    conditionExpression = = TRUE;
```

```
    cond_signal (&conditionVariable);

    mutex_unlock (&conditionMutex);
}
```

8.1.7 Broadcast a condition variable

```
int cond_broadcast (cond_t *cond)
```

The function cond_broadcast is similar to cond_signal function except that multiple threads blocked on the CV *cond* are notified of the change in the state of the desired condition expression.

```
mutex_t  conditionMutex;
cond_t   conditionVariable;
int      conditionExpression;

BroadcastCondition ()
{
   mutex_lock (&conditionMutex);

   conditionExpression = TRUE;

   cond_broadcast (&conditionVariable);

   mutex_unlock (&conditionMutex);
}
```

Let us now consider the role of a CV in a boss/worker queue model. In this case, worker threads wait on a work queue (wait on CV) for new work items to be added by a server. When the server adds a new item, then it has two choices: It can either wake up *one* worker thread or it can wake up *all* the workers. Even when multiple workers are woken up, only one of them will dequeue a work item, since only one work item was added by the server. In this case it makes sense to use cond_signal; the server, after adding a new work item, will wake up the first thread waiting on the queue to dequeue a work item. Generally, when a *single* thread has to be notified of the state change, then cond_signal is used.

Readers are advised to read Sec. 3.9 to understand the issues of race conditions and the lost wakeup problem. While reading the sections, replace all Pthreads function calls with UI threads functions (they are identical).

8.1.8 Guidelines for using condition variables

- Always use global or static variables for CVs. Do not try to use stack variables for CVs because the stack of a thread is destroyed when the thread terminates. Other threads in the process can still be referencing the CV even though the address of the CV is invalid after stack destruction.

- Initialize the CV before using it, and initialize it only once such that all threads have the same view of the CV.
- Delete a CV after it is no longer used.
- Associate a condition predicate with your CV.
- Always check the condition predicate after returning from the CV wait functions (use it in a while loop).
- When the wait functions (cond_wait or condtimed_wait) return, the mutex is locked. It is important to unlock the mutex after using a CV.

8.2 Barriers

A *barrier* is a synchronization point in a program where threads wait to synchronize with each other. It is used to ensure that cooperating threads have reached a synchronization point (SP) before they can proceed to the next step. Threads wait until the last thread reaches the synchronization point and are woken up when the last thread reaches the SP. Barriers are part of the SVR4/MP thread but are not implemented on Solaris or POSIX.1c. The reader is advised to see Sec. 9.3 on how to implement barriers using a mutex and condition variables. The SVR4/MP barrier *functions* are barrier_init, barrier_wait, and barrier_destroy.

> If *portability* is of concern, then keep in mind that POSIX.1c does not implement barriers, but it is possible to develop a barrier primitive using POSIX.1c mutex and condition variables.

8.3 Semaphore Functions

`sema_init`	Initializes a semaphore
`sema_destroy`	Destroys a semaphore
`sema_wait`	Waits on a semaphore
`sema_trywait`	Conditionally waits on a semaphore
`sema_post`	Posts a semaphore

8.3.1 Semaphores

Semaphores are used to enforce mutual exclusion and for coordinating events. Counting semaphores were invented by a Dutch professor named Edsger Dijsktra. These semaphores have a count associated with them; the count can be incremented to any high value but can only be decremented to zero. The value of the counting semaphore can never be less than zero. The *post* (*verhogen* in Dutch) operation increments the semaphore count, while the *wait* (*proberen* in Dutch) decrements the semaphore count.

UI threads implement counting semaphores and have an integer count associated with them. When a process *waits* on a semaphore and the count is greater than zero, then the process acquires the semaphore. The integer count is decremented as a result of acquiring the semaphore. When the count associated with the semaphore becomes zero, then the process blocks on the wait operation until the integer count is incremented as a result of the *post* operation by some other process. The count associated with a semaphore can never be less than zero. When a process posts a semaphore, then the semaphore count is incremented, and any thread waiting to acquire the semaphore is notified.

Counting semaphores are *useful* in restricting access to a shared resource but not necessarily in a mutually exclusive manner. You can think of a semaphore as a gate through which a variable number of threads can pass simultaneously. The maximum number of threads entering the gate can be limited, and the gate remains open as long as there are resources available. When the number of resources reaches the maximum limit, then the gate is closed and is reopened *only* when resources are freed.

> If *portability* is of concern, then keep in mind that POSIX.1c does not implement semaphores, but it is possible to develop a semaphore primitive using POSIX.1c mutex and condition variables. Binary semaphores are implemented as a part of POSIX.1b.

8.3.2 Initializing a semaphore

Just like any synchronization object, semaphores have to be created before they can be used by the threads in a process. Semaphores are defined by the data type *sema_t*.

```
int sema_init (sema_t *sem_loc, int sema_cnt, int type, void *arg)
```

The function sema_init initializes the semaphore pointed by *sema*. The second argument *sema_cnt* is the count associated with the semaphore, and it is generally initialized to the number of available resources. One can initialize the sema_cnt to zero, in which case no instance of the resource is available for use. This is generally done during some initialization phase, after which all instances of the resource are made available by calling the function sema_post.

The *type* of the semaphore can be either USYNC_THREAD or USYNC_PROCESS. Semaphores of type USYNC_THREAD can only be shared by threads within a process, while USYNC_PROCESS semaphores can be used for interprocess event synchronization. The last argument *arg* is reserved for future use and always should be passed as NULL. Do *not* initialize a semaphore more than once or when some other thread is using it.

A semaphore can be initialized statically by zero filling, in which case the sema_init function does not have to be called. Static initialization of a semaphore guarantees that the semaphore will be initialized *once* even before any thread starts execution.

```
InitializeSemaphore ()
{
   sema_t sema;

   sema = DEFAULTSEMA; /* on Solaris */
         or
   sema = calloc(1, sizeof(sema_t)); /* call free after sema_destroy */
         or
   sema_init(&sema, NULL, NULL);
}
```

8.3.3 Destroying a semaphore

When a semaphore is not needed, it can be destroyed to free up all resources used by the system. The function sema_destroy is used to delete a previously created semaphore identified by *sema*. Do not destroy semaphores when other threads are still referencing it.

```
int sema_destroy (sema_t *sema)
```

8.3.4 Wait on a semaphore

Threads must acquire a semaphore before using a shared resource that is protected by a semaphore. The function sema_wait is used to acquire a semaphore identified by *sema*. If the semaphore count associated with sema is greater than zero, then the wait is successful, and the semaphore count is decremented by one. A successful return from sema_wait guarantees that at least one instance of the shared resource is available. If the count is nonzero, then the wait operation *blocks* until some other thread or process increments the semaphore count. A nonblocking version of the function is implemented as sema_trywait, which returns EBUSY when the semaphore identified by *sema* cannot be acquired.

```
int sema_wait (sema_t *sema)

int sema_trywait (sema_t *sema)
```

8.3.5 Post a semaphore

After using the shared resource, threads must release the semaphore guarding the resource or else other threads cannot access the resource. The function sema_post is used to release a semaphore identified by *sema*. When a thread releases (posts) a semaphore, the semaphore count is incremented by one. If there are threads waiting for the semaphore to be released, then one of them is woken up. If the semaphore is acquired multiple times, then the semaphore *must* be released for each instance of the resource.

Unlike mutex locks, ownership is not tracked with semaphores, which means that the thread that acquired the semaphore does *not* have to be the thread that releases the semaphore.

```
int sema_post (sema_t *sema)
```

The following code segment illustrates the use of semaphores for the shared buffers example that we discussed early in this chapter. Two semaphores bufEmpty and bufFull are used by the producer and consumer threads to control access to the shared buffer. Assume that the routine InitSemaphores is called before either thread begins executing.

```
sema_t  bufEmpty;
sema_t  bufFull;

InitSemaphores()
{
   sema_init(&bufEmpty, 1, USYNC_THREAD, NULL);
   sema_init(&bufFull, 0, USYNC_THREAD, NULL); /* none available */
}

Producers()
{
   sema_wait(&bufEmpty);
   Produce();
   sema_post(&bufFull);
}

Consumers()
{
   sema_wait(&bufFull);
   Consume();
   sema_post(&bufEmpty);
}
```

8.4 Reader/Writer Locks

`rwlock_init`	Initializes a reader/writer lock
`rw_rdlock`	Locks a reader/writer lock in read mode
`rw_tryrdlock`	Conditionally locks a reader/writer lock in read mode
`rw_wrlock`	Locks a reader/writer lock in write mode
`rw_trywrlock`	Conditionally locks a reader/writer lock in write mode
`rw_unlock`	Unlocks a reader/writer lock
`rw_destroy`	Destroys a reader/writer lock

In certain applications, data are read much more frequently than they are modified. From an efficiency point of view, it does not make sense to lock data when multiple threads are reading data; locking should only be enforced when the data can be updated. Reader/writer (RW) lock allows multiple threads to read data simultaneously but serializes writers when data have to be updated. UI threads support RW locks with concurrent read access and exclusive write access. An RW lock can be locked in either read mode or in write mode.

One of the main advantages of reader/writer locks over mutex locks is that they allow multiple threads to share data in read mode without the overhead of locking. RW locks are better when the frequency of read operations is higher than that of write operations and the read operations are somewhat lengthy.

> If *portability* is of concern, then keep in mind that POSIX.1c does not implement reader/writer locks, but it is possible to develop a reader/writer lock primitive using POSIX.1c mutex and condition variables.

8.4.1 Creating reader/writer locks

RW locks have to be initialized before they can be used for synchronization. The UI threads library uses the data type *rwlock_t* to identify reader/writer locks.

```
int rwlock_init (rwlock_t *rwlock, int type, void *arg)
```

The function rwlock_init initializes the RW lock pointed by *rwlock,* and the initial state of the lock is UNLOCKED. The *type* of the lock can be either USYNC_THREAD or USYNC_PROCESS. RW locks of type USYNC_THREAD can only be shared by threads within a process, while locks of type USYNC_PROCESS can be used for interprocess synchronization. The third argument *arg* is reserved for future use and always should be passed as NULL. Do *not* initialize an RW lock more than once or when some other thread is using it.

An RW lock can be initialized statically by zero filling, in which case the rwlock_init function does not have to be called. Static initialization of RW locks, guarantees that the RW locks will be initialized *once* even before any thread starts execution.

```
InitializeRWLock()
{
   rwlock_t rwLock;

   rwLock = DEFAULTRWLOCK; /* on Solaris */
        or
   rwLock = calloc(1, sizeof(rwlock_t));
        or
   rwlock_init(&rwLock, NULL, NULL);
}
```

8.4.2 Destroying reader/writer locks

When an RW lock is not needed, it can be destroyed to free up all resources used by the system. The function rwlock_destroy is used to delete a previously created RW lock identified by *rwlock*. Do not destroy a lock when other threads are still referencing it.

```
int rwlock_destroy(rwlock_t *rwlock)
```

8.4.3 Lock a reader/writer lock in read mode

```
int rw_rdlock(rwlock_t *rwlock)
int rw_tryrdlock(rwlock_t *rwlock)
```

Threads must call the function rw_rdlock when they want to acquire the lock identified by *rwlock* in read mode. When a thread requests an RW lock in read mode and some other thread holds the lock in write mode, then the calling thread is suspended until the lock is released. If *no* thread holds the lock in write mode or no other thread is blocked on a lock request in write mode, then the calling thread acquires the lock irrespective of the number of read locks. The nonblocking version of the function returns EBUSY when the lock cannot be acquired in read mode.

8.4.4 Lock a reader/writer lock in write mode

```
int rw_wrlock(rwlock_t *rwlock)
int rw_trywrlock(rwlock_t *rwlock)
```

Threads must call the function rw_wrlock when they want to acquire the lock identified by *rwlock* in write mode. When a thread requests an RW lock in write mode, the lock will only be granted if *no* other thread holds the lock either in read or write mode. This means that the caller will hold the lock exclusively in write mode. When the lock is held in read or write mode by some other thread, the caller blocks until it can acquire the lock exclusively. The nonblocking version of the function returns EBUSY when the lock cannot be acquired in write mode.

A request for a lock in write mode is given *higher* preference than a request for a lock in read mode to prevent *starvation* of writers. When a lock is held in read mode and a request for a write lock is made, then all further read lock requests block until the write lock is granted to the thread requesting the lock in write mode.

The following code segment shows how readers and writers use RW locks to access a shared data structure. It is assumed that the routine RWLockInit is called once before the readers and writers start executing.

```
rwlock_t   rwLock;

InitRWLock()
{
   rwlock_init(&rwLock, USYNC_THREAD, NULL);
}

Readers()
{
   rw_rdlock(&rwLock);
   /* read the shared data structure */
   rw_unlock(&rwLock);
}

Writers()
{
   rw_wrlock(&rwLock);
   /* update the shared data structure */
   rw_unlock(&rwLock);
}
```

8.5 Choosing the Right Synchronization Object

The reader is advised to read Sec. 3.13 for more information on choosing the correct synchronization primitive. Reader/writer locks should be used only if the frequency of read operations on the entity locked by the RW lock is much more than the frequency of the write operations on the entity. Personally, I found mutexes to be the simplest, followed by semaphores, reader/writer locks, and lastly condition variables.

8.6 Thread-Specific Data

In a multithreaded application it is often required to create variables whose scope is nonglobal. There are two ways that threads can create data items whose scope is limited to a single thread. Threads can use either stack or local variables. The scope of such variables is limited to the routine in which the variable is declared. The usefulness of local variables is sometimes *limited* when these variables have to be made accessible across function calls. In a single-threaded process, the C language keyword *extern* is used to make global variables accessible across function calls. If a multithreaded application wants the same data to be maintained on a per-thread basis across function calls, then global variables *cannot* be used. What is really needed is a per-thread global variable that is accessible across function calls. The reader is advised to read Secs. 4.1 and 4.2 for more information on thread-specific data (TSD).

UI threads provide a scheme similar to POSIX threads and use a key for storing/retrieving per-thread data. To store data on a per-thread basis, the application must first create a key and then use the set/get routines to store or retrieve thread-specific data. Threads in the process use the same key, but they set and get different TSD values.

TSD Functions

`thr_keycreate`	Creates a TSD key
`thr_key_delete`	Deletes a TSD key
`thr_setspecific`	Sets a TSD associated with a specific key
`thr_getspecific`	Gets a TSD associated with a specific key

8.6.1 Creating a key

Thread-specific keys must be created before threads can use them to bind thread-specific data. The key is used to maintain association between thread and data. The key can be used by multiple threads, and a thread can bind values to multiple keys. Each thread binds a unique value to the key that is usually an address of a dynamically allocated variable.

```
int thr_keycreate (thread_key_t *key, void * (*destructor_routine) (void *))
```

The function thr_key_create is used to create a new *key* accessible to all threads within a process. When the key has to be shared by more than one thread within the process, then it is *important* to store the key identifier in a global or static variable. When a new key is created, then the TSD value is set to a value of NULL for *all* existing threads in the process. Whenever a thread is created afterwards, the TSD value for the thread is set to NULL for *all* keys in the process. The TSD value associated with a key remains NULL unless the thread binds a new value to the key.

When multiple threads use a key to maintain per-thread context, then it is important to create the key only once. The key can be created once, either by creating the key before any thread starts using it or by creating the key in the one-time initialization routine. It is a programming error to create the same key multiple times.

Destructor routines optionally can be associated with thread-specific keys and are called when the thread terminates normally. If a TSD value is a dynamically allocated variable, then these routines can be used to deallocate the thread-specific data when the thread terminates. Destructor routines are called *only* when a non-NULL value is bound to the key. When the destructor routine is called, then the current TSD value associated with a key is passed to it. Multiple keys can have either the same destructor routine or each key can have its own destructor routine. When multiple keys with their own destructor routines exist in an application, then the order in which these destructor routines are called at thread termination is unspecified.

8.6.2 Get value from a key

```
int thr_getspecific (thread_key_t key, void **value)
```

The function thr_getspecific is used to get a TSD *value* associated with a valid *key*. If no value was bound previously to the key, then a value of NULL is returned.

```
thread_key_t threadKey;

CreateKey()
{
   thr_keycreate(&threadKey, free);
}

GetThreadData ()
{
   void *threadBuffer;

   thr_getspecific (threadKey, &threadBuffer); /* assume CreateKey is called */
   if (ThreadBuffer = = NULL)
       printf ("No value set by thread \n");
}
```

8.6.3 Set value to a key

```
int thr_setspecific (thread_key_t key, void *value)
```

The function thr_setspecific is used to set a TSD *value* associated with a *key*. The value bound to the key is maintained by the threads library as long as the thread exists, assuming that the thread does not bind a new value to the key. Since TSD value is a void pointer, any kind of data can be stored (e.g., a pointer to a structure or pointer to a string). It is a bad programming practice to cast integer values to void pointers. Usually, the value is the address of a dynamically allocated variable, as shown below. Note that if a value 0 is bound to a key, then the destructor function will not run when the thread terminates.

```
thread_key_t threadKey;
SetThreadData ()
{
   char *threadBuffer;

   threadBuffer = malloc (....):
   thr_setspecific (ThreadKey, threadBuffer);
}
```

The reader is advised to read Sec. 4.2.6 to learn more about potential problems with keys and Sec. 4.2.7 for information on using TSD to write thread-safe functions.

8.7 Threads and Signals

In a single-threaded process, signals often are used to send notification between processes. In a multithreaded process, there might be multiple threads sending or receiving signals. Signals are a process resource and are installed on a *per-process basis*. This means that a signal handler that is installed for a thread is installed for all threads in the process.

In a single-threaded process, when a signal arrives, the current execution activity of the process is interrupted and the signal handler starts executing. On return from the signal handler, the process resumes execution at the location where it was interrupted. In a threaded environment, the issue of signals becomes more complex, especially when it is not clear *which* thread is interrupted when a signal is received. This depends on the *type* of the signal that is received.

In a multithreaded program, the signal-handling mechanism is different for synchronous and asynchronous signals. Synchronous signals (SIGFPE, SIGBUS) are delivered to the faulting thread, and multiple threads can handle the same synchronous signal at the same time. The mechanism for asynchronous signals is different and involves much more detail.

Signal handlers are installed on a *per-process basis,* which means that there is only one handler routine for a given signal. The handler is executed when the signal is received in any thread. If more than one thread is interested in receiving the signal, then only one of the threads will receive the signal. Which one? The thread that will receive the signal in such a case is *unspecified.* If two threads install different signal handlers for the same signal, then the signal handler registered by the last thread is used. The application should *always* use the function sigaction to install signal handlers in a threaded process. The reader is advised to read Sec. 4.6 for a more detailed description of signals in a threaded environment.

8.7.1 Thread signal mask

```
int thr_sigsetmask(int how, sigset_t *newset, sigset_t *oldset)
```

Signal masks are maintained on a *per-thread basis*. The function *thr_sigsetmask* is used to install a per-thread signal mask. When a thread blocks a signal from delivery, it does not block the signal delivery in other threads. The function sigprocmask should *never* be used in a multithreaded application for masking signals. The function thr_sigsetmask is identical in use to sigprocmask, except that it registers signal masks on a per-thread basis. The function thr_sigsetmask can be used to install signal masks in a thread and can be used to block and unblock signals. When a thread is created, it inherits the signal mask of the creating thread.

8.7.2 Sending signal to a thread

In a POSIX.1 environment it is possible to use the system call *kill* to send a signal to another process. Similarly, it is possible for one thread to send a signal to another thread within the same process, although one would seriously question this use in a threaded application.

```
int thr_kill (thread_t thread, int sig)
```

The function thread_kill sends the signal *sig* to the *thread* within the same process. If the target thread has blocked the signal from delivery, then the signal is set pending in the *thread* until it unblocks the signal from delivery. The signal should be a valid signal number; if the signal number specified by sig is 0, then no signal is actually sent, but just error checking is performed. This is similar to the POSIX.1 *kill* system call.

When the target thread is blocked on some system call and the signal *sig* is delivered to it, then the function fails and returns EINTR. Applications must be designed to handle this condition. All blocking thread functions return EINTR when they are interrupted by a signal. Check the vendor's documentation for a list of thread functions that can be called safely from the signal handler. When the target thread receives the signal, the signal handler (if any) is invoked in the context of the target thread. If a signal is sent to a suspended thread, then the signal is held pending until the target thread is resumed.

8.7.3 Waiting for signals synchronously

In a threaded process it is better to convert asynchronous signals to synchronous signals. The asynchronous signal delivery can be converted to a synchronous one by waiting for the signals to arrive at well-defined points. The well-defined point where threads must wait for signals to be delivered is at the function *sigwait*. Threads should not use the function sigaction to install signal handlers for asynchronous signals when they intend to wait for signals synchronously using sigwait.

Threads should *never* wait for synchronous signals such as SIGILL, SIGTRAP, SIGIOT, SIGEMT, SIGFPE, SIGBUS, SIGSEGV, SIGSYS, and SIGPIPE. Keep in mind that the signals SIGKILL and SIGSTOP cannot be caught by sigwait.

```
int sigwait (sigset_t *set)
```

The function sigwait can be used by a thread to wait for asynchronous signals. The first argument *set* specifies the signal mask. The thread must specify all signals to wait for in the argument *set*. The signals that are masked in *set* must be *blocked* before the thread calls sigwait. The function blocks until one of the signals currently masked in *set* arrives. When a signal arrives, the function sigwait unblocks, and the signal number is returned as the function return value.

If multiple threads call sigwait concurrently, then only one thread will be woken up when the signal arrives. This order of waking threads is *undefined* and is implementation-dependent. It is a good idea to have one dedicated thread calling sigwait on behalf of all threads.

Before a thread can call sigwait it must block all signals that it wants to receive. The following code illustrates how a dedicated thread can wait for signals to arrive. The term *sigwaiter* thread is commonly used for the dedicated thread-handling signals. In our example, the thread is only interested in receiving signals SIGUSR1 and SIGUSR2.

```
SigWaiterThread ()
{
   sigset_t  newSet;
   sigset_t  oldSet;
   int       sigReceived;

   sigemptyset (&newSet);

   sigaddset (SIGUSR1, &newSet);
   sigaddset (SIGUSR2, &newSet);

   thr_sigsetmask (SIG_BLOCK, &newSet, NULL);

   sigReceived = sigwait (&newSet);

   switch (sigReceived)
   {
     case SIGUSR1:
           /* handle SIGUSR1*/
           break;
     case SIGUSR2:
           /* handle SIGUSR2*/
           break;
     default:
           printf ("not expecting any signals\n");
           thr_exit(NULL);
   }
}
```

8.7.4 Guidelines for using signals in a multithreaded process

- Signals are a per-process resource (e.g., SIGALRM). Currently, signals are a per-LWP resource (e.g., Solaris), but this might change soon.
- Always use sigwait to wait for asynchronous signals, and do not block synchronous signals when calling sigwait.
- Threads should block all asynchronous signals they want to receive before calling sigwait.

- Do not use sigaction to install a signal handler, and also wait for the same signal synchronously using sigwait.
- Never use sigprocmask in a multithreaded process.
- Never use an alarm timer simultaneously in multiple threads.
- Always block unwanted signals in threads that are not interested in receiving them.
- The signal handler routine should be reentrant if multiple threads can call the handler routine concurrently. Also, do not call non-async-safe functions from the signal handler.
- Many thread functions are non-signal-safe and therefore should not be called from signal handlers.

8.8 Differences Between Pthreads and UI Threads

Migrating applications from UI threads to POSIX threads should be a simple affair, and only some minor adjustments need to be made. The main differences between Pthreads and UI threads are:

- No thread attributes objects in UI threads. The flags of UI threads are similar to the Pthreads attributes.
- No explicit concurrency control of LWPs in Pthreads.
- No daemon threads in Pthreads.
- No suspend/resume in Pthreads. If you are creating threads in suspended state and then initializing some state for the new thread, then it is possible to use condition variables for the same purpose.
- No pthread_once in UI threads, but it can be implemented using static mutexes.
- No thread cancellation in UI threads.
- Pthreads does not implement semaphores and reader/writer locks, but they can be implemented using the standard Pthreads synchronization primitives.
- No priority inversion mechanism in UI threads.

Chapter

9

UI Programming Examples

9.1 Compiling and Linking

Every program that uses the threads library should include the header files *thread.h* and *synch.h*. The compiler and linker options depend on the operating system. The compiler and linker options for some of the platforms are listed below.

Solaris 2.5

```
cc -D_REENTRANT foo.c -o foo -lthread
```

UNIXWARE 2.0

```
cc -D_REENTRANT foo.c -o foo -Kthread -ldl -lthread
```

9.2 Queue Implementation

Queues are a simple yet powerful interthread communication paradigm. Queues can be used effectively in applications that use worker threads to service clients. Threads, instead of waiting on semaphores or condition variables, can wait on queues for work items to be added. It should be noted that threads that use queues for servicing requests are much easier to program and test. UI threads do not provide a standard queue mechanism, but can be easily implemented using condition variables and mutexes. Queues can also be implemented by using the POSIX.1b semaphores and mutexes. The reader is advised to see Sec. 16.2 for a queue implementation using WIN32 counting semaphores.

```
#include <thread.h>
#include <synch.h>
#include <stdio.h>

typedef struct _qmsg QMSG;
struct _qmsg
{
   void  *msg;
   int   msgLen;
   QMSG  *next;
};

typedef struct _queue
{
   int      qMsgs;
   int      qMax;
   mutex_t qMutex;
   cond_t  qEmpty;
   cond_t  qFull;
   QMSG     *qHeadMsg;
   QMSG     *qTailMsg;
} QUEUE;

QUEUE   gQueue;

main(int argc, char **argv)
{
   int        numThreads;
   thread_t   threadId[MAXTHREADS];
   void       *Readers();
   void       *Writers();
   int         i;

   numThreads = NUM_WRITERS + NUM_READERS;
   if (numThreads > MAXTHREADS)
       exit(0);

   QueCreate(&gQueue, 10);

   for (i = 0; i < NUM_WRITERS; ++i)
      thr_create(0, 0, Writers, NULL, THR_NEW_LWP, &threadId[i]);

   for (i = NUM_WRITERS ; i < numThreads; ++i)
      thr_create(0, 0, Readers, NULL, THR_NEW_LWP, &threadId[i]);

   for (i = 0; i < numThreads; ++i)
      thr_join(threadId[i], NULL, NULL);
}

void *
Writers(void *pThrArg)
{
   int        i;
   int        retCode;
   thread_t   threadId;
   char       msgBuf[MSGBUF];

   threadId = thr_self();
   for (i = 0; i < NUMMSGS; ++i)
   {
       sprintf(msgBuf,"Msg %d from thread %d", i, threadId);
       retCode = QuePut(msgBuf, sizeof(msgBuf), &gQueue);
       if (retCode < 0)
       {
```

```
            fprintf(stderr,"QuePut failed [%d]\n", retCode);
            break;
        }
    }
    fprintf(stderr,"writer:thr_id[%d] msg[%d]\n",threadId, i);
    thr_exit(NULL);
}

void *
Readers(void *pThrArg)
{
    int       i;
    int       retCode;
    int       numMsgs;
    thread_t  threadId;
    char      msgBuf[MSGBUF];

    threadId = thr_self();
    numMsgs = (NUMMSGS * NUM_WRITERS) / NUM_READERS;

    for (i = 0; i < numMsgs; ++i)
    {
        retCode = QueGet(msgBuf, sizeof(msgBuf), &gQueue);
        if (retCode < 0)
        {
            fprintf(stderr,"QuePut failed [%d]\n", retCode);
            break;
        }
    }
    fprintf(stderr,"reader:thr_id[%d] msg[%d]\n",threadId, i);

    thr_exit(NULL);
}

int
QueGet(void *pmsg, int msglen, QUEUE *pQueue)
{
        mutex_lock(&pQueue->qMutex);
        while (pQueue->qMsgs == 0)
          cond_wait(&pQueue->qEmpty, &pQueue->qMutex);

        if (pQueue->qMsgs == pQueue->qMax)
             cond_broadcast(&pQueue->qFull);

        DeleteQueueMsg(pmsg, msglen, pQueue);

        --pQueue->qMsgs;

        mutex_unlock(&pQueue->qMutex);
        return(0);
}

int
QuePut(void *pmsg, int msglen, QUEUE *pQueue)
{
        mutex_lock(&pQueue->qMutex);

        while (pQueue->qMsgs == pQueue->qMax)
          cond_wait(&pQueue->qFull, &pQueue->qMutex).

        InsertQueueMsg(pmsg, msglen, pQueue);

       ++pQueue->qMsgs;

        cond_signal(&pQueue->qEmpty);
        mutex_unlock(&pQueue->qMutex);
}
```

```
QueCreate(QUEUE *pQueue, int maxMsgs)
{
   mutex_init(&pQueue->qMutex, USYNC_THREAD, NULL);
   cond_init(&pQueue->qFull, USYNC_THREAD, NULL);
   cond_init(&pQueue->qEmpty, USYNC_THREAD, NULL);
   pQueue->qMax = maxMsgs;
   pQueue->qMsgs = 0;
   pQueue->qHeadMsg = NULL;
   pQueue->qTailMsg = NULL;
}

InsertQueueMsg(void *pMsg, int msgLen, QUEUE *pQueue)
{
   QMSG *newMsg;

   newMsg = (QMSG *) calloc(1,sizeof(QMSG));
   newMsg->msgLen = msgLen;
   newMsg->msg = (void *) malloc(msgLen);

   memcpy(newMsg->msg, pMsg, msgLen);

   if (pQueue->qHeadMsg == NULL)
   {
       pQueue->qHeadMsg = newMsg;
       pQueue->qTailMsg = newMsg;
   }
   else
   {
       pQueue->qTailMsg->next = newMsg;
       pQueue->qTailMsg = newMsg;
   }
   return(0);
}

DeleteQueueMsg(void *Msg, int msgLen, QUEUE *pQueue)
{
   QMSG *currMsg;
   int  len;

   currMsg = pQueue->qHeadMsg;
   len = currMsg->msgLen;

   memcpy(Msg,currMsg->msg, currMsg->msgLen);
   if (pQueue->qHeadMsg == Queue->qTailMsg)
       pQueue->qTailMsg = NULL;

   pQueue->qHeadMsg = pQueue->qHeadMsg->next;
   free(currMsg->msg);
   free(currMsg);
   return(len); /* length of message */
}
```

9.3 Barrier Synchronization

A barrier is a synchronization point in the program where threads wait to synchronize with each other. It is used to ensure that cooperating threads have reached a point before they can proceed to the next step. All threads wait at a synchronization point until the last thread reaches the point at which all of them can proceed.

```
#include <thread.h>
#include <synch.h>
#include <stdio.h>

typedef struct _barrier
{
   int  bCount;
   int  bResetCount;
   int  bReset;
   int  bWaiters;
   mutex_t  bMutex;
   cond_t   bCond;
} BARRIER;

BARRIER  TBarrier;

main(int argc, char **argv)
{
   int        numThr;
   int        *pThrArg;
   thread_t   threadId[MAXTHREADS];
   void       *ThrRoutine();
   int        i;

   numThr = MAXTHREADS;
   pThrArg = &numThr;

   BarrierInit(&TBarrier, MAXTHREADS);
   for (i = 0; i <numThr; ++i)
       thr_create(0, 0, ThrRoutine, (void *) NULL, THR_NEW_LWP, &threadId[i]);

   for (i = 0; i <numThr; ++i)
       thr_join(threadId[i], NULL, NULL);
   exit(0);
}

void *
ThrRoutine(void *pThrArg)
{
   int i;

   for (i = 0; i < 10 ; ++i)
       BarrierSync(&TBarrier);
   thr_exit(NULL);
}

BarrierInit(BARRIER *pBarrier, int bCount)
{
   pBarrier->bCount = bCount;
   pBarrier->bResetCount = bCount;
   pBarrier->bReset = TRUE;

   mutex_init(&pBarrier->bMutex, USYNC_THREAD, NULL);
   cond_init(&pBarrier->bCond, USYNC_THREAD, NULL);
}

int
BarrierSync(BARRIER      *pBarrier)
{
   int wakingThread = 0;
   thread_t threadId;

   threadId = thr_self();
```

```
    /* this is executed by threads that have finished executing */
    /* BarrierSync and start executing again before all threads */
    /* have exited the routine BarrierSync - referred to as fast threads */

    while (pBarrier->bReset == FALSE && !pBarrier->bCount)
       thr_yield(); /* fast threads yield here */

    mutex_lock(&pBarrier->bMutex);

    --pBarrier->bCount;

    if (!pBarrier->bCount)
    {
         wakingThread = 1;
         pBarrier->bReset = FALSE;
    }

    while (pBarrier->bCount != 0)
    {
         ++pBarrier->bWaiters;
         fprintf(stderr,"thread [%d] waiting\n", threadId);
         cond_wait(&pBarrier->bCond, &pBarrier->bMutex);
         --pBarrier->bWaiters;
    }

    if (wakingThread)
    {
         pBarrier->bCount = 0;
         fprintf(stderr,"thread [%d] waking ......\n\n\n", threadId);
         mutex_unlock(&pBarrier->bMutex);
         cond_broadcast(&pBarrier->bCond);
         return (0);
    }

    if (!pBarrier->bWaiters)
    {
         fprintf(stderr,"thread [%d] reseting ......\n\n\n", threadId);
         pBarrier->bCount = pBarrier->bResetCount; /* reset barrier count */
         pBarrier->bReset = TRUE;
    }

    mutex_unlock(&pBarrier->bMutex);

    return (0);
}
```

9.4 Semaphore Synchronization

Semaphores are used to enforce mutual exclusion and for coordinating events. Each semaphore has a count associated with it; the count can be incremented to any high value but can only be decremented to zero. The value of the counting semaphore can never be less than zero. Counting semaphores are useful in restricting access to a shared resource, but not necessarily in a mutually exclusive manner. In the following example, two semaphores are used by the reader and writer threads to control access to a shared buffer. The reader is advised to see Sec. 6.4 for an implementation of semaphores using condition variables and mutexes.

```
#include <thread.h>
#include <synch.h>
```

```
#include <fcntl.h>

typedef struct _linebuf
{
   char    line[MAXLINE];
   int     lineLen;
   sema_t  lineEmpty;
   sema_t  lineFull;
} LINEBUF;

LINEBUF lineBuf[MAXBUFFERS];

main(int argc, char **argv)
{
   int       ret;
   thread_t  threadId[2];
   int       i;
   char      *fromFile;
   char      *toFile;
   void      *ConsumerThread();
   void      *ProducerThread();

   if (argc < 3)
   {
       printf("USAGE: %s input-file output-file\n");
       exit(0);
   }

   fromFile = argv[1];
   toFile = argv[2];

   for (i = 0; i < MAXBUFFERS; ++i)
   {
       sema_init(&lineBuf[i].lineEmpty, 1, USYNC_THREAD, NULL);
       sema_init(&lineBuf[i].lineFull, 0, USYNC_THREAD, NULL);
   }

   thr_create(0, 0, ProducerThread, fromFile, THR_NEW_LWP, &threadId[0]);
   thr_create(0, 0, ConsumerThread, toFile, THR_NEW_LWP, &threadId[1]);

   for (i = 0; i < 2; ++i)
       thr_join(threadId[i], NULL, NULL);
}

void *
ProducerThread(char * File)
{
   int   fileFd;
   int   nRead;
   int   i = 0;
   thread_t threadId;

   fileFd = open(File, O_RDWR, 0666);
   if (fileFd == -1)
   {
       printf("main:error opening file %s\n", File);
       perror("open");
   }
   i = 0;
   while(1)
   {
       sema_wait(&lineBuf[i].lineEmpty);

       nRead = read(fileFd, lineBuf[i].line, MAXLINE);
       lineBuf[i].lineLen = nRead;
```

```
        sema_post(&lineBuf[i].lineFull);

        if (nRead <= 0)
            break;

        if (i++ == MAXBUFFERS -1)
            i = 0;
    }
    close(fileFd);
    return(NULL);
}

void *
ConsumerThread(char * File)
{
    int   ret;
    int   fileFd;
    int   i;

    fileFd = open(File, O_RDWR|O_CREAT, 0666);
    if (fileFd == -1)
    {
        printf("error opening file %s\n", File);
        perror("open");
    }

    i = 0;
    for (;;)
    {
        int j;
        sema_wait(&lineBuf[i].lineFull);
        if (lineBuf[i].lineLen <= 0)
             break;

        j = 0;
        for (j = 0; j < lineBuf[i].lineLen; ++j)
             lineBuf[i].line[j] = toupper(lineBuf[i].line[j]);

        Ret = write(fileFd, lineBuf[i].line, lineBuf[i].lineLen);
        if (Ret == -1 ) {
             printf("error writing to file %s\n", File);
             perror("write");
        }
        sema_post(&lineBuf[i].lineEmpty);
        if (i++ == MAXBUFFERS -1)
            i = 0;
    }
    close(fileFd);
    return(NULL);
}
```

9.5 Reader/Writer Locks

In certain applications data are much more frequently read than they are modified. Reader/writer (RW) locks allow multiple threads to read data simultaneously but serialize writers when data have to be updated. One of the main advantages of reader/writer locks over mutex locks is that they allow multiple threads to share data in read mode without the overhead of locking. The payoff of RW locks over mutexes is not evident when the code guarded by the RW lock is short. RW locks are better when the frequency of read operations is higher than write operations, and the read operations are somewhat lengthy. The following implementation favors readers over writers and can cause starvation for writers. (See sample on disk for implementation favoring writers.)

```
#include <thread.h>
#include <synch.h>

typedef struct _rwlock
{
mutex_t   rwMutex;
cond_t    rwCond;
int       rwCount;
} RWLOCK;

RWLOCK    grwLock;

main(int argc, char **argv)
{
   int       numThr;
   thread_t  threadId[MAXTHREADS];
   void      *Readers();
   void      *Writers();
   int       i;

   numThr = NUM_WRITERS + NUM_READERS

   InitReadWriteLock(&grwLock);

   for (i = 0; i < NUM_WRITERS; ++i)
       thr_create(0, 0, Writers, NULL, THR_NEW_LWP, &threadId[i]);

   for (i = NUM_WRITERS ; i < numThr; ++i)
       thr_create(0, 0, Readers, NULL, THR_NEW_LWP, &threadId[i]);

   for (i = 0; i <numThr; ++i)
       thr_join(threadId[i], NULL, NULL);
}

void *
Writers(void *pThrArg)
{
   int i;
   int numLocks;

   numLocks = NUM_LOCKS;
   for (i = 0; i < numLocks; +-i)
   {
       AcquireWriteLock(&grwLock);
       /* do some update to shared data */
       ReleaseWriteLock(&grwLock);

       /* sleep for some time before updating data again */
   }
   fprintf(stderr,"thread id [%d] # writelocks [%d]\n", thr_self(), i);
   return(NULL);
}

void *
Readers(void *pThrArg)
{
   int i;
   int numLocks;
```

```
    numLocks = (NUM_LOCKS * NUM_WRITERS) / NUM_READERS;

    for (i = 0; i < numLocks; ++i)
    {
        AcquireReadLock(&grwLock);
        /* read shared data */
        ReleaseReadLock(&grwLock);
    }
    fprintf(stderr,"thread id [%d] # read locks [%d]\n", thr_self(), i);
    return(NULL);
}

int AcquireReadLock(RWLOCK *prwLock)
{
    mutex_lock(&prwLock->rwMutex);

    while( prwLock->rwCount < 0)
        cond_wait(&prwLock->rwCond, &prwLock->rwMutex);

    ++prwLock->rwCount;
    mutex_unlock(&prwLock->rwMutex);
}

int ReleaseReadLock(RWLOCK *prwLock)
{
    mutex_lock(&prwLock->rwMutex);

    --prwLock->rwCount;

    if (!prwLock->rwCount)
        cond_signal(&prwLock->rwCond);

    mutex_unlock(&prwLock->rwMutex);
}

int AcquireWriteLock(RWLOCK *prwLock)
{
    mutex_lock(&prwLock->rwMutex);

    while( prwLock->rwCount != 0)
       cond_wait(&prwLock->rwCond, &prwLock->rwMutex);

    prwLock->rwCount = -1;

    mutex_unlock(&prwLock->rwMutex);
}

int ReleaseWriteLock(RWLOCK *prwLock)
{
    mutex_lock(&prwLock->rwMutex);
    prwLock->rwCount = 0;
    mutex_unlock(&prwLock->rwMutex);
    cond_broadcast(&prwLock->rwCond);
}

int InitReadWriteLock(RWLOCK *prwLock)
{
    mutex_init(&prwLock->rwMutex, USYNC_THREAD, NULL);
    cond_init(&prwLock->rwCond, USYNC_THREAD, NULL);
    prwLock->rwCount = 0;
}
```

Chapter

10

C-Threads

10.1 Introduction to Mach

Work on the Mach operating system began in 1985 at Carnegie Mellon University (CMU). The development of Mach started out as an effort to provide a better operating system (OS) than the Berkeley UNIX operating system (4.3 BSD). In addition to providing new and advanced features, one of the main design goals was to provide compatibility with the existing BSD UNIX systems. Although the design of Mach is very different from that of the UNIX operating system, it does provide source code compatibility with the 4.3 BSD UNIX system.

Mach was designed from the ground up to support multiprocessing and multithreading. Mach was designed to be a small, extensible kernel providing basic system services such as task and thread management, scheduling, interprocess communication, and virtual memory management. Some of the system services were moved out from the kernel and implemented in user space as user processes. This greatly helped in reducing the complexity and size of the Mach kernel. It is beyond the scope of this book to discuss the Mach kernel in great detail. Keeping this in mind, the discussion will be restricted to the multithreading features of the Mach kernel.

Today, there are some successful commercial implementations of the Mach OS, such as NeXTSTEP from NeXT Computers. Open Science Foundation (OSF) chose the Mach OS as the base kernel technology for the OSF/1 system. Operating systems such as Digital's UNIX and IBM's AIX are also based on the Mach operating system. The reader is advised that if you are reading these chapters after reading earlier chapters, then you will find that some of the text has been repeated, and this has been done for the purpose of completeness.

10.1.1 Tasks, processes, and threads

In a traditional UNIX system, the unit of execution is a process. Mach divides the traditional UNIX process into two abstractions: *tasks* and *threads.* A *task* in Mach is the environment within which the process executes, and it is the basic unit of resource allocation. A task in Mach is not a scheduling entity but acts as the resource system's resource holder for things such as memory and message ports. A task in Mach can be considered to be an address space, while a process is an address space with its own stack and program counter.

In the Mach operating system, *threads* are the basic unit of execution. Mach was designed to support multiple threads of control within an address space. A task in Mach can have multiple threads each executing independently of the others. On a multiprocessor machine, these threads can even run on different processors. Each thread in Mach has its own stack and program counter. Threads within a task share a common address space and all communication rights of the task. A process in Mach can be considered to be a task with a single thread.

Each thread has a scheduling policy and priority. The priorities are in the range 0 to 31, and a higher-priority thread is always picked to run before a thread of lower priority. The highest-priority thread is chosen to run until it blocks or uses its time quantum. By default, the scheduling policy of Mach is timesharing, but it also supports the interactive and fixed-priority scheduling policies.

10.1.2 Thread execution model

The reader is advised to read Sec. 2.2 for an overview of the thread models. There is a coroutine-based implementation of the C-Threads library, in which case multiple threads are mapped to the same kernel thread (M:1 model). In NeXTSTEP (my test platform for C-Threads), the only execution model available to users is the one-to-one mapping between user and kernel threads. Since in this model there is a separate kernel thread for each user thread, it is not advisable to create too many threads in a process. In NeXTSTEP there is no support for the M:N model or the M:1 model.

10.1.3 Mach thread functions

Mach provides *two* kinds of interfaces to the programmer for thread management. One is the low-level Mach calls, while the other is a high-level interface provided in the form of a library. This library has a C-language interface and provides functions for thread management, thread synchronization, and thread-specific data. This interface is called *C-Threads,* and it is more than likely that you would be using C-Threads rather than Mach threads functions for building multithreaded applications. The Mach threads functions are low-level interfaces and are useful for building thread libraries similar to the C-Threads library. For example, if you want to implement the POSIX threads API on Mach, then you can use the Mach calls within the POSIX threads library.

When an application starts executing in Mach, a single thread is created automatically. Additional threads must be created by calling either the Mach threads or C-Threads functions. Each thread in Mach is identified by the data type *thread_t*. Let us take a look at the mechanism for creating a new thread using the low-level Mach calls.

The first thing you have to do is to call *thread_create* to create a thread within a task. These threads do not start executing, because threads are created in suspended state. After a thread is created, then the function *thread_set_state* must be called to initialize the state. You are responsible for allocating space for stack, setting up the call frames and registers before you call the function thread_set_state. After the state has been initialized, then the function *thread_resume* must be called to schedule the thread to run. Well, you must be thinking there ought to be an easier way of programming with threads rather than going through all these complicated processes. The answer is simple: Mach provides a higher-level interface for developing multi-threaded applications called *C-Threads*.

10.1.4 C-Threads

The C-Threads APIs are used to create and manage threads. The threads APIs can be broadly classified into such areas as thread management, thread synchronization, thread-specific data, and things like scheduling and priority. If you are using POSIX threads, then you can observe that the *legacy* of POSIX threads lies in C-Threads. POSIX threads are very similar to C-Threads, except they have been improved and extended with new features. If you are porting an application from C-Threads to Pthreads, then you should not have any major problem, since the basic concepts are so similar.

This chapter will cover the C-Threads APIs; any detailed discussion of some of the concepts of thread programming (e.g., mutual exclusion) will be avoided because they have already been explained in earlier chapters. If you are reading this chapter after reading the POSIX threads chapters, then you should not have any problems understanding these APIs. Readers who have not read the chapters on Pthreads will be advised to read relevant sections from the POSIX threads chapters.

10.2 Thread Management Functions

`cthread_fork`	Creates a thread
`cthread_exit`	Terminates a thread
`cthread_join`	Joins a thread
`cthread_detach`	Detaches a thread
`cthread_self`	Gets thread identifier
`cthread_yield`	Yields the CPU
`cthread_count`	Number of threads in the task
`cthread_limit`	Gets limit on number of thread creation
`cthread_set_limit`	Sets limit on number of thread creation
`cthread_errno`	Gets per-thread errno
`cthread_set_errno_self`	Sets per-thread errno
`cthread_name`	Gets string associated with a thread
`cthread_set_name`	Associates a string with a thread

10.2.1 Creating a thread

When a process begins execution, it has a single thread of control. The process is created automatically with one thread, which is commonly referred to as the *main thread*. The creation of the main thread maintains binary compatibility with single-threaded programs. If a process needs additional threads of control, then they have to be created by calling the thread creation API.

When threads are created, they begin executing a start routine. Creating a thread is somewhere in between calling a function and creating a process. The start routine specifies the entry point at which the newly created thread starts execution. Multiple threads can execute the same start routine, or each thread can have a separate start routine. If multiple threads call the same thread routine and they modify shared data within the routine, then the routine must be written to be thread-safe. All threads are created equal, and the thread does not maintain a list of created threads or have any knowledge of other threads in the process.

```
cthread_t cthread_fork(any_t (*function)(), any_t arg)
```

The function cthread_fork is used to create a new thread of control in the process. C-Threads use the data type *cthread_t* to identify threads. On success, the function returns a thread identifier of type cthread_t. Each thread within a process is identified by a thread identifier (TID). The TID of the newly created thread is only known to be usable and unique within the context of the process creating the thread.

In C-Threads, *any_t* represents a pointer to any C data type. The argument *function* is a pointer to a function that is executed as the thread's start routine. The start routine should be defined to return any_t. The second argument *arg* is a pointer to an optional argument passed to the thread's start_routine, and it can be NULL in the case where no arguments are passed to the thread routine.

The following code segment illustrates the creation of a new thread. The newly created thread is created to start executing the routine LoopThread (). The routine LoopThread executes a loop; the number of iterations to loop is specified as an argument to the thread routine.

```
typedef struct _THRARG
{
   int rows;
   int cols;
} THRARG;

main (int argc, char **argv)
{
   cthread_t  threadId;
   void       *LoopThread ();
   THRARG     thrArg;
```

```
    thrArg.Rows = 10;
    thrArg.Cols = 20;

    threadId = cthread_fork(LoopThread, &thrArg);

    /* Wait for the thread to complete */

    exit (0);
}

any_t
LoopThread (THRARG *pThrArg)
{
    int j;
    int k;
    for (j = 0; j < pThrArg->Rows; ++j)
        for (k = 0; k < pThrArg->Cols;++k)
            printf ("loop iteration j: [%d]\t k: [%d]\n", j, k);
    /* Exit Thread */
}
```

If you are new to thread programming, then I will recommend that you read Sec. 2.6. It covers topics such as passing different parameters to a thread routine and the scope of the thread argument. The maximum number of threads that can be created is implementation-specific.

10.2.2 Thread termination

Everything that is created must come to an end, and so must the life of a thread. A thread can terminate in one of the following ways:

- It exits the start_routine.
- It calls cthread_exit.

```
void cthread_exit (any_t result)
```

The function cthread_exit terminates the calling thread and stores the exit status in the variable *result* for later use. This result is later made available to any thread waiting for this thread to terminate. The function *cthread_exit* is called implicitly when a thread returns from the start routine that was used to create the thread. In such a case, the function return value serves as the exit status. The routine cthread_exit does not return to the calling thread.

When an initial thread returns from the main routine, then the exit routine is called, thus terminating *all* the threads in the process. It is a good practice to *always* call cthread_exit to terminate a thread (including a main thread). When the initial thread calls cthread_exit, it does *not* terminate the entire task. The task will only terminate when the last thread in the process terminates. Keep in mind that the *entire* task terminates when the *exit* routine is called by any thread.

10.2.3 Joining a thread

In the worker thread model it is common for a thread to suspend execution until some other thread terminates. For example, consider a program in which a master thread creates multiple worker threads to perform parallel queries on different databases. The master thread has to wait for all the worker threads to terminate before it can continue processing with the result of the queries.

```
any_t cthread_join (cthread_t thread)
```

The function cthread_join is used to wait for thread termination. It is important that the thread that is being waited on must *not* be a detached thread. The function cthread_join suspends the calling thread and waits for termination of the thread specified by *thread*. On return from a successful join, the return value contains the exit status of the terminating thread. If the thread has already terminated, then cthread_join returns the status and returns immediately without blocking.

It is important that a thread be joined only *once*. When multiple threads do a join on a target thread, then a single thread is notified of the thread termination. The rest of the threads are not notified, and they will wait *indefinitely*. Similarly, when a thread joins a detached thread, it will wait indefinitely.

The routine cthread_join along with cthread_exit also can be used to *return* some information to the calling thread. It is important that the returned variable should be valid even after the thread has terminated. Returning a pointer to a stack variable is a programming bug because the routine cthread_exit frees the stack of the thread when it exits.

In the following code segment the main thread creates a thread to execute a query. The thread returns the results of the query in a dynamically allocated buffer. On return, the main thread prints the results and then frees the buffer.

```
main (int argc, char **argv)
{
   cthread_t  threadId;
   char       *query;
   void       *QueryThread ();
   char       *queryResults;

   threadId = cthread_fork (QueryThread, (void *)query);

   queryResults = cthread_join (threadId);
   if (queryResults ! = NULL)
   {
      /*print results returned by the thread */
      free (void*) queryResults); /* assumes only one thread will do a join */
   }
   cthread_exit (NULL);
}
```

```
void *
QueryThread (void *query)
{
   int j;
   void *queryResults;

   /* QueryResults on return is either NULL or points to the result set */
   DoQuery (query, &queryResults); /* malloc is done inside this routine */

   cthread_exit (queryResults);
}
```

10.2.4 Detaching a thread

The C-Threads library maintains some information internally such as thread ID, termination status, thread-specific data, thread stack, and internal thread storage for each created thread until the thread is detached. This information is saved so that other threads can perform a successful join operation. The function cthread_detach is used to suggest to the threads library that all information maintained for the thread can be deleted after the thread terminates.

```
void cthread_detach (cthread_t thread)
```

The routine cthread_detach marks the thread specified by *thread* for deletion. Storage for the thread is reclaimed after the thread terminates. A thread may no longer be joined by another thread after it has been detached; all subsequent calls to cthread_join will result in *indefinite* postponement. If the thread has not terminated, then cthread_detach does not cause the thread to terminate but will cause the storage to be released after the thread terminates.

If you know that a thread will never be joined, then it is a good idea to detach it as soon as it is created. This lends to better performance and also guarantees that resources for the thread are freed as soon as the thread is deleted. Generally, it is used in the following manner:

```
main (int argc, char **argv)
{
   cthread_t  threadId;
   char       *query;
   void       *QueryThread ();
   char       *queryResults;

   threadId = cthread_fork (QueryThread, (void *)query);

   cthread_detach(threadId);

   /* do something */
}
```

10.2.5 Thread identifier

Each thread within a process is uniquely identified by a thread identifier. The thread identifier (TID) is only guaranteed to be unique within the context of the calling process. The TID of a new thread is returned in the call to cthread_fork. A TID is an opaque object referenced by *cthread_t*.

```
cthread_t cthread_self ()
```

The function *cthread_self* returns the TID of the calling thread. The thread identifier is returned either at creation time or by calling this function.

10.2.6 Yielding processor

```
void cthread_yield ()
```

The function *cthread_yield* can be used by the calling thread to release its processor. It allows the scheduler to determine if another thread of higher priority can be run instead of the calling thread. If no suitable thread exists, then the calling thread continues to run.

In the case of CPU-intensive threads, it is a good idea to yield the processor periodically. This will give other threads a fair chance to run. The *misuse* of this call may hurt rather than help, since it may cause lots of unnecessary context switches. For example, it does not make sense to call this function while holding a lock to a shared data structure, since the other threads might not be able to continue processing unless the shared lock is released. This can even be helpful on coroutine-based implementations of threads on Mach.

10.2.7 Number of threads in a task

An application can find out the *number* of threads that currently exist in the task by calling the function cthread_count. Some applications that want to limit the number of threads in the task can use this function to find out the current limit. This information can be useful, but it is *not* available on other operating systems such as POSIX or UNIX or WIN32.

```
int cthread_count (void)
```

10.2.8 Maximum threads allowed

Threads are much more lightweight when compared with a task. Even though threads are cheap, they are *not free*. Threads use system resources such as memory and involve scheduling overhead. The maximum number of threads allowed in a task is system-dependent; the macro THREAD_MAX is defined in the header file <*mach_param.h*>. In C-Threads, the application can set an upper limit on the number of threads that can be created in a task.

10.2.8.1 Get/set maximum threads

```
int    cthread_limit (void)
void   cthread_set_limit(int limit)
```

The function cthread_limit returns the number of threads that can potentially exist in a task. The function cthread_set_limit sets an upper limit on the maximum number of threads that can be created safely. Applications should use *cthread_count* to determine when the task is approaching the limit on the maximum number of threads. The function cthread_fork does *not* fail when the limit is reached, but a new Mach thread is not associated with the thread, and this prevents the new thread from doing anything.

10.2.9 Threads and errno

In UNIX, the variable errno is a process-wide global variable. In a multithreaded process, the variable errno is maintained in errno as well as on a per-thread basis. A thread should check the value of errno *only* when a UNIX system calls fails.

10.2.9.1 Get/set errno

```
int    cthread_errno(void)
void   cthread_set_errno_self(int error)
```

The function cthread_errno returns the value of the per-thread errno, while the function cthread_set_errno_self sets the per-thread errno to *error*. The following code segment shows how a thread should check for an error when a UNIX system call fails.

```
MakeDirectory(char *dirName)
{
   int  ret;

   ret = mkdir(dirName);

   if (ret = = -1 && cthread_errno = = EEXISTS)
        printf("The directory already exists...\n");
}
```

10.3 Thread Synchronization

In a multithreaded process, all threads execute in a single address space and hence share most of the process resources. Process resources such as open file descriptors, IPC identifiers, static variables, and dynamically allocated memory variables are shared by all the threads. For example, if one thread closes a file, then that file is considered closed for all other threads within the process. Similarly, if one thread frees a dynamically allocated buffer using the C-library *free* routine, then no other thread can safely reference the same buffer without causing an access violation.

Consider two threads running on different processors trying to update a shared variable simultaneously (e.g., ++SharedVariable). If the value of the variable before the update is 3, then the correct value after the update should be 5. If both threads update the variable concurrently, then one of the updates can be lost, and the value of the variable will be 4. Even though the statement ++SharedVariable looks atomic, keep in mind that the assembly code generated for the statement might not be atomic. This lack of atomicity can cause one of the updates to be lost.

One of the main advantages of threads is easy data sharing, but along with this comes the added responsibility to guard such data against corruption. Threads need to synchronize data that are shared and can be modified by multiple threads. If shared data are modified without any synchronization by multiple threads, then the data can become inconsistent. All access to shared resources must be protected by some mutual exclusion lock. The use of locks to synchronize access to shared data is called *data synchronization.*

In a boss/worker thread model it is common to divide work between multiple threads. In such a case, one thread might wait for another thread to reach a particular state before proceeding, or one thread might wait for a particular condition to be true before proceeding. In these cases, threads are not necessarily synchronizing on data but more on conditions or events. Data synchronization is usually for shorter duration, while event synchronization can be for much longer duration.

Let us consider an example of a producer and a consumer thread writing and reading from a shared buffer. When the threads are reading or writing from the buffer, they have exclusive access to the buffer. The producer cannot write to the buffer until the consumer has finished reading from the buffer, and the consumer cannot read from the buffer until the producer has finished writing to the buffer. Each thread waits for notification from the other thread that the buffer is available. When the producer thread is finished writing to the buffer, it notifies the consumer, and vice versa. This form of synchronization is often called *event synchronization.*

C-Threads provide mutex locks for mutual exclusion and condition variables for event synchronization. If you have already read Chap. 3, then these APIs should be very simple; otherwise, I would recommend that you read Secs. 3.1.1 through 3.1.3 to better understand some of the basic concepts of mutual exclusion and event synchronization. The concepts of critical sections and race conditions are explained in much more detail.

10.3.1 Mutual exclusion

Mutex locks generally are used to synchronize access to and ensure atomic updates of shared data. A *mutex* (mutual exclusion) lock is a data structure in memory that processes or threads use to *serialize* access to shared data. Mutex locks are meaningful only for data that can be *modified* by multiple threads or processes. This means that you do *not* need to serialize access to shared read-only data items.

The state of the mutex can be either *locked* or *unlocked*. The basic assumption behind mutexes is that threads must lock the mutex before accessing shared modifiable data and unlock the mutex after the thread has completed accessing the shared data. If one thread has acquired the mutex, then all other threads requesting to lock the mutex will *wait* until the mutex is released by the thread owning the mutex. It is important to remember that for data synchronization all threads must strictly *enforce* the mutex locking protocol. Note that if threads do not check the locks before entering the critical section, then mutex locks cannot be of any help. One possible solution to enforce mutual exclusion is to provide well-defined interfaces (functions) to allow access to shared resources and then implement the mutex locking and unlocking within these interfaces. In this way the details of locking and unlocking are hidden from the user of these interfaces.

10.3.2 Mutex functions and macros

`mutex_alloc`	Creates a mutex object
`mutex_init`	Initializes a mutex
`mutex_clear`	Clears a mutex object
`mutex_free`	Deallocates a mutex
`mutex_lock`	Locks a mutex
`mutex_trylock`	Tries to lock a mutex
`mutex_unlock`	Unlocks a mutex
`mutex_name`	Gets name associated with a mutex
`mutex_set_name`	Sets name to associate with a mutex

10.3.3 Creating and initializing a mutex object

Mutexes in C-Threads are identified by the data type *mutex_t*. Mutexes have to be created before they can be utilized for mutual exclusion.

```
mutex_t mutex_alloc(void)
```

The macro mutex_alloc is used to dynamically create a new mutex object of type mutex_t. Mutexes, by default, are created as nonrecursive, and the initial state of the mutex is *unlocked*. When the mutex has to be shared by more than one thread within the task, then it is important to store the mutex identifier in a global or static variable. A mutex variable using the same identifier should be created only *once*.

```
void mutex_init(struct mutex *M)
```

The macro mutex_init initializes an existing structure of type struct mutex. The address of this structure can be used wherever an object of type mutex_t is required (e.g., mutex_lock). The function mutex_init is used mostly in nested structures. For example,

```
typedef struct _RMUTEX
{
   int  refCnt;
   struct mutex rmutex;
} RMUTEX;
```

10.3.4 Deleting and clearing a mutex object

When dynamically created mutexes are no longer needed, they should be deleted. The library does not delete information for the mutex until the mutex is destroyed. Mutexes are *not* deleted when the thread that created the mutex terminates, since mutexes are considered to be shared resources of a process.

```
void mutex_free (mutex_t *mutex)
```

The macro mutex_free is used to delete a dynamically created mutex identified by *mutex*. This routine should be called only when the mutex is no longer referenced. You should not delete a *locked* mutex or a mutex that some other thread is trying to lock (blocked on mutex_lock).

The macro mutex_clear is used to clear the state of a static mutex object that was initialized previously by a call to mutex_init.

```
void mutex_clear (struct mutex *mutex)
```

10.3.5 Acquiring a mutex lock

Mutexes are used to guard critical sections of code. Before executing a critical section of code, the thread must *acquire* the mutex lock. After executing the critical section, the thread that locked the mutex must *release* the mutex. The locking of the mutex in C-Threads can be either blocking or nonblocking in nature.

```
int mutex_lock (mutex_t mutex)
```

The macro mutex_lock is used to acquire a lock of a valid unlocked mutex identified by *mutex*. If the mutex is currently locked by some other thread, then the calling thread is blocked until the mutex lock is released. When the function returns successfully, then the state of the mutex becomes locked, and the calling thread becomes the *owner* of the mutex. The calling thread remains the owner of the mutex lock until it unlocks the mutex later. If the mutex is never unlocked, then some other thread will block indefinitely on the mutex lock when it tries to acquire the mutex.

Any attempt by the calling thread to lock a mutex that is already locked by the calling thread will result in deadlock. It is the caller's responsibility to ensure that this function is not called while owning the mutex lock. Sometimes there is a *need* for recursive mutexes, and recursive mutexes can be built easily using the C-Threads primitives without much overhead. Any attempt to lock a mutex that has been deleted also might result in unspecified behavior.

When multiple threads call mutex_lock at the same time, they are suspended and are placed on a queue of threads waiting for the mutex to be released. Certain factors such as thread priority and scheduling determine which thread will be woken first. The thread that is woken up locks the mutex and becomes the owner of the mutex.

10.3.6 Nonblocking mutex lock

The function mutex_trylock is similar to mutex_lock except that the function returns immediately if the mutex identified by *mutex* is currently locked by any thread, and this includes the calling thread.

```
int mutex_trylock (mutex_t mutex)
```

Nonblocking mutex locks can be used to implement *spinlocks*. When the overhead of suspending and resuming a thread is higher than the time a thread would spend spinning (busy wait) on the mutex, then the use of nonblocking mutexes should be considered. Spinlocks can be helpful for short sections of the code, but they also can burn expensive CPU cycles and should only be considered on SMP machines. Spinlocks can even cause deadlocks on uniprocessor machines. Consider the following code segment that implements a version of a simple spinlock.

```
SpinLockAcquire(mutex_t SharedMutex)
{
   while(mutex_trylock(SharedMutex) == FALSE)
         ; /* busy wait */
}
```

10.3.7 Unlocking a mutex

The mutex lock should be released after the thread executes the critical section of code; otherwise, no other thread can enter the critical section guarded by the same mutex lock.

```
int mutex_unlock (mutex_t mutex)
```

The function mutex_unlock is used to unlock a *mutex* by the owner of the mutex. The results are unspecified if the mutex is unlocked or the calling thread is not the owner of the mutex. On a successful return, the state of the mutex is *unlocked*. If no threads are waiting for the mutex to be released, then the mutex is marked as having no owner. If one or more threads are waiting for the mutex to be released, then one of the waiting threads is woken up. Thread priority and scheduling determine which thread is woken up.

Let us implement the routine AddToList using mutexes to guard the critical section code.

```
typedef struct List
{
   struct List*next;
   void  *data;

}SHARED_LIST;

static SHARED_LIST *gpListHead; /* pointer to beginning of list */

mutex_t ListMutex;

InitListMutex()
{
   mutex_init(&ListMutex, NULL);
}

AddToList (SHARED_LIST *pnewEntry)
{
   /* Assume the function InitListMutex is called before */

   mutex_lock (&ListMutex);

   /* Critical Section of Code */
   pnewEntry->Next = gpListHead;
   gpListHead = pnewEntry;

   mutex_unlock (&ListMutex);
}
```

10.3.8 Mutexes and deadlocks

In a multithreaded application when one is dealing with multiple mutexes, deadlock can happen. The reader is advised to read Sec. 3.4 for a more detailed description on this topic. To avoid recursive deadlocks, implement a recursive mutex. To implement recursive mutexes, see Sec. 3.9, and replace all Pthreads calls by C-Threads calls. Note that TIDs in C-Threads are 32-bit numbers and the C-language operator = = can be used instead of pthread_equal to compare two thread identifiers.

10.3.9 Guidelines for using mutex

- Always use global or dynamic variables for storing mutex identifiers. Do not try to use stack variables for mutexes because the stack of a thread is destroyed when the thread terminates. Other threads in the process can still be referencing the mutex, and the address of the mutex identifier is invalid after the stack is destroyed.

- Initialize the mutex before using it, and initialize it only once so that all threads have the same view of the mutex.
- Delete mutexes after they are no longer used.
- Avoid locking the mutex in a recursive fashion unless you have implemented your own recursive mutex.
- While locking multiple mutexes simultaneously, be sure that all threads acquire the locks in the same order to avoid deadlocks.
- Lock mutexes for a short time. Keep the critical section of code small, and avoid any blocking operation (I/O, another synchronization lock) inside the critical sections.
- Do not use mutex locks excessively. Excessive synchronization will cause performance problems, and you will tend to lose one of the foremost benefits of multithreading, which is concurrent execution of threads. If all threads reference the shared data in *read-only* mode, then there is no need to serialize access to this piece of shared data.
- If your application runs slower on a multiprocessor machine than on a uniprocessor machine, it is very likely that your application is suffering because of excessive locking.

10.4 Condition Variable Functions and Macros

`cond_alloc`	Creates a condition object
`cond_init`	Initializes a condition object
`cond_free`	Frees a condition object
`cond_clear`	Clears a condition object
`cond_wait`	Waits on a condition
`cond_signal`	Signals a condition
`cond_broadcast`	Broadcasts a condition
`condition_name`	Gets name associated with a condition object
`condition_set_name`	Sets name to associate with a condition object

10.4.1 Condition variables

Condition variables (CVs) are yet another kind of C-Threads synchronization object that are used for event synchronization. CVs allow threads to block until a particular condition is satisfied and are most useful when multiple threads coordinate together to solve a task. A state change of a variable (condition) can be signaled to one or more threads at the same time.

The question that can be asked is: “Why can’t mutexes be used to wait until a particular condition is true?” The answer is simple: It is inefficient in terms of CPU utilization. Condition variables are used whenever the thread has to wait for *longer* periods on a specified condition. Mutexes, on the other hand, are used for implementing critical sections of code where locks are generally held for a *short* time. Condition variables should be never used for serializing access to some shared data.

Condition variables are used along with a mutex and a boolean variable (condition predicate). The three objects used together for event notification are:

- A *condition expression* to indicate whether the condition is met (e.g., X < 15 && Y > 12).
- A *condition variable* (CV) to wait for the condition.
- A *mutex variable* to synchronize access to the condition expression.

Condition variables always should be used in conjunction with mutexes. The thread *locks* the mutex and then checks if the condition expression is in the desired state. The state is defined by a boolean variable called a *predicate.* If the condition expression is not in the desired state, then the thread *waits* on the CV associated with the predicate. The mutex is atomically released when a thread waits on a CV. The atomicity of the release and wait operation ensures that no other thread can change the predicate between the operations. It is important to release the mutex because some other thread will lock the mutex before setting the condition expression to the desired state.

When the other thread sets the predicate to the desired state, then it signals the CV. The thread *relocks* the mutex after coming out of the wait because a return from the wait does not guarantee that the predicate is true or false. The thread that is woken up reexamines the predicate because more than one thread can be woken up when the condition is broadcasted and the predicate can still be false when it resumes execution after the wait.

10.4.2 Creating/initializing condition variables

Condition variables have to be created before they can be used for event notification.

```
condition_t  condition_alloc()
void         condition_init(struct condition *cond)
```

The macro condition_alloc is used to dynamically create a new condition object of type condition_t. When the condition object has to be shared by more than one thread within the task, then it is important to store the identifier in a global or static variable. A condition variable should be created only *once.*

The macro condition_init initializes an existing structure of type struct condition. The address of this structure can be used wherever an object of type condition_t is required (e.g., condition_wait).

10.4.3 Destroying/clearing condition variables

When condition objects that were created dynamically are no longer needed, they should be deleted. The library does not delete information for the object until the condition is destroyed. The condition objects are not deleted when the thread that created the condition terminates, since condition objects are considered to be shared resources of a process.

```
void condition_free(cond_t condition)
void condition_clear(struct condition *cond)
```

The macro condition_free is used to delete a dynamically created condition object identified by *cond*. This routine should be called only when the CV identified by *condition* is no longer referenced. One should not delete a condition object that is used by some other thread for waiting (blocked on condition_wait).

The macro condition_clear is used to clear a static condition object that was initialized previously by a call to condition_init.

10.4.4 Wait for a condition variable

The function cond_wait causes the thread to be suspended until the CV *cond* is signaled. The mutex should be *locked* by the calling thread before waiting on the CV. The mutex lock of *mutex* is released atomically, and the thread waits on the CV to be signaled. When the wait on the condition variable is satisfied, then the lock on the mutex variable mutex is reacquired atomically. When multiple threads are woken up as a result of some thread calling cond_broadcast, then these threads contend for the mutex lock. Note that if the CV is never signaled, then the thread will block *indefinitely* on the condition variable unless the wait is canceled after a specified time.

```
void condition_wait(condition_t cond, mutex_t mutex)
```

The following code shows a typical condition wait logic.

```
mutex_t       conditionMutex;
condition_t   conditionVariable;
int           conditionExpression;

CreateCondObjects()
{
   conditionMutex = mutex_alloc();
   conditionVariable = condition_alloc();
}

WaitForCondition ()
{
```

```
    mutex_lock (conditionMutex); /* assume CreateCondObjects has been called */

    while (conditionExpression = = FALSE)
       condition_wait (conditionVariable, conditionMutex);
    /*do something*/
    mutex_unlock (conditionMutex);
}
```

10.4.5 Signal a condition variable

```
int condition_signal (condition_t cond)
```

The function cond_signal is used to wake up a thread that is currently waiting on the condition variable *cond*. When multiple threads are waiting on a condition variable, only one of them is woken up, and the rest continue to wait on the condition variable. The scheduling policy and the priority of the thread determine which thread is woken up. After the CV is signaled, the ownership of the mutex lock is granted to the thread that is woken up. If no thread is waiting on the condition variable, then the threads library does *not* save the condition signaling. This means that the next thread calling cond_wait will block. The following code segment shows a typical condition signal logic.

```
mutex_t      conditionMutex;
condition_t  conditionVariable;
int          conditionExpression;

SignalCondition ()
{
    mutex_lock (conditionMutex); /* assume CreateCondObjects has been called */

    conditionExpression = = TRUE;

    cond_signal (conditionVariable);

    mutex_unlock (conditionMutex);
}
```

10.4.6 Broadcast a condition variable

```
int condition_broadcast (condition_t cond)
```

The function cond_broadcast is similar to the cond_signal function except that it can notify multiple threads instead of a single thread, as in the case of cond_signal. The following code segment shows a typical broadcast logic.

```
BroadcastCondition ()
{
    mutex_lock (conditionMutex); /* assume CreateCondObjects has been called */
```

```
    conditionExpression = = TRUE;

    cond_broadcast (conditionVariable);

    mutex_unlock (conditionMutex);
}
```

Readers are advised to read Sec. 3.9 to understand the issues of race conditions and the lost wakeup problem. While reading these sections, replace all Pthreads APIs with C-Threads APIs.

10.4.7 Guidelines for using condition variables

- Always use global or static variables for CVs. Do not try to use stack variables for CVs because the stack of a thread is destroyed when the thread terminates. Other threads in the process can be still referencing the CV even though the address of the CV is invalid after stack destruction.
- Initialize the CV before using it, and initialize it only once such that all threads have the same view of the CV.
- Delete CVs after they are no longer used.
- Associate a condition predicate with your CV.
- Use CVs in a while loop, as shown in Sec. 10.4.4
- When the wait function cond_wait returns, then the mutex is locked. It is important to unlock the mutex after you are done with the CV.

10.5 Threads and Variables

Threads in a process run in the same address space and have access to all process resources, including variables in memory. These variables can be of the following types:

- Static variables
- Dynamic variables
- Stack variables

Static variables have a global scope and are allocated by the compiler (e.g., static variables in the C language). Threads have access to all static variables, and they exist for the entire duration of the process. Dynamic variables can be created by calling the allocation routine (e.g., malloc routine of the C library). Any thread that knows the address of the dynamic variable can access it safely. Dynamic variables are destroyed when the deallocation routine is called (e.g., the free routine of the C library). Stack variables or automatic variables are accessible in the routine where the variable was declared, and they cease to exist when the thread returns from the routine in which the variable was declared.

10.5.1 Thread-specific data

The reader is advised to read Secs. 4.1.1 and 4.1.2 for more information on this topic.

TSD Functions

`cthread_data`	Gets thread-specific data
`cthread_set_data`	Sets thread specific data

Unlike the Pthreads mechanism, which uses a key to associate per-thread data, C-Threads only allows association of a pointer's worth of data with a thread. This is a very simple mechanism and is *not* very helpful when developing multithreaded libraries. The problem arises when two different libraries try to associate different values with a thread. Only one of the values is stored by C-Threads, while the other gets lost.

10.5.2 Get/set thread-specific data

The macro cthread_get_data returns the thread-specific data associated with the thread identified by *thread.* If no value is currently bound to the thread, then NULL is returned. This macro allows one to get the thread-specific data for any thread and not just the calling thread. This is different from the Pthreads function, in which a thread can only retrieve its own values.

```
any_t   cthread_data (cthread_t thread)
void    cthread_set_data(cthread_t thread, any_t data)
```

The function cthread_set_data associates a pointer's worth of data identified by *data* with the *thread.* Since the value set is of type any_t, you can pass an address of a string or structure to it. Since the C-Threads library only stores one value per thread, one could lose the previous association. This can lead to some disastrous results in your program.

```
SetThreadData()
{
   char  *threadData;
   threadData = malloc(....);

   cthread_set_data(cthread_self(), thrData);
}
```

The reader is advised to see the sample programs on disk where a key-based TSD scheme is implemented. This allows one to expand the thread-specific data area and allows multiple TSDs to be associated with a thread.

Chapter 11

C-Threads Programming Examples

11.1 Compiling and Linking

Every program that uses the threads library should include the header file *<mach/cthreads.h>*. The compiler and linker options for the NeXTSTEP operating system are shown below.

NeXTSTEP 3.2

```
cc foo.c -o foo -lNeXT_s -lsys_s
```

11.2 Queue Implementation

Queues are a simple yet powerful interthread communication paradigm. Queues can be used effectively in applications that use worker threads to service clients. Threads, instead of waiting on condition variables, can wait on queues for work items to be added. It should be noted that threads that use queues for servicing requests are much easier to program and test.

```
#include <stdio.h>
#include <stddef.h>
#include <mach/cthreads.h>

typedef struct _qmsg QMSG;
struct _qmsg
{
   void  *msg;
   int   msgLen;
   QMSG  *next;
};

typedef struct _queue
{
   int          qMsgs;
```

```
    int           qMax;
    mutex_t       qMutex;
    condition_t  qEmpty;
    condition_t  qFull;
    QMSG          *qHeadMsg;
    QMSG          *qTailMsg;
} QUEUE;

QUEUE   gQueue;

main(int argc, char **argv)
{
    int         numThr;
    cthread_t  threadId[MAXTHREADS];
    void        Readers();
    void        Writers();
    int         i;

    numThr = NUM_WRITERS + NUM_READERS;

    QueCreate(&gQueue, MAXTHREADS);

    for (i = 0; i < NUM_WRITERS; ++i)
        threadId[i] = cthread_fork((void *) Writers, (void *) NULL);

    for (i = NUM_WRITERS ; i < numThr; ++i)
        threadId[i] = cthread_fork((void *) Readers, (void *) NULL);

    for (i = 0; i < numThr; ++i)
        cthread_join(threadId[i]);
}

void
Writers(void *pThrArg)
{
    int         i;
    int         numMsgs;
    char        msg[256];
    cthread_t  threadId;

    numMsgs = NUMMSGS;

    threadId = cthread_self();
    sprintf(msg,"msg from thread [%d]", threadId);

    for (i = 0; i < numMsgs; ++i)
        QuePut(msg, sizeof(msg), &gQueue);

    fprintf(stderr,"writer thread:[%d] #msgs [%d] \n", threadId, numMsgs);
    cthread_exit(NULL);
}

void
Readers(void *pThrArg)
{
    int         i;
    int         numMsgs;
    cthread_t  threadId;
    char        msg[256];

    numMsgs = (NUMMSGS * NUM_WRITERS) / NUM_READERS;
    threadId = cthread_self();

    for (i = 0; i < numMsgs; ++i)
        QueGet(msg, sizeof(msg), &gQueue);
```

```
    fprintf(stderr,"reader thread:[%d] #msgs [%d] msgs\n", threadId, numMsgs);
    cthread_exit(NULL);
}

int
QueGet(void *pmsg, int msglen, QUEUE *pQueue)
{
    mutex_lock(pQueue->qMutex);

    while (pQueue->qMsgs == 0)
      condition_wait(pQueue->qEmpty, pQueue->qMutex);

    if (pQueue->qMsgs == pQueue->qMax)
      condition_broadcast(pQueue->qFull);

    DeleteQueueMsg(pmsg, msglen, pQueue);

    --pQueue->qMsgs;

    mutex_unlock(pQueue->qMutex);
}

int
QuePut(void *pmsg, int msglen, QUEUE *pQueue)
{
    mutex_lock(pQueue->qMutex);

    while (pQueue->qMsgs == pQueue->qMax)
     condition_wait(pQueue->qFull, pQueue->qMutex);

    InsertQueueMsg(pmsg, msglen, pQueue);

    ++pQueue->qMsgs;

    condition_signal(pQueue->qEmpty);

    mutex_unlock(pQueue->qMutex);
}

QueCreate(QUEUE *pQueue, int Maxmsgs)
{
   pQueue->qMutex = mutex_alloc();
   mutex_init(pQueue->qMutex);

   pQueue->qFull = condition_alloc();
   condition_init(pQueue->qFull);

   pQueue->qEmpty = condition_alloc();
   condition_init(pQueue->qEmpty);

   pQueue->qMax = Maxmsgs;
   pQueue->qMsgs = 0;
   pQueue->qHeadMsg = NULL;
   pQueue->qTailMsg = NULL;
}

InsertQueueMsg(void *pMsg, int msgLen, QUEUE *pQueue)
{
   QMSG *newMsg;

   newMsg = (QMSG *) calloc(1,sizeof(QMSG));
   newMsg->msgLen = msgLen;
   newMsg->msg = (void *) malloc(msgLen);

   memcpy(newMsg->msg, pMsg, msgLen);
```

```
    if (pQueue->qHeadMsg == NULL)
    {
        pQueue->qHeadMsg = newMsg;
        pQueue->qTailMsg = newMsg;
    }
    else
    {
        pQueue->qTailMsg->next = newMsg;
        pQueue->qTailMsg = newMsg;
    }
    return(0);
}

DeleteQueueMsg(void *Msg, int msgLen, QUEUE *pQueue)
{
    QMSG  *currMsg;
    int   len;

    currMsg = pQueue->qHeadMsg;
    len = currMsg->msgLen;

    memcpy(Msg,currMsg->msg, currMsg->msgLen);

    if (pQueue->qHeadMsg == pQueue->qTailMsg)
         pQueue->qTailMsg = NULL;

    pQueue->qHeadMsg = pQueue->qHeadMsg->next;

    free(currMsg->msg);
    free(currMsg);
    return(len); /* length of message */
}
```

11.3 Barrier Synchronization

A barrier is a synchronization point in the program where threads wait to synchronize with each other. It is used to ensure that cooperating threads have reached a point before they can proceed to the next step. All threads wait at a synchronization point until the last thread reaches the point at which all of them can proceed.

```
#include <stdio.h>
#include <stddef.h>
#include <mach/cthreads.h>

typedef struct _barrier
{
    int          bCount;
    int          bResetCount;
    int          bReset;
    int          bWaiters;
    mutex_t      bMutex;
    condition_t  bCond;
} BARRIER;

BARRIER    gBarrier;

main(int argc, char **argv)
{
    cthread_t   threadId[MAXTHREADS];
    void        BarrierThread();
    int         i;
```

```
    BarrierInit(&gBarrier, MAXTHREADS);

    for (i = 0; i < MAXTHREADS; ++i)
        threadId[i] = cthread_fork((void *) BarrierThread, NULL);

    for (i = 0; i < MAXTHREADS; ++i)
         cthread_join(threadId[i]);

    cthread_exit(NULL);
}

void
BarrierThread(void *pThrArg)
{
    int i;

    for (i = 0; i < 10; ++i)
     BarrierSync(&gBarrier);
}

int
BarrierInit(BARRIER *pBarrier, int bCount)
{
    pBarrier->bCount = bCount;
    pBarrier->bResetCount = bCount;
    pBarrier->bReset = TRUE;

    pBarrier->bMutex = mutex_alloc();
    mutex_init(pBarrier->bMutex);

    pBarrier->bCond = condition_alloc();
    condition_init(pBarrier->bCond);
}

int
BarrierSync(BARRIER *pBarrier)
{
    int wakingThread = 0;

    /* this is executed by threads that have finished executing */
    /* BarrierSync and start executing again before all threads */
    /* have exited the routine BarrierSync - referred to as fast threads */

    while (pBarrier->bReset == FALSE && !pBarrier->bCount)
       cthread_yield(); /* fast threads yield processor */

    mutex_lock(pBarrier->bMutex);

    --pBarrier->bCount;

    if (!pBarrier->bCount)
    {
       wakingThread = 1;
       pBarrier->bReset = FALSE;
    }

    while (pBarrier->bCount != 0)
    {
       ++pBarrier->bWaiters;
       fprintf(stderr,"thread [%d] waiting\n", cthread_self());
       condition_wait(pBarrier->bCond, pBarrier->bMutex);
       --pBarrier->bWaiters;
    }

    if (wakingThread)
    {
```

```
        pBarrier->bCount = 0;
        fprintf(stderr,"thread [%d] waking ......\n\n\n", cthread_self());
        mutex_unlock(pBarrier->bMutex);
        condition_broadcast(pBarrier->bCond);
        return (0);
    }

    if (!pBarrier->bWaiters)
    {
        fprintf(stderr,"barrier [%d] reset ......\n\n\n", cthread_self());
        pBarrier->bCount = pBarrier->bResetCount; /* reset barrier count */
        pBarrier->bReset = TRUE;
    }

    mutex_unlock(pBarrier->bMutex);
    return (0);
}
```

11.4 Semaphore Synchronization

```
#include <stdio.h>
#include <fcntl.h>
#include <stddef.h>
#include <mach/cthreads.h>

typedef struct _sema
{
   mutex_t      sMutex;
   int          sWaiters;
   condition_t  sCond;
   int          semCnt;
} SEMAPHORE;

typedef struct _linebuf
{
   char        line[MAXLINE];
   int         lineLen;
   SEMAPHORE   lineEmpty;
   SEMAPHORE   lineFull;
} LINEBUF;

LINEBUF lineBuf[MAX_BUFFERS];
main(int argc, char **argv)
{
   int         i;
   cthread_t   threadId[2];
   void        *ProducerThread(char * file);
   void        *ConsumerThread(char * file);
   char        *fromFile;
   char        *toFile;

   if (argc != 3)
   {
       fprintf(stderr,"USAGE: %s from-file to-file\n", argv[0]);
       exit(1);
   }
   fromFile = argv[1];
   toFile = argv[2];

   for (i = 0; i < MAX_BUFFERS; ++i)
   {
        SemaInit(&lineBuf[i].lineEmpty,1);
        SemaInit(&lineBuf[i].lineFull,0);
   }

   threadId[0] = cthread_fork((void *) ProducerThread, (void *) fromFile);
```

```
    threadId[1] = cthread_fork((void *) ConsumerThread, (void *) toFile);

    for (i = 0; i < 2; ++i)
        cthread_join(threadId[i]);
}

void *
ProducerThread(char * file)
{
    int         fileFd;
    int         nRead;
    int         i = 0;
    cthread_t   threadId;

    fileFd = open(file, O_RDWR, 0666);
    if (fileFd == -1)
    {
         printf("error opening file %s\n", file);
         perror("open");
    }

    i = 0;
    while(1)
    {
       SemaAcquire(&lineBuf[i].lineEmpty);

       nRead = read(fileFd, lineBuf[i].line, MAXLINE);
       lineBuf[i].lineLen = nRead;

       SemaRelease(&lineBuf[i].lineFull);
       if (nRead <= 0)
           break;

       if (i++ == MAX_BUFFERS -1)
           i = 0;
    }
    close(fileFd);
    return(threadId);
}

void *
ConsumerThread(char * file)
{
    int   Ret;
    int   fileFd;
    int   i;

    fileFd = open(file, O_RDWR|O_CREAT, 0666);
    if (fileFd == -1)
    {
         printf("error opening file %s\n", file);
         perror("open");
    }

    i = 0;
    for (;;)
    {
        int j;

        SemaAcquire(&lineBuf[i].lineFull);

        if (lineBuf[i].lineLen <= 0)
             break;

        j = 0;
```

```
        for (j = 0; j < lineBuf[i].lineLen; ++j)
             lineBuf[i].line[j] = toupper(lineBuf[i].line[j]);
        Ret = write(fileFd, lineBuf[i].line, lineBuf[i].lineLen);
        if (Ret == -1 ) {
             printf("error writing to file %s\n", file);
             perror("write");
        }

        SemaRelease(&lineBuf[i].lineEmpty);

        if (i++ == MAX_BUFFERS -1)
             i = 0;
   }
   close(fileFd);
   return(NULL);
}

int SemaInit(SEMAPHORE *pSema, int semCnt)
{
   pSema->sMutex = mutex_alloc();
   mutex_init(pSema->sMutex);

   pSema->sCond = condition_alloc();
   condition_init(pSema->sCond);
   pSema->semCnt = semCnt;
   pSema->sWaiters = 0;
}

int SemaAcquire(SEMAPHORE *pSema)
{
   mutex_lock(pSema->sMutex);

   while(pSema->semCnt == 0)
   {
      ttpSema->sWaiters;
      condition_wait(pSema->sCond, pSema->sMutex);
      --pSema->sWaiters;
   }

   --pSema->semCnt;

   mutex_unlock(pSema->sMutex);
}

int SemaRelease(SEMAPHORE *pSema)
{
   int userWaiting;

   mutex_lock(pSema->sMutex);

   If (pSema->sWaiters)
      condition_signal(pSema->Cond);
   mutex_unlock(pSema->sMutex);
}
```

11.5 Reader/Writer Locks

In certain applications data are much more frequently read than they are modified. Reader/writer (RW) locks allow multiple threads to read data simultaneously but serialize writers when data have to be updated. One of the main advantages of reader/writer locks over mutex locks is that they allow multiple threads to share data in read mode without the overhead of locking. The payoff of RW locks over mutexes is not evident when the code guarded by the RW lock is short. RW locks are better when the frequency of read operations is higher than write operations, and the read operations are somewhat lengthy. The following implementation favors readers over writers and can cause starvation for writers.

```
#include <stdio.h>
#include <stddef.h>
#include <mach/cthreads.h>

typedef struct _rwlock
{
mutex_t       rwMutex;
condition_t   rwCond;
int           rwCount;
} RWLOCK;

RWLOCK  grwLock;

main(int argc, char **argv)
{
   int        numThr;
   void       *Readers(void *);
   void       *Writers(void *);
   cthread_t  threadId[MAXTHREADS];
   int        i;

   numThr = MAXTHREADS;

   InitReadWriteLock(&grwLock);

   for (i = 0; i < NUM_WRITERS; ++i)
       threadId[i] = cthread_fork((void *) Writers, NULL);

   for (i = NUM_WRITERS ; i < numThr; ++i)
       threadId[i] = cthread_fork((void *) Readers, NULL);

   for (i = 0; i <numThr; ++i)
       cthread_join(threadId[i]);
}

void *
Writers(void *pThrArg)
{
   int i;
   int numLocks;

   numLocks = NUM_LOCKS;
   for (i = 0; i < numLocks; ++i)
   {
        AcquireWriteLock(&grwLock);
        /* do some update to shared data */
        ReleaseWriteLock(&grwLock);

        /* sleep for some time before updating again */
   }
   return(NULL);
}

void *
Readers(void *pThrArg)
{
```

```
    int i;
    int numLocks;

    numLocks = (NUM_LOCKS * NUM_WRITERS) / NUM_READERS;

    for (i = 0; i < numLocks; ++i)
    {
        AcquireReadLock(&grwLock);
        /* read shared data */
        ReleaseReadLock(&grwLock);
    }
    return(NULL);
}

AcquireReadLock(RWLOCK *prwLock)
{
   mutex_lock(prwLock->rwMutex);

   while( prwLock->rwCount < 0)
      condition_wait(prwLock->rwCond, prwLock->rwMutex);

  ++prwLock->rwCount;

   mutex_unlock(prwLock->rwMutex);
}

ReleaseReadLock(RWLOCK *prwLock)
{
   mutex_lock(prwLock->rwMutex);

   --prwLock->rwCount;

   mutex_unlock(prwLock->rwMutex);
   if (!prwLock->rwCount)
        condition_signal(prwLock->rwCond);
}

AcquireWriteLock(RWLOCK *prwLock)
{
   mutex_lock(prwLock->rwMutex);

   while( prwLock->rwCount != 0)
       condition_wait(prwLock->rwCond, prwLock->rwMutex);

   prwLock->rwCount = -1;

   mutex_unlock(prwLock->rwMutex);
}

ReleaseWriteLock(RWLOCK *prwLock)
{
   mutex_lock(prwLock->rwMutex);
   prwLock->rwCount = 0;
   condition_broadcast(prwLock->rwCond);
   mutex_unlock(prwLock->rwMutex);
}

InitReadWriteLock(RWLOCK *prwLock)
{
   prwLock->rwMutex = mutex_alloc();
   mutex_init(prwLock->rwMutex);
   prwLock->rwCond = condition_alloc();
   condition_init(prwLock->rwCond);
   prwLock->rwCount = 0;
}
```

Chapter

12

WIN32 Thread Management

12.1 Introduction to Windows NT

The work on Microsoft's new technology (NT) operating system started in 1988. The development of NT began with the goal of providing a reliable operating system (OS) that could establish Microsoft's presence with a new and powerful operating system for the 1990s. The NT development started as an ambitious project, and it was headed by Dave Cutler, a veteran from Digital Equipment Corporation (DEC), who while working at DEC had built some successful operating systems such as VAX/VMS and RSX-11M.

In addition to providing the new and advanced features of a modern OS, one of the main design goals of NT was to maintain compatibility with existing Microsoft systems such as DOS and Windows 3.X. Even though compatibility with legacy systems was a prime goal, Windows NT was *not* designed as some hacked-up operating system on top of DOS. One thing that is refreshing to know is that in NT finally there is no DOS. Windows NT has been designed from the ground up to be a modern 32-bit real operating system.

In addition to compatibility with existing systems, some of the other design goals of NT were to provide an operating system that was extensible, portable, secure, fast, and reliable (unlike Windows 3.1). At the time work on NT began, multiprocessor machines were becoming popular in terms of price and performance. NT is designed from the ground up to be a scalable and robust operating system supporting symmetric multiprocessing (SMP). NT is a modern 32-bit OS supporting preemptive multitasking, symmetric multiprocessing, and multithreading. Since it is beyond the scope of this book to cover the design or internals of NT in detail, the discussion will be restricted to the multiprocessing and multithreading features of NT as they relate to the WIN32 subsystem. The reader is advised that some of the text has been repeated from earlier chapters for the sake of completeness.

12.1.1 Overview of NT

The overall structure of NT can be broadly divided into two parts: protected *subsystems* and the *executive*. Windows NT is designed to support multiple operating systems (environments) such as MS-DOS, Windows 3.X, OS/2 1.X, POSIX.1, and WIN32. In NT jargon, each of these environments is referred to as a *subsystem*. NT uses a client/server model to provide the multiple programming environment to the end user. A subsystem in NT can be considered to be a personality layered on top of the NT executive (microkernel approach). This architecture was greatly influenced by the work on the Mach operating system developed at Carnegie Mellon University (CMU). Each of the subsystems calls the native services of NT to implement the different semantics and APIs of the subsystems. NT has become extensible by using the subsystem approach to layer different environments; new personalities can be added easily in the future without changing the executive or kernel portion.

NT employs a layered approach in providing the services to the subsystems. The kernel-mode component of NT is called the *executive,* and it provides basic services such as object management, virtual memory management, and interprocess communication (IPC). The executive interacts with a component called the *kernel*. The kernel, which is the heart of Windows NT, provides such services as thread scheduling, context switching, interrupt handling, and multiprocessor synchronization. The lowest level is the *hardware abstraction layer* (HAL), which insulates the executive and the kernel from hardware dependencies.

NT subsystems are implemented as user-mode NT processes that run and emulate different personalities such as MS-DOS, Windows 3.X, WIN32, POSIX, and OS/2. I feel that the WIN32 subsystem is the main subsystem and other subsystems such as POSIX and OS/2 are hardly usable and only serve as *checklist* items. Personally, I feel that it makes no sense to support OS/2 1.X when most of the current OS/2 users are running 3.X. I also believe that POSIX applications are becoming more sophisticated and require more functionality than provided by the base POSIX.1 standard. Some of the standards, such as POSIX.1b (real-time extensions) and POSIX.1c (thread extensions), provide the extensions to the base standard. It remains to be seen if Microsoft will ever support the more advanced POSIX standards. Having said this, I must add that the WIN32 environment is sufficient for application development, and one would hardly have any reason to develop a new POSIX.1 or OS/2 application on NT. A word of advice: *only* use the WIN32 environment on NT.

12.1.2 Objects and handles

Before we dive into the multithreading features of Windows NT, let us examine some of the basic concepts of NT, such as objects and handles. Borrowing from the ideas of object-oriented design, Windows NT uses object classes to represent the system resources. Even though NT uses the concept of objects, one should *not* think for a moment that NT is an object-oriented operating system.

An *object* is an abstract data type whose properties can only be manipulated through a set of services associated with the object. NT uses objects to represent system resources such as IPC, processes, threads, files, and memory. These objects are created and modified in a uniform fashion by the object manager component of the kernel. Objects in NT can either be named or unnamed. Access to each of these objects is controlled by the security manager; security information can be used to restrict access to an object.

When an object is either created or accessed in NT, then a *handle* to the object is returned. A handle can be considered to be a pointer to an opaque object. Currently, a handle is a 32-bit number, but it could change to a 64-bit number when NT is rewritten to be a 64-bit OS. The bottom line is that handles and objects are supposed to be *opaque* data types and should be considered that way. Objects in NT can reference each other by opening a handle. For example, when a thread object opens a file object, then a handle to the file object is returned that can be used later to perform I/O operations on the file.

Handles in NT are maintained on a *per-process basis*. When a process terminates, then all objects that are created by the threads are deleted *automatically* by the object manager. When a thread terminates, the system does *not* delete objects or close handles, except for objects such as windows, hooks, and Dynamic Data Exchange (DDE) objects. Since handles and objects consume memory, they should be *deleted* when they are no longer needed. Objects are deleted by closing the handle to the object.

WIN32 objects have two counters per object. One is the handle count, which is incremented for each handle pointing to an object, while the other is the pointer count, which is available in the executive and is used to reference count an object. The storage for the object is not deleted until the pointer count becomes zero. An object is created initially with a reference count of one, it is incremented by one each time a thread or a process opens the object, and it is decremented by one each time a thread or process closes the object.

12.1.3 Processes and threads

If you are not familiar with some of the basic concept of threads, I would recommend that you read Chap. 1 before you proceed to read the rest of this chapter. Chapter 1 discusses the basic concepts of multithreading and its advantages, pitfalls, and situations where using threads in your application might be useful.

In Windows NT, both processes and threads are represented as kernel objects. A process can be described to be a running instance of a program. A process in NT consists of the executable code (text and data), an address space, and possibly other system resources such as IPC objects and files. When a process is created in Windows NT, then an initial thread is created automatically by the operating system. This thread is commonly referred to as the *primary* or *main thread*. Each process in NT is uniquely identified by a process identifier (PID), and all threads within the same process share a common PID.

Threads are the basic unit of *scheduling* in NT. Each thread in Windows NT has its own stack, a set of CPU registers, and a program counter. A process in NT is defined to consist of an address space with one or more threads of control. Threads within a process share all process resources and have the same view of the address space. For example, if one thread frees a memory area, then an access violation occurs when some other thread tries to use the freed memory area. Similarly, when a file is closed by one thread, it is seen as closed by all other threads in the process.

12.1.4 WIN32 API

When the designers of Windows NT began defining the API for the WIN32 32-bit subsystem, they realized the inherent weaknesses of the 16-bit Windows 3.0 API, and thus was born the WIN32 API. Some of the design goals of the new API were

- Wherever possible, maintain compatibility with the old 16-bit API in terms of semantics and data types.
- Provide a clear migration path for the existing 16-bit applications to Windows NT.
- Change the API to use a 32-bit linear architecture.
- Make the new 32-bit APIs the same on Windows NT and MS-DOS.
- Add advanced operating system capabilities such as memory management, process and thread management, synchronization, security, and I/O capabilities.

The WIN32 API has been implemented to some *varying* degree on many Microsoft platforms such as WIN32S, Windows 95, and Windows NT, although Microsoft intends (could be by the end of the century) to port the complete set of the WIN32 APIs to all their operating environments. Note that on some platforms only a *subset* of the API is implemented. This and subsequent chapters concentrate on the APIs commonly used by multithreaded applications, and except for WIN32S, most of these APIs are implemented on Windows 95 and Windows NT. As far multithreading is concerned, some of the missing features of WIN32 in Windows 95 are support for asynchronous I/O on files, symmetric multiprocessing, and security.

The concepts and APIs discussed in the next few chapters are applicable to both Windows 95 and Windows NT. I would like to make it clear that even though the underlying OS is *different* for Windows 95 and Windows NT, you do not have to worry about it because you code to the WIN32 API. Since NT supports true multithreading and SMP, the programming bugs will show up with more frequency on NT than on Windows 95. I will try to point out the differences in the implementation of these APIs on these different operating systems wherever possible. The last chapter covers APIs such as asynchronous I/O and I/O completion ports, and today these APIs are only implemented on Windows NT. I would recommend that you should use the Microsoft

WIN32 API documentation to get a better understanding of the differences between the WIN32 implementation of Windows 95 and Windows NT.

The WIN32 APIs are used to create and manage threads. The thread APIs can be broadly classified into such areas as thread management, thread synchronization, thread-specific data, and advanced thread topics. The advanced thread topics deal with things like scheduling and priority.

For the sake of simplicity, the example code segments presented in this book do not perform any error checking. One should always *check* for error conditions, and on error use the WIN32 function *GetLastError* to find out the error code. You should consult the Microsoft WIN32 API documentation to find the error codes returned by each of the APIs. The samples in this book and some of the discussions are targeted toward the Microsoft Visual C++ compiler. If you are using some other compiler, then you should consult your compiler vendor's documentation for more information.

12.2 Thread Management Functions

`CreateThread`	Creates a new thread
`_beginthreadex`	Creates a new thread (C Library)
`_endthreadex`	Exits a thread (C Library)
`ExitThread`	Exits a thread
`GetCurrentThread`	Gets thread handle
`GetCurrentThreadId`	Gets thread identifier
`GetExitCodeThread`	Gets exit code of a thread
`GetThreadAffinityMask`	Gets processor affinity
`GetThreadTimes`	Gets thread execution time
`ResumeThread`	Resumes a suspended thread
`SuspendThread`	Suspends a thread
`SetThreadAffinityMask`	Sets processor affinity of a thread
`Sleep`	Sleeps for an interval
`SleepEx`	Alertable sleep for an interval
`TerminateThread`	Terminates a thread

12.2.1 Create a thread

When a process begins execution, it has a single thread of control. The process is created automatically with one thread that is commonly referred to as the *main thread*. The creation of the main thread maintains binary compatibility with single-threaded programs. If a process needs additional threads of control, then they have to be created either by calling the WIN32 or C-Runtime thread creation API.

When threads are created, they begin executing a start routine. Creating a thread is somewhere between calling a function and creating a process. The start routine specifies the entry point at which the newly created thread starts execution. Multiple threads can execute the same start routine, or each thread can have its own start routine. If multiple threads call the same start routine and modify shared data within the routine, then the routine *must* be written to be thread-safe. Later, in Chapter 20, strategies for developing reentrant code are explained in detail.

There is no relationship between any of the threads, nor does a thread maintain a list of all created threads or have any knowledge of other threads in the process. The process terminates when the last thread in the process terminates or some thread in the process calls the WIN32 process termination routine.

```
HANDLE CreateThread   (LPSECURITY_ATTRIBUTES lpsa, DWORD cbStack,
                       LPTHREAD_START_ROUTINE lpStartAddr,
                       LPVOID lpvThreadParam,
                       DWORD fdwCreate, LPDWORD lpIDThread)
```

The function *CreateThread* is used to create a new thread of control in the process. On success, the function returns a handle to the newly created thread object. The thread object stores all information about the newly created thread. The handle of a thread allows you to use certain APIs to access the thread. The presence of a handle does *not* affect the ability of a thread to execute. In fact if you know that you would never need to interact with the thread again, then it a good idea to close the handle of the thread immediately after calling CreateThread.

The argument *lpsa* is a pointer to a SECURITY_ATTRIBUTES structure, and it specifies if the thread handle can be inherited across child processes. It also specifies the operations that can be performed on the newly created thread. For example, if a process wants to terminate a thread, then the process should have THREAD_TERMINATE rights on the thread object. By default, the handle returned by CreateThread has THREAD_ALL_ACCESS access to the thread object. Generally, a NULL value is passed for default security attributes. By using a restrictive ACL, a thread can be created that would be hard to open using the function DuplicateHandle.

The second argument *cbStack* specifies the stack size (in bytes) that will be used by the newly created thread. The stack size of a process can be controlled by the linker's /STACK switch. By default, 1 MB of stack space is *reserved* for each thread. Initially, not all the reserved stack space is committed; rather, it starts with an initial value of one page. A page in Windows NT is the basic memory allocation unit and depends on the underlying hardware platform. The page size on DEC Alpha is 8192 bytes, and it is 4096 bytes on other systems (e.g., X86 and MIPS).

The stack is guard page protected and can grow dynamically, committing pages as required by the thread. When a thread reaches its allocated 1-MB stack limit, then an exception EXCEPTION_STACK_OVERFLOW is raised in the faulting thread. Applications can *detect* stack overflow by using the Structured Exception Handling (SEH) feature of NT. If a value of 0 (default) is passed to cbStack, then the function CreateThread creates a stack using the stack size of the process. One would use default stack size when the stack requirement is higher than the default value or when one would like to save address space in a heavily threaded application. It is more important that one should get the correct stack size for the process. In addition to the user stack, an 8-kB kernel stack is created for each new thread. The kernel stack is used whenever the thread runs in priviledged mode. Note that in NT 4.0 the kernel stack is larger than 8 kB and is manually variable.

The argument *lpStartAddr* is a pointer to a function that is executed as the thread's start routine. The start routine should be defined to accept an LPVOID as its argument, and it should return a DWORD. The argument *lpvThreadParam* is a pointer to an optional argument passed to the thread's start routine, and it can be NULL in the case when no arguments are passed to the thread routine. Passing integer values and casting them to LPVOID is a bad programming practice and should be avoided.

The argument *fdwCreate* specifies if the thread is created in a suspended state or should be scheduled for execution right away. If the value CREATE_SUSPENDED is passed to fdwCreate, then the thread is created in a suspended state and does *not* start execution until some other thread calls the function ResumeThread. When a value 0 is passed, a thread is created in runnable state.

Generally, threads are not created in suspended state, but there are certain situations where it makes sense to create them in suspended state. For example, you might want to create a thread in suspended state, alter the thread priority, and then resume the thread. Another instance in which you might want to create a thread in suspended state is when the state of the thread has to be initialized before it can run (e.g., create a mutex).

On success, the function CreateThread places the identifier of the newly created thread in *lpIDThread*. Each thread within a process is identified by a thread identifier (TID). The TID of the newly created thread is a system-wide unique identifier. This is different from many other operating systems, where thread identifiers are guaranteed only to be unique within a single process.

The system does *not* necessarily start executing the newly created thread right away. One should never depend on the order in which the new thread starts executing. The new thread can start running even before the function CreateThread returns in the calling thread; it all depends on the scheduling of both threads. Also, it is possible that the new thread would have terminated by the time the function CreateThread returns to the caller. Even when the newly created thread terminates, the TID of the terminated thread is *not* reused unless the calling thread calls CloseHandle.

There are two important things worth mentioning regarding the function CreateThread. First, the WIN32 subsystem creates a supplementary thread for itself when a thread owning a window calls the function CreateThread. This can add overhead to the WIN32 subsystem and the application. Note that in NT 4.0 a supplementary thread is *no* longer created.

Another thing worth mentioning is that when a thread is created, the system calls each of the DLL's DllMains; an important fact to know is that entry to the DLL entry point is serialized. This will restrict you from doing blocking functions in certain parts of the DllMain function. The topic of DLL and threads is covered in detail in Sec. 14.3. In NT 3.5 a process-level mutex is used to serialize access to the DLLs, while in NT 4.0 a fancy critical section is used that is partially preinitialized.

The following example illustrates the creation of a new thread. The newly created thread is created to start executing the routine LoopThread. The routine LoopThread executes a loop, and the number of iterations to loop is specified as an argument to the thread routine.

```
main (int argc, char **argv)
{
   HANDLE  hThread;
   DWORD   threadId;
   DWORD   LoopThread (LPVOID);
   int     numRows;
   int     *pThrArg;

   numRows = 1000;
   pThrArg = &numRows;

   /* create the thread to execute the routine LoopThread */
   hThread = CreateThread(NULL, 0, LoopThread, (void *) pThrArg, 0,
             & threadId);
   /* Wait for the thread to terminate. ExitProcess will terminate all
   threads */
   WaitForSingleObject(hThread, INFINITE);

   ExitProcess(0);
}

DWORD
LoopThread (void * pThrArg)
{
   int j;
   int numRows;

   numRows = *((int *) pThrArg);

   for (j = 0; j < numRows; ++j)
       printf ("loop iteration [%d]\n", j);

   return(0);
}
```

12.2.1.1 Passing multiple arguments to a thread routine. How do we pass multiple arguments to a thread routine? To pass multiple arguments to a thread routine, you should place the arguments in a structure, and pass the address of the structure as an argument to the thread's start routine. The only argument that can be passed to the thread routine is an LPVOID, and it can be the address of a string or the address of a structure.

```
typedef struct _THRARG
{
   int  rows;
   int  cols;
}THRARG;

main (int argc, char **argv)
{
```

```
    DWORD   threadId;
    HANDLE  hThread;
    DWORD   LoopThread (LPVOID);
    THRARG  thrArg;

    thrArg.Rows = 10;
    thrArg.Cols = 20;
    hThread = CreateThread(NULL, 0, LoopThread, (void *) &thrArg, 0,
                &threadId);

    WaitForSingleObject(hThread, INFINITE);

    ExitProcess(0);

}

DWORD
LoopThread (THRARG *pThrArg)
{
    int j;
    int k;

    for (j = 0; j < pThrArg->Rows; ++j)
    for (k = 0; k < pThrArg->Cols;++k)
         printf ("loop iteration j: [%d]\t k: [%d]\n", j, k);

    return(0);
}
```

12.2.1.2 Passing different parameters to a thread routine. In multithreaded applications it is common to create multiple threads to execute the same routine but with different parameters. How do you pass different parameters to a thread routine such that each thread has its own context? Dynamically allocated memory can be used to maintain context for each thread. This guarantees that each thread will have the information it needs in a unique memory area. An incorrect version of the code will be implemented first for illustration purposes, and later the correct version will be implemented.

```
main (int argc, char **argv)   /* Incorrect Version might!! work correctly */
{
    HANDLE  hThread1;
    HANDLE  hThread2;
    DWORD   threadId1;
    DWORD   threadId2;
    DWORD   LoopThread (LPVOID);
    THRARG  thrArg;

    /* Set the information for thread #1 */
    thrArg.Rows = 10;
    thrArg.Cols = 20;

    hThread1 = CreateThread(NULL, 0, LoopThread, (void *) &thrArg, 0,
                &threadId1);

    /* Set the information for thread #2 */
    thrArg.Rows = 30;
    thrArg.Cols = 40;

    hThread2 = CreateThread(NULL, 0, LoopThread, (void *) &thrArg, 0,
                &threadId2);
```

```
    /* Wait for both the threads to terminate */

    ExitProcess(0);
}

DWORD
LoopThread (THRARG *pThrArg)
{

    int j;
    int k;
    int numRows;
    int numCols;

    numRows = pThrArg->rows; /* assume T1 is preempted at this statement */
    numCols = pThrArg->cols;

    for (j = 0; j < numRows; ++j)
    for (k = 0; k < numCols;++k)
         printf ("loop iteration j: [%d]\t k: [%d]\n", j, k);

    return(0);
}
```

You would expect that when the first thread would run it would print the values 10 and 20, while the second thread would print 30 and 40. The question that arises is, "How can such a simple code not work correctly all the time?" This might work correctly depending on some other factors such as thread scheduling or the number of processors. If threads were sequential entities, then it would have worked correctly every time. Remember that threads are *concurrent* entities and can even run in parallel on an SMP machine. Let us examine the following sequence of events under which the preceding code will work incorrectly.

- The main thread creates thread T1 and is scheduled to run on the first processor P1. T1 is preempted by a higher-priority thread on P1 *before* it starts executing the assignment statements in the function LoopThread (see preceding code).
- The main thread now changes the values in the global structure and creates the second thread T2. Thread T2 starts running immediately on a different processor P2. When T2 executes the routine ThreadRoutine, it prints the values 30 and 40.
- T1 is rescheduled to run on P1 and resumes executing the routine ThreadRoutine. It will print the values 30 and 40.

You can see that under such a situation the information for the thread T1 is lost. The preceding program will work correctly if T1 executes the routine LoopThread before the main thread updates the structure with both new values for T2. This can happen if the main thread is rescheduled right after it creates the first thread, in which case the value of numRows and numCols inside LoopThread will be 10 and 20 when T1 executes both the assignment statements.

It is possible that the main thread is rescheduled after it updates one of the values, in which case when T1 runs it will print the values 30 and 20. By now you must have observed that many things can go wrong and are very much dependent on timing and scheduling of the threads. Welcome to the real world of thread programming, where all kinds of things can go *wrong* depending on thread scheduling, number of processors, and other factors (including your own programming bugs). Most of these problems can be solved by coding the application correctly.

```
main (int argc, char **argv)      /* Correct version */
{
   HANDLE    hThread1;
   HANDLE    hThread2;
   DWORD     threadId1;
   DWORD     threadId2;
   DWORD     LoopThread (LPVOID);
   THRARG    *ThrArg1;
   THRARG    *ThrArg2;

   thrArg1 = (THRARG *) malloc (sizeof (THRARG));
   thrArg1->Rows = 10;
   thrArg1->Cols = 20;

   hThread1 = CreateThread(NULL, 0, LoopThread, (void *) thrArg1, 0,
              &threadId1);

   thrArg2 = (THRARG *) malloc (sizeof (THRARG));
   thrArg2->Rows = 30;
   thrArg2->.Cols = 40;

   hThread2 = CreateThread(NULL, 0, LoopThread, (void *) thrArg2, 0,
              &threadId2);

   /* Wait for both the threads to complete using WaitforMultipleObjects */

   free ( (void *) ThreadArg1);
   free ( (void *) ThreadArg2);

   ExitProcess (0);
}
```

Now you can observe that by using different variables for each of the threads, the *race* condition associated with the use of a single variable is eliminated. When you pass dynamically allocated variables as arguments to a thread routine, you *should* deallocate the memory when the thread terminates; otherwise, you will have a memory leak in your application. It makes more sense to deallocate such variables in the thread routine unless the thread returns some result in the thread argument to the caller.

12.2.1.3 Scope of thread routine argument. The variable that is passed to the thread start routine is usually a dynamically allocated variable or a global variable. When stack variables are used, then one should make sure that the scope of the variable is *valid* throughout the execution of the thread using the variable. The scope of stack variables is limited to the routine in which the variable is declared, and these variables cease to exist after the caller returns from the routine in which the thread was declared.

The following code segment shows a programming bug that can be caused by using stack variables to pass arguments to a thread routine. The main thread calls the function DoFunc, which creates a new thread to execute the routine LoopThread. When the routine DoFunc returns, the variable thrArg is automatically *destroyed,* and this can cause problems in the thread when it begins executing the routine LoopThread. The same code might work depending on the scheduling of the threads. As a general rule, one should avoid using stack variables for passing arguments to another thread.

```
main (int argc, char **argv)
{
   void DoLoop(int, int);

   DoLoop (10, 20);
   /* do some other stuff */
}

void DoLoop (int rows, int cols)
{
   HANDLE  hThread;
   DWORD   threadId;
   DWORD   LoopThread (LPVOID);
   THRARG  thrArg;

   thrArg.Rows = Rows;
   thrArg.Cols = Cols;

   hThread = CreateThread(NULL, 0, LoopThread, (void *) &thrArg, 0,
             &threadId);

   return; /* the variable thrArg ceases to exist after the return—bug! */
}
```

To avoid this nasty bug, either declare the variable thrArg to be global or define thrArg to be a pointer and dynamically allocate the memory for the variable. I would recommend that you use the latter method, since this will ensure that the routine DoLoop can be used safely by multiple threads.

12.2.1.4 Maximum threads allowed. Threads are much more lightweight than a process. Even though threads are cheap, they are *not free*. Threads use system resources such as memory and involve scheduling overhead. The maximum number of threads that can be created successfully in a process in NT is limited by system resources. The biggest resource consumed is the system address space for the kernel stacks. For efficiency reasons, it is not a good idea to create too many threads in your application.

12.2.2 Thread termination

Everything that is created must come to an end, and so must the life of a thread. A thread can terminate in one of the following ways:

- It exits the start routine.
- It calls ExitThread to terminate itself.
- It is forcefully terminated by some other thread.

```
VOID ExitThread(DWORD fuExitCode)
```

The function ExitThread terminates the calling thread and stores the exit status in the variable *fuExitCode* for later use. This exit code is later made available to any thread calling the function GetExitCodeThread. When a thread terminates, the thread object becomes *signaled,* and all threads waiting for the thread to terminate are notified. The function ExitThread is called implicitly when a thread returns from the start routine that was used to create the thread. In such a case, the function return value serves as the exit status. The routine ExitThread does *not* return to the calling thread.

When the initial thread *returns* from the main routine, then the routine ExitProcess is implicitly called, thus terminating all threads in the process. It is a good practice to always call ExitThread to terminate a thread (including the main thread). When the initial thread calls ExitThread, it does *not* terminate the entire process. The process will only terminate when the last thread in the process terminates. When a thread terminates *naturally* (not terminated by some other thread), then the stack is destroyed and all DLLs to which the thread is attached are notified of the thread termination.

A process in WIN32 can terminate itself by calling the *ExitProcess* or the C-Runtime *_exit* routine. In a multithreaded process, the routine ExitProcess terminates the *entire* process and not just the calling thread. The routine ExitProcess in a multithreaded process should be called only when the entire process needs to be terminated. For example, on a fatal error when the integrity of the entire process is questionable, it is *better* to exit the entire process than just one thread.

12.2.2.1 Forceful termination of a thread. If a thread stops responding for some reason, then it might become necessary to terminate the thread in a forceful manner. Do *not* call this function unless you know the exact state of a thread and you know that there are no side effects. You should *always* use some interthread communication method to send a graceful termination notice to a thread. For example, a thread can check a flag periodically to see if it needs to be terminated. This logic works most of the time, except when a thread is blocked on some function such as WaitForMultipleObjects and you want to terminate that thread. In such a case, a WIN32 event object can be used for termination purposes; the handle of this object should be passed in all calls to the function WaitForMultipleObjects. When the object becomes signaled, you know that a termination request is pending. If your application processes windows messages, then use PostMsg to send a termination message. I am sure you have thought of many other ways to send termination notification to a thread.

As you can see, there are many choices, but none of them are straightforward to design in a large application. To make it easier, it is very *important* that you should code the termination logic in your application from the very beginning. There is no simple scheme that will solve the needs of all applications. Spend time thinking about forceful termination during the design phase, and code your application with termination in mind. Failure to do so might lead to deadlocks in your code. If the function TerminateThread causes *problems* in your application, it does not make sense to blame NT or the WIN32 API. Note that TerminateThread was designed only to be used as a last resort.

```
BOOL TerminateThread(HANDLE hThread, DWORD dwExitCode)
```

The function TerminateThread terminates the thread identified by *hThread* and sets its exit code to *dwExitCode*. This exit code is later made available to any thread calling the function GetExitCodeThread.

There are couple of important things to know about the function TerminateThread. The function does *not* destroy the stack of the target thread, and *none* of the DLLs are notified of the thread's termination. This is a dangerous function to use. Certain library functions like printf from the C-Runtime library can *deadlock* if a thread is terminated in the middle of executing a function.

12.2.3 Get exit code of thread termination

When a thread terminates, the system changes the exit code of the thread from STILL_ACTIVE to the code passed to the ExitThread or TerminateThread function. Other threads in the process can determine the exit code status by calling the function GetExitCodeThread.

```
BOOL GetExitCodeThread(HANDLE hThread, LPDWORD lpdwExitCode)
```

When the thread referenced by *hThread* is no longer active, then the function returns TRUE and fills *lpdwExitCode* with the exit code used by the thread at termination. If the thread referenced by hThread is still active, then the function returns FALSE and sets lpdwExitCode to STILL_ACTIVE.

The system maintains the exit code of a thread as long as the thread object is not deleted. When a thread terminates, the thread object is not deleted until the *last* handle to the thread object is closed. When you call GetExitCode on a thread whose handle has been closed, the function will fail because the handle is no longer valid.

12.2.4 Waiting for thread termination

In the worker thread model it is common for a thread to suspend execution until some other thread terminates. For example, consider a program in which a master thread creates multiple worker threads to perform parallel queries on different databases. The master thread has to wait for all the worker threads to terminate before it can continue processing with the result of the queries.

Since processes and threads in NT have built-in synchronization capabilities, the WaitForXXX (WaitforSingleObject, WaitForMultipleObjects, etc.) family of functions can be used to wait for thread termination. If you are not familiar with the WIN32 wait functions, then you should first read Sec. 13.1.5. When a thread terminates, the thread object becomes signaled, and the system wakes up any process or thread waiting for it to be signaled. Unlike some of the other kernel synchronization objects, thread objects *remain* in signaled state even after a successful return from the WIN32 WaitForXXX function.

Since the function GetExitCodeThread is a nonblocking function, one should never call this function in a polling manner (until it returns TRUE) to wait for thread termination. It is a terrible waste of CPU resources; therefore, one should always use the WaitForXXX function to wait for thread termination. The following code segment shows how to wait for a thread to terminate and then find out the termination code of the thread.

```
main (int argc, char **argv)
{
   HANDLE  hThread;
   DWORD   threadId;
   DWORD   LoopThread (LPVOID);
   int     numRows;
   int     *pthrArg;
   DWORD   status;
   BOOL    fStat;

   numRows = 1000;
   pthrArg = &NumRows;

   /* create the thread to execute the routine LoopThread */
   hThread = CreateThread(NULL ,0, LoopThread, (void *) pthrArg, 0,
             &threadId);

   /* Wait for the thread to complete */
   WaitForSingleObject(hThread, INFINITE);

   fStat = GetExitCodeThread(hThread, &status);
   if (fStat = = TRUE && status ! = 0) /* Status ! = 0 is an application
      defined protocol */
       fprintf(stderr, "Thread exited with failure status ....\n");

   CloseHandle(hThread); /* this will delete the thread object */
   ExitProcess(0);
}

DWORD
LoopThread (void * pthrArg)
{
   int j;
   int numRows;

   numRows = *((int *) pthrArg);
```

```
    if (numRows < 0 )
        ExitThread(1); /* caller should detect it as a failure */

    for (j = 0; j < numRows; ++j)
        printf ("loop iteration j: [%d]\n", j);

    return(0); /* caller considers this as a success */
}
```

12.2.5 Thread handles and identifiers

The function CreateThread returns the handle to the thread object; if the thread wants to know its own handle, it should call the function *GetCurrentThread.* The function GetCurrentThread returns a pseudohandle to the calling thread and should be used in functions that require a thread handle (e.g., SetThreadPriority). When the function CloseHandle is called with the pseudohandle, it has *no* effect. A pseudohandle is valid only within the context of the thread calling GetCurrentThread; therefore, the function DuplicateHandle should be used when an application needs the real handle.

```
HANDLE GetCurrentThread(VOID)
```

Each thread within the system is uniquely identified by a thread identifier (TID). The TID of a thread is returned in the call to CreateThread and _beginthreadex. Since NT reuses process and thread identifiers, these identifiers are only valid from the time a thread is created until it terminates. The thread can find its own TID by calling the function *GetCurrentThreadId.* Some functions such as AttachThreadInput and PostThreadMessage expect a thread identifier.

```
DWORD GetCurrentThreadId(VOID)
```

12.2.6 Thread priority

Threads in NT have 32 different priority levels. The module responsible for thread scheduling uses a *preemptive* (except in the case of Fibers) priority scheduler with different priority levels. In Windows NT, each thread is assigned a priority, and the operating system maintains an array of priority queues for each priority level. The dispatcher always picks up the highest-priority thread to run from the run queue. When multiple threads are on the same priority level, then they are chosen to run in round-robin order. In NT, a higher-priority thread can preempt a lower-priority thread, and the highest-priority thread is always chosen to run.

Priorities of threads can be broadly classified into two classes: *real-time* and *variable.* Real-time threads in NT are always scheduled ahead of other threads in the system, and the NT kernel does *not* alter the priority of real-time threads. If a thread requires fixed priority, then it should be created in the real-time class. Threads in the variable class have a *base* and a *dynamic* priority. Most applications run under the variable class. The base priority of a thread ranges from two levels above and below the process base priority. The dynamic priority of a thread is adjusted periodically by the kernel. For example, the kernel raises the dynamic priority of a thread when that thread waits on an I/O.

Threads that are CPU-bound tend to have lower dynamic priorities, while I/O-bound threads tend to have higher dynamic priority. The dynamic priority of a thread can *never* fall below the thread's base priority. Since the priority of a variable-class thread is constantly adjusted, this means that the thread can move from one priority-level queue to another during its execution. The priority of a variable-class thread is *never* boosted such that it moves to the real-time priority class.

12.2.6.1 Priority boosts The priority boost that a thread receives is small and is usually 1 or 2 points. In NT 4.0 these boosts *can* be enabled and disabled on a per-thread basis by using the functions SetThreadPriorityBoost or GetThreadPriorityBoost. The priority boost mechanism *can* be enabled or disabled on a process-wide basis by using the functions SetProcessPriorityBoost or GetProcessPriorityBoost.

```
BOOL SetThreadPriorityBoost(HANDLE hThread, BOOL bDisablePriorityBoost)
BOOL GetThreadPriorityBoost(HANDLE hThread, PBOOL pDisablePriorityBoost)
```

When running in the dynamic priority classes, the NT system will temporarily boost the priority of a thread when the thread is taken out of a wait state. The function SetThreadPriorityBoost may be used to disable this behavior for the thread *hThread*. When a value of TRUE is used for *bDisablePriorityBoost,* then dynamic priority boosting of the thread will not happen. A value of FALSE restores normal (NT 3.51 and below) behavior. The GetThreadPriorityBoost returns the priority boost control state for the thread specified by *hThread*. A value of TRUE indicates that dynamic boosting is disabled, while a value of FALSE indicates that normal (NT 3.51 and below) behavior is occurring.

12.2.7 Priority class and threads

There are basically four types of priority classes supported by the Windows NT. These are

- Idle
- Normal
- High
- Real-time

When the function CreateProcess is called, then the priority class of a process is assigned to it. Most applications run in the normal priority class (default). The priority level for the normal class ranges between 7 and 9. Foreground applications have priority level 9, while background applications have priority level 7.

In NT 4.0 this has been changed, and the normal priority class is level 8. Instead of using a priority to distinguish foreground and background applications, now quantum is used. The foreground processes get more quantum than the background processes, and the ratio is controlled by the control panel system-tasking applet. Normally, a foreground thread's quantum is three times as long as background.

The base priority of idle threads is 4 and is used mostly by low-priority system tasks such as a screen saver application or a garbage collector kind of service. You should use ideal priority class for some of your less critical background services.

High-priority class should be used rarely and usually is reserved for well-behaved and less CPU-intensive applications. If you have a communication server or a database server that does not run too frequently and does not use a lot of CPU time, then you can consider moving that server to high-priority class. By changing the priority class, there is no *guarantee* that the application will run faster. The base priority for high-priority class is 13. Keep in mind that a poorly designed high-priority application can slow down the whole system to the point that your screen might freeze.

The highest-priority class, real-time class, should be used rarely. Threads in real-time class run over all system activities. Most of the NT system in real time runs at priority level 16, while the base priority of a real-time class is 24. If you are not careful, you can interfere with the system activities. Once again, do not alter the priority of a thread unless your application is well-behaved. A process can change its priority class after it has been created. It requires special privileges to change the priority class to real-time class. When a process does not have special privileges the system ignores the request and silently puts the process in high-priority class.

```
BOOL SetPriorityClass(HANDLE hProcess, DWORD fdwPriority)
DWORD GetPriorityClass(HANDLE hProcess)
```

The function SetPriorityClass changes the priority class of the process identified by *hProcess* to *fdwPriority*. The valid values for fdwPriority are IDLE_PRIORITY_CLASS, NORMAL_PRIORITY_CLASS, HIGH_PRIORITY_CLASS, and REALTIME_PRIORITY_CLASS. You can change the priority class of any process as long you have the handle to the process and special privileges. The function GetPriorityClass returns the priority class of a process.

There are a *couple* of things that you should remember when altering the priority class to real time. First of all, changing the class does not guarantee that the application will run faster. The performance of the whole system can be degraded by one poorly performing real-time application. Also, the activities of the real-time application can interfere with system activities such as paging and cache management.

12.2.7.1 Changing thread priority. When a thread is created, it inherits the priority level of the process, which is also known as the *base priority* of a thread. A thread can increment or decrement its base priority by *2* points. For example, if the base priority of a thread is 11, then the thread can either raise its priority to 13 or lower it to 9 (max/min). If you have a CPU-intensive thread in your process, you should lower the priority level a point below other threads. Similarly, to keep the responsiveness, you can increase the priority of the GUI thread in your application.

```
BOOL SetThreadPriority(HANDLE hThread, DWORD fdwPriority)
DWORD GetThreadPriority(HANDLE hThread)
```

The function SetThreadPriority changes the relative priority of a thread identified by *hThread* to *fdwPriority*. The function GetThreadPriority returns the relative priority of a thread.

12.2.8 Thread scheduling

In Windows NT the unit of scheduling is threads, and the highest-priority thread is always scheduled to run on a CPU. Threads are scheduled according to their priority, and this is handled differently on a uniprocessor machine than on multiprocessor machines. On a uniprocessor machine, the operating system timeslices threads to run on a single processor. Each thread can run for a time quantum, and the thread is rescheduled either when it blocks, uses its total quantum, or is preempted by a higher-priority thread. On a uniprocessor machine, two threads can *never* truly run in parallel, while on SMP machines, multiple threads can run in parallel on different processors.

Scheduling of threads is also affected by the processor affinity. In NT, every process can be assigned to run on a set of processors. In the case of multiple processors, it can happen that a processor might be available but the thread cannot run on that processor even though it is the highest-priority thread. In such a case the system waits for a processor in the set to be available for the thread to run. The topic of processor affinity is discussed in Sec. 12.2.10. Windows NT uses *soft* processor affinity, which means that the system tries to run the thread on the processor it last ran on.

12.2.8.1 Thread states. A thread within a process can be in one of many system-dependent states. For the sake of simplicity, threads can be assumed to be in one of these states:

- Running
- Ready
- Waiting

A thread that is actually in the running state is utilizing the processor (CPU). On uniprocessor machines, only one thread can be in the running state, while on an SMP machine, multiple threads can be in the running state (one per CPU). For example, on a four-way SMP machine, at most four threads can be in the running state simultaneously.

A thread is classified in the ready-to-run state if the thread is waiting for an idle processor to run on. Only threads that are either in the running state or the ready-to-run state have the potential to utilize the CPU. If an application has multiple threads in the ready-to-run state, then the operating system will spend substantial time moving threads from the ready-to-run state to the running state. This process of moving threads from ready to running state is called *context switching* of threads. Context switching overhead should be minimized in order to maximize the performance gain of threads.

A thread is classified to be in the waiting state if it is waiting for some resource to be available. For example, a thread can be in the waiting state if it is waiting on I/O, mutex lock, condition variable, or even a page fault at the system level. The thread can move to the ready or running state only after the wait completes. Excessive synchronization may cause too many threads in the waiting state.

12.2.9 Suspend/Resume threads

In WIN32 a thread can be created in a suspended state when it is created by calling the function CreateThread or _beginthreadex. When a thread is suspended then it does not utilize the CPU. A suspended thread must be resumed by calling the function ResumeThread. It is also possible to suspend a thread even after it has been created by calling the function SuspendThread. Each thread has an associated suspension count. A thread can be suspended multiple times, but the requirement is that it *must* be resumed the same number of times.

These functions should *never* be used for mutual-exclusion purposes. Using thread scheduling for synchronization purposes is likely to cause you problems later. You also should know that if a thread suspends *itself* by mistake, then it will not be able to resume itself.

When a thread is suspended while holding a mutex lock and some other thread tries to acquire the same lock, then a deadlock can happen. Note that when you are using external libraries, it might *not* be possible to predict when a thread is holding a lock. For example, consider the following code segment of a function that is in some external library. If thread T1 is suspended while it is in the middle of the function DoFunc and thread T2 calls the same function, then thread T2 will block, trying to lock the mutex, until thread T1 is resumed by some other thread. If thread T1 can only be resumed by T2, then a deadlock *will* happen. Before using the function SuspendThread, be aware of the potential problems.

```
ExternalFunc()
{
   LockMutex();
   DoFunc();
   UnlockMutex();
}
```

12.2.10 Thread processor affinity

Each thread in Windows NT has a processor affinity. By default, a thread inherits this from the parent process, and it includes *all* processors. A thread in NT can choose to run on only a subset of the available processors. This subset *cannot* include a processor on which the parent process cannot run.

```
BOOL    SetThreadAffinityMask(HANDLE hThread, DWORD dwThreadAffinityMask)
DWORD   GetThreadAffinityMask(HANDLE hThread)
```

The function SetThreadAffinityMask sets a processor affinity mask of the process identified by *hThread* to *dwThreadAffinityMask*. For example, a CPU-intensive application could take advantage of the per-processor memory cache by restricting the thread to run on a specific processor. This function should be used with caution because it can lead to performance degradation and can even cause deadlocks. The following code segment shows how to restrict the thread to run on CPU 0 and 1 only.

```
LimitProcessorSet()
{
   /* note the second argument is a bitmask */
   /* restrict the thread to run on CPU 0 and 1 only */
   SetThreadAffinity(GetCurrentThread(), 3);
}
```

Another function that has been added in NT 4.0 for soft processor affinity is SetThreadIdealProcessor. The system will do its best to schedule the thread on the specified processor, allowing much of the data referenced by that thread to migrate to the caches on the specified processor.

```
DWORD   SetThreadIdealProcessor(HANDLE hThread, DWORD dwIdealProcessor)
```

The function SetThreadIdealProcessor sets the ideal processor for the thread identified by *hThread* to the processor *dwIdealProcessor*. The handle of the thread *hThread* must have THREAD_SET_INFORMATION rights. If the value passed to dwIdealProcessor is MAXIMUM_PROCESSORS, then the thread has no ideal processor. On success, the function returns either the previous ideal processor or the value MAXIMUM_PROCESSORS if the thread has no ideal processor.

12.2.11 Yielding the CPU

A thread can give up the CPU by calling the Sleep or SleepEx function. This can be used by CPU-intensive jobs to periodically give up the CPU to other processes/threads in the system.

```
VOID Sleep(DWORD cMilliSeconds)
```

The function Sleep suspends the calling thread for the time specified by *cMilliSeconds*. When a thread relinquishes the CPU, then the scheduler picks up the next thread to run on the CPU. Sleep with a value of 0 allows you to manually round-robin to other threads at your priority, but if there are no other threads, then the caller is rescheduled.

12.3 Miscellaneous Thread Functions

There are many other functions for thread management in WIN32, but these are used rarely. The function *GetThreadTimes* can be used to find out the time spent by the thread in user mode and kernel mode. Additionally, the function can give the creation and exit times of the thread. The function *CreateRemoteThread* is used to create a thread in another process, and the function *GetThreadSelectorEntry* is used to get another thread's selector table. Similarly, the functions *GetThreadContext* and *SetThreadContext* are used to get/set a thread's CONTEXT structure (CPU registers) and are used mostly by debuggers.

12.3.1 C-Runtime library and threads

The C-Runtime (CRT) library was designed initially when there was no concept or support for multiple threads within a process. With the advent of threads, the CRT functions have been rewritten to work in a multithreaded environment. If a WIN32 application calls CRT functions, then it *must* use the CRT thread functions to create/terminate any threads. The CRT functions internally allocate some memory (thread local storage) that might *not* be freed when the thread terminates using the ExitThread function. You should call the functions *_beginthreadex* and *_endthreadex,* respectively, for creating and terminating threads. The arguments to _beginthreadex are identical to CreateThread, while the argument to _endthreadex is identical to ExitThread (differences in data types). Also, *avoid* using the functions _beginthread and _endthread, which were shipped in the earlier versions of NT.

```
unsigned long _beginthreadex(void * security, unsigned int stack_size,
                      unsigned (*start_address) (void *), void *arglist,
                      unsigned int initflag, unsigned int *thraddr);

void    _endthreadex(int exitcode);
```

You must be wondering what happens if you call the function CreateThread instead of the _beginthreadex function. When a thread calls the library for the first time, the CRT detects it and allocates a per-thread data structure. This means that the threads can safely call *most* of the CRT functions. If you are planning to use the CRT function *signal,* then you have to call the _beginthreadex function because it allocates a structured exception handling frame for the thread.

For most purposes, calling either of the create functions is fine, except that the function _endthreadex has to be called to deallocate the per-thread data structure allocated by the CRT. Again, if you are using a DLL version of the CRT, then the per-thread data allocated by the CRT are freed automatically. This means that if you are using the static CRT, then you should always call _endthreadex.

Iam sure you have seen that there are some potential problems that lurk in the dark if you do not call the CRT thread creation and termination functions. I would recommend that you *always* call the function _beginthreadex and _endthreadex to create and terminate threads. When using these functions, check the error variable *errno* for errors. For example, the function _beginthreadex sets errno to EAGAIN if the system cannot create any more threads.

```
main (int argc, char **argv)
{
   unsigned long  hThread;
   unsigned int   threadId;
   unsigned int   (*LoopThread )(void *);
   int            numRows;
   int            *pthrArg;

   numRows = 1000;
   pthrArg = &numRows;

   /* create the thread to execute the routine LoopThread */
   hThread = _beginthreadex(NULL, 0, LoopThread,
                                  (void *) pthrArg, 0, &threadId);

   /* Wait for the thread to complete. ExitProcess will terminate all
      threads */
   WaitForSingleObject((HANDLE)hThread, INFINITE);

   ExitProcess(0);
}

unsigned int
LoopThread (void * pthrArg)
{
```

```
    int j;
    int numRows;

    numRows = *((int *) pthrArg);
    for (j = 0; j < numRows; ++j)
    printf ("loop iteration j: [%d]\n", j);

    return(0);
}
```

12.3.2 Fibers and Windows NT

Since WIN32 threads are preemptive it caused problems for some users (mainly UNIX database vendors) whose systems were designed to work with nonpreemptive threads (coroutines). Most of these database vendors have designed a user-level threads library on top of the UNIX process model. This was done before multithreaded UNIX kernels were popular, and they started to face problems when the code was ported to NT.

Feeling the frustration of these users, the designers of NT have introduced *nonpreemptive* threads in NT 3.5.1 called *Fibers*. A Fiber is a very lightweight execution context, and Fibers run on top of native WIN32 threads. From the WIN32 subsystem standpoint, a Fiber assumes the identity of the WIN32 thread it is running on. Fibers must be switched *manually* because they are nonpreemptive. A thread can schedule many Fibers, but the important point is that *only* a Fiber can schedule another Fiber to run. Fibers are ideal for the Windows 3.1 kind of environment and can be helpful in porting legacy Windows applications.

A Fiber is a lightweight execution context consisting of a growable stack, a set of CPU registers, and the Fiber data. Since Fibers run on top of WIN32 threads, the underlying WIN32 thread exits when a Fiber calls ExitThread. This includes all Fibers running on top of the thread. Fibers do *not* have their own thread local storage (TLS); rather, all Fibers within a thread share the TLS of the WIN32 thread.

12.3.2.1 Creating a Fiber

```
LPVOID CreateFiber(DWORD dwStackSize, LPFIBER_START_ROUTINE lpStartAddress,
                   LPVOID lpParameter)
```

This function creates a new Fiber and returns the address of the new Fiber object. CreateFiber allocates a Fiber object and sets up execution to begin at the specified start address specified by *lpStartAddress*. Unlike WIN32 threads, Fibers do *not* begin executing the routine until they are switched manually by calling the function SwitchToFiber. Note that it is the application's responsibility to manually schedule Fibers. The Fiber start routine additionally accepts a single argument *lpParameter* that is also the Fiber data returned by GetFiberData.

The function creates a stack and an initial Fiber context. The first argument *dwStackSize* controls the stack size of the Fiber, and its use is similar to the stack size argument of CreateThread. Even when a thread creates multiple Fibers *only* one of them will execute at any given time.

12.3.2.2 Address of a Fiber

```
PVOID GetCurrentFiber (VOID)
```

The function GetCurrentFiber returns the address of the current Fiber. This function is compiled in-line and is not exported from the DLL kernel32.dll.

12.3.2.3 Deleting a Fiber

```
VOID DeleteFiber (LPVOID lpFiber)
```

DeleteFiber is used to delete the stack and internal data structures associated with a Fiber pointed to by *lpFiber*. If the caller is the currently executing Fiber, then the routine ExitThread is called. If you call this function with an address of a Fiber executing on some *other* thread, then the stack of the other thread is deleted. Since this can cause an access violation in the other thread, one should be extra careful when calling this function.

12.3.2.4 Switching to a Fiber

```
VOID WINAPI SwitchToFiber (LPVOID lpFiber)
```

The function SwitchToFiber is the only way to manually schedule a Fiber. The function saves the appropriate state of the current Fiber and restores the state of the specified Fiber *lpFiber*. Note that this routine can *only* be called by a Fiber. This means that if a thread has to schedule the Fibers, then it *must* first become a Fiber by calling the function ConvertThreadToFiber.

12.3.2.5 Becoming a Fiber

```
LPVOID ConvertThreadToFiber(LPVOID lpParameter )
```

This API is used to *convert* a WIN32 thread into a Fiber. When a Win32 thread is created, it has no Fiber data structures associated with it. If the thread has a need to execute/schedule Fibers, then Fiber data structures *must* be created for the thread by calling this function. If the calling thread is not a Fiber, then this function *must* be called before the function SwitchToFiber is called.

12.3.2.6 Per-Fiber data

```
PVOID GetFiberData(VOID)
```

A Fiber in WIN32 can store a per-fiber 32-bit value. This function *returns* the per-Fiber data. When a Fiber object is created, then the data passed to the start routine are stored as the per-Fiber data. This function is compiled in-line and is not exported from the DLL kernel32.dll.

The following code segment illustrates the use of Fibers. The main thread creates a Fiber, and then they schedule each other in a round-robin fashion.

```
LPVOID mainFiber;

main(int argc, char **argv)
{
   LPVOID hFiber;
   VOID   _stdcall  RunFiber(LPVOID);

   /* convert main thread to become a fiber before scheduling */
   mainFiber = ConvertThreadToFiber(0);

   hFiber = CreateFiber(0, RunFiber, NULL); /* create a new fiber */

   for (;;)
   {
       SwitchToFiber(hFiber); /* schedule new fiber */
       fprintf(stderr,"Main Fiber Running...\n");
       DoMainFiberRoutine(); /* do something in main fiber */
   }
}
VOID _stdcall
RunFiber(LPVOID *pFiberArg)
{
   for (;;)
   {
       fprintf(stderr,"Fiber Running...\n");
       DoFiberRoutine(); /* do something in this fiber */
       SwitchToFiber(mainFiber); /* schedule main fiber */
   }
}
```

Chapter

13

WIN32 Thread Synchronization

13.1 Thread Synchronization

In a multithreaded process, all threads execute in a single address space and hence share most of the process resources. Process resources such as open file descriptors, IPC identifiers, static variables, and dynamically allocated memory variables are all shared by all the threads. For example, if one thread closes a file, then that file is considered closed for all other threads within the process. Similarly, if one thread frees a dynamically allocated buffer using the C-library *free* routine, then no other thread can safely reference the same buffer without causing an access violation.

Consider two threads running on different processors trying to update a shared variable simultaneously (e.g., ++SharedVariable). If the value of the variable before the update is 3, then the correct value after the update should be 5. If both threads update the variable concurrently, then one of the updates can be lost and the value of the variable will be 4. Even though the statement ++SharedVariable looks atomic, keep in mind that the assembly code generated for the statement might not be atomic. This lack of atomicity can cause one of the updates to be lost.

One of the main advantages of threads is easy data sharing, but along with it comes the added responsibility to guard such data against corruption. Threads need to synchronize data that are shared and can be modified by multiple threads. If shared data are modified without any synchronization by multiple threads, then the data can become inconsistent. All access to shared resources must be protected by some mutual exclusion lock. The use of locks to synchronize access to shared data is called *data synchronization.*

In a boss/worker thread model it is common to divide work between multiple threads. In such a case, one thread might wait for another thread to reach a particular state before proceeding, or one thread might wait for a particular condition to be true before proceeding. In these cases, threads are not necessarily synchronizing on data but more on conditions or events. Data synchronization is usually for shorter duration, while event synchronization can be for much longer duration.

Let us consider an example of a producer and a consumer thread writing and reading from a shared buffer. When the threads are reading or writing from the buffer, they have exclusive access to the buffer. The producer cannot write to the buffer until the consumer has finished reading from the buffer, and the consumer cannot read from the buffer until the producer has finished writing to the buffer. Each thread waits for notification from the other thread that the buffer is available. When the producer thread is finished writing to the buffer, it notifies the consumer, and vice versa. This form of synchronization is often called *event synchronization*.

13.1.1 Why mutual exclusion?

To get a better understanding of mutual exclusion, let us consider a function that adds a new item to the beginning of a list. This list is global and is shared by multiple threads within the process.

```
typedef struct _List
{
   struct _List  *next;
   void          *data;
} SHARED_LIST;

static SHARED_LIST *gpListHead; /* global variable pointing to the beginning
                                   of list */

AddToList (SHARED_LIST *pnewEntry)
{
   pnewEntry->next = gpListHead;
   gpListHead = pnewEntry;
}
```

Let us further assume that the list is empty when two threads T1 and T2 start executing the routine AddToList. Consider the following sequence of events:

- After thread T1 executes the first statement, it is preempted by the operating system.
- T2 is scheduled, and it executes both the statements. The global variable gpListHead now points to the new element added by T2.
- T1 is rescheduled, and then it executes the second statement. The global variable gpListHead now points to the element added by T1.

13.1.2 Race condition

It is obvious that in the scenario just described the item added by thread T2 will be *lost*. This is a programming bug that is caused by a race condition. A *race condition* is described as a condition in which two or more threads perform an operation and the result of the operation depends on thread scheduling (timing). The result of the operation depends on which thread wins the race to execute the statements. Race conditions are often caused by lack of proper synchronization.

In the preceding example the item added for thread T2 will be preserved if thread T1 executes the routine AddToList before thread T2 enters the routine. These kinds of timing bugs are very *difficult* to find because they do not occur with any defined frequency. Since on SMP machines threads can run in parallel, these kinds of bugs can occur with more frequency on multiprocessor machines than on uniprocessor machines.

Race conditions can happen even when proper locking strategies are used, and depending on the scheduling of the threads, the results can be different. Let us consider an example of two threads T1 and T2 sharing a global variable Total. Thread T1 executes the routine Add, while thread T2 executes the routine Multiply. If the value of Total is 10 before either thread starts execution, then depending on the scheduling of the threads, the final value of Total could be either 75 (T1 runs first) or 55 (T2 runs first). The final results depend on the scheduling of threads.

```
Add ()                                         Multiply ()
{                                          {
   Acquire mutual exclusion lock;          Acquire mutual exclusion lock;
   Total = Total + 5;                      Total = Total * 5;
   Release mutual exclusion lock;          Release mutual exclusion lock;
}                                          }
```

13.1.3 Critical section

It is obvious that the function AddToList shown above is a *critical section* of the code. A *critical section* (CS) is defined as a segment of the code in which a thread accesses shared modifiable data and where these state changes happen over several instructions. If you have to maintain data integrity, then it is important that only *one* thread should be inside the critical section of code. When one thread is executing the critical section, then all other threads must *wait* to enter the critical section until the thread inside *leaves* the critical section.

If you do not want more than one thread in the critical section, then access to the critical section should be serialized by some form of locking mechanism. The use of a lock to guard the critical section will guarantee that only one thread will execute the critical section. Failure to use such locks will result in *corruption* of the data. For performance reasons, it is important to keep the critical section of code as small as possible. Avoid calling blocking functions inside the CS code, since this might cause the preemption of the thread holding the lock to the critical section, which in turn would further delay other threads trying to enter the CS code.

Let us now consider implementation of the routine AddToList using some critical section lock. Each thread, after entering the routine, will acquire a lock, add the new entry, and then release the lock when it leaves the function. This will guarantee that only one thread will update the global variable gpListHead.

```
AddToList (LIST *pnewEntry)
{
   Acquire critical section lock;

   pnewEntry->next = gpListHead;
   gpListHead = pnewEntry;

   Release critical section lock;
}
```

Let us see how the routine AddToList serializes access to the critical section of code using some critical section lock under the scenario that we discussed earlier.

- Thread T1 acquires the CS lock on entry to the routine AddToList.
- T1 executes the first statement and is preempted by the operating system.
- T2 enters the routine AddToList and tries to acquire the CS lock. It will *block* until the lock is released by T1.
- T1 is rescheduled, and then it executes the second statement. The global variable ListHead points to the element added by T1.
- T1 releases the CS lock, which unblocks T2.
- T2 acquires the CS lock and executes the rest of the code.

Consider the example we discussed in the beginning of this chapter, where two threads execute the statement ++SharedVariable. The pseudocode for the generated assembly statements could look like

```
LOAD SharedVariable, X    /* load the value of SharedVariable into the
                          register X */
ADD X                     /* add one to it */
STORE X, SharedVariable   /* store the results into the variable
                          SharedVariable */
```

Now apply the scheduling scenario discussed in Sec. 13.1.1 to these statements, and you can see how one of the updates can be lost. Now that we have discussed some of the concepts of thread synchronization, I will present an overview of the WIN32 synchronization primitives.

13.1.4 WIN32 synchronization

The WIN32 API provides a rich set of synchronization primitives for mutual exclusion and event notification. Windows NT provides many kernel objects that can be used for interthread synchronization. The kernel objects that are used primarily for synchronization are

- Mutex
- Event

- Semaphore
- Process
- Threads
- Console input
- Change notification

Since the focus of this discussion is on data and event synchronization, the discussion will be restricted only to mutexes, events, and semaphores. WIN32 provides another form of synchronization primitive called CRITICAL_SECTION that is implemented as a nonkernel object, and it is used primarily for controlling critical sections.

In NT 4.0 a new kind of synchronization object called *waitable timers* has been added. It can be used to invoke functions when a timer expires. Waitable timers have handles and can be used in WaitForXXX functions. Refer to the manual for more information on the functions CreateWaitableTimer, OpenWaitableTimer, SetWaitableTimer, and CancelWaitableTimer.

Threads and processes in the WIN32 environment synchronize with each other by waiting on synchronization objects. A WIN32 synchronization object has two states: *signaled* or *nonsignaled*. The meaning of *signaled* and *nonsignaled* depends on the type of the object. In the case of these synchronization objects, the calling thread or process is *suspended* when it waits on a nonsignaled object. When an object becomes signaled, then the suspended thread or process is woken up. For example, when a thread waits for another thread to terminate, then the calling thread is suspended until the target thread object terminates and the target thread object becomes signaled.

WIN32 synchronization objects can be either private or public. Some of these objects can be either named or unnamed. Access to shared objects can be restricted by using a restrictive access control list (ACL). Since security is not an issue when the objects are used primarily by threads of the same process, most interthread objects are private in nature.

The operations that can be performed on synchronization objects such as mutexes, semaphores, and events are very much similar. To create the object, you call one of the Create<object> functions, where object can be one of Mutex, Semaphore, or Event. You can get a handle of an existing object by calling the Open<object> function. All these objects are deleted by calling the function CloseHandle.

All the synchronization objects and their APIs can be used for synchronization between threads and processes. Personally, I found it easy coming from the UNIX world, where you end up using two different API sets, one for thread synchronization and another for process synchronization.

13.1.5 WIN32 Wait functions

Threads use the wait functions of WIN32 to suspend their own execution until the conditions specified in the wait function are satisfied. The primary functions used for waiting are WaitForSingleObject and WaitForMultipleObjects.

These functions can be called in a *blocking* or *nonblocking manner.* The wait functions can be used to

- Wait for one object to be signaled.
- Wait for one of the objects in a list to be signaled.
- Wait for all the objects in a list to be signaled.

WIN32 also provides an alertable version of these wait functions, such as WaitForSingleObjectEx and WaitForMultipleObjectsEx. Alertable wait functions are used mostly with asynchronous I/O, and they execute an I/O completion routine when a pending I/O completes. The topic of asynchronous I/O and alertable waits will be covered in detail in Sec. 15.3. In the next few chapters the term *WaitForXXX* will be used to refer to any one of the four WIN32 wait functions.

```
DWORD   WaitForSingleObject (HANDLE hObject, DWORD dwTimeOut)

DWORD   WaitForMultipleObjects (DWORD cObjects, LPHANDLE lpHandles,
                                BOOL bWaitAll, DWORD dwTimeOut)
```

The function WaitForSingleObject waits for the object identified by *hObject* until the object is signaled or the waiting time specified by *dwTimeout* expires. The timeout value is specified in milliseconds, and it can have three values. If a value of 0 is passed, then the state of the object is checked without blocking. When a value of INFINITE is passed, the function waits until the object reaches the signaled state. This also means that if the object is never signaled then the thread will wait *indefinitely*.

When the object becomes signaled, the system unblocks the suspended thread and returns the value WAIT_OBJECT_0 (defined to be 0). The function returns WAIT_TIMEOUT on timeout (even when 0 is passed) and WAIT_FAILURE on error. As with any WIN32 API, the application should call the function GetLastError to get the extended error information. While waiting for mutex locks, the function also can return an error code of WAIT_ABANDONED, and this will be explained in the section on mutex objects (see Sec. 13.3.7).

The function WaitForMultipleObjects is similar to WaitForSingleObject except that the function works on a list of objects. The function can either wait for *one* of the objects in the list to be signaled or wait for *all* the objects in the list to be signaled.

The first argument *cObjects* specifies the number of objects in the array (list) of objects. The *maximum* number of objects that can be waited on in a single call is limited to MAXIMUM_WAIT_OBJECTS. In NT 3.5 the value of MAXIMUM_WAIT_OBJECTS is set to 64. The argument *lpHandles* is a pointer to an array of object handles. The objects in the list must be *unique* but could be of different types. For example, it is possible to wait for a mutex object and an event object in the same call to WaitForMultipleObjects.

The *dwTimeOut* argument is similar to one discussed earlier in WaitForSingleObject.

The argument *bWaitAll* specifies if the caller wants to wait for either one or all of the objects to be signaled. If the value is TRUE, then the function only returns when *all* the objects in the list are signaled, assuming the value passed to dwTimeOut is INFINITE. If the value of bWaitAll is FALSE, then the function returns when any *one* of the objects in the list becomes signaled. When you wait for any one of the objects to be signaled, then the function returns the array *index* of the objects in the list that caused the function to return.

The following code segment shows how to use WaitForMulitpleObjects to wait for two mutex objects identified by h1 and h2.

```
AcquireMultipleMutexes(HANDLE h1, HANDLE h2)
{
   DWORD   hMutex;
   HANDLE  hMux [2];
   hMux[0] = h1;
   hMux[1] = h2;

   hMutex = WaitForMultipleObjects(2, hMux, FALSE, INFINITE);
   switch(hMutex)
   {
   case WAIT_OBJECT_0 + 0:
       fprintf(stderr, "Object Handle h1 signaled...\n");
       break;
   case WAIT_OBJECT_0 + 1:
       fprintf(stderr, "Object Handle h2 signaled...\n");
       break;
   case WAIT_ABANDONED_0 + 0:
       fprintf(stderr, "Object Handle h1 abandoned...\n");
       break;
   case WAIT_ABANDONED_0 + 1:
       fprintf(stderr, "Object Handle h2 abandoned...\n");
       break;
   default:
       /* call GetLastError */
       break;
   }
}
```

As a side effect, the functions WaitForSingleObject and WaitForMultipleObjects *change* the state of objects such as mutex, semaphore, and auto-reset event to nonsignaled. Process and thread objects *remain* signaled even after the wait function returns. When the function WaitForMultipleObjects is called with a value TRUE for the argument bWaitAll, then the state of the objects in the list is *not* changed to nonsignaled until *all* objects in the list have been signaled.

Note that the function WaitForMultipleObjects sometimes can suffer from the *fairness problem*. Since the order of the objects in the array determines the completion of the wait function, this means that the objects at the top of wait list are *favored* more than the objects at the bottom of the list. If you want to add fairness to the application, then you should rotate the entries in the list after return from the wait functions.

When a thread calls WaitForMultipleObjects and waits for all the objects in the list to be signaled, then each time an object is signaled, the system checks if signaling can satisfy a pending wait. WaitForMultipleXXX is very complex, but essentially each thread has a list of objects it is waiting on, and each object has a list of threads waiting on it. When an object state change occurs, then the system computes whether or not a wait is satisfied. The most performance-intensive part is translating all the object handles into object pointers. Repeatedly calling this function for large numbers of objects is somewhat expensive.

```
BOOL  SignalObjectAndWait(HANDLE hObjectToSignal, HANDLE hObjectToWaitOn,
                        DWORD dwMilliseconds, BOOL bAlertable)
```

In NT 4.0 a new function has been added that allows the caller to atomically signal an object and wait on another object. The entire operation is atomic, and the system does not context switch the calling thread between the signal and the wait operation. The object to be signaled is specified in *hObjectToSignal,* while the object to be waited on is specified in *hObjectToWaitOn*. The object can be a semaphore, a mutex, or an event object. The timeout argument *dwMilliseconds* specifies the timeout period. When a value TRUE is passed to the flag *bAlertable,* then the operation can terminate early due to an I/O completion callback or user APC.

13.2 Critical Section Functions

`InitializeCriticalSection`	Initializes a critical section
`EnterCriticalSection`	Enters a critical section
`LeaveCriticalSection`	Exits a critical section
`DeleteCriticalSection`	Deletes a critical section

Before we move on to the kernel object synchronization objects of WIN32, let us consider a mutual exclusion primitive of WIN32 called *critical section objects*. Recall from our earlier discussion that a *critical section of code* is defined as a segment in which a thread accesses shared modifiable data and where state changes happen over several instructions. WIN32 critical section objects are one of the fastest methods for mutual exclusion. The speed of these primitives comes at the cost that they *cannot* be named, secured, or shared across processes.

13.2.1 Initializing critical section

A *critical section* (CS) in WIN32 is defined by the CRITICAL_SECTION data structure. Before a CS data structure can be used, it should be initialized by calling the function InitilializeCriticalSection. The function initializes the critical section data structure identified by *lpCriticalSection*. All CS structures must be initialized before they can be used. It is a programming *error* to initialize the same CS structure more than once without deleting the critical section.

```
VOID  InitializeCriticalSection (LPCRITICAL_SECTION lpCriticalSection)
```

13.2.2 Entering/exiting critical section

Before a thread executes some critical section (CS) of code, it *must* call the function EnterCriticalSection to serialize the code segment. When the function returns successfully, it means that the calling thread has acquired the CS and is the owner of the critical section object. It is a programming error to call EnterCriticalSection *without* initializing the critical section data structure. When a thread tries to enter the CS while some other thread is inside the CS, then the thread *waits* until the thread inside the CS leaves.

When the function EnterCriticalSection is called and contention occurs, a semaphore object is created internally by the system. The semaphore is created dynamically when contention happens for the very first time. Since the critical section data structure is implemented in user space, a switch to the kernel only happens when there is a contention, and a thread must either wait or wake a waiting thread. For locks with *low* contention this is the fastest way for data synchronization using the WIN32 API.

```
VOID  EnterCriticalSection (LPCRITICAL_SECTION lpCriticalSection)
VOID  LeaveCriticalSection (LPCRITICAL_SECTION lpCriticalSection)
```

Since ownership is tracked with critical section objects, the thread that called EnterCriticalSection *must* be the thread that calls LeaveCriticalSection. In the WIN32 environment, critical section objects can be acquired in a *recursive manner*. A thread can enter a critical section multiple times; the only requirement is that the thread should leave the CS the same number of times it entered the CS.

When multiple threads wait on the function EnterCriticalSection, only one thread is woken (FIFO) when the thread inside the critical section calls LeaveCriticalSection. If a thread enters a critical section and exits *abnormally*, then the critical section object remains *locked*. Again, use the WIN32 termination handling features and put the LeaveCriticalSection in the *finally* block. As with any other synchronization object, deadlock is possible if critical section objects are used improperly. The topic of deadlock is discussed in detail in Sec. 13.6.2.

In NT 4.0, a *new* function has been added that solves the problem of blocking associated with EnterCriticalSection. Many times it might be desirable *not* to wait if a critical section object cannot be acquired. The function TryEnterCriticalSection is similar to EnterCriticalSection except that it returns FALSE when some other thread holds the critical section object.

13.2.3 Deleting critical section

The function *DeleteCriticalSection* should be called to delete the critical section when the critical section data structure is no longer needed. The critical section structure can be reused only after it has been reinitialized. It is a programming error to delete a critical section when some other thread is *blocked* on a call to EnterCriticalSection.

```
VOID  DeleteCriticalSection (LPCRITICAL_SECTION lpCriticalSection)
```

Even though critical section is one of the fastest synchronization primitives, it can only be used for interthread synchronization. Since these functions are not implemented as kernel objects, they are unnamed and cannot be secured. The standard WaitForXXX functions cannot be used with critical sections; therefore, entry to CS is blocking in nature (changed in NT 4.0).

Continuing with the example of critical section, the segment of code AddToList will now be implemented using a WIN32 critical section object. It is assumed that the data structure is initialized by calling the function InitializeCriticalSection.

```
CRITICAL_SECTION  csList;

/* Assume that InitListCS is called once before the threads call the routine
AddToList. */

InitListCS()
{
   InitializeCriticalSection(&csList);
}

AddToList (LIST *New)
{
   EnterCriticalSection(&csList);

   New->Next = ListHead;
   ListHead = New;

   LeaveCriticalSection(&csList);
}
```

13.3 Mutual Exclusion Locks

Mutex locks generally are used to synchronize access to and ensure atomic updates of shared data. A *mutex* (mutual exclusion) lock is a data structure in memory that processes or threads use to *serialize* access to shared data. Mutex locks are meaningful only for data that can be modified by multiple threads or processes. This means that you do not need to serialize access to shared read-only data items.

The state of the mutex can be either *locked* or *unlocked*. The basic assumption behind mutexes is that threads must lock the mutex before accessing shared modifiable data and unlock the mutex after the thread has completed accessing the shared data. If one thread has acquired the mutex, then all other threads requesting to lock the mutex will wait until the mutex is released by the thread owning the mutex. It is important to remember that for data synchronization all threads must enforce the mutex locking protocol strictly. Note that if threads do not check the locks before entering the critical section, then mutex locks cannot be of any help. One possible solution to enforce mutual exclusion is to provide well-defined interfaces (functions) to allow access to shared resources and then implement the mutex locking and unlocking within these interfaces. In this way, the details of locking and unlocking are hidden from the user of these interfaces.

Acquiring a mutex is itself a critical section because it might require multiple steps such as read, test, and set the mutex. On uniprocessor and multiprocessor machines, the hardware must provide a mechanism for atomic test and set kind of operation. An atomic instruction is an instruction or a sequence of instructions that is uninterruptable. This atomic test and set instruction guarantees that the read, test, and set happen as one atomic instruction. When multiple CPUs try to get/set the same lock, only one of them will succeed. All SMP machines use this atomic operation as the basis for providing mutex locks. The following code segment is a high-level implementation of the function TestAndSet (the code below is for illustration purposes and is not atomic).

```
TestAndSet (int *lock)
{
   if (*lock == 0)
   {
       *lock = 1;
       return (1);
   }
   return (0);
}
```

13.3.1 Mutex functions

`CreateMutex`	Creates a mutex
`OpenMutex`	Opens an existing mutex
`WaitForXXX functions`	Waits for a mutex lock(s)
`CloseHandle`	Deletes a mutex object
`ReleaseMutex`	Releases a mutex

13.3.2 Creating a mutex

Mutexes have to be created before they can be used for mutual exclusion purposes. Mutexes in WIN32 can be either named or unnamed, and they can be shared across processes.

```
HANDLE  CreateMutex(LPSECURITY_ATTRIBUTES lpsa,
                    BOOL finitialOwner, LPSTR lpszMutexName);
```

The function CreateMutex is used to create a new mutex object. On success, the handle of the newly created mutex is returned to the caller. The first argument *lpsa* is the security attributes associated with a mutex, and it is NULL for default security attributes. The security attributes describe if the mutex can be inherited across child processes and the access rights other processes have on the mutex object. A mutex that is created purely for interthread synchronization is generally unnamed, in which case you should pass a NULL value to lpsa.

The argument *lpszMutexName* is either NULL or a null-terminated string identifying the mutex. Named mutexes are normally used when the mutex has to be used across processes; in the case of threads within a process, pass a NULL value. In the case of an unnamed mutex, the function CreateMutex should be called exactly *once* for each of the mutexes an application wants to create. Failure to do so can result in some difficult-to-find bugs. A named mutex variable should be created only *once*; if multiple threads try to create a mutex with the same parameter, then only one of the threads will succeed. Mutexes should be created in some once-only function (e.g., when the DLL is notified of process attachment).

As in critical section objects, *ownership* is tracked in the case of mutexes. Mutexes, by default, are created as recursive, and the initial state of the mutex is controlled by the value passed to *finitialOwner*. If the value is TRUE, then the calling thread or process creating the mutex atomically becomes the owner of the mutex. If the value is TRUE, then the mutex is created in nonsignaled state (locked state), which means that any other process or thread requesting ownership of the mutex will wait until the mutex is released by the creator of the mutex. If the value of finitialOwner is FALSE, then the mutex is created in signaled state (unlocked), which means any other thread requesting ownership of the mutex will gain ownership of the mutex object. Generally, the value passed to finitialOwner is FALSE.

13.3.3 Opening a mutex

When a mutex is created, the handle of the mutex is returned to the caller. The handle of an existing *named* mutex can be retrieved by calling the function OpenMutex. This function is used mainly when the mutex object is shared across processes, and it is *hardly ever* used by threads of the same process. Refer to the WIN32 API documentation for more details on this function.

```
HANDLE  OpenMutex(DWORD fdwAccess, BOOL fInherit, LPSTR lpszMutexName);
```

13.3.4 Destroying a mutex

When mutexes are no longer needed, they should be destroyed. Mutexes are *not* deleted when the thread that created the mutex terminates, since mutexes are considered to be shared resources of a process. Mutexes are deleted automatically when the process exits. As with any WIN32 kernel object, the function *CloseHandle* should be called to delete the object. This routine should be called *only* when the mutex is no longer referenced. Deleting a mutex allows all the resources associated with the mutex to be reclaimed.

The mutex object is not deleted until the reference count associated with the mutex becomes zero. If you call the function CloseHandle while some other thread is blocked trying to acquire the mutex, then the thread blocked on the wait function will wait *indefinitely*.

13.3.5 Acquiring a mutex lock

Before executing a critical section of code, the thread must *acquire* the mutex lock. After executing the critical section, the thread that locked the mutex must *release* the mutex. To acquire a mutex lock, use one of the standard WIN32 WaitForXXX functions. A mutex object is *signaled* when the mutex is in an unlocked state and *nonsignaled* when the mutex is locked by some thread.

The function WaitForXXX is used to acquire a lock of a valid unlocked mutex. If the mutex is currently locked by some other thread, then the calling thread is suspended until the mutex lock is released. When the function returns successfully, then the state of the mutex becomes signaled, and the calling thread becomes the owner of the mutex. The calling thread remains the owner of the mutex lock until it unlocks the mutex. If the mutex is never released, then some other thread will block indefinitely on the mutex lock when it tries to acquire the mutex lock.

In the WIN32 environment, mutex objects can be acquired in a *recursive* manner. A thread can acquire a mutex multiple times; the only requirement is that the thread should release the mutex the same number of times it acquired it. Be careful with recursive mutex locks because you can easily deadlock; in fact, most applications do *not* need recursive mutexes.

When a mutex is acquired, then the state of the mutex is *automatically* reset to nonsignaled state by the WIN32 WaitForXXX function, and this prevents more than one thread from waking up on the mutex wait. When multiple threads call the function WaitForXXX to acquire a locked mutex, they are suspended and are placed on a queue of threads waiting for the mutex to be released. The sleeping threads are woken up in a *FIFO manner* regardless of the thread priority. Mutexes, like CS objects, should only be held for a *short* duration to avoid performance problems.

For most applications, it makes sense to detect the use of recursive mutex locks as an error. Personally, I prefer to use nonrecursive mutexes for most of my applications, since this forces me to be more disciplined. The following code shows how to implement a nonrecursive mutex using the standard WIN32 APIs.

```
typedef struct _nrmutex
{
   int      lCount; /* lock count of mutex */
   HANDLE   hOwner; /* owner of mutex */
   HANDLE   hMutex; /* handle to mutex object */
} NRMUTEX;

int
CreateNrMutex(NRMUTEX *hNrMutex) /* should be only called once */
{
   hNrMutex->lCount = 0;
   hNrMutex->hMutex = CreateMutex(NULL, FALSE, NULL);
}

int
AcquireNrMutex(NRMUTEX *hNrMutex)
{
   HANDLE  myself;

   myself = GetCurrentThreadID();

   if (hNrMutex->lCount && hNrMutex->owner = = myself)
   {
        fprintf(stderr, "Error: Cannot acquire mutex in recursive manner\n");
        return(-1);
   }
   WaitForSingleObject(hNrMutex->hMutex);
   hNrMutex->owner = myself;
   hNrMutex->lCount = 1;
   return(0);
}
```

13.3.6 Releasing a mutex

The mutex lock should be released after the thread executes the critical section of the code; otherwise, no other thread can enter the critical section of code guarded by the same mutex.

```
BOOL ReleaseMutex(HANDLE hMutex)
```

The function ReleaseMutex is used to unlock the mutex identified by *hMutex*. It is an error to call this function if *hmutex* is either unlocked or the calling thread is *not* the owner of the mutex. On a successful return, the mutex lock is released, and the state of the mutex becomes *signaled*. If no thread is waiting for the mutex to be released, then the mutex remains signaled, and it is marked as having no owner. If one or more threads are waiting for the mutex to be released, then one of the waiting threads is woken up (FIFO) and the state of the mutex is changed to nonsignaled.

Let us implement the routine AddToList, which was discussed earlier, using a mutex.

```
typedef struct List
{
   struct List  *next;
   void         *data;
}SHARED_LIST;

static SHARED_LIST *gpListHead; /* pointer to beginning of list */

HANDLE hListMutex;

/* Assume that InitListMutex is called once before the threads call the rou-
tine a AddToList. */

InitListMutex()
{
   hListMutex = CreateMutex(NULL, FALSE, NULL);
}

AddToList (SHARED_LIST *pnewEntry)
{

   WaitForSingleObject(hListMutex, INFINITE);

   /*Critical Section of Code */
   pnewEntry->Next = gpListHead;
   gpListHead = pnewEntry;

   ReleaseMutex(hListMutex);
}
```

13.3.7 Abandoned mutexes

Since resource ownership is tracked for mutexes, a thread that acquires a mutex lock must be the thread that unlocks it. So what happens when the owner of the mutex terminates without releasing the lock? The mutex in this case is considered *abandoned,* since no other thread can call ReleaseMutex to release that mutex. One can use the WIN32 termination handling features and put the ReleaseMutex in the *finally* block to avoid such problems.

When an abandoned mutex is detected, then the system prevents the caller of the WaitForXXX function from indefinite postponement. The state of an abandoned mutex is restored to signaled state, and an error code is returned to the caller. All the WIN32 WaitForXXX functions return WAIT_ABANDONED_0 + X instead of WAIT_OBJECT_0 + X, where X is the index of the mutex that is abandoned. The decision to continue or exit is an application-specific one, and it usually depends on the potential damage caused by the terminating thread. One big *advantage* of mutexes over critical section objects is that abandoned mutexes are detected, while abandoned critical sections cause indefinite wait on EnterCriticalSection (unless TryEnterCriticalSection is used).

Even though the system notifies threads of abandoned mutexes, there is no guarantee that the state of the shared data guarded by the abandoned mutex is *consistent.* The terminating thread could have crashed in the middle of updating a linked list, so even if the abandoned mutex has been released, one cannot guarantee the integrity of the data. One of the best things to do in this case is to *exit* the program and then try to find the bug that crashed the thread in the critical section.

13.3.8 Guidelines for using mutexes

- Always use global or static variables for mutexes. Do not try to use stack variables for mutexes, since the stack of a thread is destroyed when the thread terminates.
- Delete mutexes after they are no longer used.
- Avoid locking mutexes in a recursive fashion unless you have valid reasons to do it.
- While locking multiple mutexes simultaneously, be sure that all threads acquire the locks in the same order to avoid deadlocks.
- Do not call CloseHandle while some other thread is blocked on a WaitForXXX function for the same mutex.
- Lock mutexes for a short time. Keep the critical section of the code small, and avoid any blocking operation (I/O, another synchronization lock) inside the critical section.
- Do not use mutex locks excessively. Excessive synchronization will cause performance problems, and you will tend to lose one of the foremost benefits of multithreading, which is concurrent execution of threads. If threads reference the shared data in read-only mode, then there is no need to serialize access to this piece of shared data.
- Carefully design your mutual exclusion locks to be either coarse- or fine-grained, since this can directly affect performance. The reader is advised to read Chap. 20 for more on design considerations.

13.4 Semaphores

Semaphores are used to enforce mutual exclusion and for coordinating events. Counting semaphores were invented by a Dutch professor named Edsger Dijsktra. These semaphores have a count associated with them; the count can be incremented to any high value but can only be decremented to zero. The value of the counting semaphore can never be less than zero. The *post* (*verhogen* in Dutch) operation increments the semaphore count, while the *wait* (*proberen* in Dutch) decrements the semaphore count.

WIN32 implements counting semaphores, and the semaphores have an integer count associated with them. When a process *waits* on a semaphore and the count is greater than zero, the process acquires the semaphore. The integer count is decremented as a result of acquiring the semaphore. When the count associated with a semaphore becomes zero, then the process blocks on the wait operation until the integer count is incremented as a result of the *post* operation by some other process. The count associated with a semaphore can never be less than zero. When a process posts a semaphore, the semaphore count is incremented, and any thread waiting to acquire the semaphore is notified. In WIN32, the term *releasing* is used instead of posting, and the standard WaitForXXX function is used to wait for a semaphore.

Counting semaphores are *useful* in restricting access to a shared resource but not necessarily in a mutually exclusive manner. You can think of semaphore as a gate through which a variable number of threads can pass simultaneously. The maximum number of threads entering the gate can be limited, and the gate remains open as long as there are resources available. When the number of resources reaches the maximum limit, then the gate is closed; it is reopened only when resources are freed.

For example, consider five threads within a process sharing three buffers. Each thread acquires a copy of the buffer when it needs it and then releases it after using the buffer. Now consider the case where all three copies of the available buffers are in use and a fourth thread tries to acquire a buffer. The thread has to wait until a copy of the buffer is released by some other thread. The choices are simple: The thread can either spin in a loop or suspend itself until a shared buffer is available. Polling or spinloops are inefficient and waste precious CPU cycles. If a thread decides to suspend itself (on a semaphore), then it is the responsibility of the thread releasing the buffer to notify the suspended thread.

The following segment of code is for illustration purposes and should *never* be used for these kinds of synchronization. This approach uses a global variable for keeping track of the resource count. In the example shown below, the variable SharedBufferCount is initialized to 3, and it is decremented by 1 when a thread acquires a copy of a buffer. The count is incremented when the thread releases the buffer back to the shared pool.

```
static  int sharedBufferCount; /* global variable to track buffers in use */
InitializeSharedBuffers()
{
   sharedBufferCount = 3;

   /* allocate memory for three buffers */
}

AcquireSharedBuffer()
{
   while (sharedBufferCount = = 0)
         ; /* busy wait */

   Acquire a shared buffer; /* assumes it is guarded by mutex */

   --SharedBufferCount; /* decrement count */

}

ReleaseSharedBuffer()
{
   Release buffer back to shared pool; /* assumes it is guarded by mutex */

   ++sharedBufferCount;
}
```

There are many *problems* with using the logic shown above. First of all, the process of busy waiting on a global counter is grossly inefficient and wastes

CPU cycles. Second, the test for sharedBufferCount in the function AcquireSharedBuffer is *not* atomic. It is possible that more than one thread can succeed on the test and proceed even though sufficient buffers may not be available. Even though in a WIN32 environment it is possible to make the test atomic by using the interlocked functions, it is hard to justify the wastage of CPU cycles. It is a bad programming practice to use global variables or flags for event synchronization. Semaphores offer a better choice for these kinds of resource synchronization.

13.4.1 Semaphore functions

`CreateSemaphore`	Creates a semaphore
`OpenSemaphore`	Opens an existing semaphore
`WaitForXXX functions`	Waits for a semaphore
`CloseHandle`	Deletes a semaphore
`ReleaseSemaphore`	Releases a semaphore

13.4.2 Creating a semaphore

Semaphores have to be created before they can be used for restricting access to a shared resource. Like mutexes, semaphores in WIN32 can be either named or unnamed, and they can be shared across processes.

```
HANDLE  CreateSemaphore(LPSECURITY_ATTRIBUTES lpsa,
                    LONG SemInitial, LONG cSemMax, LPSTR lpszSemName);
```

The function CreateSemaphore is used to create a new semaphore object. On success, the handle of the newly created semaphore is returned to the caller. The first argument *lpsa* is the security attributes associated with a semaphore. When a NULL value is passed, then default security attributes are used. The security attributes describe if the semaphore can be inherited across child processes and the access rights other processes have on the semaphore. A semaphore that is created purely for interthread synchronization is generally unnamed, in which case you should pass a NULL value to lpsa.

The argument *lpszSemName* is either NULL or a null-terminated string identifying the semaphore. Named semaphores are useful when the semaphore has to be used across processes; in the case of threads within a process, pass a NULL value. In the case of an unnamed semaphore, the function CreateSemaphore should be called *once* for each of the semaphores. A named semaphore variable should be created only *once*; if multiple threads try to create a semaphore with the same parameter, only one of the threads will succeed. Create your semaphores in a once-only function (e.g., when the DLL is notified of process attachment).

The initial count of the semaphore is controlled by the value passed to *cSemInitial.* The argument *cSemMax* specifies the maximum resource count associated with the semaphore. Generally, the value passed to cSemInitial is the *same* as the value passed to cSemMax. This means that all instances of the resource are available for use. For example, passing a value 0 would mean that none of the resources are available. This can be used to restrict the use of the resource during some initialization phase. After initialization is done, then all or some instances of the resource can be made available by calling the function ReleaseSemaphore.

13.4.3 Opening a semaphore

When a mutex is created, the handle of the semaphore is returned to the caller. The handle of an existing named semaphore can be retrieved by calling the function OpenSemaphore. This function is useful when the semaphore is shared across processes and is hardly ever used by threads of the same process. Refer to the WIN32 API documentation for more details on this function.

```
HANDLE OpenSemaphore(DWORD fdwAccess, BOOL fInherit, LPSTR lpszSemaphoreName)
```

13.4.4 Destroying a semaphore

As with any WIN32 kernel object, the function *CloseHandle* should be called to delete the semaphore. The function CloseHandle is used to delete a previously created semaphore and should be called when the semaphore is no longer referenced.

The semaphore is not deleted until the reference count associated with the semaphore becomes zero. If you call the function CloseHandle while some other thread is blocked trying to acquire a semaphore, then the thread blocked on the wait function will wait *indefinitely*.

13.4.5 Acquiring a semaphore

The function WaitForXXX is used to acquire a valid semaphore. If the count associated with the semaphore is currently zero, then the calling thread is *blocked* until the semaphore is released. When the WaitForXXX function returns successfully, then the semaphore count is decremented by 1 and the state of the semaphore is automatically *nonsignaled*. Although semaphores are not recursive they can be acquired in a *recursive* fashion. A thread can acquire a semaphore multiple times, and the thread will only block when the semaphore count reaches zero. As usual, the wait functions can be called in a blocking or nonblocking manner.

13.4.6 Releasing a semaphore

The semaphore should be released after the thread no longer needs the shared resource. After the semaphore is released, the state becomes *signaled*. If no thread is waiting for the semaphore to be signaled, then the semaphore remains signaled. If multiple threads are waiting for the semaphore to be signaled, then one or more of the waiting threads are woken up (FIFO). Unlike mutexes, there is no *ownership* associated with semaphores. This means that while one thread can acquire the semaphore, some other thread can release the semaphore.

```
BOOL ReleaseSemaphore(HANDLE hSemaphore, LONG cRelease, LPLONG lplPrevious)
```

The function ReleaseSemaphore is used to release the semaphore identified by *hSemaphore*. The argument *cRelease* is used to increment the semaphore count, and it *cannot* be negative or *greater* than the maximum count associated with the semaphore. On success, the function returns the previous semaphore count in *lpPrevious*. A value greater than 1 is useful when multiple instances of a resource have to be released in one operation. In the preceding example, if one thread acquired two copies of the buffer, then it could call ReleaseSemaphore and pass a value of 2 for cRelease (might make two blocked threads).

Note that the function to wait on a semaphore can *only* acquire one instance of a resource in a single call. To acquire two instances of a resource, you would have to call the function WaitForSingleObject twice, once for each instance.

Now that the WIN32 semaphore APIs have been covered, let us implement the example of shared buffers using semaphores. It is assumed that the function InitializeSharedBuf is called before the function AcquireSharedBuffer.

```
HANDLE  hBufSem;

InitializeSharedBuf()
{
   DWORD semCnt;

   /* initially none of the buffers are available - see malloc below */
   /* after the buffers are initialized then all 5 copies are released */

   hBufSem = CreateSemaphore(NULL, 0, 5, NULL);

   /* allocate memory for five buffers and initialize them */

   ReleaseSemaphore(hBufSem, 5, &semCnt); /* make all buffers available */
}

AcquireSharedBuffer()
{
   WaitForSingleObject(hBufSem, INFINITE);
   Find free buffer and mark it acquired;

}

ReleaseSharedBuffer()
{
   Mark the buffer free and release the buffer back to the shared pool;

   ReleaseSemaphore(hBufSem, 1, NULL);
}
```

13.4.7 Guidelines for using semaphores

- Always use global or static variables for semaphores. Do not try to use stack variables for semaphores, since the stack of a thread is destroyed when the thread terminates.
- Delete semaphores after they are no longer used.
- While locking multiple semaphores, be sure that all threads acquire the semaphores in the same order to avoid deadlocks.
- Do not call CloseHandle while some other thread is blocked on a WaitForXXX function trying to acquire a semaphore.

13.5 Event Synchronization

Consider a boss/worker thread model in which the boss thread puts new work items on a work queue and worker threads dequeue new work items from the queue. It is assumed that the threads use a mutex to guard the work queue while the actual enqueue/dequeue operation happens. The question that arises then is, "How can the worker threads know when a new work item has been placed on the queue?" The worker thread can

- Continuously check the work queue for arrival of new work items.
- Poll the work queue at specified intervals for arrival of new work items.
- Wait on the work queue for new items until the boss thread notifies the worker thread that a new work item has been placed on the work queue.

The first two methods are extremely inefficient when it comes to CPU utilization, while the last option provides the *best* solution. In this case, the worker thread is suspended when there are no work items on the queue and is only woken up when a new work item is placed on the queue. This form of event synchronization is the most efficient and highly desirable in a multithreaded environment.

13.5.1 Event objects

Event objects are yet another kind of WIN32 synchronization object that are used primarily for event synchronization. Event objects allow threads to block until a particular event or condition is satisfied and are most useful when multiple threads coordinate together to solve a task. A state change of an event can be broadcasted to multiple threads at the same time, or it can be sent to a single thread. Event objects can be used to implement barriers; many threads can wait at a barrier point, and they can all be woken up at once by some other thread. In WIN32, event objects are also used for the completion notification of a pending asynchronous I/O operation. The topic of asynchronous I/O and events will be discussed in detail in Sec. 15.2.

The question that can be asked is, "Why can't mutexes be used to wait for an event to happen?" Event objects are used whenever the thread has to wait for *longer* periods on a specified condition. Mutexes, on the other hand, are used for implementing critical sections of code where locks are generally held for a *very short* time. Event objects should be used strictly for *signaling* an event and never for serializing access to some shared data.

13.5.2 Event synchronization functions

`CreateEvent`	Creates an event object
`OpenEvent`	Opens an event object
`WaitForXXX functions`	Waits for an event
`CloseHandle`	Deletes an event object
`SetEvent`	Sets a manual event
`PulseEvent`	Sets and resets an event
`ResetEvent`	Resets an event

13.5.3 Creating an event object

Event objects have to be created before they can be used for event synchronization. Event objects in WIN32 can be either named or unnamed, and they can be shared across processes. There are two types of event objects: *manual-reset events* and *auto-reset events*. Manual reset events can be used to *broadcast* the occurrence of an event to multiple threads or processes, while auto-reset events can be used to notify the occurrence of an event or condition to a *single* thread or process.

Like mutex objects, the state of an event object can either be signaled or nonsignaled. On a successful return from the WaitForXXX function, the state of the auto-reset event is automatically *nonsignaled*. The WIN32 wait functions do *not* change the state of a manual-reset event object.

Manual-reset events should be used when multiple threads need to be notified of some event or where the state of some event has to be maintained over a period of time. Consider the implementation of a synchronization primitive called *barrier*. A barrier is a synchronization point in a program where threads must wait to proceed until all threads have reached that point in the program. A barrier can be implemented using an event object and a mutex. Each thread will lock the mutex, increment the barrier count, and wait if a sufficient number of threads have not yet reached the synchronization point. When the last thread reaches the synchronization point, it must wake up all threads blocked at the synchronization point. Since this requires waking up multiple threads, a manual-reset event should be used to implement a barrier.

Now let us turn our discussion to the boss/worker queue model that we discussed earlier and see which kinds of event objects are better suited for the purpose. In this model, worker threads wait on a work queue for new work items to be added by the server (boss) thread. When the server adds a new item, then it has two choices: it can either wake up *one* worker thread, or it can wake up *all* the worker threads. Even when multiple workers are woken up, only one of them will succeed to dequeue a work item, since only one work item was added by the server. In this case it makes sense to notify a single thread. When the server adds a new work item, it will wake up the first thread waiting on the queue to dequeue the work item. Generally, when an event is set and a *single* thread has to be notified of the state change, then auto-reset events should be used.

```
HANDLE  CreateEvent(LPSECURITY_ATTRIBUTES lpsa,
                  BOOL fManualReset, BOOL fInitialState, LPSTR lpszEventName);
```

The function CreateEvent is used to create a new event object. On a successful return, the handle of the newly created event object is returned to the caller. The first argument *lpsa* is the security attributes associated with an event. When a NULL value is passed, then default security attributes are used. The security attributes describe if the event can be inherited across child processes and the access rights other processes have on the event object. An event object that is created purely for interthread notification is generally unnamed, in which case you should pass a NULL value to lpsa.

The argument *lpszEventName* is either NULL or a null-terminated string identifying the event object. Named event objects are useful when they have to be used across processes; in the case of threads within a process, pass a NULL value. In the case of unnamed event objects, the function CreateEvent should be called *once* for each of the event objects.

The argument *fManualReset* can have the value TRUE or FALSE. This specifies whether a manual-reset or an auto-reset event should be created. If the value is TRUE, then a manual-reset object is created; otherwise, an auto-reset event is created. The initial state of the event object is controlled by the value passed to *finitialState*. If the value is FALSE, then the event object is created in a nonsignaled state, which means that any other process or thread requesting ownership of the event will suspend itself until the event object is signaled. If the value of finitialState is TRUE, then the event is created in signaled state, which means that the wait on the event object will succeed immediately. Generally, the value passed to fInitialState is FALSE.

13.5.4 Opening an event object

When an event object is created, the handle of the event is returned to the caller. The handle of an existing named event can be retrieved by calling the function OpenEvent. This function is useful when the event object is shared across processes and is hardly ever used by threads of the same process. Refer to the WIN32 API documentation for more details on this function.

```
HANDLE  OpenEvent(DWORD fdwAccess, BOOL fInherit, LPSTR lpszEventName)
```

13.5.5 Destroying an event

When events are no longer needed, they should be destroyed. Event objects are *not* deleted when the thread that created them terminates, since event objects are considered to be shared resources of a process. Event objects are deleted automatically when the process exits. As with any WIN32 kernel object, the function *CloseHandle* should be called to delete the object. This routine should be called when the event is no longer referenced.

The event object is not deleted until the reference count associated with the event becomes zero. If you call the function CloseHandle while some other thread is waiting for the event object to be signaled, then it will *deadlock*.

13.5.6 Waiting for events

An application must wait for event objects to be signaled by calling the standard WIN32 WaitForXXX function. You can wait for either *one* or *all* multiple events to happen at the same time. If the event is currently nonsignaled, then the calling thread is *blocked* until the *event* is signaled by some other thread. On return from the wait function, the auto-reset event becomes nonsignaled, while the manual-reset event remains signaled.

When multiple threads call the function WaitForXXX on a nonsignaled auto-reset event, then all threads are blocked, and they are placed on a queue of threads waiting for the event to be signaled. The sleeping threads are woken up in FIFO order when some other thread or process sets the event.

13.5.7 Setting an event

```
BOOL SetEvent(HANDLE hEvent)
```

The function SetEvent sets the event object *hEvent* to the signaled state. If no thread is waiting for the event object to be set, then the event remains signaled. If one or more threads are waiting for the event object to be signaled, then depending on the type of event object, one or more threads are notified. If the event object is a manual-reset event, then all waiting threads are notified, while in the case of an auto-reset event, only a single thread is notified.

13.5.8 Resetting an event

```
BOOL ResetEvent(HANDLE hEvent)
```

Since manual-reset events remain signaled once they are set, the state has to be explicitly cleared. The function ResetEvent sets the state of a manual reset event object identified by *hEvent* to the nonsignaled state.

With event objects sometimes you set an event, wake up all suspended threads, and then reset the state of the object to nonsignaled. In WIN32, the function PulseEvent achieves the same in one function call.

```
BOOL PulseEvent(HANDLE hEvent)
```

The function PulseEvent releases *multiple* threads in the case of manual-reset events and only one thread in the case of auto-reset events. If no threads are waiting, then the function PulseEvent simply sets the event object's state to nonsignaled and returns. PulseEvent (manual-reset) is useful in building a barrier where the last thread reaching the synchronization point has to set the event, then wake up multiple threads, and finally reset the state of the event object.

13.5.9 Guidelines for using event objects

- Always use global or static variables for event objects. Do not try to use stack variables for event objects, since the stack of a thread is destroyed when the thread terminates.
- Use manual-reset events for broadcasting an event.
- Use auto-reset events for signaling an event.
- Do not call CloseHandle while some other thread is blocked on a WaitForXXX function.

13.6 Synchronization Problems

13.6.1 Priority inversion

NT contains some anti-inversion logic that periodically boosts the priority of ready threads in the variable class that have not run for a while. The boost given to dynamic threads is a very short-term thing, so the boost can put you into an inversion state, but it will not last long and will almost always go undetected. This kind of inversion is bounded and is usually short-lived.

Priority inversion can be more of a problem for threads of the real-time priority class. Priority inversion happens when a lower-priority thread holding the mutex blocks a higher-priority thread trying to lock the same mutex lock, thus delaying execution of the higher-priority thread. When a higher-priority thread tries to acquire a lock held by a lower-priority thread, the higher-priority thread has to wait until the lock is released by the lower-priority thread. The wait time is determined by the time the lock is held by the lower-priority thread. Sometimes priority inversion can cause a higher-priority thread to block indefinitely, and this type of priority inversion is called *unbounded priority inversion.* The following example shows how unbounded priority inversion can happen.

Consider a process with three threads, namely, T1, T2, and T3, with descending priorities. The priority of thread T1 is highest, while the priority of thread T3 is lowest. Two threads T1 and T3 use a mutex to execute a critical section of the code.

```
HANDLE  csMutex;

CriticalSectionAcquire ()
{
   WaitForSingleObject(csMutex);

   /* logic inside the critical section of code */

   ReleaseMutex(csMutex);
}
```

Let us now consider the possible sequence of events: Thread T3 is scheduled and is preempted after acquiring the mutex lock. Now, when thread T1 executes the routine CriticalSectionAcquire, it blocks, since T3 owns the mutex lock. This will cause T1 to be preempted and some other thread in the process to be executed. Since T3 is a low-priority thread, it might not be rescheduled for some time; chances are that thread T2 will be scheduled before T3. If thread T2 is scheduled, then threads T1 and T3 cannot run until thread T2 ceases to run.

If your application cannot tolerate these kinds of scheduling delays, then you should implement your own priority locking strategies. For example, you can choose a mutex protocol in which each mutex is assigned a priority. The mutex priority is chosen to be the highest priority of all threads. When a thread acquires the mutex, it should decrease/increase the thread priority to the mutex priority. The thread should restore its priority after releasing the mutex. This kind of priority promotion will prevent unbounded priority inversion.

13.6.2 Deadlocks

Deadlocks occur when two threads stop execution and then wait for events that might *never* happen. For example, consider two threads T1 and T2 using two mutexes Mutex1 and Mutex2. Thread T1 acquires Mutex1, while thread T2 acquires Mutex2. Now thread T1 tries to acquire Mutex2 and thread T2 tries to acquire Mutex1. Deadlock will happen!

A deadlock happens when a thread holding a resource is waiting for a resource that is held by another thread while the other thread is waiting for a resource held by the first thread. There can be multiple threads involved in a deadlock.

WIN32 can detect potential deadlocks when threads block on the WaitForXXX function, but the deadlock detection time is set to some very high number (9 months), making it *useless* for any application. Applications *must* be coded correctly to avoid or detect deadlocks.

13.6.3 Deadlock avoidance techniques

There are a couple of ways for avoiding deadlocks with synchronization objects. If you are interested to learn more about the topic of deadlock avoidance and detection, then you should read any decent operating system book. Let us consider one of the ways to prevent deadlocks with mutexes; remember, the same discussion applies to other WIN32 synchronization objects.

In this protocol each mutex is assigned a sequence number, and the mutexes are always locked in sequence. A thread should never try to lock a mutex with a sequence number that is lower than the one of the mutex the thread holds. If a thread has to acquire a lock with a lower sequence number, it should first release all mutexes of higher sequence numbers.

The protocol is simple to understand, but in reality, this is *not* a practical solution. The unlocking of mutexes with higher sequence numbers to acquire a mutex of lower sequence number can lead to performance problems. This solution for deadlock avoidance comes at the expense of performance.

13.7 Interlocked Operations

In some applications a critical section of code might be entered frequently, yet the actual time spent inside the critical section might be small. In such cases, the cost of the context switch that arises from the frequent suspend/wakeup operations of a WIN32 mutex might be considered high. For most applications, this might not be a issue, but if you are looking for some performance gains in your application, then you should consider the use of the WIN32 interlocked operations. Keep in mind that the performance gain of the interlocked operations is greatly dependent on the underlying hardware. Also, by using the interlocked operations, portability to other operating systems is sacrificed.

Let us consider a simple example where a global variable is incremented by multiple threads. It uses mutexes to serialize access to the variable perfCounter.

```
int     perfCounter;

HANDLE  hMutex;

IncrementPerfCounters()
{
   WaitForSingleObject(hMutex, INFINITE);

   ++perfCounter;

   ReleaseMutex(hMutex);
}
```

In this code it seems that the cost of the mutex lock and unlock operation is much higher than the cost of the increment operation itself. The only reason mutexes were used is because the operation ++perfCounter cannot be assumed to be atomic. The *interlocked* APIs on WIN32 perform *atomic* instruction on long words. The functions can either add, decrement, or exchange a long word in memory. Each of these operations is noninterruptable and is considered atomic. Some additional interlocked APIs are added in NT 4.0.

```
LONG InterLockedIncrement(LPLONG lplValue);
LONG InterLockedDecrement(LPLONG lplValue);
LONG InterLockedExchange(LPLONG lplTarget, LONG lValue);
```

Let us now implement the example code we discussed earlier using the interlocked functions. Note the simplicity of the code segment.

```
int perfCounter;

IncrementPerfCounters()
{
   InterLockedIncrement(&perfCounter);
}
```

```
PVOID InterlockedCompareExchange (PVOID *Destination, PVOID Exchange,
                                  PVOID Comperand);

LONG InterlockedExchangeAdd (PLONG Addend, LONG Increment)
```

The function InterLockedCompareExchange performs an atomic compare of the variable *Destination* with *Comperand*. If the destination value is equal to the comperand value, then the exchange value is stored in the destination; otherwise, no operation is performed. The function InterLockedExchangeAdd atomically adds *Increment* to *Addend*. The initial value of the addend variable is returned as the function value.

13.7.1 Writing a once function

Sometimes in an application a piece of code must be executed once and only once; usually this is some kind of an initialization code. POSIX.1c provides a function called pthread_once (see Sec. 2.6.8) that guarantees that a function will be executed once even when multiple threads call the once function concurrently. In WIN32, one way would be to execute the once function when the process attaches to the DLL for the first time. This scheme might not be feasible at all times.

WIN32 provides the basic hooks for you to implement your own version of such a function. You can use the InterLockedExchange function to implement the function ThreadOnce. This cannot be considered as the most efficient implementation; this will work fairly well as long as your once function is a small function. A THREADONCE variable should be used for each of the once function blocks, and the variable should be initialized to THREADONCEINIT before calling the function ThreadOnce.

```
#define THREADONCEINIT {1,0}
typedef struct _THREADONCE
{
   DWORD  lock;
   DWORD  initialized;
} THREADONCE;

static THREADONCE onceData = THREADONCEINIT; /* used by caller */

VOID
ThreadOnce(void (*onceFunction)(), THREADONCE *ponceVariable)
{
   /* when one thread acquires the lock, the rest spin or sleep on the loop */
   /* while the first thread is executing the once function, others wait here */

   while(InterlockedExchange(&ponceVariable->lock,0) = = 0)
        Sleep(0); /* give up the CPU */

   if (ponceVariable->initialized = = 1) /* once function already ran */
   {
         ponceVariable->lock = 1; /* release the lock just acquired */
         return;
   }
   /* executed by only one thread in the process */
   (*onceFunction)();

   ponceVariable->initialized = 1;
   ponceVariable->lock = 1; /* release the lock just acquired */
   return;
}
```

13.7.2 Spinlocks

WIN32 interlocked operations can be used to implement *spinlocks*. When the overhead of suspending or resuming a thread is higher than the time a thread would spend spinning (busy wait) on the critical section data structure or a mutex, then the use of interlocked operations should be considered. Spinlocks are more helpful on SMP machines and should be avoided on uniprocessor machines.

Consider the following code segment, which implements a version of spinlock. In this function, the value zero is used to represent a free lock and the function InterlockedExchange is used to change the lock value to zero. When the function returns 1, this means that the lock could *not* be acquired, in which case the caller spins on the lock. In the code segment we chose to perform a busy wait after returning from InterLockedExchange, but you can choose to implement your backoff strategy. In release 4.0 of NT the new interlocked function InterlockedCompareExchange can be used instead of InterLockedExchange to implement spinlocks.

```
SpinLockAcquire(int *SharedLock)
{

   while(InterLockedExchange(SharedLock, 1) = = 1)
        ; /* busy wait could be expensive - could say Sleep(0) */
             sharedlock = 1; /* acquire lock */
}

SpinLockRelease(int *SharedLock)
```

```
{
   *SharedLock = 0;
}
```

Spinlocks can be *helpful* for short sections of the code, but they also can burn expensive CPU cycles. If you are using spinlocks, make sure that the thread owning the lock does *not* block while holding the spinlock. Even if the thread manages not to block, it is possible that the thread owning the lock can be preempted by the operating system. When either of these things happens, all other threads spin on the lock until the thread owning the lock releases the spinlock. The use of spinlocks should be evaluated *very carefully* and should be used only when the overhead of WIN32 synchronization primitives is high for your application.

13.8 Complex Synchronization Schemes

Using the basic WIN32 synchronization primitives, it is possible to build many complex synchronization schemes, such as barriers, monitors, queues, reader/writer locks, priority locks, and much more. The WIN32 API provides the basic building blocks for all your synchronization needs. You should refer to the examples in Chap. 16 for implementation of some of these complex synchronization schemes.

Chapter

14

WIN32 Thread Local Storage

14.1 Threads and Variables

Threads in a process run in the same address space and have access to all process resources, including variables in memory. These variables can be of the type

- Static variables
- Dynamic variables
- Stack variables

Static variables have a global scope and are allocated by the compiler (e.g., static variables in the C language). Threads have access to all static variables, and they exist for the entire duration of the process. Dynamic variables can be created by calling the allocation routine (e.g., malloc routine of the C library). Any thread that knows the address of the dynamic variable can access it safely. Dynamic variables are destroyed when the deallocation routine is called (e.g., the free routine of the C library). Stack variables or automatic variables are accessible in the routine where the variable is declared, and they cease to exist when the thread returns from the routine in which the variable was declared.

14.1.1 Thread local storage

In a multithreaded application it is often required to create variables whose scope is nonglobal. There are two ways that threads can create data items whose scope is limited to a single thread. Threads can use either stack or local variables. The scope of such variables is limited to the routine in which the variable was declared. The usefulness of local variables is sometimes *limited* when these variables have to be made accessible across function calls. In a single-threaded process, the C-language keyword *extern* is used to make global variables accessible across function calls. If a multithreaded application wants the same data to be maintained on a per-thread basis across function calls, then global variables *cannot* be used. What is really needed is a per-thread global variable that is accessible across function calls.

There are a couple of ways this can be achieved in a multithreaded environment. The compilers can be changed to generate a per-thread global variable (e.g., MS Visual C++). Even though these kinds of variables might require support from the operating system, it can be argued that from an application point of view it becomes real *easy* to support per-thread variables. Just a new compiler directive, and you are set! Yet another method could involve a convention among threads that would require each thread to store/retrieve variables at a well-known location reserved for each thread. While the compiler option is not portable across different operating systems, the second option is feasible as long as the application maintains the thread/data association. Third, the threads API can maintain the thread/data association for you. The last option is the most desirable and is supported by the WIN32 API.

14.1.2 Why is TLS required?

In a multithreaded environment, library functions can be called reentrantly on a per-user or a per-thread basis. Since these functions have to be thread-safe, either all variables within the function must be stack variables, or the function must use some mutual exclusion lock to serialize access to the global variables. When these functions are executed by multiple threads, then the functions sometimes maintain context information on a per-thread basis. The data or context to be maintained on a per-thread basis is referred to as *thread local storage* (TLS). On some operating systems, the concept of thread local storage is also known as *thread-specific data* (TSD on POSIX).

Let us consider an example of a multithreaded library that requires each thread to call an initialization function ThreadLibraryInit before the thread can call any other function in the library. If the thread calls any other library function before calling the function ThreadLibraryInit, then the library flags it as an error. The function ThreadLibraryInit creates a thread context structure, and this information is used by the library functions to maintain thread globals across function calls. Basically, the thread context information can be accessed by each library function in one of the two ways:

- Each library function can take an extra argument that is the pointer to the thread context structure created by ThreadLibraryInit. This becomes a bit awkward when the thread context has to be passed to each of the subsequent functions that the library function calls. Adding an additional argument also requires changing the existing functional interface of the library functions.
- Set up a TLS variable that can be accessed globally across functions with a thread scope.

Another good example for the necessity of thread local storage is the *errno* variable in the C-Runtime (CRT) library. In a single-threaded CRT library the variable *errno* is defined to be a static variable. Now consider the following situation:

- Thread T1 calls the CRT routine _open with an invalid argument. The function fails and sets errno to EINVAL.
- Thread T2 calls the CRT routine _beginthreadex to create a thread. Since the maximum allowable thread limit has been reached, the function fails and sets errno to EAGAIN.

Now, when thread T1 checks the value of errno, it might have the wrong errno value (EAGAIN). The value of errno for thread T1 is *lost* because both threads share the same global variable. This can be avoided by maintaining a per-thread errno variable. Most compilers supporting the WIN32 API redefine the variable errno to be a function returning a pointer to a per-thread errno variable. This per-thread errno is an example of a TLS variable.

14.2 WIN32 Thread Local Storage

WIN32 supports the concept of thread local storage in two different ways. The first kind of TLS is *static* TLS, in which the compiler creates variables with a per-thread scope. In the second approach, also known as *dynamic* TLS, a key (index) is used for storing and retrieving per-thread data. To store data on a per-thread basis, the application must first create a key and then use the set or get routines to store or retrieve data on a per-thread basis. Threads in the process use the *same* key, but they set and get different TLS values. TLS plays a crucial role in building multithreaded dynamic link libraries, but there are many other instances where TLS plays an equally important role. For example, consider a multithreaded socket server that creates a thread for every client that connects to it. When the server has to maintain per-client context information, then TLS plays a important role.

14.2.1 Static TLS

Static TLS can be used to create a per-thread data variable. Static TLS is very easy to use, and it depends on the compiler supporting per-thread variables using some form of compiler directive. For example, on Microsoft's Visual C++ the *__declspec(thread)* modifier is a hint to the compiler to place the variable in the *.tls* section of an executable program. Variables that are declared using the *_declspec(thread)* modifier are created and maintained on a per-thread basis.

When the program starts executing, the system allocates a block of memory to hold all the variables in the .tls section. When a new thread is created, the system creates a block of memory to hold the TLS variables for the new thread. Most of the time the system initializes these static TLS variables. All static TLS variables must be either a *global* variable or a *static* variable. Static TLS is private to a thread; therefore, one thread cannot access the static TLS of another thread in the process.

The following statement can be used to declare a static TLS variable.

```
_declspec(thread) static int    perThreadData; /* MS Visual C++ */
```

There is one *limitation* of static TLS when it is used in dynamic link libraries (DLL). Static TLS variables are initialized on a per-thread basis only when the DLL is implicitly linked. When an application calls the function LoadLibrary or LoadLibraryEx to explicitly load the DLL, then the system does *not* initialize the TLS variables. This behavior can potentially cause access violations in your application.

For example, consider the behavior of the function AppendErrorMsg that uses static TLS. The function AppendErrorMsg concatenates error messages to a per-thread buffer pointed to by the variable pErrorBuf. When the function is invoked for the first time, it allocates a buffer large enough to hold error messages. In the code segment it is assumed that the maximum size of the error message will be 1024 bytes.

```
_declspec(thread) static char *perrorBuf; /* define a static TLS variable */

AppendErrorMsg(char *perrorStr)
{
   if (perrorBuf == = NULL)
        perrorBuf = (char *) malloc(1024); /* do it once only */
   strcpy(perrorBuf, perrorStr);
}
```

Now consider the case when the function AppendErrorMsg is placed in a DLL and the function LoadLibrary is called to load the DLL explicitly. Since the variable is uninitialized, it can have a non-NULL value. When the variable perrorBuf is uninitialized to some non-NULL value, then the function will wrongly assume that memory for the variable perrorBuf has already been allocated. Later, when the function calls *strcpy,* it will have an access violation.

If you are developing a DLL that can be loaded explicitly at run time, then do *not* use static TLS. Another important thing to remember is that static TLS is *not* portable to other platforms (e.g., UNIX, OS/2); even within a WIN32 environment the compiler directive for static TLS is vendor-specific. Despite some of these shortcomings, static TLS variables are easy to use and serve their purpose well.

14.2.2 Dynamic TLS functions

`TlsAlloc`	Creates a TLS key
`TlsFree`	Frees a TLS key
`TlsSetValue`	Sets a TLS associated with a specific key
`TlsGetValue`	Gets a TLS associated with a specific key

14.2.3 Creating a key

Thread-specific keys must be created before threads can use them to bind thread local storage. The key is used to *maintain* association between a thread and its private data. The same key can be used by multiple threads, and a thread can bind the same value to multiple keys. Generally, each thread binds a unique value to the key such as an address of a dynamically allocated variable.

Let us now examine the process by which keys are allocated in the WIN32 environment. Every WIN32 process has a *minimum* of TLS_MINIMUM_AVAILABLE flags, and the index of each of these flags is considered to be a unique key. On most systems, TLS_MINIMUM_AVAILABLE is defined to be at least 64. This means that there are at least 64 slots that can be used by a process. The term *key,* which I used earlier, refers to each of these slots. Initially, the state of each of these keys is initialized to FREE.

```
DWORD TlsAlloc(VOID)
```

The function TlsAlloc is used to create a new key accessible to all threads within a process. The system scans each of the slots and then returns the index of the first free slot. Before this function returns to the caller, the state of the slot is changed to INUSE. When the system scans for a new slot, it returns the index of the first slot whose state is marked as FREE. If all the slots are in use, then the function fails, and it returns the value TLS_OUT_OF_INDEXES.

There are a couple of *important* things to know about TLS keys. When a new key is created in a process, the TLS is set to a value of NULL for *all* existing threads in the process. Whenever a thread is created afterwards, the TLS value for that thread is set to NULL for *all* existing keys in the process. The TLS value associated with a key remains NULL unless the thread binds a new value to the key.

14.2.4 Free a TLS key

When a process has finished using a key, it should free the key. This is usually done when a process detaches from the DLL. On most systems a process has only 64 slots to use, and this might seem a lot. When an application is using multiple DLLs and each of them uses a couple of keys, then soon you might run out of keys in the process.

```
BOOL  TlsFree(DWORD dwTlsIndex)
```

This function frees the key specified by *dwTlsIndex*. Internally, the function changes the state of the key identified by dwTlsIndex from INUSE to

FREE. It is the caller's responsibility to make *sure* that the key is valid and that no other thread is still using the key.

14.2.5 Get value from a key

```
LPVOID  TlsGetValue(DWORD dwTlsIndex)
```

The function TlsGetValue is used to get a TLS value associated with a key identified by *dwTlsIndex*. If no value was bound to the key previously, then a value of NULL is returned. The return value of NULL means that the thread never set a value. Keep in mind that *no* run-time checking is done to validate the value passed to dwTlsIndex, which means that it is the caller's responsibility to ensure that the key is valid.

```
DWORD  threadKey; /* slot returned by TlsAlloc */

CreateThreadKey()
{
    threadKey = TlsAlloc();
}

void *GetThreadData ()
{
    void *pthrData;

    pthrData = TlsGetValue (threadKey); /* assume CreateThreadKey is called */

    if (pthrData = = NULL)
         printf ("Null value set\n");

    return(pthrData);
}
```

14.2.6 Set value to a key

```
BOOL  TlsSetValue(dwTlsIndex, LPVOID lpTlsValue)
```

The function TlsSetValue is used to set a TLS *lpTlsValue* associated with a key identified by *dwTlsIndex*. The value bound to the key is maintained by the WIN32 system as long as the thread exists and the thread does not bind a new value to the same key.

Since TLS value is a void pointer, it is possible to store any kind of data (e.g., pointer to a structure or pointer to a string). It is a bad programming practice to cast int values to void pointers. Generally, the value is a dynamically allocated variable. The following code segment shows how to create a per-thread data variable using dynamic TLS.

```
DWORD threadKey;

SetThreadData (char *pdata)
{
   char *threadData

   threadData = TlsGetValue(threadKey); /* assume CreateThreadKey is called */

   if (!threadData)
   {
       /* no value set, thread is calling this function for the first time */
       /* malloc a buffer to store per-thread data */

       threadData = malloc (....);

       strcpy(threadData, pdata);
   }

   TlsSetValue(threadKey, threadData);
}
```

14.2.7 Potential problems with TLS

When a thread binds a new value to a key, then the old value (if any) is lost. If the TLS value associated with a key is some dynamic variable, then it is the application's *responsibility* to deallocate the storage for the old TLS value before assigning the new value. Failure to do so might result in memory leaks in the application.

The following code sample illustrates the problem of a *lost* value. For illustration purposes, I have shown two consecutive calls to TlsSetValue in the routine SetThreadData. In reality, these calls could have been made in entirely separate routines.

```
DWORD threadKey;

int CreateThreadKey ()
{
   threadKey = TlsAlloc();
}

SetThreadData () /* memory leak */
{
   void *poldData;
   void *pnewData;

   poldData = malloc (....);

   TlsSetvalue (threadKey, poldData); /* assume CreateThreadKey is called */

   /* do something */

   pnewData = malloc (....);

   TlsSetValue (threadKey, pnewData);
}
```

In this code segment it is obvious that the memory pointed to by the variable poldData will *never* be deallocated. The memory leak can be prevented easily by calling the function TlsGetValue *before* doing the second TlsSetValue.

```
SetThreadData ()
{
   void *poldData;
   void *pnewData;
   void *pcurrData;

   poldData = malloc (....);

   TlsSetValue (threadKey, poldData);

   /* check if an old TLS value is bound to the key */
   pcurrData = TlsGetValue (threadKey);

   if (pcurrData ! = NULL) /* there exists an old binding */
       free(pcurrData);

   pnewData = malloc (....);

   TlsSetValue (threadKey, pnewData);
}
```

Another area where TLS can be a problem is in cleanup handlers. In certain applications, a generic cleanup handler is called when an error happens in any thread. If the application is using a DLL, then it is important that dynamically allocated TLS variables should be deallocated only *once,* either in the cleanup handler routine or in the DllMain.

Consider the following implementation of the DLL function DllMain. This example assumes that the thread deallocates all TLS storage when it exits in the DLL. Readers who are not familiar with the concept of WIN32 DLLs are advised to read Sec. 14.3.

```
typedef struct _THRDATA
{
   void    *data;
   struct  _THRDATA *next;
} THRDATA;

BOOL DllMain(HINSTANCE hInstDll, DWORD fdwReason, LPVOID lpReserved)
{
   char  *pthrData;

   switch(fdwReason)
   {
        /* only part of the DllMain code is shown here */
        case DLL_THREAD_DETACH:
          pthrData = TlsGetValue(threadKey); /* assume ThreadKey is global */
          if (pthrData)
              FreeThreadData(pthrData); /* deallocates any thread local
          storage */ break;
   }
}

FreeThreadData (void *pthrData)
{
   THRDATA *pcurr;
   THRDATA *pnext;
```

```
    pnext = pcurr = (THRDATA *) pthrData;

    while (pcurr ! = NULL)
    {
        pnext = pcurr->next;
        free (pCurr->data);
        free (pCurr);
        pCurr = pnext;
    }
}
```

Now let us consider the following example in which the ThreadCleanup routine frees up the TLS value. Now, when the thread terminates, the DLL is notified and the thread might free variables that were already deallocated.

```
ThreadCleanup () /* potential problem */
{
    THRDATA *pthrData;

    /* logic for other thread cleanup - application specific
    ......
    */
    pthrData = TlsGetValue (ThreadKey);

    If (pthrData)
         FreeThreadData (pthrData);

    ExitThread(100); /* calls the DllMain function */
}
```

This problem can be *avoided* by setting the TLS value to NULL after the TLS has been freed. Doing so guarantees that when the thread calls TlsGetValue in the DLL, the value will be NULL. This problem also can be eliminated by deallocating all TLS variables in one routine only, either in the DLL or in the cleanup routine. If TLS variables are allocated in the DLL, then it is a better idea to deallocate such variables in the DLL itself.

```
ThreadCleanup () /* one possible implementation */
{
    char *pthrData;

    /* logic for other thread cleanup - application specific
    ......
    */
    pthrData = TlsGetValue (threadKey);

    If (pthrData)
    {
        FreeThreadData (pthrData);

        TlsSetValue (threadKey, NULL);
    }

    ExitThread(100); /* calls the DllMain function */
}
```

Whenever memory for dynamic TLS variables is deallocated in routines other than the DllMain, then the application should set TLS values to NULL.

Also, the DllMain function should *always* check for non-NULL values before using them. This will guarantee that there will be no error even if the TLS was deallocated in some routine other than the DllMain routine.

14.2.8 Using TLS to write thread-safe functions

Certain functions use static data or return a pointer to static data and therefore are considered non-thread-safe. These functions can be made thread-safe by using thread-specific data. I would *not* recommend this technique for making functions thread-safe, but sometimes you might not have much choice, especially when the functional interface of the function cannot be changed. The techniques for writing reentrant code is explained in detail later in Chapt. 20.

The following example shows how to use TLS for making a function thread-safe. In the following example, the function DbOpen opens a file and allocates a buffer for reading records. For illustration purposes, let us assume that the implementation allows only one database to be open at a time. The non-thread-safe version of the function uses a global variable pointed to by gpCurrDb to store the information.

```
#define MAXREC 512
typedef struct _dbrec
{
   int   fd;
   char  *buffer;
} DBREC;

static DBREC *gpCurrDb; /* global variable */

int DbOpen (char *DbName) /* non-thread-safe */
{
   /* assume mutex locks are used to serialize this function */
   if (gpCurrDb == NULL)
   {
      gpCurrDb = (DBREC *) malloc (sizeof (DBREC));
      gpCurrDb->fd = open (DbName.....);
      gpCurrDb->buffer = malloc (sizeof (MAXREC));
   }
   else
   {
      printf ("Error: cannot open more than one database at a time \n");
      return (-1);
   }
   return (0);
}
```

Assume the following sequence of events in a process with two threads T1 and T2:

- Thread T1 calls the functions DbOpen to open the database D1. The global variable gpCurrDb is used to store the information for the database.
- Thread T2 calls the functions DbOpen to open the database D2. Since the function DbOpen uses a global variable to store the information, the func-

tion assumes that a database was already opened by the thread and therefore returns an error to the calling thread.

Let us examine one of the ways we can make the function DbOpen thread-safe so that it can be called by multiple threads. For illustration purposes, it is assumed that the functional interface cannot be changed; therefore, the only choice is to eliminate the use of the global variable and store the information in a per-thread variable. Note that in this implementation mutual exclusion locks are not required to serialize the function DbOpen. The DbRecFree function is invoked from the DllMain function when the thread terminates.

```
DWORD dbKey;

CreateDbKey ()
{
   dbKey = TlsAlloc(); /* should be called only once */
}

DbOpen (char *pdbName) /* thread-safe */
{
   DBREC *pcurrDb;

   /* check if the key/value binding is already done */
   pcurrDb = TlsGetValue (DbKey);
   if (pcurrDb = = NULL)
   {
        pcurrDb = (DBREC *) malloc (sizeof (DBREC));
        pcurrDb->hFile = CreateFile (DbName.....);
        pcurrDb->buffer = malloc (sizeof (MAXREC));

        TlsSetValue (dbKey, pcurrDb);
   }
   else
   {
        printf ("Error: cannot open more than one database at a time\n");
        return (-1);
   }
   return (0);
}

BOOL DllMain(HINSTANCE hInstDll, DWORD fdwReason, LPVOID lpReserved)
{
   char   *pdbData;

   switch(fdwReason)
   {
       /* only part of the code is shown here */
       case DLL_THREAD_DETACH:
          pdbData = TlsGetValue(dbKey); /* assumes dbKey is global */

          if (pdbData)
              DbRecFree(pdbData); /* deallocates any thread local storage */

          break;
   }
}

DbRecFree (void *pthrDbRec)
{
   DBREC pcurrDb;
```

```
    pcurrDb = (DBREC *) pthrDbRec;
    If (pcurrDb)
    {

         CloseHandle (pcurrDb->hFile);

         free (pcurrDb->buffer);

         free (pcurrDb);
    }
 }
```

14.2.9 Guidelines for using thread local storage

- Always use global or static variables for thread keys. Do not try to use stack variables for keys because the stack of a thread is destroyed when the thread terminates. Other threads in the process can still be referencing the key, which is invalid after stack destruction.
- When dynamic TLS variables are used and a new value is bound to the key, then the memory for the old TLS (if any) should be deallocated.
- Always deallocate space for TLS variables when the thread terminates (e.g., in the DLL).
- Keep in mind that when a thread is terminated by the call to TerminateThread, then the dynamic TLS variables are not freed.

14.3 Thread Local Storage and Dynamic Link Libraries

A dynamic link library (DLL) can be mapped into a process space either *implicitly* or *explicitly*. In implicit linking the LIB files are specified to the linker at link time. In explicit linking, when an application calls either of the functions LoadLibrary or LoadLibraryEx, then at run time the DLL is mapped into the process address space. An application unloads a DLL by calling the function FreeLibrary. The load function increments the usage count associated with a DLL, and the free function decrements it by 1. When the count becomes zero, the DLL is automatically unmapped from the process address space.

Each DLL can have an optional entry and exit function, and these functions are called when a process or thread either attaches to the DLL or detaches from the DLL. In WIN32 this function is called DllMain, and it should have the following body of code:

```
static int  dllKey;
BOOL DllMain(HINSTANCE hInstDll, DWORD fdwReason, LPVOID lpvReserved)
{
   char  *pthrdata;

   switch (fdwReason)
   {
       case DLL_PROCESS_ATTACH:
           dllKey = TlsAlloc(); /* store it in a global variable */
```

```
            if (dllKey == TLS_OUT_OFINDEXES)
                 return(FALSE);

            /* do something */
            break;

        case DLL_PROCESS_DETACH:
            /* if in the above case the DllMain returned FALSE */
            /* the DllMain function is still called with DLL_PROCESS_DETACH */

            if (dllKey != TLS_OUT_OF_INDEXES)
                  TlsFree(dllKey);

            /* do something */
            break;

        case DLL_THREAD_ATTACH:
            pthrData = (char *) malloc(256); /* allocate an error buffer
            string */
            TlsSetValue(dllKey, pthrData); /* per thread error buffer */

            /* do something */
            break;
        case DLL_THREAD_DETACH:
            pthrData = TlsGetValue(dllKey);
            if (pthrData != NULL) /* always check for non-NULL value */
                free(pthrData);
            /* do something */
            break;
    }
}
```

The DllMain routine of a WIN32 DLL is called at various points during the execution of the process. When a DLL is mapped into the process's address space for the first time, the routine DllMain is called and the value of fdwReason is DLL_PROCESS_ATTACH. Since the DllMain is called with this code *once,* this becomes a natural place to perform any *process-related* initialization. For example, a multithreaded DLL might create mutexes, events, and semaphores in the initialization phase. Since all these resources are *process-based,* the handles of all these objects *should* be saved in global or static variables.

The return value of DllMain is used only when the process attaches to the DLL for the first time. For example, when the code in the process initialization function fails to create a mutex or a semaphore, then the DLL should return a value of FALSE. When DllMain returns FALSE, then the whole process is terminated. In the case of dynamic TLS, the function TlsAlloc could be called to create TLS keys when the process attaches to the DLL for the first time.

When the last thread in the process detaches from the DLL, then the DllMain routine is called with a reason code of DLL_PROCESS_DETACH. Since this is called only *once,* it serves as a natural place to perform any *process-related* cleanup. The DllMain is only called when a process calls ExitProcess and is not called if a process is terminated by a call to TerminateProcess. In the case of dynamic TLS (if any), the function TlsFree should be called to free TLS indexes.

When the process creates a new thread, then the function DllMain is called with a reason code of DLL_THREAD_ATTACH. Again, this should be used to perform any *thread-related* initialization. When a thread terminates gracefully by calling the function ExitThread or _endthreadex, then the DllMain routine is called with a reason code of DLL_THREAD_DETACH. Thread cleanup should be performed during this phase. One important thing to remember is that when threads are terminated forcefully, the DLL is *not* informed about the termination, and this might prevent the DLL from deallocating memory for any dynamic TLS.

14.3.1 Special considerations with DLL

In a WIN32 environment, the function DllMain is *serialized* by the system. In NT 3.5, the system acquires a mutual exclusion lock when a thread or process enters the DllMain routine and releases the lock when the thread leaves the routine. This mutual exclusion lock is created by the WIN32 system to serialize the DLL entry. If you do anything inside the DllMain routine that would cause the DllMain routine to be invoked in a recursive manner, you might *deadlock*.

```
BOOL DllMain(HINSTANCE hInstDll, DWORD fdwReason, LPVOID lpvReserved)
{
   char    *pThrBuffer;
   HANDLE  hSpecialThread;
   switch (fdwReason)
   {
     case DLL_PROCESS_ATTACH:
        hSpecialThread = CreateThread(.....);

        WaitForSingleObject(hSpecialThread, INFINITE); /* bug—indefinite
        wait */

        TerminateProcess(0);

        break;
     case DLL_THREAD_ATTACH:
        /* do something */
        break;
   }
}
```

In this code segment the process creates a thread for some special processing. This thread is considered critical for the entire application; it is required that if this thread should terminate, then the entire application should terminate. In our example the DllMain innocently calls WaitForSingleObject to wait for the thread object to become signaled.

When the DLL is mapped for the first time in the process, the DllMain routine is called with a reason code of DLL_PROCESS_ATTACH. The system will invoke the DllMain routine once *again* to notify of the thread creation (DLL_THREAD_ATTACH). When the newly created thread tries to enter the DllMain function, it will be blocked until the thread inside the DllMain function leaves (the main thread in our example). This is deadlock!

The main thread is blocked waiting for the new thread to terminate, while the newly created thread is blocked trying to enter the routine DllMain. The new thread can *never* start executing until the main thread returns from DllMain. All other threads trying to enter the DllMain routine will block until the main thread leaves the DllMain routine.

One should *avoid* calling any WIN32 function that would cause the DllMain routine to be called in a recursive manner. Even when you do so, make sure you do not block as in our example code segment. Note that even when the function *DisableThreadLibraryCalls* is called, the application will still deadlock.

14.4 Threads and Structured Exception Handling

WIN32 structured exception handling (SEH) is used to handle hardware and software exceptions. For example, when a thread does a divide by zero, an exception can be raised in the faulting thread. SEH allows an application to *guard* a block of code against exceptions and execute an *exception handler* if an exception occurs within a block of code.

In WIN32 there is another kind of exception handling known as *termination handling*. Termination handlers ensure that a particular block of code is *always* executed even if the guarded block of code terminates in some abnormal manner. Termination handling is useful in building robust multithreaded applications because it allows threads to release synchronization objects (like semaphores) in case of an exception. Let us now consider the following segment of code in which the function uses a semaphore to protect a shared resource.

```
HANDLE  hbufSem;
char    sharedBuffer[64];
InitializeSharedBuffer()
{
   int j;

   WaitForSingleObject(hbufSem, INFINITE);

   for (j = 0; j <= 64; ++j) /* bug - it exceeds array bounds */
        sharedBuffer [j] = `x';

   ReleaseSemaphore(hbufSem, 1, NULL);
}
```

In this code segment, when the thread exceeds the array bounds, it will get an access violation, and it will terminate *without* releasing the semaphore. Any other thread that now tries to acquire the semaphore will block waiting for the semaphore to be released. This will never happen, since the thread that acquired the semaphore has terminated, and it will lead to a *deadlock*. These kinds of deadlocks can be avoided by using the termination handling features of WIN32.

In the WIN32 environment the compiler has to do some extra work for SEH to work. The compiler introduces four keywords: *try, leave, except,* and *finally*.

The *try* keyword marks a block of code where a potential for exception exists. The *finally* keyword guards a block of code that is executed under all conditions. This body of code will be executed even when an exception occurs. Let us now implement the function shown above using the *try* and *finally* keywords. The semaphore will be released even when the exception (exceeding array bound) happens.

```
HANDLE  hBufSem;
char    SharedBuffer[64];

InitializeSharedBuffer()
{
   int j;

   try
   {
       WaitForSingleObject(hBufSem, INFINITE);

       for (j = 0; j <= 64; ++j) /* bug - it exceeds array bounds */
            SharedBuffer [j] = `x';
   }

   finally
   {
       ReleaseSemaphore(hBufSem, 1, NULL);
   }
}
```

Exception handling and termination handling are features you should *always* use in your applications. It is beyond the scope of this book to cover SEH in great detail. Interested readers should read Chap. 64 of the WIN32 programmers manual.

14.5 Potential Problems with File I/O

Now that we have covered the basic APIs used in threaded applications, let us turn our attention to input/output (I/O). In a WIN32 environment, file I/O can be performed either synchronously or asynchronously. A file has an associated file pointer that specifies the starting offset for a read operation or a write operation. When a file is created, the file pointer points to the starting offset in the file. The read and write functions, namely, ReadFile and WriteFile, change the file pointer location. The problem that we are going to discuss is not limited to file I/O but also can happen when two threads do a read from a socket. The topic of file I/O is discussed in detail in the next chapter.

Open file descriptors are shared resources of a process. In a multithreaded application, when multiple threads share an open file descriptor (e.g., file, socket, etc.), then the issue of concurrent access to these file descriptors *must* be addressed. Consider two threads T1 and T2 that share an open file descriptor, and both threads attempt to write to the end of the file at the same time by calling the function AppendToFile.

```
AppendToFile (HANDLE hFile, char *buf, int buflen)
{
   DWORD dwBytesWritten;

   SetFilePointer (hFile, 0, (LPLONG) NULL, FILE_END); /* seek to the end of
   file */
   WriteFile (hFile, buf, buflen, &dwBytesWritten, NULL);
}
```

Now, consider the following sequence of events:

- T1 seeks to the end of the file (executes call to SetFilePointer).
- T1 is preempted by the thread T2.
- T2 seeks to the end of the file (executes call to SetFilePointer) and writes to the file.
- T1 resumes execution, and now it writes to the file.

Under the scenario described above, the *WriteFile* of thread T1 will *not* be at the location as a result of the first *SetFilePointer*. The file pointer offset is changed by the *WriteFile* of thread T2. Open file descriptors are shared resources, and they should be protected by mutual exclusion locks. Things could have been much worse if the threads were doing a read, as in the following example.

The function FindRecord returns the starting offset of a record based on some key value passed to it. Let us assume that all records are fixed-size records, and threads T1 and T2 call the routine ReadRecord with different key values.

```
ReadRecord (HANDLE hFile, char *key, char *record, int recSize)
{
   LONG    offset;
   DWORD   dwBytesRead;

   offset = FindRecord (key);

   SetFilePointer (hFile, offset, (LPLONG) NULL, FILE_BEGIN);

   ReadFile (hFile, record, recSize, &dwBytesRead, NULL);
}
```

In the preceding example, if thread T1 were preempted after the call to SetFilePointer and T2 ran to completion, then thread T1 would read the wrong record. This can be avoided easily by using some mutual exclusion lock to guard the SetFilePointer/ReadFile operations. The example code below uses a mutex for mutual exclusion. It is assumed that the mutex is created in some other segment of the code.

```
ReadRecord (HANDLE hFile, char *key, char *record, int recSize)
{
   LONG   offset;
   DWORD  dwBytesRead;

   offset = FindRecord (Key);
```

```
    WaitForSingleObject(hFileMutex, INFINITE);

    SetFilePointer (hFile, offset, (LPLONG) NULL, FILE_BEGIN);

    ReadFile (hFile, record, recSize, &dwBytesRead, NULL);

    ReleaseMutex(hFileMutex);
}
```

Chapter

15

WIN32 and File I/O

15.1 Introduction

In the preceding three chapters most of the basic WIN32 concepts of thread programming were introduced. This discussion was mostly independent of the underlying operating system, and it can be applied easily to develop multithreaded applications on Windows NT as well as Windows 95. As you might recall from the earlier discussion, the complete WIN32 API has yet to be ported to all the different operating systems; this chapter introduces some of the more powerful features of WIN32 that are specific to Windows NT. The chapter will cover such topics as asynchronous I/O, asynchronous procedure calls (APCs), and I/O completion ports that are used to develop multithreaded applications.

Threads on Windows NT are often used to develop high-performance *server* applications. To build such applications, one often uses threads along with the high-performance I/O subsystem of Windows NT. The purpose of this chapter is *not* to cover all the I/O features of WIN32 but to discuss techniques for effectively using I/O in a multithreaded application. It is assumed that the reader is somewhat familiar with the concepts of WIN32 file I/O.

Even though Windows NT is gaining popularity, UNIX, with its strong networking and SMP performance, remains one of the most powerful server operating systems in the market today. Many of you are often faced with developing applications for both the platforms or you are in the process of porting an application from one system to the other. Since UNIX still enjoys so much popularity in server applications, some of the issues and strategies for porting applications to and from the UNIX operating system will be discussed later in this chapter.

15.2 WIN32 I/O

The I/O subsystem in NT is very flexible, and it supports both *synchronous* and *asynchronous* I/O. In synchronous I/O, you call an I/O function and then *wait* until the device driver completes the data transfer. When a process does synchronous I/O, then the calling thread is suspended until the I/O completes. For example, when a thread calls the function *ReadFile,* the thread blocks until the data are read into the user buffer. Similarly, when the process calls *WriteFile,* the thread waits until the operating system saves the data in the buffer cache. These cached data are later flushed to the disk by the I/O subsystem.

Many applications can get away with just using synchronous I/O, but if you are developing an efficient *server* application, then chances are very good that you will need to use asynchronous I/O. Processors have become fast, but I/O has *not* been able to keep up with the performance of these processors. Most applications are limited by I/O bottlenecks, and threads alone cannot help the responsiveness of such applications. Threads help alleviate some of the problems of synchronous I/O because only the thread calling the I/O function is blocked while the other threads continue to run. If your application cannot tolerate the I/O latency, then you should use asynchronous I/O. Asynchronous I/O can increase the throughput of applications.

Asynchronous I/O allows processing and I/O to be overlapped, and in conjunction with threads offers a powerful combination for developing efficient multithreaded applications. Server applications that have high I/O requirements are often written with asynchronous I/O in mind. These applications perform other tasks while the I/O happens asynchronously. With the fast processors that are being used, just imagine that while a device driver processes I/O requests, a processor could execute millions of instructions. This has the potential of increasing the throughput of the application manyfold.

In some cases by using asynchronous I/O it might be possible to entirely *eliminate* the need for multiple threads in your application. On multiprocessor machines, asynchronous I/O can happen on a separate processor while the thread or the process that initiated the I/O can run on a different processor. Again, this can be a performance boost on SMP machines without using extra system resources such as threads in your application.

In WIN32 jargon, the term *overlapped I/O* is used for asynchronous I/O. Asynchronous I/O is different from synchronous I/O in the sense that I/O calls do not block when called in asynchronous mode. When you call the I/O function, the device driver simply *queues* an I/O request and returns control to the caller. The application is free to do any other thing while the I/O request is handled asynchronously by the I/O subsystem. The application can check the *completion* of a pending I/O operation in one of the following ways:

- Wait synchronously for I/O completion on a WIN32 event object.
- Execute an asynchronous procedure call (APC).
- Wait on an I/O completion port.

All these completion options are explained in detail later in this chapter. One important thing to remember is that in WIN NT 3.51 there is no way to *cancel* a pending overlapped operation. In NT 4.0, a new API called CancelIo can be used to cancel overlapped operations.

15.2.1 Basic WIN32 file I/O APIs

Before looking at the asynchronous I/O capabilities of WIN32, let us take a brief look at some of the WIN32 file I/O APIs. Although some of the WIN32 I/O functions are similar to the C-Runtime (CRT) library functions, most applications hardly ever use the CRT functions. If you want to take advantage of the advanced features of the NT I/O system, then you should use the WIN32 I/O functions:

```
HANDLE   CreateFile(LPCSTR lpszName, DWORD fdwAccess,
                    DWORD fdwShareMode, LPSECURITY_ATTRIBUTES lpsa,
                    DWORD fdwCreate, DWORD fdwAttrsAndFlags,
                    HANDLE hTemplateFile)

BOOL     ReadFile(HANDLE hFile, LPVOID lpBuffer,
                  DWORD nNumberOfBytesToRead, LPDWORD lpNumberofBytesRead,
                  LPOVERLAPPED lpOverLapped)

BOOL     WriteFile(HANDLE hFile, CONST VOID *lpBuffer,
                  DWORD nNumberOfBytesToWrite, LPDWORD lpNumberofBytesWrite,
                  LPOVERLAPPED lpOverLapped)

BOOL     CloseHandle(HANDLE hFile)
```

15.2.2 Creating a file for overlapped I/O

WIN32 supports overlapped I/O on files, named pipes, sockets, and other serial communication devices. Overlapped I/O is disabled by default, but if you want to use overlapped I/O, then the file *should* be either created or opened with the overlapped I/O flag. The function *CreateFile* is used either to create a new file or to open an existing file. When a value of FILE_FLAG_OVERLAPPED is passed to *fdwAttrAndFlags,* then the system knows that the file will be accessed asynchronously.

The value passed to fdwAttrAndFlags is generally used as a hint by the operating system for system performance. For example, if you do not want to use caching, then you should pass a value of FILE_FLAG_NO_BUFFERING to CreateFile. Most applications that use overlapped I/O additionally *bypass* the cache. Refer to the WIN32 API manual for a complete listing of all the valid options to CreateFile.

15.2.3 Overlapped reads and writes

The syntax of the WIN32 functions for reading from and writing to files is similar. The first four arguments are self-explanatory, and the last argument specifies the mode of the I/O operation. All I/O operations can be performed either synchronously or asynchronously. The argument *lpOverLapped* is a pointer to an OVERLAPPED structure. If a NULL value is passed, then the I/O operation always completes synchronously, even though the file may be created or opened with the FILE_FLAG_OVERLAPPED flag.

If a non-NULL value is passed for an overlapped I/O enabled file handle, then the I/O operation has the potential to proceed asynchronously. Since the system might complete the I/O operation synchronously even though the operation was initiated in asynchronous mode, one should *always* check the return code of an I/O operation. When an I/O function returns TRUE, it means that the operation completed synchronously. When the operation continues asynchronously, then the function returns FALSE; additionally, the function GetLastError returns an error code of ERROR_IO_PENDING.

The OVERLAPPED structure is defined in WIN32 as follows:

```
typedef struct_OVERLAPPED
{
   DWORD   Internal;
   DWORD   InternalHigh;
   DWORD   Offset;
   DWORD   OffsetHigh;
   HANDLE  hEvent;
} OVERLAPPED;
```

Some of the meaningful fields within the structure are Offset, OffsetHigh, and hEvent. Offset and OffsetHigh specify the starting point for the file I/O operation. Since NT does not adjust the file pointer for asynchronous operations, you should *always* specify the starting offset for the overlapped I/O operation. Normally, the value passed to OffsetHigh is zero, and a nonzero value is only passed when the file size can be represented in 64 bits (large files). One additional advantage of overlapped I/O over synchronous I/O is that you *do not have* to worry about mutual exclusion with file handles (see Sec. 14.5). In Windows NT, event objects are used heavily for overlapped I/O notification. The member hEvent is a handle to a WIN32 *manual-reset* event object. Each asynchronous I/O operation requires a *separate* overlapped structure, and it is an *error* to reuse an overlapped structure of a pending I/O operation.

The following code segment shows how to perform I/O in both a synchronous and an asynchronous manner. The purpose of the following code segment is to show how to wait for I/O completion notification using file handles. In the next section you will see why this is *not* a good mechanism for I/O completion notification.

```
ReadData()
{
   HANDLE      hFile;
   OVERLAPPED  overLapped;
   DWORD       nRead;
   BOOL        fStatus;
   char        syncBuffer[64];
   char        asyncBuffer[64];
```

```
    hFile = CreateFile("unix.doc",
                       GENERIC_READ, FILE_SHARE_READ, NULL,
                       OPEN_ALWAYS,
                       FILE_FLAG_NORMAL | FLAG_FILE_OVERLAPPED,
                       NULL);

    ReadFile (hFile, syncBuffer, sizeof(syncBufffer), &nRead, NULL);
                                 /* synchronous I/O */

    overLapped. Offset = 0; /* start from offset 0 */
    overLapped.OffsetHigh = 0; /* not needed for 32-bit file size */
    overLapped.hEvent = NULL; /* no event object */

    fStatus = ReadFile (hFile, asyncBuffer, sizeof(asyncBuffer), &nRead,
              &overLapped);

    /* do something */

    if (!fStatus && GetLastError() = = ERROR_IO_PENDING)
        WaitForSingleObject(hFile, INFINITE);

}
```

15.2.4 Checking for asynchronous I/O completion

When a pending I/O completes, the thread that initiated the I/O is *not* asynchronously interrupted by the system. This is big departure from some of the other operating systems I have worked with, such as VMS and UNIX, which can deliver an AST or a signal when an asynchronous I/O operation completes. With asynchronous notification, the thread must be prepared to handle the notification at any given point. Signal-driven notification makes the code difficult to write and more often than not results in incorrect code.

In Windows NT, the I/O completion notification is delivered *only* at well-defined control points. This makes the coding much simpler, since the application has to handle I/O completion at certain points without sprinkling the I/O completion logic all over the code. By the way, this is similar to the POSIX *sigwait* signal delivery in multithreaded applications.

When an asynchronous operation is in progress, the thread can check for I/O completion in multiple ways. Since a WIN32 file handle is a synchronization object, it will become *signaled* when an overlapped I/O operation completes. If the calling thread calls the WaitForXXX function and passes the handle of the file, then it will be suspended until the asynchronous operation completes. When the pending I/O operation completes, the wait function returns and the file object is signaled by the system. The *problem* with using a file handle as a synchronization object arises when there are multiple overlapped I/O operations pending on the same file handle and one of them completes. In such a situation there is *no* way of finding out which operation completed. Because of this limitation, the use of file handles for notification of pending I/O operations should be avoided.

In WIN32 there are better ways to check for the completion of pending I/O operations than using file handles. The handle of an event object (*hEvent* in the OVERLAPPED structure) can be passed when any of the I/O operations are called in overlapped mode. Just before returning from an uncompleted I/O operation, the system changes the state of the event object to *nonsignaled*. The caller can *wait* on the event object to become signaled by calling the WIN32 WaitForXXX functions. The caller is woken up when the object becomes *signaled* as a result of completion of the pending I/O operation. Another way to wait for I/O completion is to call the function GetOverlappedResult. The following code illustrates the use of an event object for I/O notification.

```
ReadData()
{
   HANDLE       hFile;
   HANDLE       hAsyncCompletion;
   OVERLAPPED   overLapped;
   DWORD        nRead;
   BOOL         fStatus;
   char         asyncBuffer[64];

   hFile = CreateFile("unix.doc",
                        GENERIC_READ, FILE_SHARE_READ, NULL,
                        OPEN_ALWAYS,
                        FILE_FLAG_NORMAL | FLAG_FILE_OVERLAPPED,
                        NULL);

   hAsyncCompletion = CreateEvent (NULL, TRUE, FALSE, NULL); /* manual reset
   object */

   overLapped. Offset = 0; /* start from offset 0 */
   overLapped.OffsetHigh = 0;
   overLapped.hEvent = hAsyncCompletion; /* handle of async notification
   event */

   fStatus = ReadFile (hFile, asyncBuffer, sizeof(asyncBufffer), &nRead,
                        &overLapped);

   if (!fStatus && GetLastError() = = ERROR_IO_PENDING)
         WaitForSingleObject(hAsyncCompletion, INFINITE);

}
```

The WaitForXXX function returns when the event object passed in the OVERLAPPED structure is *signaled*. One can start *multiple* asynchronous operations and then wait for the completion of one or all of the I/O operations using the WaitForMultipleObjects function. Keep in mind that each asynchronous operation requires a unique OVERLAPPED structure, and the maximum number of objects in a single call to WaitForMultipleObjects is currently limited to 64.

There is *no* way to find out the result of the I/O operation by calling any of the standard WaitForXXX functions. When the wait function returns, the only thing you know is that a pending I/O operation has completed. Since it is possible for the I/O operation to fail, one should call the function GetOverlappedResult to check the status of the I/O operation.

```
BOOL  GetOverlappedResult(HANDLE hFile, LPOVERLAPPED lpOverlapped,
                          LPDWORD lpBytesTransferred, bWait)
```

When the value passed to *bWait* is TRUE, the function GetOverLapped-Result waits internally on the event object in the lpOverlapped structure. When the event object becomes signaled, the result of the overlapped operation is returned to the caller. The number of bytes read or written to is returned in *lpBytesTransferred*. The following code segment uses the function GetOverlappedResult instead of WaitForSingleObject to wait for the I/O completion.

```
ReadData()
{
   HANDLE       hFile;
   HANDLE       hAsyncCompletion;
   OVERLAPPED   overLapped;
   DWORD        nRead;
   DWORD        nAsyncRead;
   BOOL         fStatus;
   char         asyncBuffer[64];

   hFile = CreateFile("unix.doc",
                      GENERIC_READ, FILE_SHARE_READ, NULL,
                      OPEN_ALWAYS,
                      FILE_FLAG_NORMAL | FLAG_FILE_OVERLAPPED,
                      NULL);

   hAsyncCompletion = CreateEvent (NULL, TRUE, FALSE, NULL);

   overLapped. Offset = 0; /* start from offset 0 */
   overLapped.OffsetHigh = 0;
   overLapped.hEvent = hAsyncCompletion; /* handle of async notification
                       event */
   fStatus = ReadFile (hFile, asyncBuffer, sizeof(asyncBuffer), &nRead,
             &overLapped);

   if (!fStatus && GetLastError() == ERROR_IO_PENDING)
         GetOverlappedResult(hFile, &overLapped, &nAsyncRead, TRUE);

   if (nAsyncRead != sizeof(AsyncBuffer) /* check results of I/O completion */
         fprintf(stderr," Async I/O failed ....\n");

}
```

Either WaitForXXX function or GetOverlappedResult can be used when there is a single pending I/O operation. When there are *multiple* asynchronous operations pending and the results of each I/O operation have to be determined, then both functions have to be used together. The wait functions are used to wait until the object becomes signaled, while the GetOverlapped function is used to find out the result of the completed I/O operation.

The following code segment illustrates how to wait for multiple I/O operations on the same file handle. Note that these operations could have been on different file handles.

```
#define MAX_IO_OPERATION 2

ReadDataMultiple()
{
   HANDLE       hFile;
   HANDLE       hAsyncCompletion[MAX_IO_OPERATION];
   OVERLAPPED   overLapped[MAX_IO_OPERATION];
```

```
    HANDLE      hEvents[MAX_IO_OPERATION];
    DWORD       hSem;
    DWORD       nRead;
    DWORD       nAsyncRead;
    BOOL        fStatus;
    char        asyncBuf1[64];
    char        asyncBuf2[64];

    hFile = CreateFile("unix.doc",
                    GENERIC_READ, FILE_SHARE_READ, NULL,
                    OPEN_ALWAYS,
                    FILE_FLAG_NORMAL | FLAG_FILE_OVERLAPPED,
                    NULL);

    /* assume that all event objects are created */

    for (j = 0; j < MAX_IO_OPERATION; ++j)
    {
        hAsyncCompletion[j] = CreateEvent (NULL, TRUE, FALSE, NULL);
        overLapped[j]. Offset = 0; /* start from offset 0 */
        overLapped[j].OffsetHigh = 0;
        overLapped[j].hEvent =  hAsyncNotification[j]; /* handle of async
                                notification event */
        hEvents[j] = overLapped[j].hEvent;
    }

    fStatus = ReadFile (hFile, asyncBuf1, sizeof(asyncBuf1), &nRead,
            &overLapped[0]);
    fStatus = ReadFile (hFile, asyncBuf2, sizeof(asyncBuf2), &nRead,
            &overLapped[1]);

    /* assume none of the operations completed synchronously */
    /* this waits for both async to complete - you could wait for either */

    hSem = WaitForMultipleObjects(MAX_IO_OPERATION, hEvents, TRUE, INFINITE);

    switch(hSem)
    {
      case WAIT_OBJECT_0 + 0:
            /*since the object is already signaled pass FALSE to
            GetOverlapped */
            GetOverlappedResult(hFile, &overLapped[0], &nAsyncRead, FALSE);
            break;
      case WAIT_OBJECT_0 + 1:
            GetOverlappedResult(hFile, &overLapped[1], &nAsyncRead, FALSE);
            break;
    }
}
```

15.2.5 Guidelines for using event objects for I/O completion

- Do not reuse an overlapped structure until the pending asynchronous operation has completed.
- Use a separate overlapped structure for each asynchronous operation.
- The scope of an overlapped structure should be valid throughout the asynchronous operation.
- Use this function for moderately loaded asynchronous activity.
- Use this for multiple I/O operations on the same file.
- Do not use this for multiple I/O operations on different files.

- Only manual-reset events can be used, and they should be initialized to FALSE.

15.3 I/O Completion Functions

The preceding section covered the functions ReadFile and WriteFile for asynchronous I/O operations. WIN32 provides another version of these functions where it is possible to run a callback function when an I/O operation completes. The callback function is called *only* when the thread or the process is waiting in an *alertable* state. These I/O functions are also called the *extended I/O functions.*

```
BOOL    ReadFileEx(HANDLE hFile, LPVOID lpBuffer,
                DWORD nNumberOfBytesToRead, LPDWORD lpNumberofBytesRead,
                LPOVERLAPPED lpOverLapped,
                LPOVERLAPPED_COMPLETION_FUNCTION lpFunction)
BOOL    WriteFileEx(HANDLE hFile, CONST VOID *lpBuffer,
                DWORD nNumberOfBytesToWrite, LPDWORD lpNumberofBytesWrite,
                LPOVERLAPPED lpOverLapped,
                LPOVERLAPPED_COMPLETION_FUNCTION lpFunction)
```

The first five arguments of the extended functions are similar to ReadFile and WriteFile, and the last argument *lpFunction* is a pointer to a function that will be called by the functions ReadFileEx or WriteFileEx when an I/O operation completes. Note that the extended I/O functions do *not* return the number of bytes read from or written to the file. The callback function that is invoked when a pending I/O completes has the following prototype:

```
VOID    FileIoCompletionFunction(DWORD dwError,
                                DWORD dwBytesTransferred,
                                LPOVERLAPPED lpOverLapped)
```

When the callback is invoked, the argument *dwError* has the status of the I/O operation, and it contains the error code on failure. The argument *dwBytesTransferred* is the total number of bytes transferred in the I/O operation. The last argument *lpOverlapped* is a pointer to the OVERLAPPED structure that was passed initially to the function ReadFileEx or WriteFileEx.

15.3.1 Alertable wait functions

```
DWORD    SleepEx(DWORD dwTimeout, BOOL fAlertable)
DWORD    WaitForSingleObjectEx(HANDLE hObject, DWORD dwTimeOut,
                        BOOL fAlertable)
DWORD    WaitForMultipleObjectsEx(DWORD cObjects, LPHANDLE lphObjects,
                        BOOL fWaitAll, DWORD dwTimeOut,
                        BOOL fAlertable)
```

The alertable version of each of the preceding functions works the same way as the nonalertable version. The only *difference* between the alertable and nonalertable versions is that the last argument *fAlertable* specifies if the caller wants to enter an alertable state. If the value passed to fAlertable is TRUE, then the caller enters alertable state. When a thread is blocked in an alertable state and a pending asynchronous I/O operation completes, then the system invokes the callback function that was passed to ReadFileEx or WriteFileEx.

If the value passed to fAlertable is FALSE, then the system does *not* invoke the callback function, even if pending asynchronous I/O operations have completed. This behavior is similar to the nonalertable counterparts of these functions; in fact, the nonalertable versions of these functions call the alertable versions with a value of FALSE for fAlertable.

It is *important* that the thread that initiates the I/O operation must call the alertable wait function, since the callback function runs in the context of the calling thread. The alertable functions return WAIT_IO_COMPLETION when an I/O completes and the completion function runs.

The following code segment implements the function ReadData using completion functions.

```
#define BUFSZ 64

ReadData()
{
   HANDLE       hFile;
   HANDLE       hAsyncCompletion;
   OVERLAPPED   overLapped;
   DWORD        nRead;
   DWORD        nAsyncRead;
   BOOL         fStatus;
   char         asyncBuffer[BUFSZ];
   void         ReadCompletionFunction(DWORD, DWORD, LPOVERLAPPED);

   hFile = CreateFile("unix.doc",
                       GENERIC_READ, FILE_SHARE_READ, NULL,
                       OPEN_ALWAYS,
                       FILE_FLAG_NORMAL | FLAG_FILE_OVERLAPPED,
                       NULL);

   hAsyncCompletion = CreateEvent (NULL, TRUE, FALSE, NULL);

   overLapped. Offset = 0; /* start from offset 0 */
   overLapped.OffsetHigh = 0;
   overLapped.hEvent = hAsyncCompletion; /* handle of async notification
                       event */

   fStatus = ReadFileEx(hFile, asyncBuffer, sizeof(asyncBufffer),
                              &nRead, &overLapped, ReadComp);

   if (!fStatus && GetLastError() == = ERROR_IO_PENDING)
         SleepEx(INFINITE, TRUE);

}
VOID
ReadComp( DWORD dwError, DWORD nTransferred, LPOVERLAPPED *overLapped)
{
   if (dwError = = 0)
   {
```

```
            if (nTransferred ! = BUFSZ)
                fprintf(stderr, "Completion function: Read Error\n");
        else
            overLapped->Offset + = nTransferred; /* for next read operation */
    }
}
```

When multiple asynchronous operations are pending and an alertable wait function is called, it is possible that *all* callback functions will be invoked when the alertable wait function returns. For example, if three asynchronous read operations complete when the caller is blocked on the function SleepEx, then the callback function will be called three times even though the function SleepEx was called once. One might *not* have to call the alertable wait functions for each of the pending asynchronous operations. It would have been nice if the alertable function returned the number of times it called the callback function.

If you want to make sure that you have called the alertable wait functions *enough* times, then you should keep a count of pending asynchronous operations. Each time an asynchronous I/O operation starts, you should increment the counter, and you should decrement the counter each time the callback routine is executed. If you are calling the alertable functions just for asynchronous I/O notification, then you should make sure that you have a pending I/O operation. Failure to do so might cause an indefinite wait.

It is common to maintain context information for pending I/O operations, and one might like to pass this information to the callback routine when the I/O completes. Since the event object in the overlapped structure is *not* used when a completion function is passed to the functions *ReadFileEx* or *WriteFileEx,* one can use this field to pass user data to the callback function. You *also* can pass the address of a user-defined structure instead of the overlapped structure to the alertable I/O functions. It is dirty, but it works! I still think that WIN32 should have allowed one to pass a pointer's worth of data to the callback function cleanly.

```
typedef struct _userdata
{
   OVERLAPPED  overLapped;
   DWORD       nBytes;
   void        *pdata;
} USERDATA;

void   WINAPI   ReadCompletionFunction(DWORD, DWORD, LPOVERLAPPED);

ReadData()
{
   HANDLE      hFile;
   HANDLE      hAsyncCompletion;
   OVERLAPPED  overLapped;
   DWORD       nRead;
   BOOL        fStatus;
   char        asyncBuffer[BUFSZ];
   USERDATA    userData;

   hFile = CreateFile("unix.doc",
                        GENERIC_READ, FILE_SHARE_READ, NULL,
```

```
                          OPEN_ALWAYS,
                          FILE_FLAG_NORMAL | FLAG_FILE_OVERLAPPED,
                          NULL);

    hAsyncCompletion = CreateEvent (NULL, TRUE, FALSE, NULL);

    overLapped. Offset = 0; /* start from offset 0 */
    overLapped.OffsetHigh = 0;
    overLapped.hEvent = hAsyncCompletion; /* handle of async notification
                        event */

    userData.nBytes = sizeof(AsyncBuffer);

    /* cast the Udata structure to prevent the compiler from complaining */
    fStatus = ReadFileEx(hFile, asyncBuffer, sizeof(asyncBufffer),
                    &nRead, (LPOVERLAPPED)&userData,
                    ReadCompletionFunction);

    if (!fStatus && GetLastError() == ERROR_IO_PENDING)
        SleepEx(INFINITE, TRUE);

    }

    VOID
    ReadCompletionFunction( DWORD dwError, DWORD nTransferred, LPOVERLAPPED pOv)
  {
    USERDATA  *puserData;

    puserData = (USERDATA *) pOv;
    if (dwError == 0)
    {
       if (nTransferred != puserData->nBytes)
           fprintf(stderr, "Completion function: Read Error\n");
    }
  }
```

The completion function method for waiting for I/O completion works well in situations where there are a small number of threads and a backlog of pending I/O requests. These threads are designed to wait in an alertable state most of the time. One should *not* perform long calculations in the I/O completion function. As you might recall, one of the main requirements of the completion function is that the thread that issued the I/O function should run the completion function, and this makes it useless when a pool of worker threads service multiple clients. The event mechanisms discussed earlier work better when there is a pool of worker threads.

15.4 I/O Completion Ports

Both the notification methods we have discussed so far have their limitations. Neither of them works great for server applications (e.g., network server) that have to handle a large number of clients. To overcome the limitations of the previous models, the designers of NT designed a new mechanism in NT 3.5 for handling I/O completion. This feature is *unique* to NT and is not found on some of the other SMP operating systems such as UNIX or OS/2.

Creating an optimal number of threads is one of the crucial factors when developing a scalable multithreaded server application. The application should *not* suffer from either "too few" or "too many" threads syndrome. For servicing a small number of clients, a separate thread can be created for each client. This does not scale well under heavy loads or even for a large number of clients. Personally, I feel that a more efficient way of developing a server application is to create a pool of worker threads for servicing the clients. Later in this chapter the design of a multithreaded server (socket) will be discussed, and then the strengths and weaknesses of the various alternatives will be analyzed.

One should be aware of the fact that anytime you begin to use worker threads in your application, the design and implementation of the application code become complicated since more context information has to be maintained. When compared with a thread-per-client model, the code for the worker-thread model is more involved, but this extra work can pay off in terms of a scalable and efficient architecture. In the worker-thread model, the biggest challenge lies in creating an optimal number of worker threads. Even when you manage to create some optimal number of worker threads, it becomes *difficult* to know when any of the worker threads might block. If you do not have this information, then it is impossible to activate another worker thread to run in place of the blocked thread. The designers of NT realized this problem and in NT 3.5 came up with an easier way to program worker threads in a server application. The mechanism is called the *I/O completion port.*

I/O completion ports are designed to be used by worker threads along with asynchronous or overlapped I/O. The function CreateIoCompletionPort associates a port with file handles, and the port acts as a synchronization point for *multiple* file handles. A number of worker threads can manage I/O for clients by calling GetQueuedCompletionStatus to wait on an I/O completion port. When an I/O on any of the file handles completes, the system queues a completion packet to the completion port. This is the *most* efficient mechanism for handling overlapped I/O completion and works best for server applications using sockets or named pipes. Each file handle represents a client connection, and a pool of worker threads services the clients by waiting on the same I/O completion port. With I/O completion ports there is only one synchronization point for all I/O activity, and this lends well for designing a pool of worker threads to handle multiple clients.

The question one might ask then is, "Why can't I wait directly on event objects for asynchronous notification using WaitForMultipleObjects?" One of the problems with this approach is that a worker thread cannot monitor more than 64 objects in a single call to WaitForMultipleObject. You could get around this limitation by having each of the worker threads service a maximum of 64 clients. There are other advantages of I/O completion ports that make them *more* efficient for overlapped I/O rather than just overcoming this limitation.

The biggest advantage of I/O completion ports is that they have built-in *concurrency* control that can be programmed when the port is created. The kernel tries to limit the number of runnable threads associated with a port so as never to exceed the port's concurrency value. When a thread calls GetQueuedCompletionStatus, the function returns only when I/O is available *and* the number of runnable threads associated with a completion port is less than the port's concurrency value.

The system tracks the threads associated with a port and also tracks the number of runnable threads associated with a port. When one of the threads associated with a completion port blocks (e.g., I/O, page fault, or any other WIN32 synchronization primitive), then the kernel selects another thread waiting on the completion port to run. If there are *more* worker threads than the concurrency value of the port, then the system suspends the additional threads, which are woken up only when the number of runnable threads associated with a port drops *below* the concurrency value.

The threads that block on a completion port are woken up in LIFO order, whereas I/O requests are serviced in FIFO order. Since in a worker-thread model it does not make any difference which worker thread is woken up to service a request, the system wakes up the most recently active thread for performance reasons (e.g., processor cache). The number of threads waiting on the I/O completion port is *not* very important. If there are more worker threads than work packets, then these additional threads remain blocked. If these blocked threads do not become runnable for some time, then the memory resources for the idle threads are swapped out to disk.

The I/O completion port works *best* when there are queued I/O packets, but they cannot be serviced because the concurrency value has been reached. Running threads after completing a transaction can pick up the next request (since waiting threads are awakened LIFO) without causing any context switch. I/O completion ports are designed to work efficiently under all loads, but the performance does not suffer under heavy loads, and actually, I/O completion ports are designed to run efficiently under such situations.

15.4.1 Creating an I/O completion port

```
HANDLE  CreateIoCompletionPort(HANDLE hFile, HANDLE ExistingCompletionPort,
                               DWORD CompletionKey,
                               DWORD NumberConcurrentThreads)
```

The function CreateIoCompletionPort associates an open file handle identified by *hFile* with an input or output completion port. Since completion ports are designed to work with overlapped I/O, it is important that the file *must* be opened or created with the FILE_FLAG_OVERLAPPED flag. If you are wondering how to open a named pipe or socket in an overlapped mode, then you should not worry, since the system automatically creates sockets and named pipes with the overlapped flag set.

The completion port is created if the value passed to *ExistingCompletion Port* is NULL; otherwise, an association is made between the file handle *hFile* and an existing completion port identified by ExistingCompletionPort. The first time the function CreateIoCompletionPort is called, one should pass a NULL value for the first file handle but then use the handle of the completion port returned for future calls. This will ensure that the completion port is created only *once* and that all file handles are associated with the same I/O completion port.

The argument *CompletionKey* is a per-file completion key. Each time a file handle is associated with a completion port, one can specify a key that is returned when an I/O completes on the file handle. By using a unique key for each of the file handles, one can associate I/O completion with file handles. One also can use the completion key to find out if a read or write operation completed on the same file handle by assigning a unique key value to the read and write operations. Consider the case of a server that wants to store some context information for each of the connected clients (unique file handle), in which case the key can be used to maintain a handle/key association. If you are using a fixed-sized table for storing client information, then you can pass the index of the client entry in the table as the key or you can pass the address of a user-defined structure as the key value.

The argument *NumberofConcurrentThreads* is used to control the concurrency associated with a port, and it is used to specify the number of worker threads servicing the clients. It is a bit tricky to pick an optimal number for the number of concurrent threads. Generally, one should try to pick more than one thread per processor in the machine as the concurrency value for the I/O completion port. If the NumberofConcurrentThreads is zero, then the system finds the number of processors in the system and assigns the concurrency value equal to the number of processors in the machine (default value).

The concurrency value should never be hard coded in the application because this might limit the application's ability to exploit the multiple processors in the system. One should call the function *GetSystemInfo* to determine the number of processors at run time and pass that information to CreateIoCompletionPort. The number of worker threads is not that important; therefore, one *should* create more than one worker thread per processor. One has to account for the fact that some of the worker threads might *block,* in which case you want enough worker threads available so as to be runnable. If too many worker threads are created, then chances are that most of the time they will be idle.

For most applications it makes sense to allow for more than one thread per CPU. For example, if your application blocks too often or handles lengthy computations, it makes sense to have this number a bit higher. Personally, I feel that you should experiment with different values of concurrent threads and see their affect on the application. If you feel uncomfortable with tuning the concurrency value, then you should use the default value.

15.4.2 Waiting for completion packets

```
BOOL   GetQueuedCompletionStatus(HANDLE CompletionPort,
                                 LPDWORD lpNumberOfBytesTransferred,
                                 LPDWORD lpCompletionKey
                                 LPOVERLAPPED *lpOverLapped,
                                 DWORD dwMilliseconds)
```

This function tries to dequeue an I/O completion packet from the completion port identified by *CompletionPort*. The function can be called in a blocking manner or can be specified to time out after a specified period. The function returns TRUE on success, and it sets the variable *lpNumberOfBytes Transferred* to the number of bytes transferred during an I/O operation. The function also sets the variable *lpCompletionKey* to the completion key associated with the file handle. The completion key is the value that was passed to the function CreateIoCompletionPort.

The function also returns a pointer to an OVERLAPPED structure in *lpOverLapped*. The address of the overlapped structure is the same as that which was passed to either *ReadFile* or *WriteFile* when an overlapped I/O operation was initiated. The last argument *dwMilliseconds* specifies the time-out period the caller wants to wait for a completion packet. If the caller wants to wait until an I/O completion packet is dequeued, then pass a (DWORD) −1 value to *dwMilliseconds*. If you pass a positive nonzero value to *dwMilliseconds,* then the function waits for the time-out period specified (milliseconds). If an I/O completion packet cannot be dequeued in the specified time, then the function GetQueuedCompletionStatus returns FALSE.

The following pseudocode segment shows a typical use of completion ports by a socket server. This example assumes that the reader is familiar with Windows sockets APIs. Assume that the function ProcessWorkItem is called by each of the worker threads to handle client requests.

```
HANDLE   hIoCompletionPort;

main(int argc, char **argv)
{
   SOCKET  hListen;
   SOCKET  hConn;

   /* create socket, bind and listen for connections */

   hIoCompletionPort = NULL;
   for (;;)
   {
       OVERLAPPED *pOverlapped;

       hConn = accept(hListen....);

       /* first time CreateIoCompletionPort creates the completion port
          in this case we are using the file handle as the completion key */

       hIoCompletionPort = CreateIoCompletionPort(hConn, hIoCompletionPort,
                                                  hConn, 0);

       /* post an async operation for the new connection
       using a unique OVERLAPPED structure */

       pOverlapped = (OVERLAPPED *) calloc(1, sizeof(CVERLAPPED));
       pOverlapped->hEvent = CreateEvent (NULL, TRUE, FALSE, NULL);

       ReadFile(hConn......, pOverlapped);

       /* go back to top of loop - accept more connections */
   }
}
```

```
ProcessWorkItem()
{
   OVERLAPPED  *pOverlapped;
   DWORD       completionKey;
   DWORD       bytesTransferred;
   HANDLE      hFile;

   for (;;)
   {
      GetQueuedCompletionStatus(hPort, &bytesTransferred, &completionKey,
                                &pOverlapped, (DWORD) -1);

      /* process client request */
      HandleClientRequest(...);

      /* post another pending asynchronous operation */
      hFile = (HANDLE) completionKey; /* see call to CreateIoCompletionPort */

      ReadFile(hFile, ............,pOverlapped);
   }
}
```

15.4.3 Overriding I/O completion notification

Occasionally, one might want to temporarily override the I/O completion port notification on a file handle. This is useful when you are in the middle of doing something, but need to do a synchronous read or write operation. Assume in the above socket example that the client sends fixed-size header followed by some variable size data. The header specifies the size of the variable data. The server can call *ReadFile* and specify a large buffer to hold all possible variations, or it can perform an asynchronous read on just the fixed-size header. Once the read of the fixed-size data is successful, the server can do a synchronous read for the remaining data. It is quite likely that the synchronous read will complete immediately since the data are available in the socket buffer. Generally, some state information has to be maintained for asynchronous operations such that any worker thread can complete the transaction. By avoiding another asynchronous operation, the server can avoid the work of populating the state information. Additionally, it is more efficient since the kernel has to do less work when the operation is synchronous.

The WIN32 I/O functions *ReadFile* and *WriteFile* have been extended to *override* the I/O completion port mechanism on a per-I/O basis. If you call the function ReadFile and pass an overlapped structure that contains a valid hEvent, then you can turn off the I/O completion port notification by *setting* the low bit of the hEvent handle in the overlapped structure. When the low-order bit of the event object is set, then the system does not generate an I/O completion packet when a pending overlapped I/O completes.

```
#define MSGSZ 2048

ProcessWorkItem()
{
   OVERLAPPED  *pOverlapped;
   DWORD       completionKey;
   DWORD       bytesTransferred;
   HANDLE      hFile;
```

```
    for (;;)
    {
        GetQueuedCompletionStatus(hPort, &bytesTransferred, &completionKey,
                                  &pOverlapped, (DWORD) -1);

        /* process client request */

        hFile = (HANDLE) completionKey; /* see call to CreateIoCompletionPort
                */

        /* override completion port notification */
        if (bytesTransferred != MSGSZ) /* partial message read */
            pOverlapped->hEvent = pOverlapped->hEvent |= 0x01 ;

        ReadFile(hFile, ............,); /* do synchronous read */
    }
}
```

15.4.4 Posting special-purpose completion packets

Sometimes it might be necessary to notify a worker thread of some external event without issuing an I/O request. For example, a clean shutdown might require each thread waiting on the I/O completion port to perform thread-specific cleanup before calling ExitThread. You can post an application-defined *shutdown* packet for each worker thread. Each of the worker threads, after reading this special packet, performs a cleanup and exits the application. It is the application's responsibility to define a protocol to detect and handle these special completion packets.

```
BOOL    PostQueuedCompletionStatus(HANDLECompletionPort,
                                   DWORD lpNumberOfBytesTransferred,
                                   DWORD lpCompletionKey,
                                   LPOVERLAPPED *lpOverLapped)
```

The function PostQueuedCompletionStatus posts a special-purpose packet to the I/O completion port identified by the variable *CompletionPort*. The second argument *lpNumberOfBytesTransferred* is the size of the packet being queued to the completion port. The third argument *lpCompletionKey* associates a key value with the packet. Generally, you pass a value that the worker threads can use to detect the packet as a non-I/O packet. The following code segment shows how a worker thread can detect a shutdown message.

```
#define  NORMAL_IO_MSG  0x01
#define  SHUTDOWN_MSG   0x02

HANDLE   hIoPort;

main(int argc, char **argv)
{
   for (;;)
   {
       DWORD packet = SHUTDOWN_MSG;
       OVERLAPPED *pOverlapped;
       hConn = accept(hListen....);
```

```
            /* On Error we will post a special packet for thread cleanup */
            if (FatalError) /* post for each worker thread in a loop */
                PostQueuedCompletionStatus(hIoPort, sizeof(packet), packet, NULL);

            hIoPort = CreateIoCompletionPort(hConn, hIoPort, NORMAL_IO_MSG, 0);

            /* post an async operation for the new connection
               using a unique OVERLAPPED structure */
            /* go back to top of loop - accept more connections */
        }
    }

    ProcessWorkItem()
    {
        OVERLAPPED  *pOverlapped;
        DWORD       completionKey;
        DWORD       bytesTransferred;
        HANDLE      hFile;

        for (;;)
        {
            GetQueuedCompletionStatus(hPort, &bytesTransferred, &completionKey,
                                      &pOverlapped, (DWORD) -1);

            if (completionKey == SHUTDOWN_MSG)
            {
                ThreadCleanup();
                ExitThread(...);
            }

        if (CompletionKey == NORMAL_IO_MSG)
             HandleClientRequest();
        }
    }
```

15.5 Servers and I/O Completion Ports

For illustration purposes, the various threading models that can be used to design a multithreaded server will be considered. The server in the example is a TCP/IP-based server, but it could have been a named pipe server. It is assumed that the reader is familiar with Windows socket (WinSock) APIs on Windows NT. The main goal of any server design is to ensure that it is fast, scalable, and can work well under heavy loads. Additionally, the optimal server design should try to be fair to its client.

In the first single-threaded model, the main thread, after doing an *accept* on the socket, will service the client request. The disadvantage of this model is that while the server is processing a client request, all other requests are being queued.

In the second single-threaded model, the main thread does a *select* call on all the connected sockets. The system call select returns when data are available on any one of the connected sockets. Now multiple clients can be serviced concurrently, but as in the previous model, this does not exploit the power of multiple CPUs. The first two models are not that interesting, but if the number of clients or frequency of transactions is low, then these models can be used. It is very important to note that not all programs need threads and not all of them can benefit from them.

In the third model, the main thread would create a separate thread for each client. This model is extremely easy to program, but the disadvantage of this model is that it does not scale well for a high number of active clients. By the way, there is nothing wrong with this model except that it is inefficient, especially considering the fact that most threads could be idle. The main thread, by creating multiple threads, might be taking advantage of multiple processors, but this uses excessive system resources and causes overhead in terms of scheduling. The performance of the system degrades under "burst" traffic. In the burst mode, as the number of ready threads increases, the system spends lots of time context switching threads in and out of running state.

The previous model can be improved by using a *concurrency* semaphore to restrict the number of runnable threads in the system. Each thread will acquire the semaphore, read the transaction, process the transaction, and finally, release the semaphore. The semaphore count can be set to some optimal value based on the number of CPUs. Even though adding a concurrency semaphore introduces a slight overhead for every transaction, actually, by slowing down, we can be sure that the system will work *better* under heavy load.

In the fourth model, a pool of worker threads is created to handle client requests. The main thread does a *select* on all the connected sockets and passes the request to one of the worker threads when data arrive on any one of the connected sockets. A global work queue can be maintained to queue the incoming requests. The number of worker threads can chosen to be slightly greater than the number of processors, since some of the worker threads can block. This model uses fewer system resources than the previous model, but the disadvantage of this model is that there is a built-in context switch on every transaction between the main thread and the worker thread. The context switch might not be a problem for longer transactions, but the overhead might be high for short transactions. This model does not have built-in fairness to its clients unless the main thread does some rotation on the list of file descriptors on the select call. Also, using this model, it is difficult to service transactions in an FIFO manner.

Now let us consider the last model implemented with I/O completion ports. The main thread would create an I/O completion port and have a pool of worker threads waiting on them. This model is the most efficient of all and uses the CPU and system resources most efficiently. This model does not suffer from the overhead of context switching as in the last model, since the thread that reads the transaction services it. In the last model, if one of the worker threads were to block, then that processor would not be utilized. Completion ports always try to have the number of runnable threads equal to the concurrency value, thus utilizing all the processors much more efficiently. Since I/O requests are satisfied in FIFO order, fairness is built into the completion port model. It does not suffer from the fairness problem of the last model.

15.6 Differences between Pthreads and WIN32

This section is *only* intended for users who develop multithreaded software on UNIX as well as on Windows NT. Even though UNIX started out as a single-threaded operating system, today there are many vendors who ship an efficient SMP UNIX operating system with full multithreading support. This section assumes that the reader is using the POSIX thread API (P1003.1c) on UNIX and the WIN32 interface on NT for developing threaded applications.

Both platforms have similar APIs in terms of functionality to create and manage threads. The thread identifier of a thread is unique systemwide on NT, while in Pthreads it is guaranteed to be unique within the context of the same process. The POSIX thread supports a two-level scheduling of threads (process and system), but WIN32 only supports system scheduling. One can always use Fibers to simulate process-level threads, but remember that in Windows NT the application is responsible for the scheduling of Fibers. Threads can be suspended and resumed in WIN32, but this is not supported by Pthreads. Exception handling and termination handling are not a part of Pthreads.

The WIN32 API supports more synchronization primitives than Pthreads, and it is easy to build the Pthreads synchronization primitives using the WIN32 API. If an application is using the WIN32 critical section API, then it should be replaced by mutexes instead before it can be easily ported to Pthreads. Semaphores are not a part of Pthreads but are available as part of POSIX.1b; in fact, they also can be built using the base Pthreads primitives. The WaitForMultipleObject function of WIN32 is a powerful mechanism when multiple synchronization objects have to be monitored. The wait for multiple synchronization object mechanism is missing in the Pthreads API, and it is the caller's responsibility to build locking primitives that involve multiple synchronization objects. All WIN32 objects are acquired by calling one of the WaitForXXX functions (supports time-out), while in Pthreads each synchronization object has its own locking API. I would recommend that the locking and unlocking of these objects be done through well-defined interfaces, where the details of the implementation can be hidden. For example, consider the function LockMultipleLocks that locks two mutexes lock1 and lock2. Note that in WIN32 this is easy, while it is not straightforward to implement the same in Pthreads. The thing that makes it more difficult in Pthreads is support for time-out and the atomicity of multiple locks.

```
LockMultipleLocks(lock1, lock2)
{
   WaitForMultipleObject(, lock1..lock2,...);
}
```

```
LockMultipleLocks(lock1, lock2)
{
pthread_mutex_lock(lock1);
pthread_mutex_unlock(lock2);
}
```

In terms of thread-specific data, both are similar, except for minor differences. In POSIX jargon they are called *thread-specific data,* while in WIN32 they are called *thread local storage.* WIN32 does not support destructor functions for thread-specific keys. Note that destructor functions in Pthreads are often used to clean up any thread-specific data. If you are using a DLL, then all thread-specific cleanup can be performed when the thread terminates (DLL_THREAD_DETACH). The once-only process initialization of DLLs (DLL_PROCESS_ATTACH) can be achieved by using the function *pthread_once* in Pthreads. If an application is using static TLS, then they have to be changed to dynamic TLS before they can be ported to UNIX. POSIX supports cancellation and cleanup handlers on a thread basis. In a WIN32 environment threads should be terminated only as a last resort, and WIN32 does not support cleanup handlers. Thread termination is always a delicate issue and is not very clean even in the POSIX environment.

There many differences in the basic design philosophy of the two operating systems when it comes to I/O. On NT, most of the I/O can be done asynchronously and is often used by server applications. Most UNIX systems do not yet support the concept of asynchronous I/O, and this is where a programmer will face the biggest challenge. In the NT world, the worker-thread model along with asynchronous I/O is often used, and the reader should note that there is no equivalent of an I/O completion port in the UNIX world. The POSIX.1b asynchronous I/O model requires polling for completion of asynchronous I/O notification (when multiple I/O requests are pending).

Personally, I find that if a multithreaded application is designed correctly, then porting between the two platforms (UNIX and NT) can be a straightforward task. One should keep in mind that even though the threading APIs are different on the two operating systems, the basic thread-management functionality is very similar. The reader is advised to read Chap. 19 for more on portability of the different thread implementations.

Chapter

16

WIN32 Programming Examples

16.1 Compiling and Linking

This chapter assumes that you are using a Microsoft compiler. There are three different versions of the C-Runtime (CRT) library shipped with the MS-Visual C++ compiler. They are as follows:

```
libc.lib      Static linked library for single-threaded programs.
libcmt.lib    Static linked library for multithreaded programs.
msvcrt.lib    Import library for msvcrt.dll for single- and multithreaded
              applications.
```

To compile a multithreaded application, you should use either libcmt.lib or msvcrt.lib. You should pass the /MT option or the /MD option to the compiler; passing either of these flags causes the macro _MT to be defined. The /MT (multithreaded) uses the static version of the CRT library, while the /MD switch uses the DLL version.

16.2 Queue Implementation Using Semaphores

Queues are a simple yet powerful interthread communication paradigm. Queues can be used effectively in applications that use worker threads to service clients. Threads, instead of waiting on semaphores or condition variables, can wait on queues for work items to be added. It should be noted that threads that use queues for servicing requests are much easier to program and test.

```
#include <windows.h>
#include <stdio.h>
```

```
#define MAXHANDLES 2

typedef  struct _qmsg  QMSG;
struct _qmsg
{
   void   *msg;
   int    msgLen;
   QMSG   *next;
};

typedef struct _queue
{
   HANDLE  qMutex;
   HANDLE  qSema;
   HANDLE  qSemMutex[MAXHANDLES];
   QMSG    *qHeadMsg;
   QMSG    *qTailMsg;
} QUEUE;

QUEUE   gQueue;

void
main(int argc, char **argv)
{
   int      numThr;
   DWORD    threadId[MAXTHREADS];
   DWORD    Readers();
   DWORD    Writers();
   HANDLE   hThread[MAXTHREADS];
   int      i;

   numThr = NUM_WRITERS + NUM_READERS;
   if (numThr > MAXTHREADS)
       exit(0);

   QueCreate(&gQueue, 10);

   for (i = 0; i < NUM_WRITERS; ++i)
       hThread[i] = CreateThread(NULL, 0, (LPTHREAD_START_ROUTINE)Writers,
                                 (LPVOID)NULL, 0, &threadId[i]);

   for (i= NUM_WRITERS ; i < numThr; ++i)
       hThread[i] = CreateThread(NULL, 0, (LPTHREAD_START_ROUTINE)Readers,
                                 (LPVOID)NULL, 0, &threadId[i]);

   for (i = 0; i < numThr; ++i)
       WaitForMultipleObjects(numThr, hThread, TRUE, INFINITE);

   ExitProcess(0);
}

DWORD
Writers(void *pThrArg)
{
   DWORD  threadId;
   int    i;
   char   msg[256];

   threadId = GetCurrentThreadId();
   for (i = 0; i < NUMMSGS; ++i)
   {
       sprintf(msg,"Msg %d from thread %d", i, threadId);
       QuePut(msg, sizeof(msg), &gQueue);
   }
   fprintf(stderr,"writer [%d] put [%d] msgs\n",threadId, i);
```

```
   return(i);
}

DWORD
Readers(void *pThrArg)
{
   int    i;
   int    numMsgs;
   int    Rc;
   char   msg[256];
   DWORD  threadId;

   threadId = GetCurrentThreadId();

   numMsgs = (NUMMSGS * NUM_WRITERS)/NUM_READERS;
   for (i = 0; i < numMsgs; ++i)
        QueGet(msg, sizeof(msg), &gQueue);
   fprintf(stderr,"reader [%d] read [%d] msgs\n",threadId, i);
   return(i);
}

int
QueGet(void *pMsg, int Msglen, QUEUE *pQueue)
{
   int Rc;

   WaitForMultipleObjects(MAXHANDLES, pQueue->qSemMutex, TRUE, INFINITE);

   Rc = DeleteQueueMsg(pMsg, Msglen, pQueue);

   ReleaseMutex(pQueue->qMutex);

   return(Rc);
}

int
QuePut(void *pMsg, int Msglen, QUEUE *pQueue)
{
   int Rc;
   /* this implementation does not implement flow control */
   WaitForSingleObject(pQueue->qMutex,INFINITE);
   Rc = InsertQueueMsg(pMsg, Msglen, pQueue);

   ReleaseSemaphore(pQueue->qSema, 1, NULL);

   ReleaseMutex(pQueue->qMutex);

   return(Rc);
}

int QueCreate(QUEUE *pQueue, int MaxMsgs)
{
   pQueue->qMutex = CreateMutex(NULL, FALSE, NULL);

   /* none available */
   pQueue->qSema = CreateSemaphore(NULL, 0, 0x7fffffff, NULL);

   pQueue->qSemMutex[0] = pQueue->qMutex;
   pQueue->qSemMutex[1] = pQueue->qSema;

   pQueue->qHeadMsg = NULL;
   pQueue->qTailMsg = NULL;

   return(0);
}
```

```
InsertQueueMsg(void *pMsg, int msgLen, QUEUE *pQueue)
{
   QMSG   *newMsg;

   newMsg = (QMSG *) calloc(1,sizeof(QMSG));
   newMsg->msgLen = msgLen;
   newMsg->msg = (void *) malloc(msgLen);

   memcpy(newMsg->msg, pMsg, msgLen);

   if (pQueue->qHeadMsg == NULL)
   {
        pQueue->qHeadMsg = newMsg;
        pQueue->qTailMsg = newMsg;
   }
   else
   {
        pQueue->qTailMsg->next = newMsg;
        pQueue->qTailMsg = newMsg;
   }
   return(0);
}

DeleteQueueMsg(void *Msg, int msgLen, QUEUE *pQueue)
{
   QMSG   *currMsg;
   int    len;

   currMsg = pQueue->qHeadMsg;
   len = currMsg->msgLen;

   memcpy(Msg,currMsg->msg, currMsg->msgLen);

   if (pQueue->qHeadMsg == pQueue->qTailMsg)
        pQueue->qTailMsg = NULL;

   pQueue->qHeadMsg = pQueue->qHeadMsg->next;

   free(currMsg->msg);
   free(currMsg);
   return(len); /* length of message */
}
```

16.3 Queue Implementation using Event Objects

```
typedef struct _qmsg QMSG;

struct _qmsg
{
   void  *msg;
   int   msgLen;
   QMSG  *next;
};

typedef struct _queue
{
   int     qMsgs;
   int     qMaxMsgs;
   int     qFullReset;
   HANDLE  qMutex;
   HANDLE  qEmpty;
   HANDLE  qFull;
```

```
   QMSG    *qHeadMsg;
   QMSG    *qTailMsg;
} QUEUE;

QUEUE  qQueue;

#define   MAXHANDLES 2

int
QueGet(void *pMsg, int msgLen, QUEUE *pQueue)
{
   int   Rc;
   HANDLE muxHandle[MAXHANDLES];

   WaitForSingleObject(pQueue->qMutex, INFINITE);

   muxHandle[0] = pQueue->qMutex; /* can put these in pQueue */
   muxHandle[1] = pQueue->qEmpty;

   while (pQueue->qMsgs == 0)
   {
         ReleaseMutex(pQueue->qMutex);
         WaitForMultipleObjects(MAXHANDLES, muxHandle, TRUE, INFINITE);
   }

   Rc = DeleteQueueMsg(pMsg, msgLen, pQueue);

   if (pQueue->qMsgs == pQueue->qMaxMsgs)
        SetEvent(pQueue->qFull);

   --pQueue->qMsgs;
   ReleaseMutex(pQueue->qMutex);
   return(Rc);
}

int
QuePut(void *pMsg, int msgLen, QUEUE *pQueue)
{
   HANDLE muxHandle[MAXHANDLES];

   muxHandle[0] = pQueue->qFull; /* can put these in pQueue */
   muxHandle[1] = pQueue->qMutex;

   WaitForSingleObject(pQueue->qMutex, INFINITE);
   while (pQueue->qMsgs == pQueue->qMaxMsgs)
   {

      pQueue->qFullReset = FALSE;
      ReleaseMutex(pQueue->qMutex);
      WaitForMultipleObjects(MAXHANDLES, muxHandle, TRUE, INFINITE);
      if (pQueue->qFullReset == FALSE)
      {
         pQueue->qFullReset = TRUE;
         ResetEvent(pQueue->qFull);
      }
   }
   InsertQueueMsg(pMsg, msgLen, pQueue);
   ++pQueue->qMsgs;
   SetEvent(pQueue->qEmpty);
   ReleaseMutex(pQueue->qMutex);
   return(0);
}

int
QueCreate(QUEUE *pQueue, int maxMsgs)
```

```
{
   pQueue->qMutex = CreateMutex(NULL, FALSE, NULL);
   pQueue->qFull = CreateEvent(NULL, TRUE, FALSE, NULL);
   pQueue->qEmpty = CreateEvent(NULL, FALSE, FALSE, NULL);

   pQueue->qMaxMsgs = maxMsgs;
   pQueue->qMsgs = 0;
   pQueue->qHeadMsg = NULL;
   pQueue->qTailMsg = NULL;
   return(0);
}
```

16.4 Barrier Synchronization

A barrier is a synchronization point in the program where threads wait to synchronize with each other. It is used to ensure that cooperating threads have reached a point before they can proceed to the next step. All threads wait at a synchronization point until the last thread reaches the point at which all of them can proceed.

```
#include <windows.h>
#include <stdio.h>

#define MAXHANDLES 2

typedef struct _barrier
{
   int     bCount;
   int     bResetCount;
   int     bReset;
   int     bWaiters;
   HANDLE  bMutex;
   HANDLE  bEvent;
   HANDLE  bMuxHandle[MAXHANDLES];
} BARRIER;

BARRIER     gBarrier;

void main(int argc, char **argv)
{
   int      numThr;
   int      *pThrArg;
   DWORD    threadId[MAXTHREADS];
   HANDLE   hThread[MAXTHREADS];
   DWORD    ThrRoutine();
   int      i;

   numThr = MAXTHREADS;
   pThrArg = &numThr;

   BarrierInit(&gBarrier, MAXTHREADS);

   for (i = 0; i <numThr; ++i)
       hThread[i] = CreateThread(NULL, 0,
                      (LPTHREAD_START_ROUTINE)ThrRoutine,
                      (LPVOID)NULL, 0, &threadId[i]);

   for (i = 0; i < numThr; ++i)
       WaitForMultipleObjects(numThr, hThread, TRUE, INFINITE);

   ExitProcess(0);
}
```

```
DWORD
ThrRoutine(void *pThrArg)
{
   int i;

   for (i = 0; i < 3; ++i)
       BarrierSync(&gBarrier);

   return(0);
}

int BarrierInit(BARRIER *pBarrier, int bCount)
{
   pBarrier->bCount = bCount;
   pBarrier->bResetCount = bCount;
   pBarrier->bReset = FALSE;
   pBarrier->bWaiters = 0;

   pBarrier->bMutex = CreateMutex(NULL, FALSE, NULL);
   pBarrier->bEvent = CreateEvent(NULL, TRUE, FALSE, NULL);

   pBarrier->bMuxHandle[0] = pBarrier->bEvent;
   pBarrier->bMuxHandle[1] = pBarrier->bMutex;
   return(0);
}

int BarrierSync(BARRIER *pBarrier)
{
   int    wakingThread = 0;
   DWORD  threadId;

   threadId = GetCurrentThreadId();

   /* this is executed by threads that have finished executing */
   /* BarrierSync and start executing again before other threads */
   /* have exited the routine BarrierSync - referred to as fast threads */

   while (pBarrier->bReset == FALSE && !pBarrier->bCount)
          Sleep(0); /* fast threads yield processor */

   WaitForSingleObject(pBarrier->bMutex, INFINITE);

   --pBarrier->bCount; /* decrement barrier count */

   if (!pBarrier->bCount) /* last thread reaching barrier */
   {
        wakingThread = 1;
        pBarrier->bReset = FALSE;
   }

   while (pBarrier->bCount != 0) /* waiting threads */
   {
      ++pBarrier->bWaiters;
      ReleaseMutex(pBarrier->bMutex);
      fprintf(stderr,"Thread waiting .... %d\n", threadId);
      WaitForMultipleObjects(MAXHANDLES,
                        pBarrier->bMuxHandle, TRUE, INFINITE);
     --pBarrier->bWaiters;
   }

   if (wakingThread)
   {
      fprintf(stderr,"Thread waking .... %d\n\n", threadId);
      pBarrier->bCount = 0;
```

```
        ReleaseMutex(pBarrier->bMutex); /* wake up all threads */
        SetEvent(pBarrier->bEvent); /* wake up all threads */
        return(0);
    }

    if (!pBarrier->bWaiters) /* last thread leaving barrier */
    {
        pBarrier->bCount = pBarrier->bResetCount; /*
        ResetEvent(pBarrier->bEvent);
        pBarrier->bReset = TRUE;
        fprintf(stderr,"Thread reset .... %d\n\n", threadId);
    }

    ReleaseMutex(pBarrier->bMutex);
    return(0);
}
```

16.5 Reader/Writer Locks

In certain applications data are much more frequently read than they are modified. Reader/writer (RW) lock allows multiple threads to read data simultaneously but serializes writers when data have to be updated. One of the main advantages of reader/writer locks over mutex locks is that they allow multiple threads to share data in read mode without the overhead of locking. The payoff of RW locks over mutexes are not evident when the code guarded by the RW lock is short. RW locks are better when the frequency of read operations is higher than write operations, and the read operations are somewhat lengthy. The following implementation favors readers over writers and can cause starvation for writers. (See code on disk for implementation favoring writers.)

```
#include <windows.h>
#include <stdio.h>

typedef struct _rwlock
{
    int     lCount;
    int     lReset;
    HANDLE  lockMutex;
    HANDLE  lockEvent;
} RWLOCK;
RWLOCK  gRWLock;

main(int argc, char **argv)
{
    int     numThr;
    DWORD   threadId[MAXTHREADS];
    HANDLE  hThread[MAXTHREADS];
    DWORD   Readers();
    DWORD   Writers();
    int     i;

    numThr = NUM_WRITERS + NUM_READERS;

    InitReadWriteLock(&gRWLock);

    for (i = 0; i < NUM_WRITERS; ++i)
        hThread[i] = CreateThread(NULL, 0, (LPTHREAD_START_ROUTINE)Writers,
                                  (LPVOID)NULL, 0, &threadId[i]);
```

```
    for (i = NUM_WRITERS ; i < numThr; ++i)
        hThread[i] = CreateThread(NULL, 0, (LPTHREAD_START_ROUTINE)Readers,
                             (LPVOID)NULL, 0, &threadId[i]);

    for (i = 0; i <numThr; ++i)
        WaitForMultipleObjects(numThr, hThread, TRUE, INFINITE);
}

DWORD
Writers(void *pThrArg)
{
    int i;

    for (i = 0; i < NUMMSGS; ++i)
    {
        AcquireWriteLock(&gRWLock);
        /* do shared update */
        ReleaseWriteLock(&gRWLock);
        Sleep(50); /* simulate writer delay */
    }
    return(0);
}

DWORD
Readers(void *pThrArg)
{
    int i;
    int numMsgs;

    numMsgs = NUMMSGS / NUM_WRITERS ;
    for (i = 0; i < numMsgs; ++i)
    {
        AcquireReadLock(&gRWLock);
        /* do shared read */
        ReleaseReadLock(&gRWLock);
    }
    return(0);
}

int
AcquireReadLock(RWLOCK *pLock)
{
    HANDLE muxHandle[MAXHANDLES];

    muxHandle[0] = pLock->lockEvent;
    muxHandle[1] = pLock->lockMutex;

    WaitForSingleObject(pLock->lockMutex, INFINITE);
    while(pLock->lCount < 0)
    {
          pLock->lReset = FALSE;
          ReleaseMutex(pLock->lockMutex);
          WaitForMultipleObjects(MAXHANDLES, muxHandle, TRUE, INFINITE);
          if (pLock->lReset == = FALSE)
          {
              pLock->lReset == = TRUE;
              ResetEvent(pLock->lockEvent);
          }
    }
    ++pLock->lCount;
    return(ReleaseMutex(pLock->lockMutex));
}

int ReleaseReadLock(RWLOCK *pLock)
{
    WaitForSingleObject(pLock->lockMutex, INFINITE);
```

```
    --pLock->lCount;
    if (!pLock->lCount)
        SetEvent(pLock->lockEvent);
    return(ReleaseMutex(pLock->lockMutex));
}

int AcquireWriteLock(RWLOCK *pLock)
{
    HANDLE muxHandle[MAXHANDLES];

    muxHandle[0] = pLock->lockEvent;
    muxHandle[1] = pLock->lockMutex;

    WaitForSingleObject(pLock->lockMutex, INFINITE);
    while(pLock->lCount ! = 0)
    {
        pLock->lReset = FALSE;
        ReleaseMutex(pLock->lockMutex);
        WaitForMultipleObjects(MAXHANDLES, muxHandle, TRUE, INFINITE);
        if (pLock->lReset = = FALSE)
        {
            pLock->lReset = = TRUE;
            ResetEvent(pLock->lockEvent);
        }
    }
    pLock->lCount = -1;
    return(ReleaseMutex(pLock->lockMutex));
}

int ReleaseWriteLock(RWLOCK *pLock)
{
      WaitForSingleObject(pLock->lockMutex, INFINITE);
    --!pLock->lCount = 0;
      SetEvent(pLock->lockEvent);
      return(ReleaseMutex(pLock->lockMutex));
}

int InitReadWriteLock(RWLOCK *pLock)
{
    pLock->lockMutex = CreateMutex(NULL, FALSE, NULL);
    pLock->lockEvent = CreateEvent(NULL, TRUE, FALSE, NULL);
    pLock->lCount = 0;
    return(0);
}
```

Chapter

17

OS/2 Threads

17.1 Introduction

IBM and Microsoft jointly started out work on a new operating system (OS) some time around 1985, and it started out as an effort to provide a better operating system than the one on personal computers, namely DOS. The first release of the new 16-bit operating system called *OS/2* was delivered in 1987, and it provided some advanced OS features such as multitasking, memory management, interprocess communication, and dynamic linking. In addition to the advanced features, the new operating system ensured binary compatibility of existing DOS applications. The graphic user interface was provided in OS/2 1.1 and was called *Presentation Manager* (PM). Despite all these new features, somehow the market was slow to adopt the OS/2 technology in a big way.

IBM realized some of the earlier deficiencies of the OS/2, especially in terms of the memory requirements, and continued to work on the system before releasing OS/2 1.3 in 1990. At the same time, Microsoft announced that it would no longer codevelop the OS/2 operating system with IBM. After the split, Microsoft continued to work on the advanced OS and eventually released its new operating system, called *Windows NT*. Even though the reader might find some similarities between OS/2 and Windows NT, the reader should be cognizant of the fact that the two operating systems are *different* technologies.

In 1990 IBM finally became the sole owner of OS/2, and it assumed full responsibility for the development of the 16-bit and 32-bit versions of OS/2. With the release of OS/2 2.0, the OS finally supported a portable 32-bit programming environment. Finally, in OS/2 2.0, the DOS centric 64-kB barrier was broken. The new OS supported a list of new features and also provided support for Microsoft Windows 3.X applications. In OS/2 2.1, a new user interface called the *WorkPlace* also was introduced.

OS/2 is a modern 32-bit preemptive multitasking and multithreading operating system. Currently, OS/2 does *not* support symmetric multiprocessing (SMP), but by the time this book is released, IBM plans to introduce SMP versions of OS/2 in the market. The new version of OS/2 3.0 has been renamed, and it is now called *WARP*. The kernel in OS/2 is responsible for providing multitasking, interprocess communications, memory management, interrupt management, and I/O.

17.1.1 Processes and threads

If you are not familiar with some of the basic concepts of threads, I would recommend that you read Chap. 1 before you proceed to read the rest of this chapter. Chapter 1 discusses the basic concepts of multithreading, its advantages and pitfalls, and situations where using threads in your application might be useful.

A *process* in OS/2 can be described to be a running instance of a program. A process in OS/2 consists of the executable code, an address space, and possibly system resources such as semaphores and named pipes. A process in OS/2 is the main unit of resource sharing, while *threads* are the basic unit of scheduling. Since OS/2 threads are execution resources, a process must have at least one thread before it can begin execution on a CPU. When a process is created in OS/2, an initial thread, commonly referred to as the *main thread,* is automatically created by the operating system. Each process in OS/2 is uniquely identified by a process identifier (PID), and all threads within the same process share a common PID.

A process in OS/2 is defined to consist of an address space with one or more threads of control. Each thread has its own stack, program counter, scheduling class, and scheduling priority. Threads within a process share all process resources and have the same view of the address space. For example, if one thread frees a memory area, then a memory access violation occurs when some other thread tries to reuse the freed memory area. Similarly, when a file is closed by one thread, it is seen as closed by all other threads in the process.

17.1.2 Thread APIs

Application programming interfaces (APIs) are required to create and manage threads in a multithreaded environment. The thread APIs can be classified broadly into such areas as thread management, thread synchronization, thread-specific data, and thread scheduling. The OS/2 thread APIs are IBM-specific, and they do *not* adhere to any industry standard. The POSIX thread interface is supported as a part of DCE for OS/2. In this chapter the discussion is restricted to the 32-bit OS/2 2.X APIs. Readers are advised to read Chaps. 2 through 5 for more on POSIX threads.

The sample code segments in this book do not perform any error checking, and this has been done mainly for the sake of simplicity and to conserve space. The reader is advised to always *check* for error conditions. The reader is further advised to consult the OS/2 technical library API documentation for information on the error codes returned by each of the APIs. The samples in this book and some of the discussions assume an IBM C Set/2 compiler. If you are using some other compiler (e.g., Watcom C compiler), then you should check the compiler manual for thread-specific notes.

17.2 Thread Management Functions

`DosCreateThread`	Creates a new thread
`_beginthread`	Creates a new thread (C Library)
`_endthread`	Exits a thread (C Library)
`DosExit`	Exits a thread
`DosGetInfoBlocks`	Gets thread and process identifier
`DosWaitThread`	Waits for thread termination
`DosResumeThread`	Resumes a suspended thread
`DosSuspendThread`	Suspends a thread
`DosEnterCritSec`	Disables thread switching/scheduling in current process
`DosExitCritSec`	Restores thread switching in current process
`DosSleep`	Sleeps for an interval
`DosKillThread`	Terminates a thread

17.2.1 Create a thread

When a process begins executing, it has a single thread of control. The process is automatically created with one thread, which is commonly referred to as the *main thread*. If a process needs additional threads of control, then they have to be created by calling the OS/2 or the C-library thread creation function. Unlike the other operating systems mentioned in this book, in which all threads are treated equal, the *main* thread in OS/2 plays a significant role. If the main thread terminates in OS/2, then the entire process terminates.

When threads are created, they begin executing a start routine. Creating a thread is somewhere in between calling a function and creating a process. The start routine specifies the entry point at which the newly created thread starts execution. Multiple threads can execute the same start routine, or each thread can have its own start routine. If multiple threads call the same start routine and they modify shared data within the routine, then the routine *must* be written to be thread-safe.

```
APIRET   DosCreateThread (PTID pThreadID, PFNTHREAD pThreadAddr,
               ULONG uThreadArg, ULONG uThreadFlags, ULONG uStackSize)
```

The function DosCreateThread is used to create a new thread of control in the process. OS/2 uses the data type TID to identify threads. Each thread within a process is identified by a thread identifier (TID), and the TID is only guaranteed to be unique within the context of the same process. On success, the thread identifier of the newly created thread is stored in *pThreadID*.

The argument *pThreadAddr* is a pointer to a function that is executed as the thread's start routine. The start routine should be defined to accept a single ULONG argument and return a void. The argument *uThreadArg* is a pointer to an optional argument passed to the thread's start_routine, and it can be NULL in the case where no arguments are passed to the thread routine.

The argument *uThreadFlags* defines some of the attributes of the newly created thread. Each thread has its own stack, and by default, stack pages are not precommitted. If bit 1 of the flag uThreadFlags is set to 1, then all pages in the stack are *precommitted*; if bit 1 is set to 0, then the system uses the default stack initialization algorithm.

If bit 0 of the flag uThreadFlags is set to 1, then the thread is created in a *suspended* state. When a thread is created in suspended state, it does not begin executing the start routine until the caller or some other thread resumes the execution of the thread by calling DosResumeThread. When bit 0 is set to 0, then the thread is created in a runnable state, and it can execute the start routine. Generally, a value of 0 is passed to uThreadFlags, and this creates a thread in runnable state and uses the default stack initialization method.

Generally, threads are not created in suspended state, but there are certain situations where it makes sense to create them in suspended state. For example, you might want to create a thread in suspended state, alter the thread priority, and then resume the thread. Another case in which you might want to create a thread in suspended state is when the state of the thread has to be initialized before it can run (e.g., create a mutex).

The last argument *uStackSize* specifies the stack size (in bytes) that will be used by the new thread. It should be a multiple of a page and *must* be at least 8192 bytes. The stack size of a process also can be controlled by the linker's /ST switch. Unless the stack is precommitted by setting the flag uThreadFlags, the stack starts with a initial value of one page (4096 bytes). The stack is guard-page-protected, and it can grow dynamically, committing pages as required by the thread. When a thread reaches its maximum allocated stack limit, then an exception EXCEPTION_STACK_OVERFLOW is raised in the faulting thread. If a value of 0 is passed to uStackSize, then the function DosCreateThread creates a stack using the stack size of the process. It is more important to select the correct stack size for the process than for the thread. Unlike some other operating systems, OS/2 does *not* allow you to specify a stack address for a thread using the DosCreateThread API.

The following example illustrates the creation of a new thread. The newly created thread is created to start executing the routine LoopThread. The routine LoopThread executes a loop, and the number of iterations to loop is specified as an argument to the thread routine.

```
main (int argc, char **argv)
{
   TID          threadId;
   PFNTHREAD    LoopThread (ULONG);
   ULONG        thrArg;
   ULONG        threadFlags = 0;
```

```
    ULONG       stackSize = 8192;
    APIRET      retCode;

    thrArg = 1000;

    /* create the thread to execute the routine LoopThread */
    DosCreateThread(&threadId, LoopThread, thrArg, threadFlags, stackSize);

    /* Wait for the thread to complete. DosExit will terminate all threads */

    DosExit(EXIT_PROCESS, 0);
}

VOID
LoopThread (ULONG pthrArg)
{
    int j;
    int numRows;

    numRows = *((int *) pthrArg;
    for (j = 0; j < numRows; ++j)
        /* do something */

    return;
}
```

There is one important aspect worth mentioning regarding the function DosCreateThread. Threads created by the DosCreateThread API *cannot* safely use the C-library routines (e.g., printf) because the C run-time environment is not initialized by the function DosCreateThread. It is therefore recommended that _beginthread should *always* be used instead of DosCreateThread to create a new thread of control.

```
int   _beginthread (unsigned (*start_address) (void *), (void *) stack,
                     unsigned int stacksize, void *arglist);
```

The function _beginthread is identical to DosCreateThread in usage except for some minor differences. A thread *cannot* be created in a suspended state by calling the function _beginthread, but it can be simulated easily by using an event semaphore. The argument *start_address* is a pointer to the function at which the new thread starts execution. Unlike DosCreateThread, where the function accepts a ULONG parameter, the function accepts a void *.

The second argument *stack* is the pointer to the stack, and *stacksize* is the size of the stack that will be created for the new thread. Unlike DosCreateThread, the caller can pass the address of a user-supplied stack to _beginthread. Generally, a value NULL is passed for the stack address, in which case the system creates the stack for the thread. The last argument *arglist* is a pointer to an opaque object, and it is passed to the thread's start routine. On success, the function _beginthread returns the TID of the new thread.

In the following code segment a new thread is created, and multiple arguments are passed to the thread's start routine. To pass *multiple* arguments, place the arguments in a structure, and pass the address of the structure as an argument to the thread's start routine.

```
typedef struct _THRARG
{
   int  rows;
   int  cols;
} THRARG;

main (int argc, char **argv)
{
   unsigned long  hThread;
   void           LoopThread (void *);
   THRARG         thrArg;

   thrArg.rows = 10;
   thrArg.cols = 20;
   /* create the thread to execute the routine LoopThread */
   hThread = _beginthread (LoopThread, NULL, 8192, (void *) &thrArg);

   /* Wait for the thread to complete. DosExit will terminate all threads */

   DosExit (EXIT_PROCESS, 0);
}

void
LoopThread (THRARG *pThrArg)
{
   int j;
   int k;

   for (j = 0; j < pThrArg->Rows; ++j)
   for (k = 0; k < pThrArg->Cols;++k)
       printf ("loop iteration j: [%d]\t k: [%d]\n", j, k);

   return;
}
```

17.2.1.1 Scope of thread routine argument. The variable that is passed to the thread start routine is usually a dynamically allocated variable or a global variable. When stack variables are used, one should make sure that the scope of the variable is *valid* throughout the execution of the thread using the variable. The scope of stack variables is limited to the routine in which the variable is declared, and these variables cease to exist after the caller returns from the routine in which the thread was declared.

The following code segment shows a programming bug that can be caused by using stack variables to pass arguments to a thread routine. The main thread calls the function DoFunc, which creates a new thread to execute the routine LoopThread. When the routine DoFunc returns, the variable thrArg is automatically *destroyed,* and this can cause problems in the thread when it begins executing the routine LoopThread. The same code might work depending on the scheduling of the threads. As a general rule, one should avoid using stack variables for passing arguments to another thread.

```
main (int argc, char **argv)
{

   DoFunc ();
```

```
    /* do some other stuff */
}

DoFunc ()
{
    TID       threadId;
    void      LoopThread (void *);
    THRARG    thrArg;

    thrArg.rows = 10;
    thrArg.cols = 20;

    threadId = _beginthread (LoopThread, NULL, 8192, (void *) &thrArg);

    return; /* the variable thrArg ceases to exist after the return - bug! */
}
```

To avoid this nasty bug, either declare the variable thrArg to be global or define thrArg to be a pointer and dynamically allocate the memory for the variable. I would recommend that you use the latter method, since this will ensure that the routine DoLoop can be used safely by multiple threads.

17.2.1.2 Maximum threads allowed. Threads are much more lightweight than a process. Even though threads are cheap, they are *not free*. Threads use system resources like memory and involve scheduling overhead. For efficiency reasons, it is not a good idea to create too many threads in your application. The maximum number of threads that can be created successfully in a process in OS/2 is limited by system resources, but the total number of threads in the system cannot exceed 4095. The number of threads per process can be specified in the file *config.sys*. Generally, it is not a good idea to create too many threads. When the function DosCreateThread fails because it cannot create any more new threads, then the function returns the error code ERROR_MAX_THRDS_REACHED. In the case where the function _beginthread fails, the function returns −1, and errno is set to EAGAIN.

17.2.2 Thread termination

Everything that is created must come to an end, and so must the life of a thread. A thread can terminate in one of the following ways:

- It exits the start_routine.
- It calls DosExit or _endthread.
- It is forcefully terminated by some other thread.

```
VOID    DosExit (ULONG uActionCode, ULONG uExitCode)
void    _endthread(void )
```

The function DosExit terminates the calling thread or all the threads based on the *uActionCode* argument and stores the exit status in the variable *uExitCode* for later use. If uActionCode is equal to EXIT_THREAD, then only the calling thread is terminated; the process is terminated when uActionCode is equal to EXIT_PROCESS. The value uExitCode is later made available to the parent process calling the function DosWaitChild for this child process. The function DosExit is called implicitly when a thread returns from the start routine that was used to create the thread. In such a case, the function return value serves as the exit status.

The routine _endthread *always* should be used if you are using _beginthread to create a thread. This terminates the thread and also destroys any thread-specific data that were allocated by the C-Runtime library. Unlike DosExit, one *cannot* pass any arguments to _endthread. Unlike other operating systems, the exit status of a thread termination *cannot* be retrieved by another thread using DosExitThread. Note that the routine DosExit or _endthread does not return to the calling thread.

In OS/2, when the main thread terminates, the entire process is terminated. A word of caution: Do *not* call DosExit in the main thread when other threads are still running, since this will terminate the entire process. When the main thread returns from the main routine, then the exit routine is called, thus terminating all the threads in the process. It is good practice to always call endthread to terminate a thread. The process will terminate *only* when the main thread in the process terminates. If the thread terminates gracefully (not terminated by some other process/thread), then the stack is destroyed, and all threads waiting for the thread to terminate are notified. Note that user-supplied stacks are *not* destroyed when a thread terminates.

A process in OS/2 can terminate itself by calling the DosExit or the C-library function _exit routine. In a multithreaded process, when any thread calls DosExit with ActionCode set to EXIT_PROCESS, then it terminates the *entire* process and not just the calling thread. In a multithreaded process, this should be called only when the entire process needs to be terminated. For example, on a fatal error when the integrity of the entire process is questionable, then it is better to exit the entire process rather than just one thread.

17.2.3 Terminating a thread

If a thread stops responding for some reason, then it might become necessary to terminate the thread in a forceful manner. Do *not* call this function unless you know the exact state of a thread and you know that there are no side effects. You *should* always use some interthread communication method to send a graceful termination notice to a thread. For example, a thread can check a flag periodically to see if it needs to be terminated. This is a very dangerous API and should be used only as a last resort. When a thread is terminated using DosKillThread, then an exception XCPT_ASYNC_PROCESS_TERMINATE is raised in the terminated thread and can be used to release resources held by the terminated thread.

```
APIRET  DosKillThread(TID idThread)
```

The function DosKillThread terminates the thread identified by *idThread* in the current process. Certain library functions such as printf from the C-Runtime library can *deadlock* if a thread is terminated in the middle of executing the function. Additionally, if the thread to be terminated is executing 16-bit code or has been created by a 16-bit request, then the DosKillThread() call will fail and return the error code ERROR_BUSY. The function DosKillThread cannot be used by the caller to terminate the current thread. A thread always should call _endthread to terminate itself.

17.2.4 Waiting for thread termination

In the worker-thread model it is common for a thread to suspend execution until some other thread terminates. For example, consider a program in which a master thread creates multiple worker threads to perform parallel queries on different databases. The master thread has to wait for all the worker threads to terminate before it can continue processing with the result of the queries. Unlike UNIX or NT, one *cannot* get the termination status of threads when they exit using any OS/2 API.

```
APIRET  DosWaitThread(PTID pThreadId, ULONG uWaitOption)
```

In OS/2 the function DosWaitThread can be used to wait for thread termination of any or a specific thread in the process. When a thread terminates, all threads that have a DosWaitThread pending on the terminating thread are notified of the thread's termination. If *pThreadId* is zero, then the calling thread waits for the next thread in the process to terminate. If pThreadId is nonzero, then the calling thread waits until the thread identified by pThreadId has terminated. On success, the thread identifier of the terminating thread is returned in the variable pThreadId.

The function can be invoked either in a blocking or a nonblocking manner. If the argument *uWaitOption* is DCWW_WAIT, then the current thread waits blocked until the thread terminates. If the WaitOption is DCWW_NOWAIT, then the current thread returns immediately irrespective of whether the thread has terminated. If the thread is still running, then the function returns ERROR_THREAD_NOT_TERMINATED. The nonblocking call can be used to poll for the existence of a given thread. It is a programming error to wait for the termination of the calling thread itself. It is *bad* programming practice to call this function repetitively in a nonblocking manner for a running thread because this will waste a lot of CPU cycles.

```
main (int argc, char **argv)
{
   TID     threadId;
   void    LoopThread (void *);
   int     thrArg;
   int     *pthrArg;
```

```
    thrArg = 100
    pthrArg = &thrArg;
    /* create the thread to execute the routine LoopThread */
    threadId = _beginthread (LoopThread, NULL, 8192, (void *) pthrArg);

    /* Wait for the thread identified by threadId to complete */
    DosWaitThread(&threadId, DCWW_WAIT);
    threadId = 0;
    DosWaitThread(&threadId, DCWW_WAIT);
    DosExit(EXIT_PROCESS, 0);
}

void
LoopThread(void *pArg)
{
    /* do something */

    DosExit(EXIT_THREAD, 0);
}
```

17.2.5 Thread identifiers

The operating system creates and maintains a thread information block (TIB) for each thread in the process. The TIB *contains* information such as thread ID, stack address, thread priority class, and thread priority level. A thread can access it own TIB by calling the function DosGetInfoBlocks. The function DosGetInfoBlocks also returns the address of the process information block (PIB) of the process to which the current thread belongs.

```
APIRET  DosGetInfoBlocks(PTIB ptib, PPIB ppib)
```

Each thread within a process is uniquely identified by a thread identifier (TID). When a thread is created, the TID is returned by the functions DosCreateThread and _beginthread. Since OS/2 reuses process and thread identifiers, these identifiers are only valid from the time a thread is created until it terminates. The thread can find its own TID by calling the function DosGetInfoBlocks. The following code segment extracts the TID from the thread information block.

```
TID
GetCurrentTID()
{
    PTIB   ptib;
    PPIB   ppib;

    DosGetInfoBlocks (&ptib, &ppib);

    return ((TID) ptib->tib_ptib2->tib2_ultid));
}
```

17.2.6 Priority class and threads

There are basically four types of priority classes supported by OS/2. They are

- Time-critical
- Fixed-high
- Regular
- Idle

Most applications run in the regular priority class (default). Idle-time class is used mostly by low-priority system tasks; a good example could be a screen saver application. Fixed-high-priority class should be used rarely and usually is reserved for well-behaved and less CPU-intensive applications. If you have a communication server or a database server that does not run too frequently or does not use a lot of CPU time, then you can consider moving that server to fixed-high class. Keep in mind that a poorly designed high-priority application can slow down the whole system and even freeze your screen. The highest-priority class, time-critical, should be used only if your application response time is critical.

17.2.7 Thread priority

Threads in OS/2 have 32 different priority levels within each priority class. The module responsible for thread scheduling uses a preemptive priority scheduler with different priority levels. Threads are scheduled according to priority class and priority level. In OS/2 each thread is assigned a priority, and the operating system maintains an array of priority queues for each priority level. The scheduler always picks up the highest-priority thread to run from the run queue. When multiple threads are on the same priority level, they are chosen to run in round-robin fashion. When multiple threads within a priority class are on the same priority level, they are chosen to run in round-robin order. In OS/2, the highest-priority thread from the highest-priority class is always chosen to run.

The priority of threads running in the time-critical class is fixed, and it is *never* adjusted by the operating system. The priority of the threads running in the fixed-high and regular classes can be varied dynamically if the priority statement in the file *config.sys* is set to DYNAMIC. If the priority value is set to ABSOLUTE, then the thread priorities remain fixed. When the value is set to DYNAMIC, the priority of threads in the fixed-high and regular priority classes are constantly adjusted by the operating system.

17.2.8 Changing thread priority

When a thread is created, it *inherits* the priority class and base priority of the creator. Most applications would hardly ever need to alter priorities or classes of threads, but in certain cases doing so might be very helpful. If you have a CPU-intensive thread in your process, you should lower the priority level below that of other threads. Similarly, to keep the responsiveness, you could increase the priority of the PM (presentation manager) thread in your application.

The priority of a thread in the variable class can be adjusted constantly during its execution. The thread periodically gets a temporary boost from the kernel. For example, when a pending I/O for a thread completes, the priority is boosted, and it is restored after the thread runs for a timeslice.

```
APIRET  DosSetPriority (ULONG Scope, ULONG PriorityClass,
                                     ULONG PriorityDelta, ULONG ID)
```

The function DosSetPriority changes the priority class and/or priority of a thread in the current process or in the child process. The first argument *Scope* is used to specify if the scope is limited to a single thread or all threads within the process. The valid values for scope are PRTYS_PROCESS, PRTYS_PROCESSTREE, and PRTYS_THREAD. To change the priority of a given thread, use the value PRTYS_THREAD.

The second argument *PriorityClass* is used to change the priority class of the process. If you do want to change the priority class, then pass the value PRTYC_NOCHANGE. The other valid values for priority class are PRTYC_SFOREGROUNDSERVER, PRTYC_IDLETIME, and PRTYC_REGULAR. The third argument *PriorityDelta* is the change in the priority value, and it is added to the current priority. A positive value increments the priority, while a negative value decrements the priority. The last argument *ID* is either the thread identifier or process identifier depending on the scope of the operation. TID is used only when the scope is PRTYS_THREAD; otherwise, the PID is used.

In OS/2 there is *no* direct API to get the priority of a thread. The priority of the thread is stored in the TIB, and it can be retrieved by calling the function DosGetInfoBlocks. The following code segment retrieves the priority class and priority value of a thread.

```
GetThreadPriority()
{
   PTIB   pTib;
   PPIB   pPib;
   ULONG prioClass;
   ULONG priority;

   DosGetInfoBlocks (&pTib, pPib);

   prioClass = pTib->pptib_ptib2->ultib2_ulpri >> 8;
   priority = pTib->pptib_ptib2->ultib2_ulpri & 0xff;
}
```

17.2.9 Suspend/resume threads

In OS/2 a thread can be created in a suspended state. A suspended thread must be resumed by calling the function DosResumeThread. It is also possible to suspend a thread even after it has been created by calling the function DosSuspendThread. Keep in mind that it is *not* possible to create a thread in suspended state by calling _beginthread; therefore, you have to suspend the thread by calling the function DosSuspendThread. These functions should never be used for synchronization purposes. Using thread scheduling behavior for synchronization purposes is likely to cause problems later.

When suspending threads, make sure that the suspended thread does *not* hold any mutex or synchronization objects, because if some other thread tries to lock the same mutex, the thread will *deadlock*. It is *not* easy to predict if a thread is holding a locked resource, especially when using non-user-supplied libraries (e.g., C library). The following code segment illustrates the problem. Consider the situation where a thread T1 is suspended while executing the routine DoSomething. Now, when some other thread calls the routine ExternalFunc, the calling thread *will* wait indefinitely trying to acquire the mutex lock. The wait will be terminated only when thread T1 is resumed.

```
ExternalFunc()
{
   Lock Mutex;

   DoSomething();

   Unlock Mutex;
}
```

DosSuspendThread temporarily suspends, while DosResumeThread resumes the execution of a thread specified by the argument *ThreadID*. The function DosSuspendThread suspends only one thread at a time. When a thread needs to suspend *all* threads except the calling thread, and then it must call DosEnterCritSec and DosExitCritSec. It is a programming error to resume a thread that was *never* suspended in the first place.

```
APIRET   DosSuspendThread(TID ThreadID)
APIRET   DosResumeThread(TID ThreadID)
APIRET   DosEnterCritSec()
APIRET   DosExitCritSec()
```

DosEnterCritSec *disables* the scheduling of all threads in the current process. Only the thread that called DosEnterCritSec is scheduled to run until a corresponding call to DosExitCritSec is made. Since no other thread can run when one thread calls DosEnterCritSec, it can be a big performance loss, especially on a multiprocessor machine. I would recommend that one should *not* use this function except for some specialized needs (e.g., implementing a once-only function semantic).

When a thread calls DosEnterCritSec, it *cannot* call any DLL function until it enables thread switching by calling DosExitCritSec. Doing so could cause a deadlock state if the thread requests a resource that is being held by another thread in the process. The DosEnterCritSec call can be made recursively; the only requirement is that DosExitCritSec should be called the same number of times the function DosEnterCritSec was called.

The following code segment creates a thread and then alters the priority of the thread before resuming the thread.

```
main (int argc, char **argv)
{
   TID   threadId;
   void  LoopThread (void *);
   int   thrArg;
   LONG  priorityDelta;

   thrArg = 1000;

   /* create the thread to execute the routine LoopThread */
   threadId = _beginthread (LoopThread, NULL, 8192, (void *) &thrArg);

   /* since _beginthread one cannot create a thread in suspended state
      use DosSuspendThread to suspend execution of the threads */

   DosSuspendThread(threadId);

   /* call DosGetInfoBlocks to retrieve the priority in priorityDelta */

   /* now increase the priority of thread by 5 */
   priorityDelta += 5;
   DosSetPriority(PRTYS_THREAD, 0, priorityDelta, threadId);

   DosResumeThread(threadId);

   /* wait for thread to terminate */

   DosExit(EXIT_PROCESS, 0);
}

LoopThread(void *pArg)
{
   /* do something */

   DosExit(EXIT_THREAD, 0);
}
```

17.2.10 Yielding the CPU

A thread can give up the CPU by calling the DosSleep function. This can be used by CPU-intensive jobs to periodically give up the CPU to other processes/threads in the system.

```
APIRET   DosSleep(ULONG uMilliSeconds)
```

The function DosSleep *suspends* the calling thread for the time specified by *uMilliSeconds*. A value of zero can be used to give up the remainder of the thread's timeslice. When a thread relinquishes the CPU, then the scheduler picks up the next highest priority thread to run on the CPU. After expiration of the sleep interval, the thread is woken up and is reconsidered for scheduling by the scheduler.

17.3 Thread Synchronization

In a multithreaded process, *all* threads of a process run in the same address space and hence share most of the process resources. All process resources such as open files descriptors, ipc identifiers, static variables, and dynamically allocated memory variables are shared by all the threads. For example, if one thread closes a file, then that file is considered closed for all other threads within the process. Similarly, if one thread frees a dynamically allocated buffer using the C-library *free* routine, then no other thread can safely reference the same buffer without causing an access violation.

Consider, for example, two threads running on different processors trying to update a shared variable simultaneously (e.g., ++SharedVariable). If the value of the variable before the update is 3, then the correct value after the update should be 5. If both threads update the variable concurrently, then one of the updates can be lost, and the value of the variable will be 4. Even though the statement ++SharedVariable looks atomic, the assembly code generated for the statement might not be atomic. This lack of atomicity can cause one of the updates to be lost.

One of the main advantages of threads is easy data sharing, but along with this comes the added responsibility to guard such data against corruption. Threads need to synchronize data that are shared and modified by multiple threads. In the absence of any synchronization, shared data can be inconsistent if they are updated by multiple threads simultaneously. All access to shared resources must be protected by mutual exclusion locks. The use of locks to synchronize access to shared data is called *data synchronization.*

In a boss/worker thread model it is common to divide work between multiple threads. In such a case, one thread might wait for another thread to reach a particular state before proceeding, or one thread might wait for a particular condition to be true before proceeding. In these cases, threads are not necessarily synchronizing on data but more on conditions or events. Data synchronization is usually for shorter durations, while event synchronization can be for longer durations.

Let us consider an example of a producer and a consumer thread writing and reading from a shared buffer. When the threads are reading or writing from the buffer, they have exclusive access to the buffer. The producer cannot write to the buffer until the consumer has finished reading from the buffer, and the consumer cannot read from the buffer until the producer has finished writing to the buffer. Each thread waits for notification from the other thread that the buffer is available. When the producer thread is finished writing to the buffer, it notifies the consumer, and vice versa. This form of synchronization is often called *event synchronization.*

If you have already read Chap. 13, then most of these APIs should be very simple; otherwise, I would recommend that you read Secs. 13.1.1 through 13.1.3 to better understand some of the basic concepts of mutual exclusion and event synchronization.

17.3.1 Semaphores

OS/2 provides three kinds of semaphores as the synchronization primitives. Semaphores are of two types: *private* semaphores and *shared* semaphores. Private semaphores are used for interthread synchronization, while shared semaphores are used mainly for interprocess synchronization. Semaphores in OS/2 are accessed by a 32-bit semaphore handle. The kernel uses these handles to distinguish between private and public semaphores and for accessing the semaphore structure. Private semaphores are *unnamed* and are accessible by using the semaphore handle. Shared semaphores *can* be either named or unnamed. When creating a named semaphore, the name should begin with *SEM32*\\ and must follow the OS/2 file naming convention.

The private and shared semaphores are *mutex* semaphores, *event* semaphores, and *muxwait* semaphores. Mutex semaphores are used primarily for data synchronization, event semaphores are used for event synchronization, and muxwait semaphores are used for synchronizing on multiple mutex or event semaphores.

17.4 Mutex Semaphores

`DosCreateMutexSem`	Creates a mutex semaphore
`DosDestroyMutexSem`	Destroys a mutex semaphore
`DosWaitMutexSem`	Acquires a mutex semaphore
`DosReleaseMutexSem`	Releases a mutex semaphore
`DosQueryMutexSem`	Queries a mutex semaphore

17.4.1 Mutual exclusion

Mutex semaphores generally are used to synchronize access to and ensure atomic updates of shared data. A *mutex* (mutual exclusion) semaphore is used by processes or threads to *serialize* access to shared data.

The state of the mutex semaphore can be either *locked* or *unlocked*. The basic assumption behind mutexes is that threads must lock the mutex before accessing shared data and unlock the mutex after the thread has completed accessing the shared data. If one thread has acquired the mutex, then all other threads requesting to lock the mutex will *wait* until the mutex is released by the thread owning the mutex. It is important to remember that for data synchronization all threads must *enforce* the mutex locking protocol strictly; if threads do not check the locks before entering the critical section, then no mutex mechanism will ever help. One possible solution to enforce mutual exclusion is to provide well-defined interfaces to allow access to shared resources and implement the mutex locking and unlocking within these interfaces. In this way the details of locking and unlocking are hidden from the users of these interfaces.

17.4.2 Creating a mutex

Mutex semaphores have to be created before they can be used for mutual exclusion purposes. Normally, they are created in some initialization code of the process. Mutexes in OS/2 can be either named or unnamed and can be shared across processes.

```
APIRET   DosCreateMutex(PSZ pName, PHMTX phMutex,
                        ULONG uAttr, BOOL32 fState)
```

The function DosCreateMutex is used to create a new mutex semaphore. The argument *pName* is either NULL or a null-terminated string identifying the mutex. A named mutex is normally employed when the mutex has to be used across processes; in the case of threads within a process, pass a NULL value. In the case of an unnamed mutex, the function DosCreateMutex should be called exactly once for each of the mutexes an application wants to create. Failure to do can result in some difficult-to-find bugs.

On success, the handle of the newly created mutex semaphore is returned in *phMutex*. The attributes of the semaphore are defined by the *uAttr* flags. If the value passed to uAttr is DC_SEM_SHARED, then the semaphore is a shared semaphore and is used only when the semaphore is unnamed.

In the case of mutex semaphores, *ownership* is tracked, which means that the thread that locked the mutex must be the thread that unlocks it. Mutexes are *recursive,* and the initial state of the mutex is controlled by the value passed to *fState*. If the value is TRUE, then the calling thread or process creating the mutex atomically becomes the owner of the mutex. If the value is TRUE, then the mutex is created in *locked* state, which means that any other process or thread requesting ownership of the mutex will wait until the mutex is released by the creator of the mutex. If the value of fState is FALSE, then the mutex is created in *unlocked* state, which means that any other thread requesting ownership of the mutex will gain ownership of the mutex object. Generally, the value passed to fState is FALSE.

17.4.3 Opening a mutex semaphore

When a mutex semaphore is created, the handle of the mutex is returned to the caller. One also can get the handle of an existing *named* mutex by calling the function DosOpenMutex. This function is useful mainly when the mutex object is shared across processes and is hardly ever used by threads of the same process. Refer to the OS/2 API documentation for more details on this function.

```
APIRET   DosOpenMutexSem(PSZ pName, PHMTX phMtx)
```

17.4.4 Closing a mutex semaphore

When mutexes are no longer needed, they should be closed. Mutexes are not deleted when the thread that created the mutexes terminates, since mutexes are considered to be shared resources of a process.

```
APIRET   DosCloseMutexSem(HMTX hMutex)
```

The function DosCloseMutexSem closes the mutex semaphore identified by *hMutex*. The operation DosCloseMutexSem decrements the reference count and automatically deletes the mutex semaphore when the reference count becomes zero. It is a programming *error* to close a mutex semaphore when some other thread is still referencing it.

17.4.5 Acquiring a mutex lock

Before executing a *critical* section of code, the thread must acquire the mutex lock. After executing the critical section, the thread that locked the mutex must *release* the mutex. The function DosRequestMutexSem is used to acquire a lock of a valid unlocked mutex. If the mutex is currently locked by some other thread, then the calling thread is *suspended* until the mutex lock is released. When the function returns successfully, then the state of the mutex becomes locked, and the calling thread becomes the *owner* of the mutex. The calling thread remains the owner of the mutex lock until it unlocks the mutex. If the mutex is never released, then some other thread will block *indefinitely* on the mutex lock when it tries to acquire the same mutex lock.

In OS/2 mutex semaphores can be acquired in a *recursive* manner. A thread can acquire a mutex multiple times; the only requirement is that the thread should release the mutex the same number of times it acquired it. Be careful with recursive mutex locks because you can easily deadlock; in fact, most applications do *not* need recursive mutexes.

When multiple threads call DosRequestMutexSem to acquire a locked mutex, then they are suspended and are placed on a queue of threads waiting for the mutex to be released. The highest-priority thread is woken up when multiple threads are waiting for the mutex to be released. It is good programming practice not to rely on the order in which threads are woken up. Mutex semaphores should be held for only a *short* duration to avoid performance problems.

```
APIRET   DosRequestMutexSem(HMTX hMutex, ULONG uTimeOut)
```

The function DosRequestMutexSem is used to acquire the lock of the mutex semaphore identified by *hMutex*. The function can be called in either a blocking or a nonblocking manner. If the value passed to *uTimeOut* is SEM_INDEFINITE_WAIT, then the calling thread blocks until the mutex can be locked by the calling thread. If the value passed to *uTimeOut* is SEM_IMMEDIATE_RETURN, then the function returns immediately if the mutex semaphore cannot be locked. The calling thread also can block for a specified time in milliseconds by passing a nonzero value to *uTimeOut*.

17.4.5.1 Nonrecursive mutex locks. For most applications, it makes sense to detect the use of recursive mutex locks as an error. Personally, I prefer to use nonrecursive mutexes for most of my applications because this forces me to be more disciplined. The following code segment shows how to implement a nonrecursive mutex using the standard OS/2 APIs.

```
typedef struct _nrmutex
{
   int   lCount; /* lock count of mutex */
   TID   owner; /* owner of mutex */
   HMTX  hMutex; /* handle to mutex object */
}NRMUTEX;

int
CreateNrMutex(NRMUTEX *pMutex) /* should be only called once */
{
   pMutex->lCount = 0;
   /* create an unnamed semaphore in unlocked state */
   DosCreateMutex(NULL, &pMutex->hMutex, 0, FALSE);
}

int
AcquireNrMutex(NRMUTEX *pMutex)
{
   TID   mySelf;

   /* could have used the DosQueryMutexSem function to find owner of mutex */

   mySelf = GetCurrentTID(); /* see section 17.2.5 */

   if (pMutex->lCount && pMutex->owner == mySelf)
   {
        fprintf(stderr, "Error: Cannot acquire mutex in recursive manner\n");
        return(-1);
   }
   DosRequestMutexSem(pMutex->hMutex, SEM_INDEFINITE_WAIT);
   pMutex->owner = mySelf;
   pMutex->lCount = 1;
   return(0);
}
```

17.4.6 Releasing a mutex

The mutex lock should be released *after* the thread executes the critical section of the code; otherwise, no other thread can enter the critical section guarded by the same mutex.

```
APIRET   DosReleaseMutex(HMTX hMutex)
```

The function DosReleaseMutex is used to *unlock* the mutex identified by *hMutex.* It is an error to call this function if hMutex is either unlocked or the calling thread is *not* the owner of the mutex. On a successful return, the mutex lock is released, and the state of the mutex becomes unlocked. If no thread is waiting for the mutex to be released, then the mutex remains unlocked and is marked as having no owner. If one or more threads are waiting for the mutex to be released, then the highest-priority thread is woken up, and ownership is granted to the thread acquiring the mutex.

Let us consider a function that adds a new item to the beginning of a list. This list is shared by multiple threads within the process. For a detailed description of critical sections and race conditions, please refer to Sec. 13.1.

```
typedef struct List
{
   struct List  *next;
   void         *data;
}SHARED_LIST;

static SHARED_LIST *gpListHead; /* pointer to beginning of list */

HMTX hListMutex;

InitListMutex()
{
   /* create an unnamed semaphore in unlocked state */
   DosCreateMutex(NULL, &hListMutex, 0, FALSE);
}

AddToList (SHARED_LIST *pNewEntry)
{
   /* Assume the function InitListMutex is called before */

   DosRequestSem(hListMutex, SEM_INDEFINITE_WAIT);

   /* Critical Section of Code */
   pnewEntry->Next = gpListHead;
   gpListHead = pnewEntry;

   DosReleaseMutexSem(hListMutex);
}
```

17.4.7 Abandoned mutexes

A thread that acquires a mutex lock *must* be the thread that unlocks it, since resource ownership is tracked for mutexes. So what happens when the owner of the mutex terminates without releasing the lock? The mutex in this case is considered *abandoned,* because no other thread can call DosReleaseMutex to release that mutex.

When an abandoned mutex is detected and threads are blocked on DosRequestSem, then the system prevents the caller from indefinite postponement and returns the error code SEM_OWNER_DIED. The decision to continue or exit is an application-specific one and usually depends on the potential damage caused by the terminating thread. Even though the system notifies you, there is *no* guarantee that the state of the shared data guarded by the abandoned mutex is consistent. The terminating thread could have crashed in the middle of updating a linked list, so even if the abandoned mutex has been released, it does *not* ensure data integrity. One of the best things to do in this case is to exit the program and then try to find the bug that crashed the thread in the critical section.

17.4.8 Query a mutex semaphore

OS/2 provides a function to query run-time information about mutex semaphores. The function DosQueryMutexSem is used to query the information for a valid open semaphore. The function returns the PID and TID of the thread holding the mutex semaphore. The function also returns the request count associated with the mutex semaphore. This count is the number of times the mutex was locked minus the number of times the mutex was unlocked. The request count is zero when the semaphore is unlocked.

17.4.9 Mutexes, deadlocks, and priority inversion

In a multithreaded application, when you are dealing with multiple mutexes, deadlock can happen. Similarly, some applications might be affected by priority inversion. The topics of deadlock and priority inversion are explained in detail in Sec. 13.6. The reader is advised to replace all WIN32 APIs with OS/2 mutex APIs.

17.4.10 Guidelines for using mutexes

- Always use global or static variables for mutexes. Do not try to use stack variables for mutexes because the stack of a thread is destroyed when the thread terminates.
- Close mutexes after they are no longer used.
- Avoid locking the mutex in a recursive fashion unless you have valid reasons to do it.
- While locking multiple mutexes simultaneously, be sure that all threads acquire the locks in the same order to avoid deadlocks.
- Do not call DosCloseMutexSem while some other thread is still referencing the mutex semaphore.
- Lock mutexes for a short time. Keep the critical section of code small, and avoid any blocking operation (I/O, another synchronization lock) inside the critical section.
- Do not use mutex locks excessively. Excessive synchronization will cause performance problems, and you will tend to lose one of the foremost benefits of multithreading, which is concurrent execution of threads. If threads reference the shared data in read-only mode, then there is no need to serialize access to this piece of shared data.

- Carefully design your mutual exclusion locks to be either coarse- or fine-grained, since this can directly affect performance.

17.5 Event Semaphores

`DosCreateEventSem`	Creates an event semaphore
`DosDestroyEventSem`	Closes an event semaphore
`DosWaitEventSem`	Acquires an event semaphore
`DosReleaseEventSem`	Releases an event semaphore
`DosQueryEventSem`	Queries an event semaphore

Consider a boss/worker thread model in which the boss thread puts new work items on a work queue and one of the worker threads dequeues new work items from the queue. It is assumed that the threads use a mutex to guard the work queue while the actual enqueue/dequeue operation happens. The question is, "How does the worker thread know that a new work item has been placed on the queue?" The worker thread can

- Continuously check the work queue for arrival of new work items.
- Poll the work queue at specified intervals for arrival of new work items.
- Wait on the work queue for new items until the boss thread notifies the worker thread that a new work item has been placed on the work queue.

The first two methods are extremely *inefficient* when it comes to CPU utilization, while the last option provides the best solution. In this case, the worker thread is suspended when there are no work items on the queue and is only woken up when a new work item is placed on the queue. This form of event synchronization is the most efficient and highly desirable in a multithreaded environment. Do *not* use global flags or shared variables to implement event synchronization.

In OS/2, *event* semaphores are used for event notification and synchronization. An event semaphore has two states: *set* (posted) and *clear* (reset). When threads have to synchronize on events, they wait for the event semaphore to be posted. Event semaphores can be used to broadcast events to multiple threads. When an event semaphore is set and multiple threads are waiting for the event to be set, then all threads are notified of the event. In addition to the binary state of event semaphores (set/cleared), the semaphores also have a count associated with them and act more like counting semaphores.

The OS/2 event semaphores are unlike the counting semaphores of UNIX or NT. Personally, I found it very confusing that even though all synchronization primitives in OS/2 are called semaphores, OS/2 does not implement the classic counting semaphores. In the case of classic counting semaphores, when multiple threads are waiting for the semaphore to be set, then only *one* thread is woken up, but in the case of OS/2 threads, *all* threads are woken up.

17.5.1 Creating an event semaphore

Event semaphores have to be created before they can be used for mutual exclusion purposes. Event semaphores in OS/2 can be either named or unnamed and can be used for interprocess event synchronization.

```
APIRET   DosCreateEventSem(PSZ pName, PHEV phEvent,
                               ULONG uAttr, BOOL32 fState);
```

The function DosCreateEventSem is used to create a new event semaphore. The argument *pName* is either NULL or a null-terminated string identifying the semaphore. A named semaphore normally is used when the semaphore has to be used across processes; in the case of threads within a process, pass a NULL value. In the case of an unnamed semaphore, the function DosCreateEventSem should be called exactly *once* for each of the semaphores an application wants to create. Failure to do can result in some difficult-to-find bugs.

On success, the handle of the newly created semaphore is returned in *phEvent*. The attributes of the semaphore are defined by the *uAttr* flags. If the value passed to uAttr is DC_SEM_SHARED, then the semaphore is a shared semaphore, and this is used only when the semaphore is unnamed.

Unlike mutex semaphores, ownership is *not* tracked for event semaphores. The *initial* state of the semaphore is controlled by the value passed to *fState*. If the value is TRUE, then the calling thread or process creates the semaphore in posted state. If the value of *fState* is FALSE, then the semaphore is created in nonposted (clear) state, which means that any other thread that will wait on the semaphore will wait until the semaphore is posted. Generally, the value passed to *fState* is FALSE.

17.5.2 Opening an event semaphore

When a semaphore is created, the handle of the semaphore is returned to the caller. One also can get the handle of an existing named event semaphore by calling the function DosOpenEventSem. This function is useful when the semaphore is shared across processes and is hardly ever used by threads of the same process. Refer to the OS/2 API documentation for more details on this function.

```
APIRET   DosOpenEventSem(PSZ pName, PHEV phEvent)
```

17.5.3 Closing an event semaphore

When event semaphores are no longer needed, they should be closed. They are not deleted when the thread that created them terminates because semaphores are considered to be shared resources of a process.

```
APIRET    DosCloseEventSem(HEV hEvent)
```

The function DosCloseEventSem closes the mutex semaphore identified by *hEvent*. The operation DosCloseEventSem decrements the reference count and automatically deletes the semaphore when the reference count becomes zero. It is a programming error to close a semaphore when some other thread is still referencing it.

17.5.4 Waiting for an event semaphore

An application must wait for a semaphore to be set by calling the function DosWaitEventSem. If the semaphore is currently in nonposted state, then the calling thread is *blocked* until the semaphore is posted by some other thread. On return from the wait function, the state of the semaphore *remains* posted unless it is reset by calling the function DosResetEventSem.

When multiple threads call the function DosWaitEventSem on a nonposted semaphore, then all threads are *blocked* and are placed on a queue of threads waiting for the event to be posted. When some other thread posts the event semaphore, then *all* waiting threads are woken up.

```
APIRET    DosWaitEventSem(HEV hEvent, ULONG uTimeOut)
```

The function DosWaitEventSem waits for the semaphore identified by *hEvent* to be posted. The function can be called in either a blocking or a non-blocking manner. If the value passed to *uTimeOut* is SEM_INDEFINITE_WAIT, then the calling thread blocks until the state of the semaphore becomes posted. If the value passed to *uTimeOut* is SEM_IMMEDIATE_RETURN, then the function returns immediately if the semaphore cannot be acquired. The calling thread also can block for a specified time in milliseconds by passing a nonzero value to *uTimeOut*. If the semaphore is in a set (posted) state, then the function returns *without* blocking.

17.5.5 Posting an event semaphore

The function DosPostEventSem is used to post an event semaphore. All threads blocked on the call to DosWaitEventSem are notified, and the semaphore remains in posted state. After posting a semaphore, if one wants to clear the state of the semaphore, then is must be *reset* by calling the function DosResetEventSem. When multiple threads are waiting and you only want to wake up a single thread, then you have to build your own complex synchronization primitive using the base OS/2 APIs.

```
APIRET    DosPostEventSem(HEV hEvent)
```

This function posts the event semaphore identified by *hEvent*. If the semaphore is already in posted state, then the post count associated with the semaphore is incremented, and the error code ERROR_ALREADY_POSTED is returned to the caller.

17.5.6 Resetting an event semaphore

When the state of the semaphore becomes posted as a result of DosPostEventSem, then the state is *retained* until it is explicitly reset by the caller. The post operation on a semaphore wakes up all blocked threads waiting on the semaphore. After the semaphore is posted, any thread that waits on the semaphore does *not* block because the semaphore is in a posted state. If subsequent wait operations have to block, then the state of the semaphore has to be cleared.

```
APIRET   DosResetEventSem(HEV hEvent, PULONG puCount)
```

The function DosResetEventSem resets the state of the semaphore identified by *hEvent* and returns the post count associated with the semaphore in *puCount*. The number puCount is the number of times DosPostEventSem was called before the state of the semaphore was cleared. After a semaphore is reset, all subsequent wait operations on the semaphore will *block* until it is posted again. When DosResetEventSem is called on an already reset semaphore, the function fails and returns ERROR_ALREADY_SET without resetting the semaphore.

17.5.7 Querying an event semaphore

The function DosQueryEventSem returns the post count *puCount* associated with the event semaphore identified by *hEvent*.

```
APIRET   DosQueryEventSem(HEV hEvent, PULONG puCount)
```

The following code segment shows how producer and consumer threads can synchronize with each other for new work packets. In the following example, consumer threads wait for the event semaphore identified by *bufFull* to be set before they can start reading the data from the shared buffer; the producers then wait for the consumer to read the data from the shared buffer before it can reuse the shared buffer. When consumer threads finish reading the data from the buffer, then they post the semaphore identified by *bufEmpty,* and this wakes up the producer threads. Note that each thread resets the semaphore after a successful return from the wait operation to ensure that next time it blocks. It is assumed that the routine InitializeEvents is called before the producer or consumer thread starts running.

```
HEV bufFull;
HEV bufEmpty;

InitializeEvents()
{
   DosCreateMutexSem(NULL, &bufFull, 0, FALSE); /* create in nonposted
   state */
   DosCreateMutexSem(NULL, &bufEmpty, 0, FALSE); /* create in nonposted
   state */
}

Producer ()
{
   ULONG   postCount;
   for (;;)
   {
         /* put data into shared buffer */
         DosPostEventSem(bufFull); /* signal consumer to read work packet */

         DosWaitEventSem(bufEmpty); /* wait for consumer to consume work
         packet */
         DosResetEventSem(bufEmpty, &postCount);
   }
}

Consumer ()
{
   ULONG   postCount;
   for (;;)
   {
         DosWaitEventSem(bufFull); /* wait for producer to produce work
         packet */
         DosResetEventSem(BufFull, &postCount); /* ensure next time the
         thread blocks */

         /* get data from shared buffer */
         DosPostEventSem(bufEmpty); /* signal producer so it can use buffer */
   }
}
```

17.6 Muxwait Semaphores

Muxwait (multiple wait) semaphores are used when a thread or process needs to wait on *multiple* semaphores. Muxwait semaphores allow one to wait on multiple event or mutex semaphores in a list. A list can contain up to a maximum of 64 event or mutex semaphores, and it is required that each member of the list be of the *same* type. This means that in a single muxwait semaphore one *cannot* mix mutex and event semaphores. Also, shared muxwait semaphores must include *only* shared semaphores. When waiting on muxwait semaphores, two types of wait semantics are supported by OS/2. A thread can wait for *any* or *all* of the semaphores in the list. Using this, a thread or process can wait for

- Any event semaphore in the list
- All event semaphores in the list

- Any mutex semaphore in the list
- All mutex semaphores in the list

When threads wait on all mutex or event semaphores to be set, then the wait function waits until all semaphores are either released (mutex) or posted (event) at the same time. One important point to remember is that a muxwait semaphore *cannot* be included in another muxwait semaphore.

17.6.1 Creating a muxwait semaphore

Muxwait semaphores have to be created before they can be used for synchronization purposes. Muxwait semaphores in OS/2 can either be named or unnamed, and they also can be used for interprocess event synchronization. Before a muxwait semaphore can be created, each of the semaphores in the muxwait semaphore *must* be created.

```
APIRET   DosCreateMuxWaitSem(PSZ pName, PHMUX phMuxSem,
                    ULONG uSemRec, PSEMRECORD pSemRec, ULONG uAttr)
```

The function DosCreateMuxWaitSem is used to create a new muxwait semaphore. The argument *pName* is either NULL or a null-terminated string identifying the semaphore. Named semaphores normally are used when the semaphore has to be used across processes; in the case of threads within a process, pass a NULL value. In the case of an unnamed semaphore, the function DosCreateMuxWaitSem should be called exactly *once* for each of the semaphores an application wants to create. Failure to do can result in some difficult-to-find bugs.

On success, the handle of the newly created semaphore is returned in *phMuxSem*. The attributes of the semaphore are defined by the *uAttr* flags. If the value passed to uAttr is DC_SEM_SHARED, then the semaphore is a shared semaphore, and it is only used when the semaphore is unnamed. If the value passed to uAttr is DCMW_WAIT_ANY, then the muxwait semaphore clears when *any* of the semaphores in the list are released (mutex) or posted (event). If the value passed is DCMW_WAIT_ALL, then the muxwait semaphore will clear only when *all* the semaphores in the list are either released or posted.

Personally, I would have preferred that the decision to wait for any or all semaphores in the list be delayed until the wait function is called, since this would have added more flexibility. If one has to make the decision to wait for any or all semaphores in the list based on some condition, then in OS/2 one has to create two muxwait semaphores, one with the DCMW_WAIT_ANY bit set and the other with the DCMW_WAIT_ALL bit set, and then use the appropriate muxwait semaphore.

The argument *uSemRec* specifies the number of event or mutex semaphores in the list. The argument *pSemRec* is a pointer to an array of semaphores of type SEMRECORD. Each semaphore added to the array *must* be a valid existing semaphore.

17.6.2 Opening a muxwait semaphore

When a semaphore is created, the handle of the semaphore is returned to the caller. One also can get the handle of an existing named muxwait semaphore by calling the function DosOpenMuxWaitSem. This function is useful when the semaphore is shared across processes and is hardly ever used by threads of the same process. Refer to the OS/2 API documentation for more details on this function.

```
APIRET  DosOpenMuxWaitSem(PSZ pName, HMUX hMuxSem)
```

17.6.3 Closing a muxwait semaphore

```
APIRET  DosCloseMuxWaitSem(HMUX hMux)
```

The function DosCloseMuxWaitSem closes the muxwait semaphore identified by *hMux*. The operation DosCloseMuxWaitSem decrements the reference count and automatically deletes the semaphore when the reference count becomes zero. It is a programming *error* to close a semaphore when some other thread is still referencing it. When you close a muxwait semaphore, it does *not* close the semaphores in the list; each semaphore in the list *must* be closed explicitly by calling either DosCloseEventSem or DosCloseMutexSem.

17.6.4 Waiting for a muxwait semaphore

When threads wait on the muxwait semaphore, then they *wait* for either one or all objects in the list to be released or posted. The function DosWaitMutexSem is used to wait on a muxwait semaphore identified by *hMux*.

```
APIRET   DosWaitMuxWaitSem(HMUX hMux, ULONG uTimeOut, PULONG phSem)
```

When threads wait on muxwait semaphores, the behavior is different depending on the type of semaphore contained within the muxwait semaphore. When the thread blocks with wait-any semantics on muxwait semaphores containing *mutex* semaphores, then the semaphore handle of the mutex that was released is returned in *phSem*. When the thread blocks with wait-all semantics, then the function blocks until *all* the mutexes in the list are released. The semaphore handle of the last mutex to be released is returned in phSem. When the function DosWaitMutexSem returns, then the calling thread becomes *owner* of either one or all the mutex semaphores depending on the wait semantics used. After the thread uses the mutexes, then ownership of each of the mutex semaphores *must* be explicitly released.

When the thread blocks with wait-any semantics on muxwait semaphores containing *event* semaphore(s), then the semaphore handle of the event semaphore that is posted is returned in *phSem*. When the thread blocks with wait-all semantics, then the function blocks until all the event semaphores in the list are posted. It is still the caller's responsibility to reset each of the event semaphores in the list as required by the application.

Since muxwait event semaphores are *level*-triggered, each of the semaphores *must* be in the posted state at the same time (for wait-all semantics) before the function DosWaitMuxWaitSem will return to the caller. Consider, for example, a thread blocked on a muxwait semaphore consisting of three event semaphores S1, S2, and S3. Now some other thread posts and resets semaphore S1 before S2 and S3 are posted. The function DosWaitMuxWaitSem will block even when S2 and S3 are posted because the state of S1 has become nonposted.

17.6.5 Adding/deleting a muxwait semaphore

Semaphores can be added to the muxwait list even after a muxwait semaphore has been created. The function DosAddMuxWaitSem can be called to *add* event semaphores or mutex semaphores to an already existing list, while the function DosDeleteMuxWaitSem must be called to *delete* a semaphore from a muxwait list. When an event semaphore or mutex semaphore that is a member of the muxwait list is closed, then the corresponding entry *should* be deleted from the muxwait list. The function DosQueryMuxWaitSem can be used to *query* a muxwait semaphore.

```
APIRET   DosAddMuxWaitSem(HMUX hMux, PSEMRECORD pSemRec)
APIRET   DosDeleteMuxWaitSem(HMUX hMux, HSEM hSem)
```

The following code segment illustrates the use of muxwait semaphores. A muxwait semaphore is created containing two mutex semaphores. The main thread does a wait for the muxwait semaphore with wait-all semantics.

```
HMTX   hMutex1;
HMTX   hMutex2;

CreateMutexSems()
{
   DosCreateMutexSem(NULL, &hMutex1, 0, FALSE); /* create in nonposted
   state */
   DosCreateMutexSem(NULL, &hMutex2, 0, FALSE); /* create in nonposted
   state */
}
```

```
WaitForMultipleMutexes()
{
    SEMRECORD   muxList[2];
    HMUX   hMuxSem;

    muxList[0].hsemCurr = hMutex1; /* assume CreateMutexSems has been
    called */
    muxList[1].hsemCurr = hMutex2;

    DosCreateMuxSem(NULL, &hMuxSem, 2, muxList, DCMW_WAIT_ALL); /* wait for
    both */

    for (;;)
    {
          DosWaitMuxWaitSem(hMuxSem, SEM_INDEFINITE_WAIT, &RetSem);

          /* at this point both mutexes are locked */
          DoFunc(); /* do func requires lock to both mutexes */

          DosReleaseMutexSem(hMutex1);

          DosReleaseMutexSem(hMutex2);
    }
}
```

17.7 Thread-Specific Data

In a multithreaded application it is often required to create variables whose scope is nonglobal. There are two ways that threads can create data items whose scope is limited to a single thread. Threads can use either stack or local variables, and the scope of such variables is limited to the routine in which the variable is declared. The usefulness of local variables is sometimes *limited* when these variables have to be made accessible across function calls. In a single-threaded process, the C-language keyword extern is used to make global variables accessible across function calls. If a multithreaded application wants the same data to be maintained on a per-thread basis across function calls, then it is obvious that static (global) variables *cannot* be used. What is really needed is a per-thread global variable that is accessible across function calls. The reader is advised to read Sec. 14.1 to get a better understanding of thread-specific data (TSD).

Personally, I found it surprising that OS/2 does not provide any useful API for managing per-thread data. It is often the programmer's responsibility to manage data association for threads. The C library provides a simple function *_threadstore* to associate per-thread data, but it is not useful because it can store only one pointer value for a thread. For example, this cannot be used safely when two different libraries might need to store a per-thread variable. If the function _threadstore is called twice, then the older value is lost, and this can cause serious problems in the application. I would recommend that you *not* use this function for storing per-thread data.

In OS/2 3.0 a new API called DosAllocThreadLocalMemory has been introduced for managing thread local memory. This is still not as flexible as in WIN32 or POSIX, but it allows a process to store up to 128 bytes of thread local memory. The reader is advised to read the documentation on the functions DosAllocThreadLocalMemory and DosFreeThreadLocalMemory for more details. The reader is advised to see the sample code on the disk in the OS/2 directory for a possible implementation of TSD that is similar in concept to POSIX thread-specific data.

17.8 Exceptions, Signals, and Timers

Most *exceptions* are conditions that one does *not* expect during normal program execution. For example, when a thread accesses a memory location that is not its address space, then an exception is raised. Exceptions are synchronous when they are caused by the same event in the executing thread and are asynchronous when some external event causes the exception. Events such as a user pressing CTRL-C or some other process issuing a call to DosKillProcess can raise an asynchronous exception and are called *signal* exceptions.

When an exception happens in a application, then the default action is to terminate the application. An application can have routines that the operating system calls when an exception happens and that are called *exception handlers*. Exception handlers allow a thread to terminate gracefully; for example, it can unlock a locked mutex in its exception handler. It is sometimes desirable to *defer* the exception handling process, and OS/2 provides the concept of must-complete sections. A must-complete section is a critical section of code during which the system does *not* deliver the exceptions.

When a thread calls the function DosSleep, the calling thread is suspended, and it ceases to run on the CPU for the duration of the sleep interval. When applications need asynchronous *timers,* they can use either the one-shot or repeated timer facility. When a thread calls the asynchronous timer function, it is not suspended, and it is free to perform other tasks while the timer elapses. When the timer interval expires, an event semaphore is *set* by the operating system. The function DosAsyncTimer starts a *single-shot* asynchronous timer, while the function DosStartTimer starts a *repeated-interval* asynchronous timer. The function DosStopTimer is used to stop an asynchronous timer. Since it is beyond the scope of this book to cover exceptions, signals, and timers in detail, the reader is advised to read the OS/2 documentation for more details.

Chapter

18

OS/2 Programming Examples

18.1 Queue Implementation

Queues are a simple yet powerful interthread communication paradigm. Queues can be used effectively in applications that use worker threads to service clients. Threads, instead of waiting on semaphores, can wait on queues for work items to be added. It should be noted that threads that use queues for servicing requests are much easier to program and test.

```
#define INCL_DOSPROCESS
#define INCL_DOSSEMAPHORES
#include <os2.h>
#include <stdio.h>

typedef struct _qmsg QMESG;

struct _qmsg
{
   void    *msg;
   int     msgLen;
   QMESG   *next;
};

typedef struct _queue
{
   int     qMsgs;
   int     qMax;
   HMTX    qMutex;
   HEV     qEmpty;
   HEV     qFull;
   QMESG   *qHeadMsg;
   QMESG   *qTailMsg;
} QUEUE;

QUEUE  gQueue;
```

```
main(int argc, char **argv)
{
   int     numThr;
   TID     threadId[MAXTHREADS];
   void    Readers();
   void    Writers();
   int     i;

   numThr = NUM_WRITERS + NUM_READERS;
   if (numThr > MAXTHREADS)
        exit(0);

   QueCreate(&gQueue, 10);

   for (i = 0; i < NUM_WRITERS; ++i)
        threadId[i] = _beginthread(Writers, NULL, 8192, NULL);

   for (i = NUM_WRITERS; i < numThr; ++i)
        threadId[i] = _beginthread(Readers, NULL, 8192, NULL);

   for (i = 0; i < numThr; ++i)
        DosWaitThread(&threadId[i], DCWW_WAIT);

   exit(0);
}

void
Writers(void *pThrArg)
{
   TID   threadId;
   int   i;
   char  msg[256];

   threadId = GetCurrentThreadId();
   for (i = 0; i < NUMMSGS; ++i)
   {
        sprintf(msg,"Msg %d from thread %d", i, threadId);
        QuePut(msg, sizeof(msg), &gQueue);
   }
   fprintf(stderr,"writer [%d] put [%d] msgs\n", threadId, i);
   return;
}

void
Readers(void *pThrArg)
{
   int   i;
   int   nMsgs;
   int   Rc;
   char  msg[256];
   TID   threadId;

   threadId = GetCurrentThreadId();

   nMsgs = (NUMMSGS * NUM_WRITERS) / NUM_READERS;

   for (i = 0; i < nMsgs; ++i)
        Rc = QueGet(msg, sizeof(msg), &gQueue);

   fprintf(stderr,"reader [%d] get [%d] msgs\n",threadId, i);
   return;
}

int
QueGet(void *pMsg, int msglen, QUEUE *pQueue)
{
```

```
    int rc;
    ULONG semPostCnt;

    DosRequestMutexSem(pQueue->qMutex, SEM_INDEFINITE_WAIT);
    while (pQueue->qMsgs == 0)
    {

        DosReleaseMutexSem(pQueue->qMutex);
        DosWaitEventSem(pQueue->qEmpty, SEM_INDEFINITE_WAIT);
        DosResetEventSem(pQueue->qEmpty, &semPostCnt);
        DosRequestMutexSem(pQueue->qMutex, SEM_INDEFINITE_WAIT);
    }

  if (pQueue->qMsgs == pQueue->qMax)
      DosPostEventSem(pQueue->qFull);

  rc = DeleteQueueMsg(pMsg, msglen, pQueue);
  --pQueue->qMsgs;
  DosReleaseMutexSem(pQueue->qMutex);
  return(rc);
}

int
QuePut(void *pMsg, int msglen, QUEUE *pQueue)
{
  ULONG SemPostCnt;

  DosRequestMutexSem(pQueue->qMutex, SEM_INDEFINITE_WAIT);
  while (pQueue->qMsgs == pQueue->qMax)
  {
      DosReleaseMutexSem(pQueue->qMutex);
      DosWaitEventSem(pQueue->qFull, SEM_INDEFINITE_WAIT);
      DosResetEventSem(pQueue->qFull, &SemPostCnt);
      DosRequestMutexSem(pQueue->qMutex, SEM_INDEFINITE_WAIT);
  }

  InsertQueueMsg(pMsg, msglen, pQueue);

  ++pQueue->qMsgs;
  DosPostEventSem(pQueue->qEmpty);
  DosReleaseMutexSem(pQueue->qMutex);
}

QueCreate(QUEUE *pQueue, int maxMsgs)
{
  DosCreateMutexSem(NULL, &pQueue->qMutex, 0, FALSE);
  DosCreateEventSem(NULL, &pQueue->qFull, 0, FALSE);
  DosCreateEventSem(NULL, &pQueue->qEmpty, 0, FALSE);

  pQueue->qMax = maxMsgs;
  pQueue->qMsgs = 0;
  pQueue->qHeadMsg = NULL;
  pQueue->qTailMsg = NULL;
}

InsertQueueMsg(void *pMsg, int msgLen, QUEUE *pQueue)
{
  QMESG *newMsg;

  newMsg = (QMESG *) calloc(1,sizeof(QMESG));
  newMsg->msgLen = msgLen;
  newMsg->msg = (void *) malloc(msgLen);

  memcpy(newMsg->msg, pMsg, msgLen);

  if (pQueue->qHeadMsg == NULL)
  {
```

```
        pQueue->qHeadMsg = newMsg;
        pQueue->qTailMsg = newMsg;
    }
    else
    {
        pQueue->qTailMsg->next = newMsg;
        pQueue->qTailMsg = newMsg;
    }
    return(0);
}

DeleteQueueMsg(void *Msg, int msgLen, QUEUE *pQueue)
{
    QMESG *currMsg;
    int   len;

    currMsg = pQueue->qHeadMsg;
    len = currMsg->msgLen;

    memcpy(Msg,currMsg->msg, currMsg->msgLen);

    if (pQueue->qHeadMsg == pQueue->qTailMsg)
        pQueue->qTailMsg = NULL;
    pQueue->qHeadMsg = pQueue->qHeadMsg->next;
    free(currMsg->msg);
    free(currMsg);
    return(len); /* length of message */
}

TID
GetCurrentThreadId()
{
    TIB  *ptib;
    PIB  *ppib;

    DosGetInfoBlocks(&ptib, &ppib);

    return((TID)ptib->tib_ptib2->tib2_ultid);
}
```

18.2 Barrier Synchronization

A barrier is a synchronization point in the program where threads wait to synchronize with each other. It is used to ensure that cooperating threads have reached a point before they can proceed to the next step. All threads wait at a synchronization point until the last thread reaches the point at which all of them can proceed.

```
#include <stdio.h>
#define INCL_DOSPROCESS
#define INCL_DOSSEMAPHORES
#include <os2.h>

typedef struct _barrier
{
    int   bCount;
    int   bResetCount;
    int   bReset;
    int   bWaiters;
    HMTX  bMutex;
    HEV   bEvent;
} BARRIER;
```

```
BARRIER   TBarrier;

void main(int argc, char **argv)
{
   volatile int  numThr;
   volatile int  *pThrArg;
   TID           tid[MAXTHREADS];
   void          ThrRoutine();
   int           i;

   numThr = MAXTHREADS;
   pThrArg = &numThr;

   BarrierInit(&TBarrier, MAXTHREADS);

   for (i = 0; i <numThr; ++i)
       tid[i] = _beginthread(ThrRoutine, NULL, 8192, NULL);

   for (i = 0; i <numThr; ++i)
       DosWaitThread(&tid[i], DCWW_WAIT);

   exit(0);
}

void
ThrRoutine(void *pThrArg)
{
   int i;

   for (i = 0; i < 3; ++i)
       BarrierSync(&TBarrier);

   fprintf(stderr,"Thread exiting.....\n");
   return;
}

int BarrierInit(BARRIER *pBarrier, int bCount)
{
   pBarrier->bCount = bCount;
   pBarrier->bResetCount = bCount;
   pBarrier->bReset = FALSE;
   pBarrier->bWaiters = 0;

   DosCreateMutexSem(NULL, &pBarrier->bMutex, 0, FALSE);
   DosCreateEventSem(NULL, &pBarrier->bEvent, 0, FALSE);

   return(0);
}

int BarrierSync(BARRIER *pBarrier)
{
   int wakingThread = 0;
   ULONG SemPostCnt;

   while (pBarrier->bReset == FALSE && !pBarrier->bCount)
       DosSleep(0); /* fast threads yield processor */

   DosRequestMutexSem(pBarrier->bMutex, SEM_INDEFINITE_WAIT);

   --pBarrier->bCount;
   if (!pBarrier->bCount) /* last thread reaching barrier */
   {
        wakingThread = 1;
        pBarrier->bReset = FALSE;
   }
```

```
    while (pBarrier->bCount ! = 0) /* waiting threads */
    {
        ++pBarrier->bWaiters;
        DosReleaseMutexSem(pBarrier->bMutex);
        fprintf(stderr,"Thread waiting ....\n");
        DosWaitEventSem(pBarrier->bEvent, SEM_INDEFINITE_WAIT);
        --pBarrier->bWaiters;
    }

    if (wakingThread)
    {
        fprintf(stderr,"Thread waking .... \n\n");
        pBarrier->bCount = 0;
        DosReleaseMutexSem(pBarrier->bMutex);
        DosPostEventSem(pBarrier->bEvent);
        return(0);
    }

    if (!pBarrier->bWaiters) /* last waiting thread */
    {
        pBarrier->bCount = pBarrier->bResetCount;
        DosResetEventSem(pBarrier->bEvent, &SemPostCnt);
        pBarrier->bReset = TRUE;
    }
    DosReleaseMutexSem(pBarrier->bMutex);
    return(0);
}
```

18.3 Reader/Writer Locks

In certain applications data are much more frequently read than they are modified. Reader/writer (RW) locks allow multiple threads to read data simultaneously but serialize writers when data have to be updated. One of the main advantages of reader/writer locks over mutex locks is that they allow multiple threads to share data in read mode without the overhead of locking. The payoff of RW locks over mutexes is not evident when the code guarded by the RW lock is short. RW locks are better when the frequency of read operations is higher than write operations, and the read operations are somewhat lengthy. The following implementation favors readers over writers and can cause starvation for writers. (See code on disk for implementation favoring writers.)

```
#define INCL_DOSPROCESS
#define INCL_DOSSEMAPHORES
#include <os2.h>
#include <stdio.h>

typedef struct _rwlock
{
   HMTX  Mutex;
   HEV   Event;
   int   Count;
} RWLOCK;

RWLOCK  gRWLock;

main(int argc, char **argv)
{
   int   NumThr;
   TID   Tid[MAXTHREADS];
```

```
    void  Readers();
    void  Writers();
    int   i;

    NumThr = NUM_WRITERS + NUM_READERS;

    InitReadWriteLock(&gRWLock);

    for (i = 0; i < NUM_WRITERS; ++i)
        Tid[i] = _beginthread(Writers, NULL, 8192, NULL);

    for (i= NUM_WRITERS ; i < NumThr; ++i)
        Tid[i] = _beginthread(Readers, NULL, 8192, NULL);

    for (i = 0; i <NumThr; ++i)
        DosWaitThread(&Tid[i], DCWW_WAIT);
}

void
Writers(void *pThrArg)
{
    in   *Arg;
    int  i;
    for (i = 0; i < NUMMSGS; ++i)
    {
        AcquireWriteLock(&gRWLock);
        /* Update some shared buffer */

        ReleaseWriteLock(&gRWLock);
    }
    fprintf(stderr, "Write [%d] msgs: TID = %d\n", i, GetCurrentThreadId());
    return;
}

void
Readers(void *pThrArg)
{
    int  i;
    int  nMsgs;

    nMsgs = (NUMMSGS * NUM_WRITERS) / NUM_READERS;
    for (i = 0; i < nMsgs; ++i)
    {
        AcquireReadLock(&gRWLock);
        /* read some shared buffer */
        ReleaseReadLock(&gRWLock);
    }
    fprintf(stderr, "Read [%d] msgs: TID = %d\n", i, GetCurrentThreadId());
    return;
}

AcquireReadLock(RWLOCK *pLock)
{
    ULONG SemPostCnt;

    DosRequestMutexSem(pLock->Mutex, SEM_INDEFINITE_WAIT);
    while(pLock->Count < 0)
    {
        DosReleaseMutexSem(pLock->Mutex);
        DosWaitEventSem(pLock->Event, SEM_INDEFINITE_WAIT);
        DosResetEventSem(pLock->Event, &SemPostCnt);
        DosRequestMutexSem(pLock->Mutex, SEM_INDEFINITE_WAIT);
    }
    ++pLock->Count;
    DosReleaseMutexSem(pLock->Mutex);
}
```

```
ReleaseReadLock(RWLOCK *pLock)
{
   DosRequestMutexSem(pLock->Mutex, SEM_INDEFINITE_WAIT);
   --pLock->Count;
   if (!pLock->Count)
        DosPostEventSem(pLock->Event);
   DosReleaseMutexSem(pLock->Mutex);
}

AcquireWriteLock(RWLOCK *pLock)
{
   ULONG SemPostCnt;

   DosRequestMutexSem(pLock->Mutex, SEM_INDEFINITE_WAIT);
   while(pLock->Count ! = 0)
   {
       DosReleaseMutexSem(pLock->Mutex);
       DosWaitEventSem(pLock->Event, SEM_INDEFINITE_WAIT);
       DosResetEventSem(pLock->Event, &SemPostCnt);
       DosRequestMutexSem(pLock->Mutex, SEM_INDEFINITE_WAIT);
   }
   pLock->Count = -1;
   DosReleaseMutexSem(pLock->Mutex);
}

ReleaseWriteLock(RWLOCK *pLock)
{
   DosRequestMutexSem(pLock->Mutex, SEM_INDEFINITE_WAIT);
   pLock->Count = 0;
   DosPostEventSem(pLock->Event);
   DosReleaseMutexSem(pLock->Mutex);
}

InitReadWriteLock(RWLOCK *pLock)
{
   DosCreateMutexSem(NULL, &pLock->Mutex, 0, FALSE);
   DosCreateEventSem(NULL, &pLock->Event, 0, FALSE);
   pLock->Count = 0;
}

TID
GetCurrentThreadId()
{
   TIB   *ptib;
   PIB   *ppib;

   DosGetInfoBlocks(&ptib, &ppib);

   return((TID)ptib->tib_ptib2->tib2_ultid);
}
```

Chapter

19

Portable Threads Interface

19.1 Introduction

Multiplatform computing is not a choice but a reality. Developers are developing software for multiple operating systems. Each of the operating systems covered in this book has its own application programming interface for thread programming. This causes a lot of grief for developers and independent software vendors (ISVs) and adds to the cost of software development. The fact is that even though the APIs are different across systems, they are very *similar* in functionality. If you are prepared to use just the common features of thread programming, then it is not too difficult to develop portable thread functions. This means that you might *not* be able to use operating system–dependent functionality such as signals in UNIX.

This chapter introduces an abstraction layer for threads programming that can be used across multiple operating systems. This exercise is to illustrate portability and is *not* intended as a replacement for the operating system APIs. This layer is called *Mthread,* and it employs abstract data types (ADTs) to hide the operating system details. In this chapter only two functions are illustrated, but a listing of all the functions implemented in Mthread is given at the end of the chapter. Readers who are interested in the details of other functions should refer to the code on the disk.

Some of the additional functions that *can* be implemented easily in Mthread are functions for semaphores, barriers, queues, reader/writer locks, etc. This is left as an exercise for the reader, who should use the code samples in the disk to implement a Mthread interface for these primitives.

19.2 Thread Management

Thread management deals with creating and managing threads. One of the more common functions of thread management is to create threads. The three *most* important things that any thread creation function should provide are the ability to execute a start routine, provision for passing arguments to the routine, and provision to return the thread identifier of the newly created thread.

In the function MthreadCreate many more options are provided. Note that such features as creating threads in suspended state have been purposefully avoided. The prototype of the function is shown below, and most of the arguments are self-explanatory.

```
MthreadCreate (MTHREADROUTINE (*ThreadRoutine)(), /* routine to start
                                                     executing in thread */
              ANY         *ThreadArg, /* argument passed to thread */
              MTHREADID   *MThreadId, /* OS dependent information about
                          Thread */
              MTHREADINT  StackSize, /* Stack Size of Thread */
              MTHREADINT  DetachFlag, /* Is the thread joinable (POSIX + UI
                          only) */
              MTHREADINT  KernelThread,/* Bound or unbound thread :POSIX +
                          UI only */
              MTHREADINT  *Errno) /* Error code returned by operating system
                          */
```

19.2.1 POSIX thread

```
typedef struct _mthreadid
{
   pthread_t  ThreadId; /* handle of system thread_id */
   int        DetachState;
}MTHREADID;

MthreadCreate(........)

   MTHREADINT       Ret;
   pthread_t        Tid;
   pthread_attr_t   ThreadAttr;

   pthread_attr_init(&ThreadAttr);

   if (DetachFlag = = 0)
       pthread_attr_setdetachstate(&ThreadAttr,PTHREAD_CREATE_JOINABLE);

   if (KernelThread = = 1)
       pthread_attr_setscope(&ThreadAttr, PTHREAD_SCOPE_SYSTEM);

   Ret = pthread_create(&MThreadid->ThreadId, & ThreadAttr,
                        ThreadRoutine, ThreadArg);
   if (Ret ! = 0)
   {
       *Errno = Ret;
       return(MTHREAD_ER_SYSERR);
   }

   if (DetachFlag = = 1)
       MThreadId->DetachState = 1;
   else
       MThreadId->DetachState = 0;

   return(MTHREAD_SUCCESS);
}
```

19.2.2 UI Thread

```
typedef struct _mthreadid
{
   thread_t   ThreadId; /* handle of system thread_id */
   int        DetachState; /* detached-thread = 1 else 0 */
}MTHREADID;

MTHREADINT
MthreadCreate (.....)
{
   MTHREADINT   Ret;
   int          BoundFlag = 0;

   if (KernelThread == 1)
       BoundFlag = THR_BOUND;

   if (DetachFlag == 1)
       BoundFlag = BoundFlag | THR_DETACHED;

   Ret = thr_create(NULL, NULL, ThreadRoutine, ThreadArg,
       BoundFlag, &MThreadId->ThreadId);
   if (Ret == -1)
   {
       *Errno = errno;
       return(MTHREAD_ER_SYSERR);
   }

   if (DetachFlag == 1)
       MThreadId->DetachState = 1;
   else
       MThreadId->DetachState = 0;

   return(MTHREAD_SUCCESS);
}
```

19.2.3 C-Thread

```
typedef struct _mthreadid
{
   cthread_t  ThreadId; /* handle of system thread_id */
   int        DetachState; /* detached = 1; nondetached = 0 */
}MTHREADID;

MTHREADINT
MthreadCreate (.....)
{
   cthread_t  Tid;

   Tid = cthread_fork(ThreadRoutine, ThreadArg);
   if (DetachFlag == 1)
   {
       cthread_detach(Tid);
       MThreadId->DetachState = 1;
   }
   else
       MThreadId->DetachState = 0;
   MThreadId->ThreadId = Tid;
   return(MTHREAD_SUCCESS);
}
```

19.2.4 WIN32 thread

```
typedef struct  _mthreadid
{
   DWORD   ThreadId; /* handle of system thread_id */
   HANDLE  ThreadHandle; /* pseudo handle of thread */
}MTHREADID

MTHREADINT
MthreadCreate (.....)
{
   HANDLE   hThread;

   hThread = CreateThread(NULL, StackSize,
                  (LPTHREAD_START_ROUTINE) ThreadRoutine,
                  (LPVOID) ThreadArg, 0, &MThreadId->ThreadId);
   if (hThread == NULL)
   {
      *Errno = (DWORD) GetLastError();
      return(MTHREAD_ER_SYSERR);
   }
   If (DetachFlag == 1)
      CloseHandle (hThread)
   MThreadId->ThreadHandle = hThread;
   return(MTHREAD_SUCCESS);
}
```

19.2.5 OS/2 thread

```
typedef struct   _mthreadid
{
   TID   ThreadId; /* handle of system thread_id */
}MTHREADID;

MTHREADINT
MthreadCreate (.....)
{
   TID   Tid;

   Tid = _beginthread (ThreadRoutine, NULL, StackSize, ThreadArg);
   if (Tid < 0)
   {
       *Errno = Tid;
       return (MTHREAD_ER_SYSERR);
   }
   MThreadId->ThreadId = Tid;
   return (MTHREAD_SUCCESS);
}
```

19.3 Thread Synchronization

Data synchronization is a necessary part of thread programming. Mutex locks are one of the main forms of mutual exclusion locks used. Mutex functions on any operating system should provide these basic functionalities: create, lock, unlock, and destroy. Mutexes can be recursive or nonrecursive. The Mthread functions shown below support both kinds of mutexes. Ownership is tracked, and a recursion count is maintained for each mutex. When used as a nonrecursive mutex, the locking functions can detect recursive deadlocks. The mutex destroy function is left as an exercise for the reader.

```
MthreadMutexCreate(MTHREADMUTEX *MThreadMutex,
                  MTHREADINT MutexType, MTHREADINT *Errno)
MthreadMutexLock(MTHREADMUTEX *MThreadMutex, MTHREADINT *Errno)
MthreadMutexUnlock(MTHREADMUTEX *MThreadMutex, MTHREADINT *Errno)
```

19.3.1 POSIX thread

```
typedef struct _mthread_mutex
{
   int               Type; /* 0 = nonrecursive : 1 = recursive */
   int               LCnt; /* number of locks acquired by owner of mutex */
   pthread_t         Owner; /* owner of mutex */
   pthread_mutex_t   Mutex; /* handle of system mutex */
} MTHREADMUTEX;

MTHREADINT
MthreadMutexCreate(...)
{
   pthread_mutexattr_t  mutexAttr;
   MTHREADINT           retCode;

   mutexAttr = pthread_mutexattr_default;
   retCode = pthread_mutex_init(&MThreadMutex->Mutex, mutexAttr);
   if (retCode != 0)
   {
       *Errno = retCode;
       return(MTHREAD_ER_SYSERR);
   }
   MThreadMutex->Type = MutexType; /* can be recursive or non-recursive */
   MThreadMutex->LCnt = 0; /* initialize lock cnt to no owner */
   return(MTHREAD_SUCCESS);
}

MTHREADINT
MthreadMutexLock(...)
{
   MTHREADINT   retCode;
   pthread_t    mySelf;

   mySelf = pthread_self();

   if (MThreadMutex->LCnt && pthread_equal(MThreadMutex->Owner,mySelf))
   {
       if (MThreadMutex->Type == MTHREAD_NON_RECURSIVE_MUTEX)
       {
           *Errno = MTHREAD_ER_INTERNAL;
           return(MTHREAD_ER_MUTEX_LOCKED);
       }
       else /* default is recursive-mutex */
       {
           MThreadMutex->LCnt += 1; /* increment lock count */
           return(MTHREAD_SUCCESS);
       }
   }
   retCode = pthread_mutex_lock(&MThreadMutex->Mutex);
   if (retCode != 0)
   {
       *Errno = retCode;
       return(MTHREAD_ER_SYSERR);
   }
   MThreadMutex->Owner = mySelf;
```

```
    MThreadMutex->LCnt = 1;
    return(MTHREAD_SUCCESS);
}

MTHREADINT
MthreadMutexUnlock(...)
{
    pthread_t      mySelf;
    MTHREADINT     retCode;

    mySelf = pthread_self();

    if (!MThreadMutex->LCnt)
    {
        *Errno = MTHREAD_ER_INTERNAL;
        return(MTHREAD_ER_MUTEX_UNLOCKED);
    }

    if (MThreadMutex->LCnt && !pthread_equal(MThreadMutex->Owner,mySelf))
    {
        *Errno = MTHREAD_ER_INTERNAL;
        return(MTHREAD_ER_MUTEX_NOTOWNER);
    }
    --MThreadMutex->LCnt;
    /* Should set owner field to 0 */
    if (!MThreadMutex->LCnt)
    {
        retCode = pthread_mutex_unlock(&MThreadMutex->Mutex);
        if (retCode ! = 0)
        {
            *Errno = retCode;
            return(MTHREAD_ER_SYSERR);
        }
    }
    return(MTHREAD_SUCCESS);
}
```

19.3.2 UI thread

```
typedef struct _mthread_mutex
{
    int         Type; /* 0 = nonrecursive : 1 = recursive */
    int         LCnt; /* number of locks acquired by owner of mutex */
    thread_t    Owner; /* owner of mutex */
    mutex_t     Mutex; /* handle of system mutex */
} MTHREADMUTEX;

MTHREADINT
MthreadMutexCreate(...)
{
    MTHREADINT   retCode;

    retCode = mutex_init(&MThreadMutex->Mutex, USYNC_THREAD, NULL);
    if (retCode = = -1)
    {
        *Errno = errno;
        return(MTHREAD_ER_SYSERR);
    }
    MThreadMutex->Type = MutexType; /* recursive or non-recursive */
    MThreadMutex->LCnt = 0; /* initialize lock cnt to no owner */
    return(MTHREAD_SUCCESS);
}
```

```
MTHREADINT
MthreadMutexLock(...)
{
   MTHREADINT   retCode;
   thread_t mySelf;

   mySelf = thr_self();

   if (MThreadMutex->LCnt && MThreadMutex->Owner == mySelf)
   {
       if (MThreadMutex->Type == MTHREAD_NON_RECURSIVE_MUTEX)
       {
           *Errno = MTHREAD_ER_INTERNAL;
           return(MTHREAD_ER_MUTEX_LOCKED);
       }
       else /* default is recursive-mutex */
       {
           MThreadMutex->LCnt += 1; /* increment lock count */
           return(MTHREAD_SUCCESS);
        }
   }
   retCode = mutex_lock(&MThreadMutex->Mutex);
   if (retCode == -1)
   {
          *Errno = errno;
          return(MTHREAD_ER_SYSERR);
   }
   MThreadMutex->Owner = mySelf;
   MThreadMutex->LCnt = 1;
   return(MTHREAD_SUCCESS);
}

MTHREADINT
MthreadMutexUnlock(...)
{
   thread_t     mySelf;
   MTHREADINT   retCode;

   mySelf = thr_self();

   if (!MThreadMutex->LCnt)
   {
        *Errno = MTHREAD_ER_INTERNAL;
        return(MTHREAD_ER_MUTEX_UNLOCKED);
   }

   if (MThreadMutex->LCnt && MThreadMutex->Owner != mySelf)
   {
        *Errno = MTHREAD_ER_INTERNAL;
        return(MTHREAD_ER_MUTEX_NOTOWNER);
   }
   --MThreadMutex->LCnt;
   if (!MThreadMutex->LCnt)
   {    /* Should set owner field to 0 */.
        retCode = mutex_unlock(&MThreadMutex->Mutex);
        if (retCode == -1)
        {
             *Errno = errno;
             return(MTHREAD_ER_SYSERR);
        }
   }
   return(MTHREAD_SUCCESS);
}
```

19.3.3 C-Thread

```
typedef struct _mthread_mutex
{
   int         Type; /* 0 = non-recursive : 1 = recursive */
   int         LCnt; /* number of locks acquired by owner of mutex */
   cthread_t   Owner; /* ownwer of mutex */
   mutex_t     Mutex; /* handle of system mutex */
} MTHREADMUTEX;

MTHREADINT
MthreadMutexCreate(...)
{
   MThreadMutex->Mutex = mutex_alloc();
   MThreadMutex->Type = MutexType;
   MThreadMutex->LCnt = 0; /* initialize lock cnt to no owner */
   return(MTHREAD_SUCCESS);
}

MTHREADINT
MthreadMutexLock(...)
{
   MTHREADINT   retCode;
   cthread_t    mySelf;

   mySelf = cthread_self();

   if (MThreadMutex->LCnt && MThreadMutex->Owner == mySelf)
   {
       if (MThreadMutex->Type == MTHREAD_NON_RECURSIVE_MUTEX)
       {
           *Errno = MTHREAD_ER_INTERNAL;
           return(MTHREAD_ER_MUTEX_LOCKED);
       }
       else /* default is recursive-mutex */
       {
           MThreadMutex->LCnt += 1; /* increment lock count */
           return(MTHREAD_SUCCESS);
       }
   }
   mutex_lock(MThreadMutex->Mutex);
   MThreadMutex->Owner = mySelf;
   MThreadMutex->LCnt = 1;
   return(MTHREAD_SUCCESS);
}

MTHREADINT
MthreadMutexUnlock(...)
{
   MTHREADINT   retCode;
   cthread_t    mySelf;

   mySelf = cthread_self();

   if (!MThreadMutex->LCnt)
   {
       *Errno = MTHREAD_ER_INTERNAL;
       return(MTHREAD_ER_MUTEX_UNLOCKED);
   }

   if (MThreadMutex->LCnt && MThreadMutex->Owner != mySelf)
   {
       *Errno = MTHREAD_ER_INTERNAL;
       return(MTHREAD_ER_MUTEX_NOTOWNER);
   }
```

```
    --MThreadMutex->LCnt;
    /* Should reset owner field */.
    if (!MThreadMutex->LCnt)
         mutex_unlock(MThreadMutex->Mutex);

    return(MTHREAD_SUCCESS);
}
```

19.3.4 WIN32 thread

```
typedef struct _mthread_mutex
{
    int       Type; /* 0 = nonrecursive : 1 = recursive */
    int       LCnt; /* number of locks acquired by owner of mutex */
    DWORD     Owner; /* owner of mutex */
    HANDLE    Mutex; /* handle of system mutex */
} MTHREADMUTEX;

MTHREADINT
MthreadMutexCreate(...)
{
    MThreadMutex->Mutex = CreateMutex(NULL, FALSE, NULL);
    if (MThreadMutex->Mutex == NULL)
    {
        *Errno = (DWORD) GetLastError();
        return(MTHREAD_ER_SYSERR);
    }
    MThreadMutex->Type = MutexType;
    MThreadMutex->LCnt = 0; /* lock cnt == 0 : means no owner */
    return(MTHREAD_SUCCESS);
}

MTHREADINT
MthreadMutexLock(...)
{
    DWORD mySelf;
    DWORD retCode;
    DWORD dwTimeOut;

    mySelf = GetCurrentThreadId();
    if (MThreadMutex->LCnt && MThreadMutex->Owner == mySelf)
    {
        if (MThreadMutex->Type == MTHREAD_NON_RECURSIVE_MUTEX)
        {
            *Errno = MTHREAD_ER_INTERNAL;
            return(MTHREAD_ER_MUTEX_LOCKED);
        }
        else
        {
            MThreadMutex->LCnt += 1; /* increment lock count */
            return(MTHREAD_SUCCESS);
        }
    }
    dwTimeOut = INFINITE;

    retCode = WaitForSingleObject(MThreadMutex->Mutex, dwTimeOut);
    if (retCode == 0xffffffff)
    {
        *Errno = (DWORD) GetLastError();
        return(MTHREAD_ER_SYSERR);
    }

    MThreadMutex->Owner = mySelf;
    MThreadMutex->LCnt = 1;
```

```
    return(MTHREAD_SUCCESS);
}

MTHREADINT
MthreadMutexUnlock(...)
{
    DWORD   mySelf;
    BOOL    FlagReleased;

    mySelf = GetCurrentThreadId();

    if (!MThreadMutex->LCnt)
    {
         *Errno = MTHREAD_ER_INTERNAL;
         return(MTHREAD_ER_MUTEX_UNLOCKED);
    }

    if (MThreadMutex->LCnt && MThreadMutex->Owner != mySelf)
    {
        *Errno = MTHREAD_ER_INTERNAL;
        return(MTHREAD_ER_MUTEX_NOTOWNER);
    }

    --MThreadMutex->LCnt;

    if (!MThreadMutex->LCnt)
    {
        /* Should reset owner field */.
        FlagReleased = ReleaseMutex(MThreadMutex->Mutex);
        if (FlagReleased == FALSE)
        {
             *Errno = (DWORD) GetLastError();
             return(MTHREAD_ER_SYSERR);
        }
    }
    return(MTHREAD_SUCCESS);
}
```

19.3.5 OS/2 thread

```
typedef struct _mthread_mutex
{
    int   Type; /* 0 = nonrecursive : 1 = recursive */
    int   LCnt; /* number of locks acquired by owner of mutex */
    TID   Owner; /* owner of mutex */
    HMTX  Mutex; /* handle of system mutex */
} MTHREADMUTEX;

MTHREADINT
MthreadMutexCreate (...)
{
    APIRET retCode;

    retCode = DosCreateMutexSem (NULL, &MThreadMutex->Mutex,
                                 DC_SEM_SHARED, FALSE);
    if (retCode != 0)
    {
        *Errno = retCode;
        return (MTHREAD_ER_SYSERR);
    }
    MThreadMutex->Type = MutexType;
    MThreadMutex->LCnt = 0; /* Initialize Lock Cnt to 0 i.e No Owner */
    return (MTHREAD_SUCCESS);
}
```

```
MTHREADINT
MthreadMutexLock (...)
{
   APIRET   retCode;
   ULONG    TimeOut = SEM_INDEFINITE_WAIT;
   TID      mySelf;

   mySelf = MThreadGetthreadId ();

   if (MThreadMutex->LCnt && MThreadMutex->Owner == mySelf)
   {
       if (MThreadMutex->Type == MTHREAD_NON_RECURSIVE_MUTEX)
       {
           *Errno = MTHREAD_ER_INTERNAL;
           return (MTHREAD_ER_MUTEX_LOCKED);
       }
       else /* default is recursive-mutex */
       {
           MThreadMutex->LCnt += 1; /* increment lock count */
           return (MTHREAD_SUCCESS);
       }
   }
   retCode = DosRequestMutexSem (MThreadMutex->Mutex, TimeOut);
   if (retCode != 0)
   {
       *Errno = retCode;
       return (MTHREAD_ER_SYSERR);
   }
   MThreadMutex->Owner = mySelf;
   MThreadMutex->LCnt = 1;
   return (MTHREAD_SUCCESS);
}

MTHREADINT
MthreadMutexUnlock (...)
{
   TID      mySelf;
   APIRET   retCode;

   mySelf = MThreadGetthreadId ();

   if (MThreadMutex->LCnt == 0)
   {
       *Errno = MTHREAD_ER_INTERNAL;
       return (MTHREAD_ER_MUTEX_UNLOCKED);
   }

   if (MThreadMutex->LCnt && MThreadMutex->Owner != mySelf)
   {
       *Errno = MTHREAD_ER_INTERNAL;
       return (MTHREAD_ER_MUTEX_NOTOWNER);
   }
   --MThreadMutex->LCnt;

   if (MThreadMutex->LCnt == 0)
   {
       /* Should reset owner field */
       retCode = DosReleaseMutexSem (MThreadMutex->Mutex);
       if (retCode != 0)
       {
           *Errno = retCode;
           return (MTHREAD_ER_SYSERR);
       }
   }
   return (MTHREAD_SUCCESS);
}
```

19.4 Additional Functions

`MthreadExit`	Exit a thread
`MthreadYield`	Yield to other threads
`MthreadSelf`	Get thread identifier
`MthreadKill`	Terminate a thread
`MthreadWait`	Wait for thread termination
`MthreadOnce`	Execute a funtion once
`MthreadKeyCreate`	Create a TSD or TLS key
`MthreadSetValue`	Set TSD or TLS value
`MthreadGetValue`	Get TSD or TLS value
`MthreadCondCreate`	Create a condition variable
`MthreadCondWait`	Wait on a condition variable
`MthreadCondBroadcast`	Broadcast a condition
`MthreadCondSignal`	Signal a condition

19.5 Conclusion

Many people think that portable code runs slower than native interfaces. As you can see from the examples discussed in this chapter, developing portable code is not that difficult, and contrary to belief, it can be fast and efficient. One key aspect of developing portable code is to rely on common aspects across the different operating systems. This might mean that one cannot architect applications with any one operating system in mind. Portability should never be taken to an extreme; rather, it should be limited to common services across operating systems. Keep in mind that a properly architected application can be ported easily from one operating system to another. This can mean faster time to market new products, and this means a lot in today's competitive world.

Chapter

20

Design Considerations

20.1 Introduction

Developing threaded applications is one thing, but designing efficient multithreaded (MT) applications is yet another thing. Developing an MT program requires the developer to think in terms of concurrent rather than sequential execution. You might face obstacles while developing threaded applications, but keep in mind that most of them can be resolved by using some simple design guidelines. This chapter introduces some of the common problems faced in threaded development, techniques for avoiding these problems, design guidelines, and objectives when developing an efficient MT application.

20.2 Reentrant and Thread-Safe Libraries

Before multithreading became generally accepted, developers never had to worry about developing code for multiple threads of execution. In traditional programs, since there is only one thread of execution, a function can *never* be executed by more than one thread at the same time. In a multithreaded program, a function *can* be executed concurrently by multiple threads, and this introduces the problems of reentrancy and thread safety. If you are either developing library functions that can be invoked simultaneously by multiple threads or using libraries in a multithreaded application, then you *should* definitely understand the issues of reentrant and thread-safe software.

In an MT application, all threads share the same address space and have access to all process resources, including data. In order for the data to be consistent, all access to such shared data *must* be serialized by some form of mutual exclusion lock. A function is said to be *thread-safe* when it can be used safely in a multithreaded application. A thread-safe function serializes internally access to shared resources and does *not* require the caller to do anything special when calling the functions. Any function that does not use static data or does not manipulate shared data can be called thread-safe. For example, the function Add2Numbers shown below is an example of a function that is thread-safe.

```
int
Add2Numbers (int num1, int num2)
{
int total;

total = num1 + num2;

return(total);
}
```

A function is said to be *non-thread-safe* when it uses static data or accesses shared data *without* using any mutual exclusion locks. For example, the following code segment is non-thread-safe.

```
int
FindGreatestNum(int num)
{
   static int greatestNum;

   if (num > greatestNum)
        greatestNum = num;
}
```

This function *can* be made thread-safe by serializing access to the shared global data (greatestNum), as shown below.

```
int
FindGreatestNum(int num)
{
   static int greatestNum;

   MThreadMutexLock(...); /* OS Dependent */

   if (num > greatestNum)
        greatestNum = num;

   MThreadMutexUnlock(...); /* OS Dependent */
}
```

A function is said to be a *reentrant* when it can be executed safely by multiple threads concurrently. Reentrant functions share these properties: They do *not* return pointer to static data, and they do *not* hold static data when called successively. When the C-library functions were developed, issues of multiple threads were *never* considered, and this makes many C-library functions non-reentrant.

The C-library function *ctime* cannot be classified as reentrant because it returns the pointer to static data. This makes the invocation of *ctime* unsafe when two threads call the function simultaneously. Even if mutex locks could be used internally by *ctime* to serialize access to the static buffer, the output of one thread's call to *ctime* would overwrite the data stored in the static area.

Similarly, the function *strtok* cannot be considered thread-safe because it maintains state information between calls and also modifies the buffer passed to the routine each time it is called. This means that while one thread is calling *strtok* in a repetitive manner, no other thread can call the function *strtok* using the same buffer. Functions can be defined to be either thread-safe, reentrant, or both. Thread safety does *not* necessarily imply reentrancy, while reentrancy *always* implies thread safety.

The code segment of the function *FindGreatestNum* shown above is not reentrant because it uses static data internally. The function cannot be called safely by multiple threads when each thread wants to have its own copy of the variable *greatestNum*. The function *FindGreatestNum can* be made reentrant by eliminating the use of the static variable. A function *can* be made reentrant by using one of the two following approaches: If the function returns the pointer to some static area, then it can be changed to return a pointer to a per-thread data area. Alternatively, the interface of the function can be changed to take an extra argument for returning the data to the user. The code segment shown above can be made reentrant by using either approach.

```
int
FindGreatestNum(int num)
{
   int *greatestNum;

   MThreadGetValue(greatestNum,...); /* OS Dependent */

   if (greatestNum == NULL) /* NO per thread data set */
        greatestNum = (int *) calloc(1,sizeof(int)).

   if (num > *greatestNum)
   {
      *greatestNum = num;
      MThreadSetValue(greatestNum,...); /* OS Dependent */
   }
}
```

In this code segment, the functions *MThreadGetValue* and *MThreadSetValue* are operating system–dependent, and they allow one to get and set data on a per-thread basis. For example, the function *MThread SetValue* can call *pthread_setspecific* on POSIX systems and *TlsSetValue* on WIN32-based systems (see Chap. 19 for implementation). The only *problem* with dynamically allocating per-thread data is that they must be deallocated when the thread exits. This means that threads must call some termination function when the per-thread data are deallocated. This approach is used by C-library functions such as _endthreadex on NT and OS/2 to deallocate any per-thread data that were allocated dynamically by the C-library functions. If you are developing an MT library and you know for sure that *all* the threads will call a library routine before terminating, then this approach will work fine.

Alternatively, the function *can* be made reentrant by changing the interface of the function. The preceding function can be redefined to take a user-supplied buffer that the function will use to store the results of the operation.

This will require that each thread initialize the buffer pointed to by greatestNum to zero before the function is called for the first time. Note that even though this approach is cleaner than the previous approach, it requires that the developers *have* to change their application code to adhere to the new calling convention. Keep in mind that this approach may or may *not* be always possible, and this depends on the dependence of the code on the old calling interface. Personally, I would recommend that you use this approach to make functions reentrant, even if it means that you might have to maintain two versions of the library.

```
int
FindGreatestNum(int num, int *greatestNum)
{
   if (num > *greatestNum)
       *greatestNum = num;
}
```

This approach is used by library developers on POSIX systems to make functions reentrant. Reentrant functions in POSIX follow the convention of redefining the reentrant versions to end with an *_r* suffix. For example, below are the two versions of the functions *ctime* as defined on some POSIX systems. The reader is advised to refer to his or her vendor's documentation for all reentrant versions of library functions. If you are a library developer, then it *is* important that you document your functions to be either non-thread-safe, thread-safe, or reentrant.

```
int  ctime(time_t *clock)
int  ctime_r(time_t *clock, char *buffer)
```

20.2.1 Using non-thread-safe libraries

In a multithreaded application, if you are using libraries that you did *not* develop, then you *have* to verify that the library functions can be used safely in an MT environment. If functions are documented to be reentrant, then there is *no* problem with using these functions. However, if some or all of the functions are non-thread-safe, then there could be potential problems. Mixing thread-safe and non-thread-safe code is always dangerous, but sometimes there might be simple ways to work around the limitations of non-thread-safe code.

It is important to understand that there is *no* problem in using non-thread-safe code in a threaded application as long as *only* one thread executes the non-thread-safe code. For example, even though the GUI libraries are non-thread-safe on most systems that implement X-Windows, it is perfectly safe for a single thread to use the non-thread-safe code. Using this scheme, one can still use multiple threads in a program but dedicate a separate thread to access each of the non-thread-safe libraries. On UNIX platforms, if you are using some non-thread-safe code that relies on the *signal* mechanism, then you *should* be very careful using it (see Sec. 4.6).

One way to use non-thread-safe functions is to *serialize* access to the functions by using some kind of global locking scheme. Note that in this scheme it is the caller's responsibility to ensure that only one thread executes the non-thread-safe function at a time. The problem with this kind of locking scheme is that it prevents more than one thread from calling a function in the library concurrently. This kind of locking should *only* be used for nonfrequently accessed routines. If performance is an issue, then change the locking granularity by providing separate locks for functions in the libraries rather than providing a single lock for the entire library. The following code segment illustrates the use of global locks to access non-thread-safe functions.

```
int
SerializeLibraryCalls()
{
   LockLibraryMutex(); /* OS Dependent */

   CallUnsafeFunction(); /* non-thread-safe function */

   UnlockLibraryMutex(); /* OS Dependent */
}
```

Many applications are developed using third-party libraries (e.g., DBMS, TP monitors) that are supplied by system vendors. Some of you might be very surprised to know that many of the more commonly used commercial products do *not* support threaded versions of their libraries yet; thus one has to be very careful when using them in MT applications.

Today, most DBMS vendors do *not* support native multithreading with their libraries. Most of these DBMS vendors rely on their own nonpreemptive user-level thread implementation, and it is difficult, if not impossible, to use native threads with these libraries. The biggest problem I have with these threading packages is that they prevent applications from exploiting the potential of SMP architecture. If you have ever been involved in making large code segments multithreaded, then you can understand the impasse of these vendors. The reality is that it takes a *lot* of development and testing time to release an MT library, especially when there is so much legacy code base. Knowing the effort involved, it is encouraging to learn that most DBMS vendors now plan to support native threads in their upcoming releases.

Personally, I found that I could *not* use threads where I felt their use would have helped me the most, such as database, internet (NSAPI or ISAPI), or transaction-processing applications. This was so mainly because they had some component such as a legacy TP monitor or DBMS that made it difficult to use native threading. Multithreading is still in its infancy, but I am confident that many more vendors will start shipping multithreaded libraries in the coming years. Once vendors of these popular products support threads, only *then* will multithreading become popular. A word of caution: Be prepared to find bugs when the early versions of these libraries are introduced. Also, remember that it takes considerable time to tune the performance of MT libraries; therefore, some of these libraries might suffer from early performance problems.

20.2.2 Converting non-thread-safe libraries

Even when you are developing new libraries, you will always be required to convert existing libraries to be thread-safe. The task of conversion could be simple, or it could be very painful and simply *not* worth the effort. There are a couple of steps required in making libraries thread-safe. Some libraries might rely too much on globals and static data; thus it might be better to *rewrite* a much cleaner and MT-safe library (especially true for legacy code).

The first step would be to identify global variables, static variables, and other shared resources in the application. Avoid static variables as much as possible; use dynamically allocated varaibles instead. Global variables should be made per-thread data, unless they require a process scope. If the variables require a process scope, then some form of mutual exclusion locks should be used to ensure data integrity. Access to all shared data and resources *should* be serialized; otherwise, data can be corrupted. It is important that considerable time *should* be spent in identifying per-thread data variables. Do *not* take all process-based data structures and make them thread-based. Sure, you can port your library faster that way, but remember that it is *not* an efficient design. One should carefully isolate the process and thread data structures, pack related data structures together, and minimize the locking of shared data. Always think of the locking issues while designing MT libraries.

When making a function reentrant, one should be careful *not* to call the operating system thread functions to get/set per-thread data too often, since this can have a performance impact on the applications. Do not rely too much on the TSD or TLS mechanisms for making functions reentrant. The TSD or TLS mechanisms are *not* very fast calls on most operating systems. I have seen many UNIX developers falling victim to this when converting their *legacy* nonthreaded libraries to be thread-safe or reentrant. This is so mainly because most of these companies rush to get their MT libraries released. If you follow the same practice, then your libraries can be inefficient and will suffer from serious performance problems. Spend time in designing the MT version of the library, and be prepared to rearchitect some parts of your library. As a developer, your goal *should* be to make libraries MT-efficient and not just MT-safe.

Even when you rely on per-thread data for making functions reentrant, you should call these functions minimally. For example, consider the function *LibraryFunc* that does not provide a reentrant version of the function; rather, it uses thread-specific data to maintain the per-thread context data. Also, assume that the function internally calls some other nonexported function, namely, *InternalFunc1,* which also needs to access the per-thread data. Assume that the non-thread-safe versions of the functions *LibraryFunc* and *InternalFunc1* rely on global data.

Method 1

```
int
LibraryFunc(...)
{
   void *pThreadData;

   pThreadData = GetThreadData(.....); /* OS Dependent */

   InternalFunc1();
}

int
InternalFunc1()
{
   void *pThreadData;

   pThreadData = GetThreadData(.....); /* OS Dependent */

   DoSomething(pThreadData...);
}
```

Method 2

```
int
LibraryFunc(...)
{
   void *pThreadData;

   pThreadData = GetThreadData(.....); /* OS Dependent */

   InternalFunc1(pThreadData); /* note: functional interface changed */
}

int
InternalFunc1(void *pThreadData)
{
   DoSomething(pThreadData...);
}
```

Both versions of the functions will work, but I would recommend that you use the second method, since it eliminates the need to get the per-thread data in the function *InternalFunc1*. Even though it requires that you change the functional interface of your internal library functions, it is well worth the effort. The new interface is cleaner because it does not rely on global data and also can be used when you develop a single-threaded version of the library.

While developing MT libraries on some platforms, one might have to consider issues other than reentrancy and thread safety. If you are developing MT libraries for the POSIX threads environment, then you *should* consider the issues of cancellation and fork safety and document your functions accordingly.

20.3 SMP Issues

Let me start this section with an anecdote. A customer once called me to ask me why his multithreaded application was suddenly running slower on a four-processor SMP machine when the company had *just* moved from an older two-processor machine. He asked me if I could take a look at the application and help him identify some of the performance bottlenecks. Since I was busy at that time, I offered to visit the location later and discuss the application design with the developers.

I am sure you have often heard your hardware salesperson telling that you need to buy more memory in order to increase performance. Trust me, *sometimes* these expensive solutions work with no change to the application code. Sure enough, a couple of days later I received a call from an engineer at the same company who told me that the performance of the applications had improved dramatically. He told me that they bought *more* cache memory because their salesperson recommended it as a quick solution. He also added that since the performance problems were more or less solved, his boss would reschedule my meeting with the developers at some later date (not yet!).

The lesson I learned from this incident was that applications can behave differently when ported to SMP machines for reasons well beyond the programmer's control. I also realized that there were many things that one does *not* think about when developing multithreaded applications on SMP machines. This section will describe *some* of the issues of SMP machines and how a programmer can develop efficient SMP-aware applications.

In an SMP machine, memory is shared by all processors, and this causes bus contention when memory locations are updated. The contention can have a serious performance impact on applications and, in turn, on the scalability of SMP machines. If every processor relied on the main memory for memory access, then the performance of most SMP machines would be horrific. Today, most SMP systems have a memory *cache* between the CPU and the main memory. A cache is high-speed memory that is used to store frequently accessed data. Cache memory is static RAM (SRAM) and is much faster and more expensive than the main memory. Main memory is dynamic RAM (DRAM) and is much slower compared with the cache memory.

There are *many* advantages to cache memory; in fact, without cache memory, the performance of SMP machines would be simply horrible. In addition to providing fast access to data, it also helps in reducing the contention for memory access. When a data item is accessed and it is found in the cache, then there is no need to access the main memory. This works fine for data items that are read, but when items are modified, this introduces yet another problem. Since each CPU has its own cache, the system *has* to keep the caches consistent across all the processors if each processor has to have the same view of memory. Operating systems use different kinds of cache consistency protocols, such as write-invalidate and write-broadcast, to keep the cache consistent across all processors. It is beyond the scope of this book to cover these protocols in much more detail.

Cache memory plays a important role in the performance of applications on SMP machines. Memory caches are divided into smaller pieces, and each piece is called a cache *line*. The sizes of cache lines can vary anywhere from 16 to 256 bytes. When data is accessed and they are found in the cache, then it is called a cache *hit*. When the data are not found in the cache, then the system reads the data from the main memory into the cache, and this is called a cache *miss*. Ideally, one would like to always access data from the cache, but the sheer cost of cache memory makes this infeasible. It is not uncommon to see a cache hit ratio of 90 percent on many modern systems. From a programmer's prospective, most operating systems do not provide sufficient (if any) tools that can pinpoint the reasons for bad cache performance in programs. Detecting cache problems is not simple, but if you detect (using some profiling tool) that functions run slower as more processors are added, then it might be a symptom of a cache problem.

On most systems when a cache line has to be updated, then the processor takes exclusive control of the cache and then invalidates (write-invalidate protocol) all other copies in the other processors' caches. The process of updating all the other caches means that a processor has to gain exclusive access to the cache line, and when this happens, it means that all the other processors stop running momentarily. When a cache line is constantly updated, then the system might face the problem of cache *sloshing,* a situation in which the data keep moving from one cache line to another.

For example, consider a global counter that is constantly updated by threads on different processors. The update causes the cache line to be updated constantly on all processors, which can be an expensive process. One way to *solve* this problem is by using variables local to each thread and updating the global counter either when the thread exits or at some well-defined interval.

Another problem that can happen with cache is the *false sharing* of data. When a data item is accessed and it is not found in the cache line, then the data are fetched from main memory. When a cache line is updated, the *entire* cache line is updated with the new data. This means that when a cache line is being shared by two different variables and the variables are being updated by different processors, it will cause the cache line to be updated constantly. One way to *avoid* this problem is to ensure that frequently accessed variables do *not* share the same cache line. Ideally, structures should be padded to fit on a cache line. Having said this, I must admit that coding applications in such a manner makes the code *nonportable* and also dependent on the architecture of the machine. However, if you are in the business of writing efficient MT programs, this might be a worthwhile price to pay. Note that even though most cache lines are either 16 or 32 bytes, you should check your vendor's manual for exact details.

20.4 Locking and Synchronization

In an MT process, threads share a common address space and have equal access to all shared resources, including data. To prevent data corruption, applications use some form of mutual exclusion locks to serialize access to shared data. Locking is necessary in thread programming and *cannot* be avoided, but the overhead of locking *can* be minimized by avoiding locking and using efficient synchronization primitives. Locking and synchronization are the most important aspects of multithreaded application development.

Applications can use either

- Code-based locks
- Data-based locks

Code-based locks are coarse-grained and lock pieces of code generally known as *critical-section code.* Basically, a lock is acquired when a thread enters the critical section code, and it is released when the thread exits the critical section. Code-based locks are simple to implement, but the *contention* for such locks can be high when the time for which the lock is held is long. These kinds of locks work better when the critical section of code is small (locks held for a short time).

Data-based locks are associated with data structures and are used to ensure the integrity of data. The application is responsible for locking the data structure before modifying it and releasing the lock when it is done. These locks can be coarse-grained, medium-grained, or fine-grained. For example, consider a simple data structure, an array of 100 integers. One might choose to lock the entire array using a single lock (coarse-grained), lock 20 elements of the array at a time (medium-grained), or lock each element of the array separately (fine-grained).

Consider an MT-safe implementation of the function *InsertListElement* that inserts new items in a list that is shared by multiple threads. The function *can* be made thread-safe either by using code or data locks. In the code-based locking scheme, a mutex is used to serialize access to the function InsertListElement. This means that while one thread is executing the function, other threads will block until the thread executing the function unlocks the mutex. This will be true even when two separate threads are inserting elements into different lists.

In the data-based locking scheme, since each list has its own mutex, it allows multiple threads to insert elements into different lists in parallel (potentially without the overhead of blocking/unblocking). The advantage of a data-based lock will be that it will allow two threads to operate on separate lists at the same time, but if both threads are inserting elements in the same list, then it has no particular advantage over a code-based lock. As you can see, data-based locks can be much *more* efficient in terms of allowing parallel execution of threads. Data locks are more efficient when data structures are independent and do not need to access data locks of other data structures during synchronization.

Code-Based Locking

```
MUTEX InsertListMutex; /* OS Dependent */

int InsertListElement(void *pElement, LIST *pHead)
{
   LockListMutex(InsertListMutex); /* OS dependent */

   AddElementToList(pElement, pHead); /* actual function that adds element */
```

```
    UnlockListMutex(InsertListMutex); /* OS Dependent */
}
```

Data-Based Locking

```
typedef struct _listhead
{
    LIST    *pHead; /* pointer to beginning of list */
    MUTEX   listMutex; /* OS dependent */
} PLIST;

int InsertListElement(void *pElement, PLIST *pList)
{
    LockListMutex(pList->listMutex); /* OS Dependent */

    AddElementToList(pElement, pList->pHead); /* actual function that adds
    element */

    UnlockListMutex(pList->listMutex); /* OS Dependent */
}
```

Choosing the optimal lock type and selecting lock granularity are two important factors that *must* be considered when developing efficient locking strategies. Even though both types of locking can be used to develop thread-safe functions, data locks can be *more* efficient than code locks.

While considering lock granularity, one can easily conclude that fine-grained locks are the most efficient, since locks are held for a short time. This might not be true for many reasons. If locks are too coarse-grained, then wait time for a lock can increase, while too fine-grained locks have the associated overhead of blocking/unblocking. It is a classic tradeoff between fewer locks and higher contention. On most SMP machines, locking and unlocking operations are not cheap and can add to the overhead even when *no* blocking occurs. Personally, I found that selecting the optimal lock granularity is usually a trial-and-error process, and it may require some experimentation. One should start with low- or medium-grained locks and then refine the granularity based on the results.

20.4.1 Blocking versus spinning

The overhead of locking is one of the factors that can slow down the performance of applications on uniprocessor as well as SMP machines. The time to acquire a lock depends on the frequency of request and the average time the lock is held by the owner of the lock. The wait time *increases* nonlinearly as locks get more busy. When a thread tries to acquire a lock that is held by some other thread, then it has one of two options: It can either wait or it can spinloop. Spinlocks should only be used on SMP machines, and they are suitable only when the locks are held for a short duration. When locks are held for longer durations, then blocking is the preferred alternative.

On most SMP platforms the processor has special instructions for *atomic* updates. Spinlocks can be built using the hardware atomic instruction such as test and set, compare and swap, or the load reserved and store conditional.

Sometimes it might be better to use these instructions for implementing your own locking primitives rather than use the operating system locking primitives. If the wait time for locks is less than the context switching time of a thread, then spinlocks can be helpful because they can save lots of processor cycles. The following code segment illustrates the use of such a lock using the hardware TestAndSet instruction.

```
int Spinlock(int *pLock)
{
   while (TestAndSet(*pLock) = = 0)
     ; /* could sleep for a small period */
}
```

In the code segment shown below, the routine Spinlock has been changed, and this works better from the perspective of cache consistency.

```
int Spinlock(int *pLock)
{
   int retCode;

   for(;;)
   {
      while (*pLock  = = 0)
      ; /* could sleep for a small period */

      retCode = TestAndSet(*pLock);
      if (retCode)
           break;

   }
}
```

Sometimes it might be better for the threads to *sleep* for a small period before retrying to acquire the lock. The sleeping reduces the unnecessary traffic on the memory bus, especially when multiple threads block on the same lock. The efficiency of spinlocks depends on many factors such as the processor, memory bus, and cache. Since starvation is possible with spinloops, the use of spinlocks should be evaluated carefully. Note, AIX users using the *cs* function should use the _check_lock and _clear_lock functions instead on AIX 4.1.

20.4.2 Locking guidelines

- Do not hold locks for long duration.
- Do not have too fine-grained locks, since this might affect performance.
- Do not perform blocking operations (e.g., I/O operations) while holding locks.
- To avoid deadlocks with multiple threads, acquire resource locks in the same order.
- Keep critical-section code small, and do not perform noncritical code inside the critical section of code.

- Avoid putting multiple locks on the same cache line, since this might increase the chances of false sharing.
- If data are read more than written, then consider complex locks such as reader/writer locks.
- Avoid the double-wakeup problem. When data are modified in some critical section of code and some other thread has to be notified of the update, then it is better to unlock the lock and then notify the thread. For example, in a POSIX threaded environment one should unlock the mutex before signaling the condition variable.

20.5 Thread Creation Guidelines

For most developers, one of the main reasons for developing a multithreaded application is to increase performance, especially on an SMP machine. One of the challenging problems that developers often face is regarding the number of threads that are created in an application. The issue is much more relevant when one is developing multithreaded server processes to service many clients. Too few threads or too many threads *both* can have performance ramifications. By creating too few threads, the application is not fully utilizing the power of available CPUs, while creating more threads than available CPUs might not give the performance boost. Usually, an optimal balance *should* be achieved in order to maximize performance on an SMP machine.

It is true that threads are much cheaper than traditional processes, but remember, they are *not free*. Threads utilize system resources and memory and involve some scheduling overhead. Threads should *not* be created just to execute a small section of code. Similarly, for efficiency purposes, one should *not* create too many threads in a process. The number of threads that can be created in a process depends on such factors as available memory and number of processors.

On most systems there is a one-to-one mapping between a user and a kernel thread. The POSIX and UI threading models support the two-level threading model, while systems such as Windows NT and OS/2 only support the 1:1 model. When there are too many threads in a system, the context-switching overhead can be significant. If an application has too many threads but only a few of them are active at the same time, then the context-switching overhead might not be so high, even though the design might be inefficient in terms of resource consumption. However, if most of these threads are active, then the context-switching overhead might cause performance problems. On systems that support two-level thread scheduling (user and kernel), one should always create user-level threads and adjust (if possible) the concurrency of kernel threads according to the application requirement. This can be relevant if the number of threads in the application is high. Note that the context-switching overhead of user-level threads is much lower than that of kernel threads. On systems that support two-level thread scheduling, it is more efficient to create more user-level threads and fewer kernel threads.

Also, on systems that support the concept of detached threads, it might be faster to create detached threads than nondetached threads. Keep in mind that when you depend on two-level scheduling of threads, then you lose portability between operating systems.

Proper use of threads in the design of a multithreaded server process is crucial. Rather than create a thread for every client that connects to the server, a *better* design is to use the worker-thread model. For example, a TCP/IP server process can create a separate thread for every client that connects to it, or it can create a pool of worker threads to service all clients. The 1:1 model can be inefficient, while the worker-thread model is a much better scalable design. Note that the 1:1 model is simple to program, while design of the worker-thread model might be much more complicated.

Keep in mind that the efficiency of the worker-thread model might *not* be the same on different operating systems. One of the requirements to keep the system responsive is to ensure that none of the worker threads blocks for a long time (e.g., I/O). Personally, among all the operating systems that I have worked on, I found Windows NT to have the best programming support for designing applications that involve I/O and worker threads. The asynchronous I/O of Windows NT, along with I/O completion port, can be used to design highly scalable servers. On UNIX, even though the POSIX.1b asynchronous model can be used for I/O purposes, the notification part of POSIX.1b can still be a polling mechanism. Personally, I think that the POSIX interface *should* have notified which pending I/O completed when a thread had multiple asynchronous I/O requests pending (aio_return).

Threads should *not* be created and destroyed frequently in an application. Some operating systems maintain a *cache* of threads, thus speeding up the thread creation process, but this is *not* a universal design across operating systems. One of the more time-consuming process in thread creation/destruction is the time spent in allocating/deallocating the *stack* of a thread. If it is possible, pass a user-supplied stack to threads (on creation) and cache the stacks when threads exit. The effort is not worth it unless you have too many threads or threads are created and destroyed frequently. When passing your own stack address to thread creation functions, be careful with the stack management. It is important that stacks should *not* be shared or reused until the thread that is using the stack has exited.

Operating systems often take advantage of the thread context in the *cache* if a thread can be scheduled to run on the same processor it last ran on. Most operating systems use soft processor affinity, meaning that the system makes a best effort to schedule the thread to run on the same processor it last ran on. Many operating systems (e.g., Solaris, AIX, and NT) allow a thread to be permanently bound to certain processor and *prevent* the scheduler from scheduling the thread to run on any other processor. The process of binding a thread to run on a processor is also known as *processor affinity*. The scheduler usually does a good job of finding the right processor to execute the thread; therefore, binding threads to run on a certain processor generally should be avoided.

20.6 Debugging MT Applications

In theory, debugging an MT application is no different from debugging a single-threaded application. Debugging MT applications can be challenging and frustrating without the support of decent thread-aware debuggers. Nowadays, most operating systems support thread-aware debuggers as part of their programming environment. These debuggers are capable of showing objects such as threads, mutexes, and other synchronization primitives. Most of these debuggers allow you to suspend and resume threads and also allow you to inspect variables, stacks, and registers on a per-thread basis. Whenever a thread hits a breakpoint, *all* other threads in the process are suspended, and this ensures that while the thread is being debugged, no other thread is manipulating the data. What is *not* possible with debuggers is concurrent execution of threads when a breakpoint is reached. Some of the more subtle bugs are caused by concurrent executions. Even though I would have preferred, it is beyond the scope of this book to cover the different debuggers of the numerous operating systems covered in this book. Refer to the documentation of your popular debugger for information on the commands for MT debugging.

Software testing of MT programs can be tricky because it might *not* be easy to reproduce bugs easily. Many of the bugs are timing bugs and are often caused by concurrent execution of multiple threads. I have talked to numerous managers in software companies that dread to develop or support MT applications because the first and only thing that comes to their mind is those nasty MT bugs! This is one of the main reasons that so many software practitioners strongly feel (with some merit) that manual multithreading should be used only by experienced programmers and multithreading should be restricted only to certain classes of applications such as DBMS systems, transaction-processing (TP) monitors, and some specialized servers.

Manual multithreading is the technique where it is the programmer's responsibility to ensure proper locking and unlocking. All threading techniques described in this book are examples of manual threading. Some languages such as *Java* support multithreading at the language level and are considered to greatly reduce the chances of errors due to bad programming practices. Language support of threads makes it much easier to use threads in applications. More about Java threads in the next edition of this book.

Many MT bugs are caused by *improper* locking techniques used to access shared data. By the term *improper* I mean either not using mutual exclusion locks at all or prematurely (not) releasing mutual exclusion locks. Use object-oriented techniques such as data abstraction and hiding, and provide well-defined interfaces (methods) to access elements of a data structure. In this way, the details of locking and unlocking *can* be confined to the interfaces only. Techniques for detecting other locking problems such as deadlocks (recursive and hierarchical) were discussed earlier in this book.

An important goal of locking primitives should be simplicity. Export well-defined interfaces or class libraries for synchronization. The details of locking should be hidden within these interfaces. Also, keeping these primitives simple can be very helpful while debugging code. Making the interaction between threads overly complicated can cause difficult-to-find bugs. Do not try to optimize thread interaction unless your code is debugged. It does not pay to optimize the code if it adds extra complexity to the code and makes the code less maintainable. Remember, maintaining the code is as important as performance. Keeping this in mind, design simple but efficient interthread communication and synchronization primitives.

On certain platforms compiler optimization also *can* cause subtle bugs in MT programs. If you have a global variable that is shared by two threads and the compiler as part of the optmization decides to store the variable in a register, then this can cause difficult-to-find bugs. When the variable is placed in a register, the changes made by one thread are not visible to the other thread. One way to avoid such problems is to employ the C-language *volatile* identifier with the variable. Use of the *volatile* identifier is a hint to the compiler not to place the variable in the register. Since this problem can cause nasty bugs, it is advisable to use the volatile identifier for global variables.

On many occasions I found that indefinite waits on mutex locks were caused by error-handling code segments of a function that did *not* release a mutex lock. To prevent this from happening, one can always call some well-defined function when any kind of error is detected. The function can be written to unlock the mutex (if locked), and this will prevent the caller from sprinkling code all over to explicitly unlock the mutex on error conditions.

Often, depending on the effort required, I develop two versions of the application (single-threaded and multithreaded). Only when the single-threaded application works fine do I start debugging the MT version. Make sure that all thread-safe functions can be executed safely by a single thread. The effects of memory leaks in an MT application can cause more problems than in the case of single-threaded systems. Many vendors are providing tools as part of their application development environment that can help in detecting memory leaks.

Use of the C-language *printf* statements in an MT application can be frustrating. I experienced that inserting the *printf* statement often caused interesting results. Sometimes a program that ran fine earlier crashed, while at other times programs that crashed earlier ran fine when *printf* was introduced. Some bugs in MT programs are also caused by stack overflow, especially if the stack size of the thread is insufficient.

20.7 Designing Efficient MT Applications

Multithreading has been *hyped* too much by vendors, and this has caused some developers to think that MT is the best solution to most of their performance problems. If performance is the objective, then be aware that only certain kinds of applications and environments are suited for multithreading. Personally, I recommend that inexperienced folks avoid multithreading unless they have sufficient time designing threaded applications. Know your reasons for using threads in the application; please do *not* use them just because someone else in the group is using them.

Optimizing threaded programs requires careful *design* and run-time *analysis* of programs. If you are experiencing performance problems, then follow some of these steps. Make sure that the work is equally divided between the threads. If the design is such that one thread has to do much more work than the other, then it is possible that some threads will be idle while others will be disproportionately busy. Application partitioning is important in the development of MT applications. If you create too many threads to solve a relatively small problem, then it is possible that *more* time will be spent on interthread communication and synchronization and less on actually solving the problem.

The number of CPUs and the number of active threads can cause yet another kind of imbalance. If you have more runnable threads than the number of CPUs, then the context-switching overhead will cause performance problems. In case you have too many threads, it might be a better idea to make the algorithm more coarse-grained.

The overhead of locking and contention for locks is detrimental to performance of MT applications. Both these things cannot be eliminated completely in MT programs but definitely can be reduced. Avoid lock contention, and measure the time spent by threads trying to acquire the lock. The best areas to optimize are the sections where most of the time is spent. Once you identify these hot spots, then apply some of the locking guidelines discussed earlier in this chapter. Another problem that threads might experience with locking is priority *inversion*. The topic of priority inversion was discussed in detail earlier in this book.

Profiling tools can be very helpful in identifying code bottlenecks. Traditional tools (such as gprof on UNIX) can be used for profiling MT applications. Certain operating systems provide analyzing tools that can measure the time required to acquire locks (e.g., Thread Analyzer on Solaris). On NT 4.0, a new tool called APIMON can be used for profiling MT applications. The key to optimizing the application speed is finding the code segment(s) causing the bottleneck. One should spend considerable time in optimizing the body of the application, the code segment where most of the time is spent by the application. In addition to profiling tools, some operating systems provide noninterfering tracing tools that can be used to instrument the application code and system libraries. They can measure context-switch time and time wait for mutex locks and also can trace many other system activities (e.g., page faults, etc.). These tracing tools can be either graphic or nongraphic in nature (e.g., Solaris supports a tool called *tnfview*).

20.8 Conclusion

Developing MT programs can be a fun and effective means of solving problems, but the key is to know the limitations and the pitfalls of the MT environment. Always keep in mind that threads alone cannot solve all your problems, but they *can* go a long way in helping some of them. Once you are convinced that you need threads, then you *should* use them in the most effective manner. Keep in mind that operating systems alone cannot be responsible for delivering the performance of SMP applications; instead, applications *must* be designed properly to utilize the system resources (e.g., processors) most effectively. By following some of the design guidelines mentioned in this chapter, you can reap the benefits of multithreading. Good luck with all your multithreading projects!

Appendix

A

References and Recommended Readings

M. Bach, *Design of UNIX Operating System,* Prentice Hall, 1986.

A. Birell, *An Introduction to Programming with Threads*, A White Paper, Digital Equipment Corporation.

J. Boykin, D. Kirschen, A. Langermand, S. LoVerso, *Programming under Mach*, Addison Wesley, 1993.

D. Box, "Introducing Distributed COM and the New OLE Features in Windows NT 4.0," *Microsoft Systems Journal*, May 1996.

M. Brain, *WIN32 System Services*, Prentice Hall, 1994.

B. Catanzaro, *Multiprocessor Systems Architecture*, SunSoft Press.

E. Cooper and R. Draves, *C Threads*, Department of Computer Science, Carnegie Mellon University, 1988.

H. Custer, *Inside Windows NT*, Microsoft Press, 1993.

R. Davis, *Windows NT Network Programming*, Addison Wesley, 1994.

H. Deitel and M. Kogan, *The Design of OS/2*, Addison Wesley, 1992.

Digital Equipment Corporation, *DECthreads: Guide to DECthreads*.

L. Dorfman and M. Neuberger, *Effective Multithreading in OS/2*, McGraw-Hill, 1994.

J. Dugger, "Multithreading in C++," *C/C++Users Journal*, November 1995.

B. Gallmeister, *POSIX4: Programming for the Real World*, O'Reilly & Associates, 1995.

D. Glasser, "Efficient Synchronization Techniques for Multithreaded WIN32-based Applications," *Microsoft Systems Journal*, February 1995.

B. Goodheart and J. Cox, *The Magic Garden Explained*, Prentice Hall, 1994.

J. Graham, *Solaris 2.X: Internals and Architecture*, McGraw-Hill, 1995.

J. Graham, "An Introduction to Threads," *SunExpert*, February 1996.

J. Gray and A. Reuter, *Transaction Processing: Concepts and Techniques*, Morgan Kaufman Publishers, 1993.

M. Heller, "Tips and Tricks on Developing Killer Server Applications for Windows NT," *Microsoft Systems Journal*, August 1995.

C. Hoare, *Communicating Sequential Processes*, Prentice Hall, 1985.

IBM Corporation, *AIX Version 4 General Programming Concepts: Writing and Debugging Programs*.

IBM Corporation, *Operating System/2 Technical Reference*, Volume 2.

S. Kleiman, D. Shah, and B. Smaalders, *Programming with Threads*, Prentice Hall, 1996.

D. Lewine, *POSIX Programmer's Guide*, O'Reilly & Associates, 1991.

B. Lewis and D. Berg, *Threads Primer*, SunSoft Press, 1995.

H. Lockhart, *OSF DCE: Guide to Developing Distributed Applications,* McGraw-Hill, 1994.

W. Neilsen, "Breaking up the Task," *Advanced Systems*, April 1994.

NeXT Computer Inc., *NeXTSTEP Operating System Software*.

C. Northrup, *Programming with UNIX Threads*, John Wiley & Sons, 1996.
Novell Inc., *UnixWare 2.0 Operating System API Reference Manual,* 1995.
R. Orfali and D. Harkey, *Client-Server Programming with OS/2 Extended Edition*, Van Nostrand Reinhold, 1990.
M. Peterson, *DCE: A Guide to Developing Portable Applications*, McGraw-Hill, 1994.
T. Pham and P. Garg, *Multithreading Programming with Windows NT*, Prentice Hall, 1996.
M. Pietrik, "Poking Around Under the Hood: A Programmer's View of Windows NT 4.0," *Microsoft Systems Journal*, August 1996.
S. Prasad, "Weaving a Thread," *BYTE*, October 1995.
S. Prasad, "Windows NT Threads," *BYTE*, November 1995.
J. Richter, *Advanced Windows*, Microsoft Press, 1995.
K. Robbins, S. Robbins, *Practical UNIX Programming: A Guide to Concurrency, Communication, and Multithreading,* Prentice Hall, 1996.
W. Rosenberry and Teague, *Distributing Applications Across DCE and Windows NT*, O'Reilly & Associates, 1993.
J. D. Schank, *Novell's Guide to Client-Server Applications and Architecture,* Novell Press.
C. Shimmel, *UNIX Systems for Modern Architectures: Symmetric Multiprocessing and Caching for Kernel Programmers,* Addison Wesley, 1994.
W. Stallings, *Operating Systems*, Prentice Hall, 1995.
SunSoft Inc., *SUNOS 5.2: Guide to Multi-thread Programming.*
C. Tamarisa, "Introduction to Multithreaded Programming," *AIXpert*, November 1994.
C. Tamarisa, "Porting DCE Threads Program to 4.1," *AIXpert*, October 1994.
A. Tanenbaum, *Distributed Operating Systems*, Prentice Hall, 1995.
U. Vahalia, *Unix Internals: the New Frontiers*, Prentice Hall, 1995.
J. Vest, "Writing Scalable Applications for Windows NT," Microsoft Corporation, 1995.

Appendix B
Net Sources

- newsgroup:comp.programming.threads
- http://www.sun.com/sunsoft/Developer-products/sig/threads
- http://www.austin.ibm.com/aix/library/diff/df4threa.html
- http://www.microsoft.com/win32dev/
- http://www.microsoft.com/win32dev/wcnt.htm
- http://www.cs.cmu.edu/afs/cs/cmu.edu/project/mach/public/www/mach.html
- http://www.unix.digital.com/unix/smp
- http://www.osf.org/dce/qna/contents.html
- http://liinwww.ira.uka.de/bibliography/Os/threads.html
- http://savines.imag.fr/threadedcomm/threadedcomm_3.html
- http://www.mit.edu:8001/people/proven/pthreads.html
- http://siesta.cs.wustl.edu/~ schmidt/

Index